Extending and Embedding PHP

Extending and Embedding PHP

Sara Golemon

DEVELOPER'S
LIBRARY

Sams Publishing, 800 East 96th Street, Indianapolis, Indiana 46240 USA

Extending and Embedding PHP

International Standard Book Number: 0-672-32704-X
Library of Congress Catalog Card Number: 2004093741
Printed in the United States of America

This product is printed digitally on demand.

Trademarks

Warning and Disclaimer

Bulk Sales

Sams Publishing offers excellent discounts on this book when ordered in quantity for bulk purchases or special sales. For more information, please contact

U.S. Corporate and Government Sales
1-800-382-3419
corpsales@pearsontechgroup.com

For sales outside of the U.S., please contact
International Sales
international@pearsoned.com

Acquisitions Editors
Betsy Brown
Shelley Johnston

Development Editor
Damon Jordan

Managing Editor
Charlotte Clapp

Project Editor
Dan Knott

Copy Editor
Kate Givens

Indexer
Erika Millen

Proofreader
Susan Eldridge

Technical Editor
Brian France

Publishing Coordinator
Vanessa Evans

Multimedia Developer
Dan Scherf

Interior Designer
Gary Adair

Cover Designer
Alan Clements

Page Layout
Juli Cook

❖

*To my partner Angela, who waited with patience and
constancy while I ignored her night after night making this
title a reality. And to my family, who gave me strength,
courage, and confidence, and made me the person
I am today.*

❖

Contents at a Glance

Table of Contents

Foreword

If you had told me when I submitted my first patch to the PHP project that I'd be writing a book on the topic just three years later, I'd have called you something unpleasant and placed you on /ignore. However, the culture surrounding PHP development is so welcoming, and so thoroughly entrapping, that looking back my only question is "Why aren't there more extension developers?"

The short (easy) answer, of course, is that while PHP's documentation of userspace syntax and functions is—in every way—second to none, the documentation of its internals is far from complete and consistently out of date. Even now, the march of progress towards full Unicode support in PHP6 is introducing dozens of new API calls and changing the way everyone from userspace scripters to core developers looks at strings and binary safety.

The response from those of us working on PHP who are most familiar with its quirks is usually, "Use the source." To be fair, that's a valid answer because nearly every method in the core, and the extensions (both bundled and PECL), are generously peppered with comments and formatted according to strict, well followed standards that are easy to read…once you're used to it.

But where do new developers start? How do they find out what PHP_LONG_ MACRO_NAME() does? And what, precisely, is the difference between a zval and a pval? (Hint: There isn't one; they're the same variable type). This book aims to bring the PHP internals a step closer to the level of accessibility that has made the userspace language so popular. By exposing the well planned and powerful APIs of PHP and the Zend Engine, we'll all benefit from a richer pool of talented developers both from the commercial ranks and within the open source community.

About the Author

Sara Golemon is a self-described terminal geek (pun intended). She has been involved in the PHP project as a core developer for nearly four years and is best known for approaching the language "a little bit differently than everyone else"; a quote you're welcome to take as either praise or criticism. She has worked as a programmer/analyst at the University of California, Berkeley for the past six years after serving the United States District Courts for several years prior. Sara is also the developer and lead maintainer of a dozen PECL extensions as well as libssh2, a non-PHP related project providing easy access to the SSH2 protocol. At the time of this writing, she is actively involved with migrating the streams layer for Unicode compatibility in PHP6.

We Want to Hear from You!

As the reader of this book, *you* are our most important critic and commentator. We value your opinion and want to know what we're doing right, what we could do better, what areas you'd like to see us publish in, and any other words of wisdom you're willing to pass our way.

You can email or write me directly to let me know what you did or didn't like about this book—as well as what we can do to make our books stronger.

Please note that I cannot help you with technical problems related to the topic of this book, and that due to the high volume of mail I receive, I might not be able to reply to every message.

When you write, please be sure to include this book's title and author as well as your name and phone or email address. I will carefully review your comments and share them with the author and editors who worked on the book.

Email: opensource@samspublishing.com
Mail: Mark Taber
            Associate Publisher
            Sams Publishing
            800 East 96th Street
            Indianapolis, IN 46240 USA

Reader Services

Visit our website and register this book at www.samspublishing.com/register for convenient access to any updates, downloads, or errata that might be available for this book.

Introduction

Should You Read This Book?

You probably picked this book off the shelf because you have some level of interest in the PHP language. If you are new to programming in general and are looking to get into the industry with a robust but easy-to-use language, this is not the title for you. Have a look at *PHP and MySQL Web Development* or *Teach Yourself PHP in 24 Hours*. Both titles will get you accustomed to using PHP and have you writing applications in no time.

After you become familiar with the syntax and structure of the PHP scripts, you'll be ready to delve into this title. Encyclopedic knowledge of the userspace functions available within PHP won't be necessary, but it will help to know what wheels don't need reinventing, and what proven design concepts can be followed.

Because the PHP interpreter was written in C, its extension and embedding API was written from a C language perspective. Although it is certainly possible to extend from or embed into another language, doing so is outside of the scope of this book. Knowing basic C syntax, datatypes, and pointer management is vital.

It will be helpful if you are familiar with autoconf syntax. Don't worry about it if you aren't; you'll only need to know a few basic rules of thumb to get by and you'll be introduced to these rules in Chapters 17, "Configuration and Linking" and 18, "Extension Generators."

Why Should You Read This Book?

This book aims to teach you how to do two things. First, it will show you how to extend the PHP language by adding functions, classes, resources, and stream implementations. Second, it will teach you how to embed the PHP language itself into other applications, making them more versatile and useful to your users and customers.

Why Would You Want to Extend PHP?

There are four common reasons for wanting to extend PHP. By far, the most common reason is to link against an external library and expose its API to userspace scripts. This motivation is seen in extensions like mysql, which links against the libmysqlclient library to provide the mysql_*() family of functions to PHP scripts.

These types of extensions are what developers are referring to when they describe PHP as "glue." The code that makes up the extension performs no significant degree of work on its own; rather, it creates an interpretation bridge between PHP's extension API and the API exposed by the library. Without this, PHP and libraries like libmysqlclient would not be able to communicate on a common level. Figure I.1 shows how this type of extension bridges the gap between third-party libraries and the PHP core.

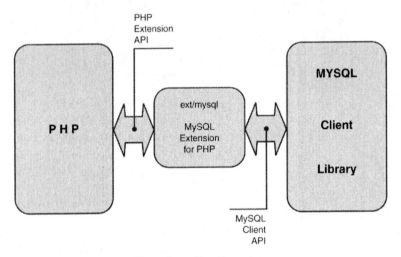

Figure I.1   Glue Extensions

Another common reason to extend PHP is performing special internal operations like declaring superglobals, which cannot be done from userspace because of security restrictions or design limitations. Extensions such as apd (Advanced PHP Debugger) and runkit perform this kind of "internal only" work by exposing bits of the virtual machine's execution stack that are ordinarily hidden from view.

Coming in third is the sheer need for speed. PHP code has to be tokenized, compiled, and stepped through in a virtual machine environment, which can never be as fast as native code. Certain utilities (known as Opcode Caches) can allow scripts to skip the tokenization and compilation step on repeated execution, but they can never speed up the execution step. By translating it to C code, the maintainer sacrifices some of the ease of design that makes PHP so powerful, but gains a speed increase on the order of several multiples.

Lastly, a script author may have put years of work into a particularly clever subroutine and now wants to sell it to another party, but doesn't want to reveal the source code. One approach would be to use an opcode encryption program; however, this approach is more easily decoded than a machine code extension. After all, in order to be useful to the licensed party, their PHP build must, at some point, have access to the compiled bytecode. After the decrypted bytecode is in memory, it's a short road to extracting it to disk and displaying the code. Bytecode, in turn, is much easier to parse into source script than a native binary. What's worse, rather than having a speed advantage, it's actually slightly slower because of the decryption phase.

What Does Embedding Actually Accomplish?

Let's say you've written an entire application in a nice, fast, lean, compiled language like C. To make the application more useful to your users or clients, you'd like to provide a means for them to script certain behaviors using a simple high-level language where they don't have to worry about memory management, or pointers, or linking, or any of that complicated stuff.

If the usefulness of such a feature isn't immediately obvious, consider what your office productivity applications would be without macros, or your command shell without batch files. What sorts of behavior would be impossible in a web browser without JavaScript? Would you be able to capture the magic Hula-Hoop and rescue the prince without being able to program your F1 key to fire a triple shot from your rocket launcher at just the right time to defeat the angry monkey? Well, maybe, but your thumbs would hurt.

So let's say you want to build customizable scripting into your application; you could write your own compiler, build an execution framework, and spend thousands of hours debugging it, or you could take a ready-made enterprise class language like PHP and embed its interpreter right into your application. Tough choice, isn't it?

What's Inside?

This book is split into three primary topics. First you'll be reintroduced to PHP from the inside out in Part I, "Getting to Know PHP All Over Again."

You'll see how the building blocks of the PHP interpreter fit together, and learn how familiar concepts from userspace map to their internal representations.

In Part II, "Extensions", you'll start to construct a functional PHP extension and learn how to use additional features of the PHPAPI. By the end of this section, you should be able to translate nearly any PHP script to faster, leaner C code. You'll also be ready to link against external libraries and perform actions not possible from userspace.

In Part III, "Embedding", you'll approach PHP from the opposite angle. Here, you'll start with an ordinary application and add PHP scripting support into it. You'll learn how to leverage safe_mode and other security features to execute user-supplied code safely, and coordinate multiple requests simultaneously.

Finally, you'll find a set of appendices containing a reference guide to API calls, solutions to common problems, and where to find existing extensions to crib from.

PHP Versus Zend

The first thing you need to know about PHP is that it's actually made up of five separate pieces shown in Figure I.2.

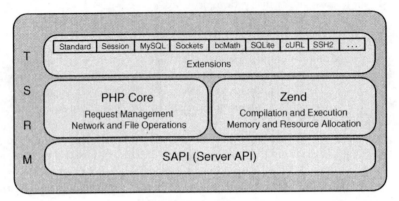

Figure I.2   Anatomy of PHP.

At the bottom of the heap is the *SAPI (Server API)* layer, which coordinates the lifecycle process you'll see in Chapter 1, "The PHP Lifecycle." This layer is what interfaces to web servers like Apache (through `mod_php5.so`) or the command line (through bin/php). In Part III, you'll be linking against the embed SAPI which operates at this layer.

Above the SAPI layer is the *PHP Core*. The core provides a binding layer for key events and handles certain low-level operations like file streams, error handling, and start-up/shutdown triggering.

Right next to the core you'll find the *Zend Engine*, which parses and compiles human readable scripts into machine readable bytecode. Zend also executes that bytecode inside a virtual machine where it reads and writes userspace variables, manages program flow, and periodically passes control to one of the other layers such as during a function call. Zend also provides per-request memory management and a robust API for environment manipulation.

Lying above PHP and Zend is the extension layer where you'll find all the functions available from userspace. Several of these extensions (such as standard, pcre, and session) are compiled in by default and are often not even thought of as extensions. Others are optionally built into PHP using `./configure` options like –with-mysql or –enable-sockets, or built as shared modules and then loaded in the `php.ini` with `extension=` or in userspace scripts using the `dl()` function. You'll be developing in this layer in Part II and Part III when you start to perform simultaneous embedding and extending.

Wrapped up around and threaded through all of this is the TSRM (Thread Safe Resource Management) layer. This portion of the PHP interpreter is what allows a single instance of PHP to execute multiple independent requests at the same time without stepping all over each other. Fortunately most of this layer is hidden from view through a range of macro functions that you'll gradually come to be familiar with through the course of this book.

What Is an Extension?

An extension is a discrete bundle of code that can be plugged into the PHP interpreter in order to provide additional functionality to userspace scripts. Extensions typically export at least one function, class, resource type, or stream implementation, often a dozen or more of these in some combination.

The most widely used extension is the `standard` extension, which defines more than 500 functions, 10 resource types, 2 classes, and 5 stream wrappers. This extension, along with the `zend_builtin_functions` extension, is always compiled into the PHP interpreter regardless of any other configuration options. Additional extensions, such as `session`, `spl`, `pcre`, `mysql`, and `sockets`, are enabled or disabled with configuration options, or built separately using the phpize tool.

One structure that each extension (or module) shares in common is the `zend_module_entry` struct defined in the PHP source tarball under `Zend/zend_modules.h`. This structure is the "start point" where PHP introduces itself to your extension and defines the startup and shutdown methods used by the lifecycle process described in Chapter 1 (see Figure I.3). This structure also references an array of `zend_function_entry` structures, defined in `Zend/zend_API.h`. This array, as the data type suggests, lists the built-in functions exported by the extension.

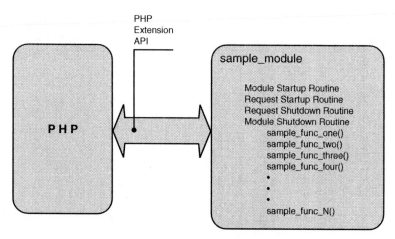

Figure I.3 PHP extension entry point.

You'll examine this structure in more depth starting with Chapter 6, "Returning Values," when you begin to build a functioning extension.

How Is Embedding Accomplished with PHP?

Ordinarily, the PHP interpreter is linked into a process that shuttles script requests into the interpreter and passes the results back out.

The CLI SAPI does this in the form of a thin wrapper between the interpreter and the command line shell while the Apache SAPI exports the right hooks as an apxs module.

It might be tempting to embed PHP into your application using a custom written SAPI module. Fortunately, it's completely unnecessary! Since version 4.3, the standard PHP distribution has included a SAPI called *embed*, which allows the PHP interpreter to act like an ordinary dynamic link library that you can include in any application.

In Part III, you'll see how any application can leverage the power and flexibility of PHP code through the use of this simple and concise library.

Terms Used Throughout This Book

PHP	Refers to the PHP interpreter as a whole including Zend, TSRM, the SAPI layer, and any extensions.
PHP Core	A smaller subset of the PHP interpreter as defined in the "PHP Versus Zend" section earlier in this chapter.
Zend	The Zend Engine, which handles parsing, compiling, and executing script opcodes.
PEAR	The PHP Extension and Application Repository. The PEAR project (http://pear.php.net) is the official home for community-generated open source free projects. PEAR houses several hundred object-oriented classes written in PHP script, providing drop-in solutions to common programming tasks. Despite its name, PEAR does not include C-language PHP extensions.
PECL	The PHP Extension Code Library, pronounced "pickle." PECL (http://pecl.php.net) is the C-code offshoot of the PEAR project that uses many of the same packaging, deployment, and installation systems. PECL packages are usually PHP extensions, but may include Zend extensions or SAPI implementations.

PHP extension	Also known as a module. A discrete bundle of compiled code defining userspace-accessible functions, classes, stream implementations, constants, ini options, and specialized resource types. Anywhere you see the term extension used elsewhere in the text, you may assume it is referring to a PHP extension.
Zend extension	A variant of the PHP extension used by specialized systems such as OpCode caches and encoders. Zend extensions are beyond the scope of this book.
Userspace	The environment and API library visible to scripts actually written in the PHP language. Userspace has no access to PHP internals or data structures not explicitly granted to it by the workings of the Zend Engine and the various PHP extensions.
Internals (C-space)	Engine and extension code. This term is used to refer to all those things that are not directly accessible to userspace code.

The PHP Life Cycle

IN A COMMON WEB SERVER ENVIRONMENT, YOU'LL NEVER explicitly start the PHP interpreter; you'll start Apache or some other web server that will load PHP and process scripts as needed—that is, as .php documents are requested.

It All Starts with the SAPI

Though it may look very different, the CLI binary actually behaves just the same way. A php command, entered at the system prompt starts up the "command line sapi," which acts like a mini–web server designed to service a single request. When the script is done running, this mini–PHP-web server shuts down and returns control to the shell.

Starting Up and Shutting Down

This startup and shutdown process happens in two separate startup phases and two separate shutdown phases. One cycle is for the PHP interpreter as a whole to perform an initial setup of structures and values that will persist for the life of the SAPI. The second is for transient settings that only last as long as a single page request.

During the initial startup, before any request has been made, PHP calls every extension's MINIT (Module Initialization) method. Here, extensions are expected to declare constants, define classes, and register resource, stream, and filter handlers that all future script requests will use. Features such as these, which are designed to exist across all requests, are referred to as being *persistent*.

A common MINIT method might look like the following:

```
/* Initialize the myextension module
 * This will happen immediately upon SAPI startup
 */
PHP_MINIT_FUNCTION(myextension)
{
    /* Globals: Chapter 12 */
```

```
#ifdef ZTS
    ts_allocate_id(&myextension_globals_id,
        sizeof(php_myextension_globals),
        (ts_allocate_ctor) myextension_globals_ctor,
        (ts_allocate_dtor) myextension_globals_dtor);
#else
    myextension_globals_ctor(&myextension_globals TSRMLS_CC);
#endif

    /* REGISTER_INI_ENTRIES() refers to a global
     * structure that will be covered in
     * Chapter 13 "INI Settings"
     */
    REGISTER_INI_ENTRIES();

    /* define('MYEXT_MEANING', 42); */
    REGISTER_LONG_CONSTANT("MYEXT_MEANING", 42, CONST_CS | CONST_PERSISTENT);
    /* define('MYEXT_FOO', 'bar'); */
    REGISTER_STRING_CONSTANT("MYEXT_FOO", "bar", CONST_CS | CONST_PERSISTENT);

    /* Resources: chapter 9 */
    le_myresource = zend_register_list_destructors_ex(
                    php_myext_myresource_dtor, NULL,
                    "My Resource Type", module_number);
    le_myresource_persist = zend_register_list_destructors_ex(
                    NULL, php_myext_myresource_dtor,
                    "My Resource Type", module_number);

    /* Stream Filters: Chapter 16 */
    if (FAILURE == php_stream_filter_register_factory("myfilter",
                    &php_myextension_filter_factory TSRMLS_CC)) {
        return FAILURE;
    }

    /* Stream Wrappers: Chapter 15 */
    if (FAILURE == php_register_url_stream_wrapper ("myproto",
                    &php_myextension_stream_wrapper TSRMLS_CC)) {
        return FAILURE;
    }

    /* Autoglobals: Chapter 12 */
#ifdef ZEND_ENGINE_2
    if (zend_register_auto_global("_MYEXTENSION", sizeof("_MYEXTENSION") - 1,
                                        NULL TSRMLS_CC) == FAILURE) {
        return FAILURE;
    }
```

```
    zend_auto_global_disable_jit ("_MYEXTENSION", sizeof("_MYEXTENSION") - 1
                                                    TSRMLS_CC);
#else
    if (zend_register_auto_global("_MYEXTENSION", sizeof("_MYEXTENSION") - 1
                                                    TSRMLS_CC) == FAILURE) {
        return FAILURE;
    }
#endif
    return SUCCESS;
}
```

After a request has been made, PHP sets up an operating environment including a symbol table (where variables are stored) and synchronizes per-directory configuration values. PHP then loops through its extensions again, this time calling each one's RINIT (Request Initialization) method. Here, an extension may reset global variables to default values, prepopulate variables into the script's symbol table, or perform other tasks such as logging the page request to a file. RINIT can be thought of as a kind of auto_prepend_file directive for all scripts requested.

An RINIT method might be expected to look like this:

```
/* Run at the start of every page request
 */
PHP_RINIT_FUNCTION(myextension)
{
    zval *myext_autoglobal;

    /* Initialize the autoglobal variable
     * declared in the MINIT function
     * as an empty array.
     * This is equivalent to performing:
     * $_MYEXTENSION = array();
     */
    ALLOC_INIT_ZVAL(myext_autoglobal);
    array_init(myext_autoglobal);
    zend_hash_add(&EG(symbol_table), "_MYEXTENSION", sizeof("_MYEXTENSION") - 1,
                        (void**)&myext_autoglobal, sizeof(zval*), NULL);

    return SUCCESS;
}
```

After a request has completed processing, either by reaching the end of the script file or by exiting through a die() or exit() statement, PHP starts the cleanup process by calling each extension's RSHUTDOWN (Request Shutdown) method. RSHUTDOWN corresponds to auto_append_file in much the same was as RINIT corresponds to auto_prepend_file. The most important difference between RSHUTDOWN and auto_append_file, however, is that RSHUTDOWN will always be executed, whereas a call to die() or exit() inside the userspace script will skip any auto_append_file.

Any last minute tasks that need to be performed can be handled in RSHUTDOWN before the symbol table and other resources are destroyed. After all RSHUTDOWN methods have completed, every variable in the symbol table is implicitly unset(), during which all non-persistent resource and object destructors are called in order to free resources gracefully.

```
/* Run at the end of every page request
 */
PHP_RSHUTDOWN_FUNCTION(myextension)
{
    zval **myext_autoglobal;

    if (zend_hash_find(&EG(symbol_table), "_MYEXTENSION", sizeof("_MYEXTENSION"),
                                        (void**)&myext_autoglobal) == SUCCESS) {
        /* Do something meaningful
         * with the values of the
         * $_MYEXTENSION array
         */
        php_myextension_handle_values(myext_autoglobal TSRMLS_CC);
    }
    return SUCCESS;
}
```

Finally, when all requests have been fulfilled and the web server or other SAPI is ready to shut down, PHP loops through each extension's MSHUTDOWN (Module Shutdown) method. This is an extension's last chance to unregister handlers and free persistent memory allocated during the MINIT cycle.

```
/* This module is being unloaded
 * constants and functions will be
 * automatically purged,
 * persistent resources, class entries,
 * and stream handlers must be
 * manually unregistered.
 */
PHP_MSHUTDOWN_FUNCTION(myextension)
{
    UNREGISTER_INI_ENTRIES();
    php_unregister_url_stream_wrapper ("myproto" TSRMLS_CC);
    php_stream_filter_unregister_factory ("myfilter" TSRMLS_CC);
    return SUCCESS;
}
```

Life Cycles

Each PHP instance, whether started from an `init` script, or from the command line, follows a series of events involving both the Request/Module Init/Shutdown events covered previously, and the actual execution of scripts themselves. How many times, and how frequently each startup and shutdown phase is executed, depends on the SAPI in use. The four most common SAPI configurations are CLI/CGI, Multiprocess Module, Multithreaded Module, and Embedded.

CLI Life Cycle

The CLI (and CGI) SAPI is fairly unique in its single-request life cycle; however, the Module versus Requests steps are still cycles in discrete loops. Figure 1.1 shows the progression of the PHP interpreter when called from the command line for the script `test.php`.

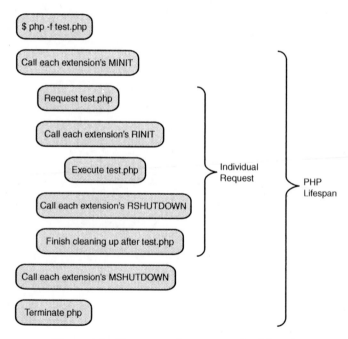

Figure 1.1   Requests cycles versus engine life cycle.

The Multiprocess Life Cycle

The most common configuration of PHP embedded into a web server is using PHP built as an APXS module for Apache 1, or Apache 2 using the Pre-fork MPM. Many other web server configurations fit into this same category, which will be referred to as the *multiprocess model* through the rest of this book.

It's called the multiprocess model because when Apache starts up, it immediately forks several child processes, each of which has its own process space and functions independently from each another. Within a given child, the life cycle of that PHP instance looks immediately familiar as shown in Figure 1.2. The only variation here is that multiple requests are sandwiched between a single MINIT/MSHUTDOWN pair.

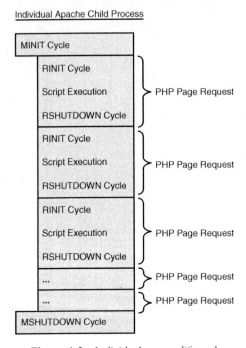

Figure 1.2   Individual process life cycle.

This model does not allow any one child to be aware of data owned by another child, although it does allow children to die and be replaced at will without compromising the stability of any other child. Figure 1.3 shows multiple children of a single Apache invocation and the calls to each of their MINIT, RINIT, RSHUTDOWN, and MSHUTDOWN methods.

Multiprocess
Apache
Webserver

Apache Child Process	Apache Child Process	Apache Child Process	Apache Child Process
MINIT	MINIT	MINIT	MINIT
RINIT	RINIT	RINIT	RINIT
Script	Script	Script	Script
RSHUTDOWN	RSHUTDOWN	RSHUTDOWN	RSHUTDOWN
RINIT	RINIT	RINIT	RINIT
Script	Script	Script	Script
RSHUTDOWN	RSHUTDOWN	RSHUTDOWN	RSHUTDOWN
RINIT	RINIT	RINIT	RINIT
Script	Script	Script	Script
RSHUTDOWN	RSHUTDOWN	RSHUTDOWN	RSHUTDOWN
...	...	...	...
...	...	...	...
...	...	...	...
MSHUTDOWN	MSHUTDOWN	MSHUTDOWN	MSHUTDOWN

Figure 1.3   Multiprocess life cycles.

The Multithreaded Life Cycle

Increasingly, PHP is being seen in a number of multithreaded web server configurations such as the ISAPI interface to IIS and the Apache 2 Worker MPM. Under a multithreaded web server only one process runs at any given time, but multiple threads execute within that process space simultaneously. This allows several bits of overhead, including the repeated calls to MINIT/MSHUTDOWN to be avoided, true global data to be allocated and initialized only once, and potentially opens the door for multiple requests to deterministically share information. Figure 1.4 shows the parallel process flow that occurs within PHP when run from a multithreaded web server such as Apache 2.

The Embed Life Cycle

Recalling that the Embed SAPI is just another SAPI implementation following the same rules as the CLI, APXS, or ISAPI interfaces, it's easy to imagine that the life cycle of a request will follow the same basic path: Module Init => Request Init => Request => Request Shutdown => Module Shutdown. Indeed, the Embed SAPI follows each of these steps in perfect time with its siblings.

What makes the Embed SAPI appear unique is that the request may be fed in multiple script segments that function as part of a single whole request. Control will also pass back and forth between PHP and the calling application multiple times under most configurations.

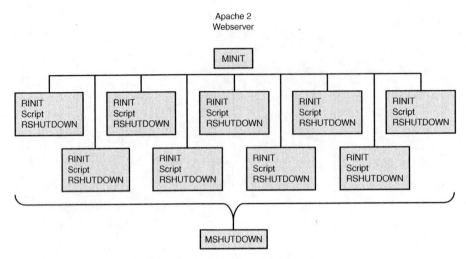

Figure 1.4   Multithreaded life cycles.

Although an Embed request may consist of one or more code elements, embed applications are subject to the same request isolation requirements as web servers. In order to process two or more simultaneous embed environments, your application will either need to fork like Apache1 or thread like Apache2. Attempting to process two separate request environments within a single non-threaded process space will lead to unexpected, and certainly undesired, results.

Zend Thread Safety

When PHP was in its infancy, it ran as a single process CGI and had no concern for thread safety because no process space could outlive a single request. An internal variable could be declared in the global scope and accessed or changed at will without consequence so long as its contents were properly initialized. Any resources that weren't cleaned up properly would be released when the CGI process terminated.

Later on, PHP was embedded into multiprocess web servers like Apache. A given internal variable could still be defined globally and safely accessed by the active request so long as it was properly initialized at the start of each request and cleaned up at the end because only one request per process space could ever be active at one time. At this point per-request memory management was added to keep resource leaks from growing out of control.

As single-process multithreaded web servers started to appear, however, a new approach to handling global data became necessary. Eventually this would emerge as a new layer called *TSRM (Thread Safe Resource Management)*.

Thread-Safe Versus Non–Thread-Safe Declaration

In a simple non-threaded application, you would most likely declare global variables by placing them at the top of your source file. The compiler would then allocate a block of memory in your program's data segment to hold that unit of information.

In a multithreaded application where each thread needs its own version of that data element, it's necessary to allocate a separate block of memory for each thread. A given thread then picks the correct block of memory when it needs to access its data, and references from that pointer.

Thread-Safe Data Pools

During an extension's MINIT phase, the TSRM layer is notified how much data will need to be stored by that extension using one or more calls to the ts_allocate_id() function. TSRM adds that byte count to its running total of data space requirements, and returns a new, unique identifier for that segment's portion of the thread's data pool.

```
typedef struct {
    int sampleint;
    char *samplestring;
} php_sample_globals;
int sample_globals_id;
PHP_MINIT_FUNCTION(sample)
{
    ts_allocate_id(&sample_globals_id,
        sizeof(php_sample_globals),
        (ts_allocate_ctor) php_sample_globals_ctor,
        (ts_allocate_dtor) php_sample_globals_dtor);
    return SUCCESS;
}
```

When it comes time to access that data segment during a request, the extension requests a pointer from the TSRM layer for the current thread's resource pool, offset by the appropriate index suggested by the resource ID returned by ts_allocate_id().

Put another way, in terms of code flow, the following statement
SAMPLE_G(sampleint) = 5; is one that you might see in the module associated with the previous MINIT statement. Under a thread-safe build, this statement expands through a number of intermediary macros to the following:

```
(((php_sample_globals*)(*((void ***)tsrm_ls))[sample_globals_id-1])->sampleint =
5;
```

Don't be concerned if you have trouble parsing that statement; it's so well integrated into the PHPAPI that some developers never bother to learn how it works.

When Not to Thread

Because accessing global resources within a thread-safe build of PHP involves the overhead of looking up the correct offset into the right data pool, it ends up being slower than its non-threaded counterpart, in which data is simply plucked out of a true global whose address is computed at compile time.

Consider the prior example again, this time under a non-threaded build:

```
typedef struct {
    int sampleint;
    char *samplestring;
} php_sample_globals;
php_sample_globals sample_globals;
PHP_MINIT_FUNCTION(sample)
{
    php_sample_globals_ctor(&sample_globals TSRMLS_CC);
    return SUCCESS;
}
```

The first thing you'll notice here is that rather than declaring an `int` to identify a reference to a globals struct declared elsewhere, you're simply defining the structure right in the process's global scope. This means that the `SAMPLE_G(sampleint) = 5;` statement from before only needs to expand out as `sample_globals.sampleint = 5;`. Simple, fast, and efficient.

Non-threaded builds also have the advantage of process isolation so that if a given request encounters completely unexpected circumstances, it can bail all the way out or even segfault without bringing the entire web server to its knees. In fact, Apache's `MaxRequestsPerChild` directive is designed to take advantage of this effect by deliberately killing its children every so often and spawning fresh ones in their place.

Agnostic Globals Access

When creating an extension, you won't necessarily know whether the environment it gets built for will require thread safety or not. Fortunately, part of the standard set of include files that you'll use conditionally define the `ZTS` preprocessor token. When PHP is built for thread safety, either because the SAPI requires it, or through the —enable-maintainer-zts option, this value is automatically defined and can be tested with the usual set of directives such as `#ifdef ZTS`.

As you saw a moment ago, it only makes sense to allocate space in the thread safety pool if the pool actually exists, and it will only exist if PHP was compiled for thread safety. That's why in the previous examples it's wrapped in checks for `ZTS`, with a non-threaded alternative being called for non-ZTS builds.

In the `PHP_MINIT_FUNCTION(myextension)` example you saw much earlier in this chapter, `#ifdef ZTS` was used to conditionally call the correct version of global initialization code. For ZTS mode it used `ts_allocate_id()` to populate the `myextension_globals_id` variable, and non-ZTS mode just called the initialization method for `myextension_globals` directly. These two variables would have been declared in your extensions source file using a Zend macro: `DECLARE_MODULE_GLOBALS` `(myextension);` which automatically handles testing for ZTS and declaring the correct host variable of the appropriate type depending on whether ZTS is enabled.

When it comes time to access these global variables, you'll use a self-defined macro like `SAMPLE_G()` shown earlier. In Chapter 12, you'll learn how to design this macro to expand to the correct form depending on whether ZTS is enabled.

Threading Even When You Don't Have To

A normal PHP build has thread safety turned off by default and only enables it if the SAPI being built is known to require thread safety, or if thread safety is explicitly turned on by a `./configure` switch.

Given the speed issues with global lookups and the lack of process isolation you might wonder why anyone would deliberately turn the TSRM layer on when it's not required. For the most part, it's extension and SAPI developers—like you're about to become—who turn thread safety on in order to ensure that new code will run correctly in all environments.

When thread safety is enabled, a special pointer, called `tsrm_ls`, is added to the prototype of many internal functions. It's this pointer that allows PHP to differentiate the data associated with one thread from another. You may recall seeing it used with the `SAMPLE_G()` macro under ZTS mode earlier in this chapter. Without it, an executing function wouldn't know whose symbol table to look up and set a particular value in; it wouldn't even know which script was being executed, and the engine would be completely unable to track its internal registers. This one pointer keeps one thread handling page request from running right over the top of another.

The way this pointer parameter is optionally included in prototypes is through a set of defines. When ZTS is disabled, these defines all evaluate to blank; when it's turned on, however, they look like the following:

```
#define TSRMLS_D    void ***tsrm_ls
#define TSRMLS_DC   , void ***tsrm_ls
#define TSRMLS_C    tsrm_ls
#define TSRMLS_CC   , tsrm_ls
```

A non-ZTS build would see the first line in the following code as having two parameters, an `int` and a `char*`. Under a ZTS build, on the other hand, the prototype contains three parameters: an `int`, a `char*`, and a `void***`. When your program calls this function, it will need to pass in that parameter, but only for ZTS-enabled builds. The second line in the following code shows how the CC macro accomplishes exactly that.

```
int php_myext_action(int action_id, char *message TSRMLS_DC);
php_myext_action(42, "The meaning of life" TSRMLS_CC);
```

By including this special variable in the function call, `php_myext_action` will be able to use the value of `tsrm_ls` together with the `MYEXT_G()` macro to access its thread-specific global data. On a non-ZTS build, `tsrm_ls` will be unavailable, but that's okay because `MYEXT_G()`, and other similar macros, will have no use for it.

Now imagine that you're working on a new extension and you've got the following function that works beautifully under your local build using the CLI SAPI, and even when you compile it using the apxs SAPI for Apache 1:

```
static int php_myext_isset(char *varname, int varname_len)
{
    zval **dummy;

    if (zend_hash_find(EG(active_symbol_table),
        varname, varname_len + 1,
        (void**)&dummy) == SUCCESS) {
        /* Variable exists */
        return 1;
    } else {
        /* Undefined variable */
        return 0;
    }
}
```

Satisfied that everything is working well, you package up your extension and send it to another office to be built and run on the production servers. To your dismay, the remote office reports that the extension failed to compile.

It turns out that they're using Apache 2.0 in threaded mode so their build of PHP has ZTS enabled. When the compiler encountered your use of the `EG()` macro, it tried to find `tsrm_ls` in the local scope and couldn't because you never declared it and never passed it to your function.

The fix is simple of course; just add `TSRMLS_DC` to the declaration of `php_myext_isset()` and toss a `TSRMLS_CC` onto every line that calls it. Unfortunately, the production team in the remote office is a little less certain of your extension's quality now and would like to put off the rollout for another couple of weeks. If only this problem could have been caught sooner!

That's where `–enable-maintainer-zts` comes in. By adding this one line to your `./configure` statement when building PHP, your build will automatically include ZTS even if your current SAPI, such as CLI, doesn't require it. Enabling this switch, you can avoid this common and unnecessary programming mistake.

Note

In PHP4, the `–enable-maintainer-zts` flag was known as `–enable-experimental-zts`; be sure to use the correct flag for your version of PHP.

Finding a Lost `tsrm_ls`

Occasionally, it's just not possible to pass the `tsrm_ls` pointer into a function that needs it. Usually this is because your extension is interfacing with a library that uses callbacks and doesn't provide room for an abstract pointer to be returned. Consider the following piece of code:

```
void php_myext_event_callback(int eventtype, char *message)
{
    zval *event;

    /* $event = array('event'=>$eventtype,
                      'message'=>$message) */
    MAKE_STD_ZVAL(event);
    array_init(event);
    add_assoc_long(event, "type", eventtype);
    add_assoc_string(event, "message", message, 1);

    /* $eventlog[] = $event; */
    add_next_index_zval(EXT_G(eventlog), event);
}
PHP_FUNCTION(myext_startloop)
{
    /* The eventlib_loopme() function,
     * exported by an external library,
     * waits for an event to happen,
     * then dispatches it to the
     * callback handler specified.
     */
    eventlib_loopme(php_myext_event_callback);
}
```

Although not all of this code segment will make sense yet, you will notice right away that the callback function uses the `EXT_G()` macro, which is known to need the `tsrm_ls` pointer under threaded builds. Changing the function prototype will do no good because the external library has no notion of PHP's thread-safety model, nor should it. So how can `tsrm_ls` be recovered in such a way that it can be used?

The solution comes in the form of a Zend macro called `TSRMLS_FETCH()`. When placed at the top of a code segment, this macro will perform a lookup based on the current threading context, and declare a local copy of the `tsrm_ls` pointer.

Although it will be tempting to use this macro everywhere and not bother with passing `tsrm_ls` via function calls, it's important to note that a `TSRMLS_FETCH()` call takes a fair amount of processing time to complete. Not noticeable on a single iteration certainly, but as your thread count increases, and the number of instances in which you call `TSRMLS_FETCH()` grows, your extension will gradually begin to show this bottleneck for what it is. Be sure to use it sparingly.

Note

To ensure compatibility with C++ compilers, be sure to place `TSRMLS_FETCH()` —and all variable declarations for that matter—at the top of a given block scope before any statements. Because the `TSRMLS_FETCH()` macro itself can resolve in a couple of different ways, it's best to make this the last variable declared within a given declaration header.

Summary

In this chapter you glimpsed several of the concepts that you'll explore in later chapters. You also built a foundation for understanding what goes on, not only under the hood of the extensions you'll come to build, but behind the scenes of the Zend Engine and TSRM layer, which you'll take advantage of as you embed and deploy PHP in your applications.

2

Variables from the Inside Out

ONE THING EVERY PROGRAMMING LANGUAGE SHARES IN COMMON is a means to store and retrieve information; PHP is no exception. Although many languages require all variables to be declared beforehand and that the type of information they will hold be fixed, PHP permits the programmer to create variables on the fly and store any type of information that the language is capable of expressing. When the stored information is needed, it is automatically converted to whatever type is appropriate at the time.

Because you've used PHP from the userspace side already, this concept, known as *loose typing*, shouldn't be unfamiliar to you. In this chapter, you'll look at how this information is encoded internally by PHP's parent language, C, which requires strict typecasting.

Of course, encoding data is only half of the equation. To keep track of all these pieces of information, each one needs a label and a container. From the userspace realm, you'll recognize these concepts as variable names and scope.

Data Types

The fundamental unit of data storage in PHP is known as the `zval`, or Zend Value. It's a small, four member struct defined in `Zend/zend.h` with the following format:

```
typedef struct _zval_struct {
    zvalue_value value;
    zend_uint refcount;
    zend_uchar type;
    zend_uchar is_ref;
} zval;
```

It should be a simple matter to intuit the basic storage type for most of these members: unsigned integer for `refcount`, and unsigned character for `type` and `is_ref`. The `value` member however, is actually a union structure defined, as of PHP5, as:

```
typedef union _zvalue_value {
    long lval;
    double dval;
    struct {
        char *val;
        int len;
    } str;
    HashTable *ht;
    zend_object_value obj;
} zvalue_value;
```

This union allows Zend to store the many different types of data a PHP variable is capable of holding in a single, unified structure.

Zend currently defines the eight data types listed in Table 2.1.

Table 2.1   **Data Types Used by Zend/PHP**

Type Value	Purpose
IS_NULL	This type is automatically assigned to uninitialized variables upon their first use and can also be explicitly assigned in userspace using the built-in NULL constant. This variable type provides a special "non-value," which is distinct from a Boolean FALSE or an integer 0.
IS_BOOL	Boolean variables can have one of two possible states, either TRUE or FALSE. Conditional expressions in userspace control structures—if, while, ternary, for—are implicitly typecast to Boolean during evaluation.
IS_LONG	Integer data types in PHP are stored using the host system's signed long data type. On most 32-bit platforms this yields a storage range of -2147483648 to +2147483647. With a few exceptions, whenever a userspace script attempts to store an integer value outside of this range, it is automatically converted to a double-precision floating point type (IS_DOUBLE).
IS_DOUBLE	Floating point data types use the host system's signed double data type. Floating point numbers are not stored with exact precision; rather, a formula is used to express the value as a fraction of limited precision (mantissa) times 2 raised to a certain power (exponent). This representation allows the computer to store a wide range of values (positive or negative) from as small as $2.225 \times 10^{(-308)}$ to an upper limit of around 1.798×10^{308} in only 8 bytes. Unfortunately, numbers that evaluate to exact figures in decimal don't always store cleanly as binary fractions. For example, the decimal expression 0.5 evaluates to an exact binary figure of 0.1, while decimal 0.8 becomes a repeating binary representation of 0.1100110011.... When converted back to decimal, the truncated binary digits yield a slightly offset value because they are not able to store the entire figure. Think of it like trying to express the

Table 2.1   **Continued**

Type Value	Purpose
	number 1/3 as a decimal: 0.333333 comes very close, but it's not precise as evidenced by the fact that 3 ★ 0.333333 is not 1.0. This imprecision often leads to confusion when dealing with floating point numbers on computers. (These range limits are based on common 32-bit platforms; range may vary from system to system.)
IS_STRING	PHP's most universal data type is the string which is stored in just the way an experienced C programmer would expect. A block of memory, sufficiently large to hold all the bytes/characters of the string, is allocated and a pointer to that string is stored in the host zval.
	What's worth noting about PHP strings is that the length of the string is always explicitly stated in the zval structure. This allows strings to contain NULL bytes without being truncated. This aspect of PHP strings will be referred to hereafter as *binary safety* because it makes them safe to contain any type of binary data.
	Note that the amount of memory allocated for a given PHP string is always, at minimum, its length plus one. This last byte is populated with a terminating NULL character so that functions that do not require binary safety can simply pass the string pointer through to their underlying method.
IS_ARRAY	An array is a special purpose variable whose sole function is to carry around other variables. Unlike C's notion of an array, a PHP array is not a vector of a uniform data type (such as zval arrayofzvals[];). Instead, a PHP array is a complex set of data buckets linked into a structure known as a HashTable. Each HashTable element (bucket) contains two relevant pieces of information: label and data. In the case of PHP arrays, the label is the associative or numeric index within the array, and the data is the variable (zval) to which that key refers.
IS_OBJECT	Objects take the multi-element data storage of arrays and go one further by adding methods, access modifiers, scoped constants, and special event handlers. As an extension developer, building object-oriented code that functions equally well in PHP4 and PHP5 presents a special challenge because the internal object model has changed so much between Zend Engine 1 (PHP4) and Zend Engine 2 (PHP5).
IS_RESOURCE	Some data types simply cannot be mapped to userspace. For example, stdio's FILE pointer or libmysqlclient's connection handle can't be simply mapped to an array of scalar values, nor would they make sense if they could. To shield the userspace script writer from having to deal with these issues, PHP provides a generic resource data type. The details of how resources are implemented will be covered in Chapter 9, "The Resource Datatype"; for now just be aware that they exist.

The IS_* constants listed in Table 2.1 are stored in the type element of the zval struct and determine which part of the value element of the zval struct should be looked at when examining its value.

The most obvious way to inspect the value of type would probably be to dereference it from a given zval as in the following code snippet:

```
void describe_zval(zval *foo)
{
    if (foo->type == IS_NULL) {
        php_printf("The variable is NULL");
    } else {
        php_printf("The variable is of type %d", foo->type);
    }
}
```

Obvious, but wrong.

Well, not wrong, but certainly not the preferred approach. The Zend header files contain a large block of zval access macros that extension authors are expected to use when examining zval data. The primary reason for this is to avoid incompatibilities when and if the engine's API changes, but as a side benefit the code often becomes easier to read. Here's that same code snippet again, this time using the Z_TYPE_P() macro:

```
void describe_zval(zval *foo)
{
    if (Z_TYPE_P(foo) == IS_NULL) {
        php_printf("The variable is NULL");
    } else {
        php_printf("The variable is of type %d",
                        Z_TYPE_P(foo));
    }
}
```

The _P suffix to this macro indicates that the parameter passed contains a single level of indirection. Two more macros exist in this set, Z_TYPE() and Z_TYPE_PP(), which expect parameters of type zval (no indirection), and zval** (two levels of indirection) respectively.

Note

In this example a special output function, php_printf(), was used to display a piece of data. This function is syntactically identical to stdio's printf() function; however, it handles special processing for web server SAPIs and takes advantage of PHP's output buffering mechanism. You'll learn more about this function and its cousin PHPWRITE() in Chapter 5, "Your First Extension."

Data Values

As with type, the value of zvals can be inspected using a triplet of macros. These macros also begin with Z_, and optionally end with _P or _PP depending on their degree of indirection.

For the simple scalar types, Boolean, long, and double, the macros are short and consistent: BVAL, LVAL, and DVAL.

```
void display_values(zval boolzv, zval *longpzv,
            zval **doubleppzv)
{
    if (Z_TYPE(boolzv) == IS_BOOL) {
        php_printf("The value of the boolean is: %s\n",
            Z_BVAL(boolzv) ? "true" : "false");
    }
    if (Z_TYPE_P(longpzv) == IS_LONG) {
        php_printf("The value of the long is: %ld\n",
            Z_LVAL_P(longpzv));
    }
    if (Z_TYPE_PP(doubleppzv) == IS_DOUBLE) {
        php_printf("The value of the double is: %f\n",
            Z_DVAL_PP(doubleppzv));
    }
}
```

String variables, because they contain two attributes, have a pair of macro triplets representing the char* (STRVAL) and int (STRLEN) elements:

```
void display_string(zval *zstr)
{
    if (Z_TYPE_P(zstr) != IS_STRING) {
        php_printf("The wrong datatype was passed!\n");
        return;
    }
    PHPWRITE(Z_STRVAL_P(zstr), Z_STRLEN_P(zstr));
}
```

The array data type is stored internally as a HashTable* that can be accessed using the ARRVAL triplet: Z_ARRVAL(zv), Z_ARRVAL_P(pzv), Z_ARRVAL_PP(ppzv). When looking through old code in the PHP core and PECL modules, you might encounter the HASH_OF() macro, which expects a zval*. This macro is generally the equivalent of the Z_ARRVAL_P() macro; however, its use is deprecated and should not be used with new code.

Objects represent complex internal structures and have a number of access macros: OBJ_HANDLE, which returns the handle identifier, OBJ_HT for the handler table, OBJCE for the class definition, OBJPROP for the property HashTable, and OBJ_HANDLER for manipulating a specific handler method in the OBJ_HT table. Don't worry about the meaning of these various object macros just yet; they'll be covered in detail in Chapter 10, "PHP4 Objects," and Chapter 11, "PHP5 Objects."

Within a zval, a resource data type is stored as a simple integer that can be accessed with the RESVAL tripplet. This integer is passed on to the zend_fetch_resource() function which looks up the registered resource from its numeric identifier. The resource data type will be covered in depth in Chapter 9.

Data Creation

Now that you've seen how to pull data out of a zval, it's time to create some of your own. Although a zval could be simply declared as a direct variable at the top of a function, it would make the variable's data storage local and it would have to be copied in order to leave the function and reach userspace.

Because you will almost always want zvals that you create to reach userspace in some form, you'll want to allocate a block of memory for it and assign that block to a zval* pointer. Once again the "obvious" solution of using malloc(sizeof(zval)) is not the right answer. Instead you'll use another Zend macro: MAKE_STD_ZVAL(pzv). This macro will allocate space in an optimized chunk of memory near other zvals, automatically handle out-of-memory errors (which you'll explore further in the next chapter), and initialize the refcount and is_ref properties of your new zval.

> **Note**
>
> In addition to MAKE_STD_ZVAL(), you will often see another zval* creation macro used in PHP sources: ALLOC_INIT_ZVAL(). This macro only differs from MAKE_STD_ZVAL() in that it initializes the data type of the zval* to IS_NULL.

Once data storage space is available, it's time to populate your brand-new zval with some information. After reading the section on data storage earlier, you're probably all primed to use those Z_TYPE_P() and Z_SOMEVAL_P() macros to set up your new variable. Seems the "obvious" solution right?

Again, obviousness falls short!

Zend exposes yet another set of macros for setting zval* values. Following are these new macros and how they expand to the ones you're already familiar with.

```
ZVAL_NULL(pvz);                    Z_TYPE_P(pzv) = IS_NULL;
```

Although this macro doesn't provide any savings over using the more direct version, it's included for completeness.

```
ZVAL_BOOL(pzv, b);                 Z_TYPE_P(pzv) = IS_BOOL;
                                   Z_BVAL_P(pzv) = b ? 1 : 0;

ZVAL_TRUE(pzv);                    ZVAL_BOOL(pzv, 1);

ZVAL_FALSE(pzv);                   ZVAL_BOOL(pzv, 0);
```

Notice that any non-zero value provided to ZVAL_BOOL() will result in a truth value. This makes sense of course, because any non-zero value type casted to Boolean in user-space will exhibit the same behavior. When hardcoding values into internal code, it's considered good practice to explicitly use the value 1 for truth. The macros ZVAL_TRUE() and ZVAL_FALSE() are provided as a convenience and can sometimes lend to code readability.

```
ZVAL_LONG(pzv, 1);            Z_TYPE_P(pzv)   = IS_LONG;
                              Z_LVAL_P(pzv)   = 1;
ZVAL_DOUBLE(pzv, d);          Z_TYPE_P(pzv)   = IS_DOUBLE;
                              Z_DVAL_P(pzv)   = d;
```

The basic scalar macros are as simple as they come. Set the zval's type, and assign a numeric value to it.

```
ZVAL_STRINGL(pzv,str,len,dup);   Z_TYPE_P(pzv)  = IS_STRING;
                                 Z_STRLEN_P(pzv) = len;
                                 if (dup) {
                                     Z_STRVAL_P(pzv) =
                                             estrndup(str, len + 1);
                                 } else {
                                     Z_STRVAL_P(pzv) = str;
                                 }
ZVAL_STRING(pzv, str, dup);      ZVAL_STRINGL(pzv, str,
                                             strlen(str), dup);
```

Here's where zval creation starts to get interesting. Strings, like arrays, objects, and resources, need to allocate additional memory for their data storage. You'll explore the pitfalls of memory management in the next chapter; for now, just notice that a dup value of 1 will allocate new memory and copy the string's contents, while a value of 0 will simply point the zval at the already existing string data.

```
ZVAL_RESOURCE(pzv, res);         Z_TYPE_P(pzv)   = IS_RESOURCE;
                                 Z_RESVAL_P(pzv) = res;
```

Recall from earlier that a resource is stored in a zval as a simple integer that refers to a lookup table managed by Zend. The ZVAL_RESOURCE() macro therefore acts much like the ZVAL_LONG() macro, but using a different type.

Data Storage

You've used PHP from the userspace side of things, so you're already familiar with the concept of an array. Any number of PHP variables (zvals) can be dropped into a single container (array) and be given names (labels) in the form of numbers or strings.

What's hopefully not surprising is that every single variable in a PHP script can be found in an array. When you create a variable, by assigning a value to it, Zend stores that value into an internal array known as a symbol table.

One symbol table, the one that defines the global scope, is initialized upon request startup just before extension RINIT methods are called, and then destroyed after script completion and subsequent RSHUTDOWN methods have executed.

When a userspace function or object method is called, a new symbol table is allocated for the life of that function or method and is defined as the active symbol table. If current script execution is not in a function or method, the global symbol table is considered active.

Taking a look at the execution globals structure (defined in Zend/zend_globals.h), you'll find the following two elements defined:

```
struct _zend_execution_globals {
    ...
    HashTable symbol_table;
    HashTable *active_symbol_table;
    ...
};
```

The symbol_table, accessed as EG(symbol_table), is always the global variable scope much like the $GLOBALS variable in userspace always corresponds to the global scope for PHP scripts. In fact, the $GLOBALS variable is just a userspace wrapper around the EG(symbol_table) variable seen from the internals.

The other part of this pair, active_symbol_table, is similarly accessed as EG(active_symbol_table), and represents whatever variable scope is active at the time.

The key difference to notice here is that EG(symbol_table), unlike nearly every other HashTable you'll use and encounter while working with the PHP and Zend APIs, is a direct variable. Nearly all functions that operate on HashTables, however, expect an indirect HashTable* as their parameter. Therefore, you'll have to dereference EG(symbol_table) with an ampersand when using it.

Consider the following two code blocks, which are functionally identical:
In PHP:

```
<?php $foo = 'bar'; ?>
```

In C:

```
{
    zval *fooval;

    MAKE_STD_ZVAL(fooval);
    ZVAL_STRING(fooval, "bar", 1);
    ZEND_SET_SYMBOL(EG(active_symbol_table), "foo", fooval);
}
```

First, a new zval was allocated using MAKE_STD_ZVAL() and its value was initialized to the string "bar". Then a new macro, which roughly equates with the assignment operator (=), combines that value with a label (foo), and adds it to the active symbol table. Because no userspace function is active at the time, EG(active_symbol_table) == &EG(symbol_table), which ultimately means that this variable is stored in the global scope.

Data Retrieval

In order to retrieve a variable from userspace, you'll need to look in whatever symbol table it's stored in. The following code segment shows using the zend_hash_find() function for this purpose:

```
{
    zval **fooval;

    if (zend_hash_find(EG(active_symbol_table),
                    "foo", sizeof("foo"),
                    (void**)&fooval) == SUCCESS) {
        php_printf("Got the value of $foo!");
    } else {
        php_printf("$foo is not defined.");
    }
}
```

A few parts of this example should look a little funny. Why is fooval defined to two levels of indirection? Why is sizeof() used for determining the length of "foo"? Why is &fooval, which would evaluate to a zval***, cast to a void**? If you asked yourself all three of these questions, pat yourself on the back.

First, it's worth knowing that HashTables aren't only used for userspace variables. The HashTable structure is so versatile that it's used all over the engine and in some cases it makes perfect sense to want to store a non-pointer value. A HashTable bucket is a fixed size, however, so in order to store data of any size, a HashTable will allocate a block of memory to wrap the data being stored. In the case of variables, it's a zval* being stored, so the HashTable storage mechanism allocates a block of memory big enough to hold a pointer. The HashTable's bucket uses that new pointer to carry around the zval* and you effectively wind up with a zval** inside the HashTable. The reason for storing a zval* when HashTables are clearly capable of storing a full zval will be covered in the next chapter.

When trying to retrieve that data, the HashTable only knows that it has a pointer to something. In order to populate that pointer into a calling function's local storage, the calling function will naturally dereference the local pointer, resulting in a variable of indeterminate type with two levels of indirection (such as void**). Knowing that your "indeterminate type" in this case is zval*, you can see where the type being passed into zend_hash_find() will look different to the compiler, having three levels of indirection rather than two. This is done on purpose here so a simple typecast is added to the function call to silence compiler warnings.

The reason sizeof() was used in the previous example was to include the terminating NULL in the "foo" constant used for the variable's label. Using 4 here would have worked equally well; however, it is discouraged because changes to the label name may affect its length, and it's much easier to find places where the length is hard-coded if it contains the label text that's being replaced anyway. (strlen("foo")+1) could have also solved this problem; however, some compilers do not optimize this step and the resulting binary might end up performing a pointless string length loop—what would be the fun in that?

If zend_hash_find() locates the item you're looking for, it populates the dereferenced pointer provided with the address of the bucket pointer it allocated when the requested data was first added to the HashTable and returns an integer value matching the SUCCESS constant. If zend_hash_find() cannot locate the data, it leaves the pointer untouched and returns an integer value matching the FAILURE constant.

In the case of userspace variables stored in a symbol table, SUCCESS or FAILURE effectively means that the variable is or is not set.

Data Conversion

Now that you can fetch variables from symbol tables, you'll want to do something with them. A direct, but painful, approach might be to examine the variable and perform a specific action depending on type. A simple switch statement like the following might work:

```
void display_zval(zval *value)
{
    switch (Z_TYPE_P(value)) {
        case IS_NULL:
            /* NULLs are echoed as nothing */
            break;
        case IS_BOOL:
            if (Z_BVAL_P(value)) {
                php_printf("1");
            }
            break;
        case IS_LONG:
            php_printf("%ld", Z_LVAL_P(value));
            break;
        case IS_DOUBLE:
```

```
            php_printf("%f", Z_DVAL_P(value));
            break;
        case IS_STRING:
            PHPWRITE(Z_STRVAL_P(value), Z_STRLEN_P(value));
            break;
        case IS_RESOURCE:
            php_printf("Resource #%ld", Z_RESVAL_P(value));
            break;
        case IS_ARRAY:
            php_printf("Array");
            break;
        case IS_OBJECT:
            php_printf("Object");
            break;
        default:
            /* Should never happen in practice,
             * but it's dangerous to make assumptions
             */
            php_printf("Unknown");
            break;
    }
}
```

Yeah, right, simple. Compared with the ease of `<?php echo $value; ?>` it's not hard to imagine this code becoming unmanageable. Fortunately, the very same routine used by the engine when a script performs the action of echoing a variable is also available to an extension or embed environment. Using one of the `convert_to_*()` functions exported by Zend, this sample could be reduced to simply:

```
void display_zval(zval *value)
{
    convert_to_string(value);
    PHPWRITE(Z_STRVAL_P(value), Z_STRLEN_P(value));
}
```

As you can probably guess, there are a collection of functions for converting to most of the data types. One notable exception is `convert_to_resource()`, which wouldn't make sense because resources are, by definition, incapable of mapping to a real userspace expressible value.

It's good if you're worried about the fact that the `convert_to_string()` call irrevocably changed the value of the zval passed into the function. In a real code segment this would typically be a bad idea, and of course it's not what the engine does when echoing a variable. In the next chapter you'll take a look at ways of using the convert functions to safely change a value's contents to something usable without destroying its existing contents.

Summary

In this chapter you looked at the internal representation of PHP variables. You learned to distinguish types, set and retrieve values, and add variables into symbol tables and fetch them back out. In the next chapter you'll build on this knowledge by learning how to make copies of a zval, how to destroy them when they're no longer needed, and most importantly, how to avoid making copies when you don't need to.

You'll also take a look at Zend's per-request memory management layer, and examine persistent versus non-persistent allocations. By the end of the next chapter you'll have the solid foundation necessary to begin creating a working extension and experimenting with your own code variations.

3

Memory Management

ONE OF THE MOST JARRING DIFFERENCES BETWEEN A MANAGED language like PHP, and an unmanaged language like C is control over memory pointers.

Memory

In PHP, populating a string variable is as simple as `<?php $str = 'hello world'; ?>` and the string can be freely modified, copied, and moved around. In C, on the other hand, although you could start with a simple static string such as `char *str = "hello world";`, that string cannot be modified because it lives in program space. To create a manipulable string, you'd have to allocate a block of memory and copy the contents in using a function such as `strdup()`.

```
{
    char *str;

    str = strdup("hello world");
    if (!str) {
        fprintf(stderr, "Unable to allocate memory!");
    }
}
```

For reasons you'll explore through the course of this chapter, the traditional memory management functions (`malloc()`, `free()`, `strdup()`, `realloc()`, `calloc()`, and so on) are almost never used directly by the PHP source code.

Free the Mallocs

Memory management on nearly all platforms is handled in a request and release fashion. An application says to the layer above it (usually the operating system) "I want some number of bytes of memory to use as I please." If there is space available, the operating system offers it to the program and makes a note not to give that chunk of memory out to anyone else.

When the application is done using the memory, it's expected to give it back to the OS so that it can be allocated elsewhere. If the program doesn't give the memory back, the OS has no way of knowing that it's no longer being used and can be allocated again by another process. If a block of memory is not freed, and the owning application has lost track of it, then it's said to have "leaked" because it's simply no longer available to anyone.

In a typical client application, small infrequent leaks are sometimes tolerated with the knowledge that the process will end after a short period of time and the leaked memory will be implicitly returned to the OS. This is no great feat as the OS knows which program it gave that memory to, and it can be certain that the memory is no longer needed when the program terminates.

With long running server daemons, including web servers like Apache and by extension mod_php, the process is designed to run for much longer periods, often indefinitely. Because the OS can't clean up memory usage, any degree of leakage—no matter how small—will tend to build up over time and eventually exhaust all system resources.

Consider the userspace stristr() function; in order to find a string using a case-insensitive search, it actually creates a lowercase copy of both the haystack and the needle, and then performs a more traditional case-sensitive search to find the relative offset. After the offset of the string has been located, however, it no longer has use for the lowercase versions of the haystack and needle strings. If it didn't free these copies, then every script that used stristr() would leak some memory every time it was called. Eventually the web server process would own all the system memory, but not be able to use it.

The ideal solution, I can hear you shouting, is to write good, clean, consistent code, and that's absolutely true. In an environment like the PHP interpreter, however, that's only half the solution.

Error Handling

In order to provide the ability to bail out of an active request to userspace scripts and the extension functions they rely on, a means needs to exist to jump out of an active request entirely. The way this is handled within the Zend Engine is to set a bailout address at the beginning of a request, and then on any die() or exit() call, or on encountering any critical error (E_ERROR) perform a longjmp() to that bailout address.

Although this bailout process simplifies program flow, it almost invariably means that resource cleanup code (such as free() calls) will be skipped and memory could get leaked. Consider this simplified version of the engine code that handles function calls:

```
void call_function(const char *fname, int fname_len TSRMLS_DC)
{
    zend_function *fe;
    char *lcase_fname;
```

```
/* PHP function names are case-insensitive
 * to simplify locating them in the function tables
 * all function names are implicitly
 * translated to lowercase
 */
lcase_fname = estrndup(fname, fname_len);
zend_str_tolower(lcase_fname, fname_len);

if (zend_hash_find(EG(function_table),
        lcase_fname, fname_len + 1, (void **)&fe) == FAILURE) {
    zend_execute(fe->op_array TSRMLS_CC);
} else {
    php_error_docref(NULL TSRMLS_CC, E_ERROR,
                    "Call to undefined function: %s()", fname);
}
    efree(lcase_fname);
}
```

When the `php_error_docref()` line is encountered, the internal error handler sees that the error level is critical and invokes `longjmp()` to interrupt the current program flow and leave `call_function()` without ever reaching the `efree(lcase_fname)` line. Again, you're probably thinking that the `efree()` line could just be moved above the `zend_error()` line, but what about the code that called this `call_function()` routine in the first place? Most likely `fname` itself was an allocated string and you can't free that before it has been used in the error message.

Note

The `php_error_docref()` function is an internals equivalent to `trigger_error()`. The first parameter is an optional documentation reference that will be appended to `docref.root` if such is enabled in `php.ini`. The third parameter can be any of the familiar `E_*` family of constants indicating severity. The fourth and later parameters follow `printf()` style formatting and variable argument lists.

Zend Memory Manager

The solution to memory leaks during request bailout is the Zend Memory Management (ZendMM) layer. This portion of the engine acts in much the same way the operating system would normally act, allocating memory to calling applications. The difference is that it is low enough in the process space to be request-aware so that when one request dies, it can perform the same action the OS would perform when a process dies. That is, it implicitly frees all the memory owned by that request. Figure 3.1 shows ZendMM in relation to the OS and the PHP process.

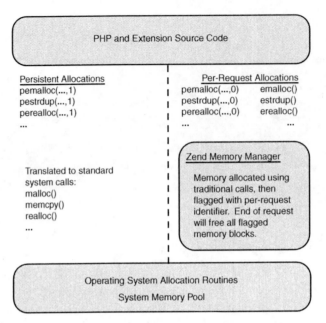

Figure 3.1   Zend Memory Manager replaces system calls for per-request
allocations.

In addition to providing implicit memory cleanup, ZendMM also controls the per-
request memory usage according to the php.ini setting: memory_limit. If a script
attempts to ask for more memory than is available to the system as a whole, or more
than is remaining in its per-request limit, ZendMM will automatically issue an
E_ERROR message and begin the bailout process. An added benefit of this is that the
return value of most memory allocation calls doesn't need to be checked because failure
results in an immediate longjmp() to the shutdown part of the engine.

Hooking itself in between PHP internal code and the OS's actual memory management layer is accomplished by nothing more complex than requiring that all memory
allocated internally is requested using an alternative set of functions. For example,
rather than allocate a 16-byte block of memory using malloc(16), PHP code will use
emalloc(16). In addition to performing the actual memory allocation task, ZendMM
will flag that block with information concerning what request it's bound to so that
when a request bails out, ZendMM can implicitly free it.

Often, memory needs to be allocated for longer than the duration of a single request.
These types of allocations, called persistent allocations because they persist beyond the
end of a request, could be performed using the traditional memory allocators because
these do not add the additional per-request information used by ZendMM. Sometimes,
however, it's not known until runtime whether a particular allocation will need to be

persistent or not, so ZendMM exports a set of helper macros that act just like the other memory allocation functions, but have an additional parameter at the end to indicate persistence.

If you genuinely want a persistent allocation, this parameter should be set to one, in which case the request will be passed through to the traditional `malloc()` family of allocators. If runtime logic has determined that this block does not need to be persistent however, this parameter may be set to zero, and the call will be channeled to the per-request memory allocator functions.

For example, `pemalloc(buffer_len, 1)` maps to `malloc(buffer_len)`, whereas `pemalloc(buffer_len, 0)` maps to `emalloc(buffer_len)` using the following `#define` in `Zend/zend_alloc.h`:

```
#define pemalloc(size, persistent) \
        ((persistent)?malloc(size):emalloc(size))
```

Each of the allocator functions found in ZendMM can be found below along with their more traditional counterparts.

Table 3.1 shows each of the allocator functions supported by ZendMM and their e/pe counterparts:

Table 3.1   **Traditional versus PHP-specific allocators**

Allocator funtion	e/pe counterpart
`void *malloc(size_t count);`	`void *emalloc(size_t count);`
	`void *pemalloc(size_t count,` `                char persistent);`
`void *calloc(size_t count);`	`void *ecalloc(size_t count);`
	`void *pecalloc(size_t count,` `                char persistent);`
`void *realloc(void *ptr,` `              size_t count);`	`void *erealloc(void *ptr,` `                size_t count);`

	`void *perealloc(void *ptr,`
	`                 size_t count,`
	`                 char persistent);`

`void *strdup(void *ptr);`	`void *estrdup(void *ptr);`
	`void *pestrdup(void *ptr,` `                char persistent);`
`void free(void *ptr);`	`void efree(void *ptr);`
	`void pefree(void *ptr,` `             char persistent);`

You'll notice that even `pefree()` requires the persistency flag. This is because at the time that `pefree()` is called, it doesn't actually know if `ptr` was a persistent allocation or not. Calling `free()` on a non-persistent allocation could lead to a messy double free, whereas

calling `efree()` on a persistent one will most likely lead to a segmentation fault as the
memory manager attempts to look for management information that doesn't exist. Your
code is expected to remember whether the data structure it allocated was persistent or
not.

In addition to the core set of allocator functions, a few additional and quite handy
ZendMM specific functions exist:

```
void *estrndup(void *ptr, int len);
```

Allocate `len+1` bytes of memory and copy `len` bytes from `ptr` to the newly allocated
block. The behavior of `estrndup()` is roughly the following:

```
void *estrndup(void *ptr, int len)
{
    char *dst = emalloc(len + 1);
    memcpy(dst, ptr, len);
    dst[len] = 0;
    return dst;
}
```

The terminating NULL byte implicitly placed at the end of the buffer here ensures that
any function that uses `estrndup()` for string duplication doesn't need to worry about
passing the resulting buffer to a function that expects NULL terminated strings such as
`printf()`. When using `estrndup()` to copy non-string data, this last byte is essentially
wasted, but more often than not, the convenience outweighs the minor inefficiency.

```
void *safe_emalloc(size_t size, size_t count, size_t addtl);
void *safe_pemalloc(size_t size, size_t count, size_t addtl, char persistent);
```

The amount of memory allocated by these functions is the result of `((size * count)
+ addtl)`. You may be asking, "Why an extra function at all? Why not just use
emalloc/pemalloc and do the math myself?" The reason comes in the name: *safe*.
Although the circumstances leading up to it would be exceedingly unlikely, it's possible
that the end result of such an equation might overflow the integer limits of the host
platform. This could result in an allocation for a negative number of bytes, or worse, a
positive number that is significantly smaller than what the calling program believed it
requested. `safe_emalloc()` avoids this type of trap by checking for integer overflow and
explicitly failing if such an overflow occurs.

> **Note**
>
> Not all memory allocation routines have a p* counterpart. For example, there is no `pestrndup()`, and
> `safe_pemalloc()` does not exist prior to PHP 5.1. Occasionally you'll need to work around these gaps
> in the ZendAPI.

Reference Counting

Careful memory allocation and freeing is vital to the long term performance of a multirequest process like PHP, but it's only half the picture. In order for a server that handles thousands of hits per second to function efficiently, each request needs to use as little memory as possible and perform the bare minimum amount of unnecessary data copying. Consider the following PHP code snippet:

```
<?php
    $a = 'Hello World';
    $b = $a;
    unset($a);
?>
```

After the first call, a single variable has been created, and a 12 byte block of memory has been assigned to it holding the string 'Hello World' along with a trailing NULL. Now look at the next two lines: $b is set to the same value as $a, and then $a is unset (freed).

If PHP treated every variable assignment as a reason to copy variable contents, an extra 12 bytes would need to be copied for the duplicated string and additional processor load would be consumed during the data copy. This action starts to look ridiculous when the third line has come along and the original variable is unset making the duplication of data completely unnecessary. Now take that one further and imagine what could happen when the contents of a 10MB file are loaded into two variables. That could take up 20MB where 10 would have been sufficient. Would the engine waste so much time and memory on such a useless endeavor?

You know PHP is smarter than that.

Remember that variable names and their values are actually two different concepts within the engine. The value itself is a nameless zval* holding, in this case, a string value. It was assigned to the variable $a using zend _hash_add(). What if two variable names could point to the same value?

```
{
    zval *helloval;
    MAKE_STD_ZVAL(helloval);
    ZVAL_STRING(helloval, "Hello World", 1);
    zend_hash_add(EG(active_symbol_table), "a", sizeof("a"),
                                            &helloval, sizeof(zval*), NULL);
    zend_hash_add(EG(active_symbol_table), "b", sizeof("b"),
                                            &helloval, sizeof(zval*), NULL);
}
```

At this point you could actually inspect either $a or $b and see that they both contain the string "Hello World". Unfortunately, you then come to the third line: unset($a);. In this situation, unset() doesn't know that the data pointed to by the $a variable is also in use by another one so it just frees the memory blindly. Any subsequent accesses to $b will be looking at already freed memory space and cause the engine to crash. Hint: You don't want to crash the engine.

This is solved by the third of a zval's four members: refcount. When a variable is first created and set, its refcount is initialized to 1 because it's assumed to only be in use by the variable it is being created for. When your code snippet gets around to assigning helloval to $b, it needs to increase that refcount to 2 because the value is now "referenced" by two variables:

```
{
    zval *helloval;
    MAKE_STD_ZVAL(helloval);
    ZVAL_STRING(helloval, "Hello World", 1);
    zend_hash_add(EG(active_symbol_table), "a", sizeof("a"),
                                      &helloval, sizeof(zval*), NULL);
    ZVAL_ADDREF(helloval);
    zend_hash_add(EG(active_symbol_table), "b", sizeof("b"),
                                      &helloval, sizeof(zval*), NULL);
}
```

Now when unset() deletes the $a copy of the variable, it can see from the refcount parameter that someone else is interested in that data and it should actually just decrement the refcount and otherwise leave it alone.

Copy on Write

Saving memory through refcounting is a great idea, but what happens when you only want to change one of those variables? Consider this code snippet:

```
<?php
    $a = 1;
    $b = $a;
    $b += 5;
?>
```

Looking at the logic flow you would of course expect $a to still equal 1, and $b to now be 6. At this point you also know that Zend is doing its best to save memory by having $a and $b refer to the same zval after the second line, so what happens when the third line is reached and $b must be changed?

The answer is that Zend looks at refcount, sees that it's greater than one and separates it. Separation in the Zend engine is the process of destroying a reference pair and is the opposite of the process you just saw:

```
zval *get_var_and_separate(char *varname, int varname_len TSRMLS_DC)
{
    zval **varval, *varcopy;
    if (zend_hash_find(EG(active_symbol_table),
                    varname, varname_len + 1, (void**)&varval) == FAILURE) {
```

```
        /* Variable doesn't actually exist - fail out */
        return NULL;
    }
    if ((*varval)->refcount < 2) {
        /* varname is the only actual reference,
         * no separating to do
         */
        return *varval;
    }
    /* Otherwise, make a copy of the zval* value */
    MAKE_STD_ZVAL(varcopy);
    varcopy = *varval;
    /* Duplicate any allocated structures within the zval* */
    zval_copy_ctor(varcopy);

    /* Remove the old version of varname
     * This will decrease the refcount of varval in the process
     */
    zend_hash_del(EG(active_symbol_table), varname, varname_len + 1);

    /* Initialize the reference count of the
     * newly created value and attach it to
     * the varname variable
     */
    varcopy->refcount = 1;
    varcopy->is_ref = 0;
    zend_hash_add(EG(active_symbol_table), varname, varname_len + 1,
                                   &varcopy, sizeof(zval*), NULL);

    /* Return the new zval* */
    return varcopy;
}
```

Now that the engine has a zval* that it knows is only owned by the $b variable, it can convert it to a long and increment it by 5 according to the script's request.

Change on Write

The concept of reference counting also creates a new possibility for data manipulation in the form of what userspace scripters actually think of in terms of "referencing". Consider the following snippet of userspace code:

```
<?php
    $a = 1;
    $b = &$a;
    $b += 5;
?>
```

Being experienced in the ways of PHP code, you'll instinctively recognize that the value of $a will now be 6 even though it was initialized to 1 and never (directly) changed. This happens because when the engine goes to increment the value of $b by 5, it notices that $b is a reference to $a and says, "It's okay for me to change the value without separating it, because I want all reference variables to see the change."

But how does the engine know? Simple, it looks at the fourth and final element of the zval struct: is_ref. This is just a simple on/off bit value that defines whether the value is, in fact, part of a userspace-style reference set. In the previous code snippet, when the first line is executed, the value created for $a gets a refcount of 1, and an is_ref value of 0 because its only owned by one variable ($a), and no other variables have a change on write reference to it. At the second line, the refcount element of this value is incremented to 2 as before, except that this time, because the script included an ampersand to indicate full-reference, the is_ref element is set to 1.

Finally, at the third line, the engine once again fetches the value associated with $b and checks if separation is necessary. This time the value is not separated because of a check not included earlier. Here's the refcount check portion of get_var_and_separate() again, with an extra condition:

```
if ((*varval)->is_ref || (*varval)->refcount < 2) {
    /* varname is the only actual reference,
     * or it's a full reference to other variables
     * either way: no separating to be done
     */
    return *varval;
}
```

This time, even though the refcount is 2, the separation process is short-circuited by the fact that this value is a full reference. The engine can freely modify it with no concern about the values of other variables appearing to change magically on their own.

Separation Anxiety

With all this copying and referencing, there are a couple of combinations of events that can't be handled by clever manipulation of is_ref and refcount. Consider this block of PHP code:

```
<?php
    $a = 1;
    $b = $a;
    $c = &$a;
?>
```

Here you have a single value that needs to be associated with three different variables, two in a change-on-write full reference pair, and the third in a separable copy-on-write context. Using just is_ref and refcount to describe this relationship, what values will work?

The answer is: none. In this case, the value must be duplicated into two discrete `zval*`s, even though both will contain the exact same data (see Figure 3.2).

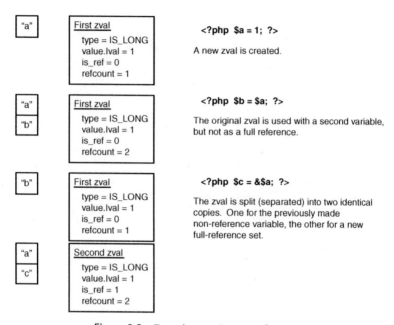

Figure 3.2   Forced separation on reference.

Similarly, the following code block will cause the same conflict and force the value to separate into a copy (see Figure 3.3).

```php
<?php
    $a = 1;
    $b = &$a;
    $c = $a;
?>
```

Notice here that in both cases here, $b is associated with the original zval object because at the time separation occurs, the engine doesn't know the name of the third variable involved in the operation.

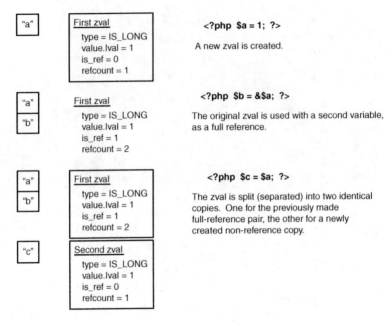

Figure 3.3   Forced separation on copy.

Summary

PHP is a managed language. On the userspace side of things, this careful control of resources and memory means easier prototyping and fewer crashes. After you delve under the hood though, all bets are off and it's up to the responsible developer to maintain the integrity of the runtime environment.

4

Setting Up a Build Environment

BY NOW YOU PROBABLY ALREADY HAVE A VERSION OF PHP installed on at least one system and you've been using it to develop web-based applications. You might have downloaded the Win32 build from php.net to run on IIS or Apache for Windows, or used your *nix distribution's (Linux, BSD, or another POSIX-compliant distribution) packaging system to install binaries created by a third party.

Building PHP

Unless you downloaded the source code as a tarball from php.net and compiled it yourself, however, you're most likely missing at least one component.

*nix Tools

The first piece of equipment in any C developer's toolkit is an actual C compiler. There's a good chance your distribution included one by default, and a very good chance that it included gcc (GNU Compiler Collection). You can easily check whether or not a compiler is installed by issuing gcc -version or cc -version, one of which will hopefully run successfully and respond with version information for the compiler installed.

If you don't have a compiler yet, check with your distribution's website for instructions on downloading and installing gcc. Typically this will amount to downloading an .rpm or .deb file and issuing a command to install it. Depending on your specific distribution, one of the following commands may simply work out of the box without requiring further research: urpmi gcc, apt-get install gcc, pkg-add -r gcc, or perhaps emerge gcc.

In addition to a compiler you'll also need the following programs and utilities: make, autoconf, automake, and libtool. These utilities can be installed using the same per-distribution methods you used for gcc, or they can be compiled from their source using tarballs available from gnu.org.

For best results, libtool version 1.4.3 and autoconf 2.13 with automake version 1.4 or 1.5 are recommended. Using newer versions of these packages will quite probably work as well, but only these versions are certified.

If you plan on using CVS to check out the latest and most up-to-date version of PHP to develop with, you'll also need `bison` and `flex` for constructing the language parser. Like the others, these two packages may either be installed using your distribution's packaging system, or downloaded from `gnu.org` and compiled from source.

If you choose to go the CVS route, you'll also need the `cvs` client itself. Again, this may be installed by your distribution, or downloaded and compiled. Unlike the other packages, however, this one is found at `cvshome.org`.

Win32 Tools

The Win32/PHP5 build system is a complete rewrite and represents a significant leap forward from the PHP4 build system. Instructions for compiling PHP4 under Windows are available on php.net, only the PHP5 build system—which requires Windows 2000, Windows 2003, or Windows XP—will be discussed here.

First, you'll need to grab libraries and development headers used by many of the core PHP extensions. Fortunately, many of these files are redistributed from php.net as a single `.zip` file located at http://www.php.net/extra/win32build.zip.

Create a new directory named `C:\PHPDEV\` and unzip `win32build.zip` using your favorite zip management program into this location. The folder structure contained in the zip file will create a subdirectory, `C:\PHPDEV\win32build`, which will contain further subfolders and files. It's not necessary to name your root folder `PHPDEV`; the only important thing is that win32build and the PHP source tree are both children of the same parent folder.

Next you'll need a compiler. If you've already got Visual C++ .NET you have what you need; otherwise, download Visual C++ Express from Microsoft at http://lab.msdn.microsoft.com/express/.

The installer, once you've downloaded and run it, will display the usual welcome, EULA (End-User License Agreement), and identification dialogs. Read through these screens and proceed using the Next buttons after you've agreed to the terms of the EULA and entered any appropriate information.

Installation location is of course up to you, and a typical installation will work just fine. If you'd like to create a leaner installation, you may deselect the three optional components—GUI, MSDN, and SQL Server.

The final package is the Platform SDK, also available for download from Microsoft at http://www.microsoft.com/downloads/details.aspx?FamilyId=A55B6B43-E24F-4EA3-A93E-40C0EC4F68E5. The site currently lists three download options: PSDK-x86.exe, PSDK-ia64.exe, and PSDK-amd64.exe. These options refer to x86 compatible 32bit, Intel64bit, and AMD64bit processors respectively. If you're not sure which one applies to your processor, select PSDK-x86.exe, which should work cleanly, albeit less efficiently, with both 64 bit variants.

As before, proceed through the first few screens as you would with any other installer package until you are prompted to select between Typical and Custom installation. A Typical installation includes the Core SDK package, which is sufficient for the purposes of building PHP. Other packages can be deselected by choosing a Custom installation, but if you have the hard disk space to spare, you might as well install it all. The other packages may come in handy later on.

So unless you're byte conscious, select Typical and proceed through the next couple of standard issue screens until the installer begins copying and registering files. This process should take a few minutes so grab some popcorn.

Once installation is complete you'll have a new item on your Start menu—Microsoft Platform SDK for Windows Server 2003 SP1.

Obtaining the PHP Source Code

When downloading PHP, you have a few options. First, if your distribution supports the concept, you can download it from them using a command such as `apt-get source php5`. The advantage to this approach is that your distribution might have some known quirks that require modifications to the PHP source code. By downloading from them, you can be certain that these quirks have been patched for and your builds will have fewer issues. The disadvantage is that most distributions lag weeks, if not months, behind the official PHP releases, making the version you download outdated before it ever reaches your hard drive.

The next option, which is generally preferred, is to download php-$x.y.z$.tar.gz (where $x.y.z$ is the currently released version) from www.php.net. This release of PHP will have been tested by countless other PHP users around the globe and will be quite up-to-date without pushing the absolute bleeding edge.

You could also go a small step further and download a snapshot tarball from snaps.php.net. On this site, the latest revisions of all the source code files in the PHP repository are packaged up every few hours. An accidental commit by a core developer might make one of these bundles unusable occasionally, but if you need the latest PHP 6.0 features before it has been officially released, this is the easier place to go looking.

Lastly, you can use CVS to fetch the individual files that make up the PHP source tree directly from the development repository used by the PHP core development team. For the purposes of extension and embedding development, this offers no significant advantage over using an official release tarball or a snapshot. However, if you plan to publish your extension or other application in a CVS repository, it will be helpful to be familiar with the checkout process.

Performing a CVS Checkout

The entire PHP project, from the Zend Engine and the core to the smallest PEAR component, is hosted at cvs.php.net. From here, hundreds of developers develop and maintain the bits and pieces that make up the whole of PHP and its related projects.

Among the other parts housed here, the core PHP package is available in the php-src module and can be downloaded to a workstation with two simple commands. First you'll want to introduce yourself to the php.net CVS server by logging in.

```
$ cvs -d:pserver:cvsread@cvs.php.net:/repository login
```

The cvsread account is a public use (read-only) account with a password of phpfi—an homage to a much earlier version of what we know today as PHP. Once logged in, the PHP sources may be checked out using

```
$ cvs -d:pserver:cvsread@cvs.php.net:/repository co php-src
```

Variations of this command can be used to check out specific versions of PHP going back as far as PHP2. For more information, refer to the anonymous cvs instructions at http://www.php.net/anoncvs.

Configuring PHP for Development

As covered in Chapter 1, there are two special ./configure switches you'll want to use when building a development-friendly PHP whether you plan to write an extension to PHP or embed PHP in another application. These two switches should be used in addition to the other switches you'd normally use while building PHP.

—enable-debug

The enable debug switch turns on a few critical functions within the PHP and Zend source trees. First, it enables reporting of leaked memory at the end of every request.

Recall from Chapter 3, "Memory Management," that the Zend Memory Manager will implicitly free per-request memory that was allocated but not explicitly freed prior to script end. By running a series of aggressive regression tests against newly developed code, leak points can be easily spotted and plugged prior to any public release. Take a look at the following code snippet:

```
void show_value(int n)
{
    char *message = emalloc(1024);

    sprintf(message, "The value of n is %d\n", n);
    php_printf("%s", message);
}
```

If this—admittedly silly—block of code were executed during the course of a PHP request, it would leak 1,024 bytes of memory. Under ordinary circumstances ZendMM would quietly free that block at the end of script execution and not complain.

With —enable-debug turned on, however, developers are treated to an error message giving them a clue about what needs to be addressed.

```
/cvs/php5/ext/sample/sample.c(33) :  Freeing 0x084504B8 (1024 bytes), script=-
=== Total 1 memory leaks detected ===
```

This short but informative message tells you that ZendMM had to clean up after your mess and identifies exactly from where the lost memory block was allocated. Using this information, it's a simple matter to open the file, scroll down to the line in question, and add an appropriate call to `efree(message)` at the end of the function.

Memory leaks aren't the only problems you'll run into that are hard to track down, of course. Sometimes the problems are much more insidious, and far less telling. Let's say you've been working all night on a big patch that requires hitting a dozen files and changing a ton of code. When everything is in place, you confidently issue `make`, try out a sample script, and are treated to the following output:

```
$ sapi/cli/php -r 'myext_samplefunc();'
Segmentation Fault
```

Well...that's just swell, but where could the problem be? Looking at your implementation of `myext_samplefunc()` doesn't reveal any obvious clues, and running it through gdb only shows a bunch of unknown symbols.

Once again, –enable-debug lends a hand. By adding this switch to `./configure`, the resulting PHP binary will contain all the debugging symbols needed by gdb or another core file examination program to show you where the problem occurred.

Rebuilding with this option, and triggering the crash through gdb, you're now treated to something like the following:

```
#0 0x1234567 php_myext_find_delimiter(str=0x1234567 "foo@#(FHVN)@\x98\xE0...",
                                      strlen=3, tsrm_ls=0x1234567)
    p = strchr(str, ',');
```

Suddenly the cause is clear. The `str` string is not a NULL terminated string, as evidenced by the garbage at the end, but a non–binary-safe function was used on it. The underlying `strchr()` implementation tried scanning past the end of `str`'s allocated memory and got into regions it didn't own, causing a segfault. A quick replacement using `memchr()` and the `strlen` parameter will prevent the crash.

–enable-maintainer-zts

This second `./configure` option forces PHP to be built with the Thread Safe Resource Manager(TSRM)/Zend Thread Safety(ZTS) layer enabled. This switch will add complexity and processing time when it's not otherwise needed, but for the purposes of development, you'll find that's a good thing. For a detailed description of what ZTS is and why you want to develop with it turned on, refer to Chapter 1.

–enable-embed

One last `./configure` switch of importance is only necessary if you'll be embedding PHP into another application. This option identifies that `libphp5.so` should be built as the selected SAPI in the same way that –with-apxs will build `mod_php5.so` for embedding PHP specifically into Apache.

Compiling on UNIX

Now that you've got all the necessary tools together, you've downloaded the PHP source tarball, and you've identified all the necessary ./configure switches, it's time to actually compile PHP.

Assuming that you've downloaded php-5.1.0.tar.gz to your home directory, you'll enter the following series of commands to unpack the tarball and switch to the PHP source directory:

```
[/home/sarag]$ tar -zxf php-5.1.0.tar.gz
[/home/sarag]$ cd php-5.1.0
```

If you're using a tool other than GNU tar, you might need to use a slightly different command:

```
[/home/sarag]$ gzip -d php-5.1.0.tar.gz | tar -xf -
```

Now, issue the ./configure command with the required switches and any other options you want enabled or disabled:

```
[/home/sarag/php-5.1.0]$ ./configure —enable-debug \
—enable-maintainer-zts —disable-cgi —enable-cli \
—disable-pear —disable-xml —disable-sqlite \
—without-mysql —enable-embed
```

After a lengthy process, during which dozens of lines of informational text will scroll up your screen, you'll be ready to start the compilation process:

```
[/home/sarag]$ make all install
```

At this point, get up and grab a cup of coffee. Compile times can range from anywhere between a couple minutes on a high-end powerhouse system to half an hour on an old overloaded 486. When the build process has finished, you'll have a functional build of PHP with all the right configuration ready for use in development.

Compiling on Win32

As with the UNIX build, the first step to preparing a Windows build is to unpack the source tarball. By default, Windows doesn't know what to do with a .tar.gz file. In fact, if you downloaded PHP using Internet Explorer, you probably noticed that it changed the name of the tarball file to php-5.1.0.tar.tar. This isn't IE craving a plate of fish sticks or—depending on who you ask—a bug, it's a "feature."

Start by renaming the file back to php-5.1.0.tar.gz (if necessary). If you have a program installed that is capable of reading .tar.gz files, you'll notice the icon immediately change. You can now double-click on the file to open up the decompression program. If the icon doesn't change, or if nothing happens when you double-click the icon, it means that you have no tar/gzip compatible decompression program installed. Check your favorite search engine for WinZIP, WinRAR, or any other application that is suitable for extracting .tar.gz archives.

Whatever decompression program you use, have it decompress `php-5.1.0.tar.gz` to the root development folder you created earlier. This section will assume you have extracted it to `C:\PHPDEV\` which, because the zip file contains a folder structure, will result in the source tree residing in `C:\PHPDEV\php-5.1.0`.

After it's unpacked, open up a build environment window by choosing Start, All Programs, Microsoft Platform SDK for Windows Server 2003 SP1, Open Build Environment Window, Windows 2000 Build Environment, Set Windows 2000 Build Environment (Debug). The specific path to this shortcut might be slightly different depending on the version of the Platform SDK you have installed and the target platform you will be building for (2000, XP, 2003).

A simple command prompt window will open up stating the target build platform. This command prompt has most, but not all, necessary environment variables set up. You'll need to run one extra batch file in order to let the PHP build system know where Visual C++ Express is. If you accepted the default installation location this batch file will be located at `C:\Program Files\Microsoft Visual Studio 8\VC\bin\vcvars32.bat`. If you can't find `vcvars32.bat`, check the same directory—or its parent—for `vcvarsall.bat`. Just be sure to run it inside the same command prompt window you just opened. It will set additional environment variables that the build process will need.

Now, change the directory to the location where you unpacked PHP— `C:\PHPDEV\php-5.1.0`— and run `buildconf.bat`.

```
C:\Program Files\Microsoft Platform SDK> cd \PHPDEV\php-5.1.0
C:\PHPDEV\php-5.1.0> buildconf.bat
```

If all is going well so far you'll see the following two lines of output:

```
Rebuilding configure.js
Now run 'cscript /nologo configure.js —help'
```

At this point, you can do as the message says and see what options are available. The `—enable-maintainer-zts` option is not necessary here because the Win32 build automatically assumes that ZTS will be required by any SAPI. If you wanted to turn it off, you could issue `—disable-zts`, but that's not the case here because you're building for a development environment anyway.

In this example I've removed a few other extensions that aren't relevant to extension and embedding development for the sake of simplicity. If you'd like to rebuild PHP using additional extensions, you'll need to hunt down the libraries on which they depend.

```
C:\php-5.1.0> cscript /nologo configure.js —without-xml —without-wddx \
—without-simplexml —without-dom —without-libxml —disable-zlib \
—without-sqlite —disable-odbc —disable-cgi —enable-cli \
—enable-debug —without-iconv
```

Again, a stream of informative output will scroll by, followed by instructions to execute the final command:

```
C:\php-5.1.0> nmake
```

Finally, a working build of PHP compiled for the Win32 platform.

Summary

Now that PHP is installed with all the right options, you're ready to move on to generating a real, functional extension. In the next few chapters you'll be introduced to the anatomy of a PHP extension. Even if you only plan on embedding PHP into your application without extending the language any, you'll want to read through this section because it explains the mechanics of interfacing with the PHP environment in full detail.

5

Your First Extension

Every PHP extension is built from at least two files: a configuration file, which tells the compiler what files to build and what external libraries will be needed, and at least one source file, which does the actual work.

Anatomy of an Extension

In practice, there is typically a second or third configuration file and one or more header files as well. For your first extension, you'll be working with one of each of these types of files and adding from there.

Configuration File

To start out, create a directory under the `ext/` dir in your PHP source tree called "`sample`". In reality this new directory could be placed anywhere, but in order to demonstrate Win32 and static build options later in this chapter, I'll be asking you to put it here this one time.

Next, enter this directory and create a file called `config.m4` with the following contents:

```
PHP_ARG_ENABLE(sample,
  [Whether to enable the "sample" extension],
  [  —enable-sample        Enable "sample" extension support])

if test $PHP_SAMPLE != "no"; then
  PHP_SUBST(SAMPLE_SHARED_LIBADD)
  PHP_NEW_EXTENSION(sample, sample.c, $ext_shared)
fi
```

This minimalist configuration sets up a `./configure` option called —enable-sample. The second parameter to `PHP_ARG_ENABLE` will be displayed during the `./configure` process as it reaches this extension's configuration file. The third parameter will be displayed as an available option if the end-user issues `./configure —help`.

If an end user calls ./configure using the —enable-sample option, then a local environment variable, $PHP_SAMPLE, will be set to yes. PHP_SUBST() is a PHP-modified version of the standard autoconf AC_SUBST() macro and is necessary to enable building the extension as a shared module.

Last but not least, PHP_NEW_EXTENSION() declares the module and enumerates all the source files that must be compiled as part of the extension. If multiple files were required, they would be listed in the second parameter using a space as a delimiter, for example:

```
PHP_NEW_EXTENSION(sample, sample.c sample2.c sample3.c, $ext_shared)
```

The final parameter is a counterpart to the PHP_SUBST(SAMPLE_SHARED_LIBADD) command and is likewise necessary for building as a shared module.

Header

When developing in C, it almost always makes sense to segregate certain types of data into external header files that are then included by the source files. Although PHP does not require this, it lends simplicity when a module grows beyond the scope of a single source file.

You'll start with the following contents in your new header file, called php_sample.h:

```
#ifndef PHP_SAMPLE_H
/* Prevent double inclusion */
#define PHP_SAMPLE_H

/* Define Extension Properties */
#define PHP_SAMPLE_EXTNAME   "sample"
#define PHP_SAMPLE_EXTVER    "1.0"

/* Import configure options
   when building outside of
   the PHP source tree */
#ifdef HAVE_CONFIG_H
#include "config.h"
#endif
```

```
/* Include PHP Standard Header */
#include "php.h"

/* Define the entry point symbol
 * Zend will use when loading this module
 */
extern zend_module_entry sample_module_entry;
#define phpext_sample_ptr &sample_module_entry

#endif /* PHP_SAMPLE_H */
```

This header file accomplishes two primary tasks: If the extension is being built using the phpize tool—which is how you'll be building it through most of this book—then HAVE_CONFIG_H gets defined and config.h will be included as well. Regardless of how the extension is being compiled, it also includes php.h from the PHP source tree. This header file subsequently includes several other headers spread across the PHP sources providing access to the bulk of the PHPAPI.

Next, the zend_module_entry struct used by your extension is declared external so that it can be picked up by Zend using dlopen() and dlsym() when this module is loaded using an extension= line.

This header file also includes a few preprocessor defines that will be used in the source file shortly.

Source

Last, and by no means least, you'll create a simple source skeleton in the file sample.c:

```
#include "php_sample.h"

zend_module_entry sample_module_entry = {
#if ZEND_MODULE_API_NO >= 20010901
    STANDARD_MODULE_HEADER,
#endif
    PHP_SAMPLE_EXTNAME,
    NULL, /* Functions */
    NULL, /* MINIT */
    NULL, /* MSHUTDOWN */
    NULL, /* RINIT */
    NULL, /* RSHUTDOWN */
    NULL, /* MINFO */
#if ZEND_MODULE_API_NO >= 20010901
    PHP_SAMPLE_EXTVER,
#endif
    STANDARD_MODULE_PROPERTIES
};
```

```
#ifdef COMPILE_DL_SAMPLE
ZEND_GET_MODULE(sample)
#endif
```

And that's it! These three files are everything needed to create a module skeleton. Granted, it doesn't do anything useful, but it's a place to start and you'll be adding functionality through the rest of this section. First though, let's go through what's happening.

The opening line is simple enough: Include the header file you just created, and by extension all the other PHP core header files from the source tree.

Next, create the `zend_module_entry` struct you declared in the header file. You'll notice that the first element of the module entry is conditional based on the current `ZEND_MODULE_API_NO` definition. This API number roughly equates to PHP 4.2.0, so if you know for certain that your extension will never be built on any version older than this, you could eschew the `#ifdef` lines entirely and just include the `STANDARD_MODULE_HEADER` element directly.

Consider, however, that it costs you very little in terms of compile time and nothing in terms of the resulting binary or the time it takes to process, so in most cases it will be best to just leave this condition in. The same applies to the version property near the end of this structure.

The other six elements of this structure you've initially set to NULL for now; you can see a hint from the comments next to these lines as to what they'll eventually be used for.

Finally, at the bottom you'll find a short element common to every PHP extension, which is able to be built as a shared module. This brief conditional simply adds a reference used by Zend when your extension is loaded dynamically. Don't worry about what it does or how it does it too much; just make sure that it's around or the next section won't work.

Building Your First Extension

Now that you've got all the files in place, it's time to make it go. As with building the main PHP binary, there are different steps to be taken depending on whether you're compiling for *nix or for Windows.

Building Under *nix

The first step is to generate a `./configure` script using the information in `config.m4` as a template. This can be done by running the `phpize` program installed when you compiled the main PHP binary.

```
$ phpize
PHP Api Version: 20041225
Zend Module Api No: 20050617
Zend Extension Api No: 220050617
```

> **Note**
>
> The extra 2 at the start of `Zend Extension Api No` isn't a typo; it corresponds to the Zend Engine 2 version and is meant to keep this API number greater than its ZE1 counterpart.

If you look in the current directory at this point, you'll notice a lot more files than you had there a moment ago. The `phpize` program combined the information in your extension's `config.m4` file with data collected from your PHP build and laid out all the pieces necessary to make a compile happen. This means that you don't have to struggle with makefiles and locating the PHP headers you'll be compiling against. PHP has already done that job for you.

The next step is a simple `./configure` that you might perform with any other OSS package. You're not configuring the entire PHP bundle here, just your one extension, so all you need to type in is the following:

```
$ ./configure —enable-sample
```

Notice that not even —`enable-debug` and —`enable-maintainer-zts` were used here. That's because phpize has already taken those values from the main PHP build and applied them to your extension's `./configure` script.

Now build it! Like any other package, you can just type **make** and the generated script files will handle the rest.

When the build process finishes, you'll be treated to a message stating that `sample.so` has been compiled and placed in a directory called "`modules`" within your current build directory.

Building Under Windows

The `config.m4` file you created earlier was actually specific to the *nix build. In order to make your extension compile under Windows, you'll need to create a separate—but similar—configuration file for it.

Add `config.w32` with the following contents to your `ext/sample` directory:

```
ARG_ENABLE("sample", "enable sample extension", "no");
if (PHP_SAMPLE != "no") {
    EXTENSION("sample", "sample.c");
}
```

As you can see, this file bears a resemblance on a high level to `config.m4`. The option is declared, tested, and conditionally used to enable the build of your extension.

Now you'll repeat a few of the steps you performed in Chapter 4, "Setting Up a Build Environment," when you built the PHP core. Start by opening up a build window from the Start menu by selecting All Programs, Microsoft Platform SDK for Windows Server 2003 SP1, Open Build Environment Window, Windows 2000 Build Environment, Set Windows 2000 Build Environment (Debug), and running the `C:\Program Files\Microsoft Visual Studio 8\VC\bin\vcvars32.bat` batch file.

Remember, your installation might require you to select a different build target or run a slightly different batch file. Refer to the notes in the corresponding section of Chapter 4 to refresh your memory.

Again, you'll want to go to the root of your build directory and rebuild the configure script.

```
C:\Program Files\Microsoft Platform SDK> cd \PHPDEV\php-5.1.0
C:\PHPDEV\php-5.1.0> buildconf.bat
Rebuilding configure.js
Now run 'cscript /nologo configure.js —help'
```

This time, you'll run the configure script with an abridged set of options. Because you'll be focusing on just your extension and not the whole of PHP, you can leave out options pertaining to other extensions; however, unlike the Unix build, you do need to include the —enable-debug switch explicitly even though the core build already has it.

The only crucial switch you'll need here—apart from debug of course—is —enable-sample=shared. The shared option is required here because configure.js doesn't know that you're planning to build sample as a loadable extension. Your configure line should therefore look something like this:

```
C:\PHPDEV\php-5.1.0> cscript /nologo configure.js \
—enable-debug —enable-sample=shared
```

> **Note**
> Recall that —enable-maintainer-zts is not required here as all Win32 builds assume that ZTS must be enabled. Options relating to SAPIs—such as embed—are also not required here as the SAPI layer is independent from the extension layer.

Lastly, you're ready to build the extension. Because this build is based from the core—unlike the Unix extension build, which was based from the extension—you'll need to specify the target name in your build line.

```
C:\PHPDEV\php-5.1.0> nmake php_sample.dll
```

Once compilation is complete, you should have a working php_sample.dll binary ready to be used in the next step. Remember, because this book focuses on *nix development, the extension will be referred to as sample.so rather than php_sample.dll in all following text.

Loading an Extension Built as a Shared Module

In order for PHP to locate this module when requested, it needs to be located in the same directory as specified in your php.ini setting: extension_dir. By default, php.ini is located in /usr/local/lib/php.ini; however, this default can be changed and often is with distribution packaging systems. Check the output of php -i to see where PHP is looking for your config file.

This setting, in an unmodified `php.ini`, is an unhelpful `./`. If you don't already have extensions being loaded, or just don't have any extensions other than `sample.so` anyway, you can change this value to the location where `make` put your module. Otherwise, just copy `sample.so` to the directory where this setting is pointing.

After `extension_dir` is pointing to the right place, there are two ways to tell PHP to load your module. The first is using the `dl()` function within your script:

```php
<?php
    dl('sample.so');
    var_dump(get_loaded_modules());
?>
```

If this script doesn't show `sample` as a loaded module, something has gone wrong. Look for error messages above the output for a clue, or refer to your `error_log` if one is defined in your `php.ini`.

The second, and much more common, method is to specify the module in your `php.ini` using the `extension` directive. The extension setting is relatively unique among `php.ini` settings in that it can be specified multiple times with different values. So if you already have an extension setting in your `php.ini`, don't add it to the same line like a delimited list; instead insert an additional line containing just `sample.so`. At this point your `php.ini` should look something like this:

```
extension_dir=/usr/local/lib/php/modules/
extension=sample.so
```

Now you could run the same script without the `dl()` line, or just issue the command `php -m` and still see "sample" in the list of loaded modules.

> **Note**
> All sample code in this and the following chapters will assume you've loaded the current extension using this method. If you plan on using `dl()` instead, be sure to add the appropriate load line to the sample scripts.

Building Statically

In the list of loaded modules, you probably noticed that several modules were listed that were not included using the extension directive in `php.ini`. These modules are built directly into PHP and are compiled as part of the main build process.

Building Static Under *nix

At this point, if you tried navigating up a couple directories to the PHP source tree root, you could run `./configure —help` and see that although your sample extension is located in the `ext/` directory along with all the other modules, it's not listed as an

option. This is because, at the time that the ./configure script was generated, your
extension was unknown. To regenerate ./configure and have it locate your new
extension all you need to do is issue one command:

```
$ ./buildconf
```

> **Note**
>
> If you're using a production release of PHP to do development against, you'll find that ./buildconf by
> itself doesn't actually work. In this case you'll need to issue: ./buildconf —force to bypass some
> minor protection built into the ./configure command.

Now you can issue ./configure —help and see that —enable-sample is an available
option. From here, you could re-issue ./configure with all the options you used in the
main PHP build plus —enable-sample to create a single, ready-to-go binary containing
a full PHP interpreter and your custom extension.

Of course, it's probably a bit early to be doing that. Your extension still needs to do
something besides take up space. Let's stick to building a nice lean shared object for
now.

Building Statically Under Windows

Regenerating the configure.js script for Windows follows the same pattern as
regenerating the ./configure script for *nix. Navigate to the root of the PHP source
tree and reissue buildconf.bat as you did in Chapter 4.

The PHP build system will scan for config.w32 files, including the one you just
made for ext/sample, and generate a new configure.js script with which to build a
static php binary.

Functional Functions

The quickest link between userspace and extension code is the PHP_FUNCTION(). Start
by adding the following code block near the top of your sample.c file just after
#include "php_sample.h":

```
PHP_FUNCTION(sample_hello_world)
{
    php_printf("Hello World!\n");
}
```

The PHP_FUNCTION() macro functions just like a normal C function declaration because
that's exactly how it expands:

```
#define PHP_FUNCTION(name)        \
    void zif_##name(INTERNAL_FUNCTION_PARAMETERS)
```

which in this case evaluates out to:

```
void zif_sample_hello_world(zval *return_value,
    char return_value_used, zval *this_ptr TSRMLS_DC)
```

Simply declaring the function isn't enough, of course. The engine needs to know the address of the function as well as how the function name should be exported to user space. This is accomplished by the next code block, which you'll want to place immediately after the PHP_FUNCTION() block:

```
static function_entry php_sample_functions[] = {
    PHP_FE(sample_hello_world,        NULL)
    { NULL, NULL, NULL }
};
```

The php_sample_functions vector is a simple NULL terminated vector that will grow as you continue to add functionality to the sample extension. Every function you export will appear as an item in this vector. Taking apart the PHP_FE() macro, you see that it expands to

```
{ "sample_hello_world", zif_sample_hello_world, NULL},
```

thus providing both a name for the new function, as well as a pointer to its implementation function. The third parameter in this set is used to provide argument hinting information such as requiring certain arguments to be passed by reference. You'll see this feature in use in Chapter 7, "Accepting Parameters."

So now you've got a list of exportable functions, but still nothing connecting it to the engine. This is accomplished with the last change to sample.c, which amounts to simply replacing the NULL, /* Functions */ line in your sample_module_entry structure with php_sample_functions, (be sure to keep that comma there!)

Now rebuild according to the instructions earlier and test it out using the -r option to the php command line, which allows running simple code fragments without having to create an entire file:

```
$ php -r 'sample_hello_world();'
```

If all has gone well, you'll see the words "Hello World!" output almost immediately.

Zend Internal Functions

The zif_ string prefixed to internal function names stands for "Zend Internal Function" and is used to avoid probable symbol conflicts. For example, the userspace strlen() function could not be implemented as void strlen(INTERNAL_FUNCTION_PARAMTERS) as it would conflict with the C library's implementation of strlen.

Sometimes even the default prefix of zif_ simply won't do. Usually this is because the function name expands another macro and gets misinterpreted by the C compiler. In these cases, an internal function may be given an arbitrary name using the

`PHP_NAMED_FUNCTION()` macro; for example, `PHP_NAMED_FUNCTION(zif_`
`sample_hello_world)` is identical to the earlier use of
`PHP_FUNCTION(sample_hello_world)`.

When adding an implementation declared using `PHP_NAMED_FUNCTION()`, the
`PHP_NAMED_FE()` macro is used to link it into the `function_entry` vector. So if you
declared your function as `PHP_NAMED_FUNCTION(purplefunc)`, you'd use
`PHP_NAMED_FE(sample_hello_world, purplefunc, NULL)` rather than using
`PHP_FE(sample_hello_world, NULL)`.

This practice can been seen in `ext/standard/file.c` where the `fopen()` function is
actually declared using `PHP_NAMED_FUNCTION(php_if_fopen)`. As far as userspace is
concerned, there's nothing usual about the function; it's still called as simply `fopen()`.
Internally, however, the function is protected from being mangled by preprocessor
macros and over-helpful compilers.

Function Aliases

Some functions can be referred to by more than one name. Recalling that ordinary
functions are declared internally as the function's userspace name with `zif_` prepended,
it's easy to see that the `PHP_NAMED_FE()` macro could be used to create this alternative
mapping:

```
PHP_FE(sample_hello_world,      NULL)
PHP_NAMED_FE(sample_hi,    zif_sample_hello_world,      NULL)
```

The `PHP_FE()` macro associates the userspace function name `sample_hello_world` with
`zif_sample_hello_world`—the expansion of `PHP_FUNCTION(sample_hello_world)`.
The `PHP_NAMED_FE()` macro then associates the userspace function name `sample_hi`
with this same internal implementation.

Now pretend that, because of a major change in the Zend engine, the standard prefix
for internal functions changes from `zif_` to `pif_`. Your extension will suddenly stop
being able to compile because when the `PHP_NAMED_FE()` function is reached,
`zif_sample_hello_world` is undefined.

This sort of unusual but troublesome case can be avoided by using the `PHP_FNAME()`
macro to expand `sample_hello_world` for you:

```
PHP_NAMED_FE(sample_hi, PHP_FNAME(sample_hello_world), NULL)
```

This way, if the function prefix ever changes, the function entry will update
automatically using the macro expansions defined in the PHP Core.

Now that you've got this entry working, guess what? It's not necessary. PHP exports
yet another macro designed specifically for creating function aliases. The previous
example could be rewritten as simply:

```
PHP_FALIAS(sample_hi, sample_hello_world, NULL)
```

Indeed this is the official way to create function aliases, and how you'll see it done nearly
everywhere else in the PHP source tree.

Summary

In this chapter you created a simple working PHP extension and learned the steps necessary to build it for most major platforms. In the coming chapters, you'll add to this extension, ultimately including every type of PHP feature.

The PHP source tree and the tools it relies on to compile and build on the many platforms it supports is constantly changing. If something in this chapter failed to work, refer to the `php.net` online manual under `Installation` to see if your version has special needs.

6

Returning Values

U SERSPACE FUNCTIONS MAKE USE OF THE return keyword to pass information back to their calling scope in the same manner that you're probably familiar with doing in a C
application, for example:

```
function sample_long() {
  return 42;
}
$bar = sample_long();
```

When sample_long() is called, the number 42 is returned and populated into the $bar variable. In C this might be done using a nearly identical code base:

```
int sample_long(void) {
  return 42;
}
void main(void) {
  int bar = sample_long();
}
```

Of course, in C you always know what the function being called is going to return based on its function prototype so you can declare the variable the result will be stored in accordingly. When dealing with PHP userspace, however, the variable type is dynamic and you have to fall back on the zval type introduced in Chapter 2, "Variables from the Inside Out."

The return_value **Variable**

You'll probably be tempted to believe that your internal function should return an immediate zval, or—more likely—allocate memory for a zval and return a zval* such as in the following code block:

```
PHP_FUNCTION(sample_long_wrong)
{
    zval *retval;

    MAKE_STD_ZVAL(retval);
    ZVAL_LONG(retval, 42);

    return retval;
}
```

Unfortunately, you'll be close, but ultimately wrong. Rather than forcing every function implementation to allocate a zval and return it, the Zend Engine pre-allocates this space before the method is called. It then initializes the zval's type to IS_NULL, and passes that value in the form of a parameter named return_value. Here's that same function again, done correctly:

```
PHP_FUNCTION(sample_long)
{
    ZVAL_LONG(return_value, 42);
    return;
}
```

Notice that nothing is directly returned by the PHP_FUNCTION() implementation. Instead, the return_value parameter is populated with appropriate data directly and the Zend Engine will process this into the value after the internal function has finished executing.

As a reminder, the ZVAL_LONG() macro is a simple wrapper around a set of assignment operations, in this case:

```
Z_TYPE_P(return_value) = IS_LONG;
Z_LVAL_P(return_value) = 42;
```

Or more primitively:

```
return_value->type = IS_LONG;
return_value->value.lval = 42;
```

> **Note**
> The is_ref and refcount properties of the return_value variable should almost never be modified by an internal function directly. These values are initialized and processed by the Zend Engine when it calls your function.

Let's take a look at this particular function in action by adding it to the sample extension from Chapter 5, "Your First Extension," just below the sample_hello_world() function. You'll also need to expand the php_sample_functions struct to contain a function entry for sample_long() as shown:

```
static function_entry php_sample_functions[] = {
    PHP_FE(sample_hello_world, NULL)
    PHP_FE(sample_long, NULL)
    { NULL, NULL, NULL }
};
```

At this point the extension can be rebuilt by issuing `make` from the source directory or `nmake php_sample.dll` from the PHP source root for Windows.

If all has gone well, you can now run PHP and exercise your new function:

```
$ php -r 'var_dump(sample_long());'
```

Wrap Your Macros Tightly

In the interest of readable, maintainable code, the `ZVAL_*()` macros have duplicated counterparts that are specific to the `return_value` variable. In each case, the `ZVAL` portion of the macro is replaced with the term `RETVAL`, and the initial parameter—which would otherwise denote the variable being modified—is omitted.

In the prior example, the implementation of `sample_long()` can be reduced to the following:

```
PHP_FUNCTION(sample_long)
{
    RETVAL_LONG(42);
    return;
}
```

Table 6.1 lists the `RETVAL` family of macros as defined by the Zend Engine. In all cases except two, the `RETVAL` macro is identical to its `ZVAL` counterpart with the initial `return_value` parameter removed.

Table 6.1 **Return Value Macros**

Generic ZVAL **Macro**	return_value **Specific Counterpart**
`ZVAL_NULL(return_value)`	`RETVAL_NULL()`
`ZVAL_BOOL(return_value, bval)`	`RETVAL_BOOL(bval)`
`ZVAL_TRUE(return_value)`	`RETVAL_TRUE`
`ZVAL_FALSE(return_value)`	`RETVAL_FALSE`
`ZVAL_LONG(return_value, lval)`	`RETVAL_LONG(lval)`
`ZVAL_DOUBLE(return_value, dval)`	`RETVAL_DOUBLE(dval)`
`ZVAL_STRING(return_value, str, dup)`	`RETVAL_STRING(str, dup)`
`ZVAL_STRINGL(return_value, str, len, dup)`	`RETVAL_STRINGL(str,len,dup)`
`ZVAL_RESOURCE(return_value, rval)`	`RETVAL_RESOURCE(rval)`

Quite often, after your function has come up with a return value it will be ready to exit and return control to the calling scope. For this reason there exists one more set of macros designed specifically for internal functions: The RETURN_*() family.

```
PHP_FUNCTION(sample_long)
{
    RETURN_LONG(42);
}
```

Although it's not actually visible, this function still explicitly returns at the end of the RETURN_LONG() macro call. This can be tested by adding a php_printf() call to the end of the function:

```
PHP_FUNCTION(sample_long)
{
    RETURN_LONG(42);
    php_printf("I will never be reached.\n");
}
```

The php_printf(), as its contents suggest, will never be executed because the call to RETURN_LONG() implicitly leaves the function.

Like the RETVAL series, a RETURN counterpart exists for each of the simple types shown in Table 6.1. Also like the RETVAL series, the RETURN_TRUE and RETURN_FALSE macros do not use parentheses.

More complex types, such as objects and arrays, are also returned through the return_value parameter; however, their nature precludes a simple macro based approach to creation. Even the resource type, while it has a RETVAL macro, requires additional work to generate. You'll see how to return these types later on in Chapters 8 through 11.

Is It Worth the Trouble?

One underused feature of the Zend Internal Function is the return_value_used parameter. Consider the following piece of userspace code:

```
function sample_array_range() {
    $ret = array();
    for($i = 0; $i < 1000; $i++) {
        $ret[] = $i;
    }
    return $ret;
}
sample_array_range();
```

Because `sample_array_range()` is called without storing the result into a variable, the work—and memory—being used to create a 1,000 element array is completely wasted. Of course, calling `sample_array_range()` in this manner is silly, but wouldn't it be nice to know ahead of time that its efforts will be in vain?

Although it's not accessible to userspace functions, an internal function can conditionally skip otherwise pointless behavior like this depending on the setting of the `return_value_used` parameter common to all internal functions.

```
PHP_FUNCTION(sample_array_range)
{
    if (return_value_used) {
        int i;
        /* Return an array from 0 - 999 */
        array_init(return_value);
        for(i = 0; i < 1000; i++) {
            add_next_index_long(return_value, i);
        }
        return;
    } else {
        /* Save yourself the effort */
        php_error_docref(NULL TSRMLS_CC, E_NOTICE,
                "Static return-only function called without processing output");
        RETURN_NULL();
    }
}
```

To see this function operate, just add it to your growing `sample.c` source file and toss in a matching entry to your `php_sample_functions` struct:

```
    PHP_FE(sample_array_range,    NULL)
```

Returning Reference Values

As you already know from working in userspace, a PHP function may also return a value by reference. Due to implementation problems, returning references from an internal function should be avoided in versions of PHP prior to 5.1 as it simply doesn't work. Consider the following userspace code fragment:

```
function &sample_reference_a() {
    /* If $a does not exist in the global scope yet,
     * create it with an initial value of NULL
     */
    if (!isset($GLOBALS['a'])) {
        $GLOBALS['a'] = NULL;
    }
    return $GLOBALS['a'];
```

```
}
$a = 'Foo';
$b = sample_reference_a();
$b = 'Bar';
```

In this code fragment, $b is created as a reference of $a just as if it had been set using
$b = &$GLOBALS['a']; or—because it's being done in the global scope anyway—just
$b = &$a;.

When the final line is reached, both $a and $b—which you'll recall from Chapter 3,
"Memory Management," are looking at the same actual value—contain the value 'Bar'.
Let's look at that same function again using an internals implementation:

```
#if (PHP_MAJOR_VERSION > 5) || (PHP_MAJOR_VERSION == 5 && \
                          PHP_MINOR_VERSION > 0)
PHP_FUNCTION(sample_reference_a)
{
    zval **a_ptr, *a;

    /* Fetch $a from the global symbol table */
    if (zend_hash_find(&EG(symbol_table), "a", sizeof("a"),
                                        (void**)&a_ptr) == SUCCESS) {
        a = *a_ptr;
    } else {
        /* $GLOBALS['a'] doesn't exist yet, create it */
        ALLOC_INIT_ZVAL(a);
        zend_hash_add(&EG(symbol_table), "a", sizeof("a"), &a,
                                        sizeof(zval*), NULL);
    }
    /* Toss out the old return_value */
    zval_ptr_dtor(return_value_ptr);
    if (!a->is_ref && a->refcount > 1) {
        /* $a is in a copy-on-write reference set
         * It must be separated before it can be used
         */
        zval *newa;
        MAKE_STD_ZVAL(newa);
        *newa = *a;
        zval_copy_ctor(newa);
        newa->is_ref = 0;
        newa->refcount = 1;
        zend_hash_update(&EG(symbol_table), "a", sizeof("a"), &newa,
                                        sizeof(zval*), NULL);
        a = newa;
    }
    /* Promote to full-reference and increase refcount */
    a->is_ref = 1;
```

```
    a->refcount++;
    *return_value_ptr = a;
}
#endif /* PHP >= 5.1.0 */
```

The `return_value_ptr` parameter is another common parameter passed to all internal functions and is a `zval**` containing a pointer to `return_value`. By calling `zval_ptr_dtor()` on it, the default `return_value zval*` is freed. You're then free to replace it with a new `zval*` of your choosing, in this case the variable `$a`, which has been promoted to `is_ref` and optionally separated from any non-full reference pairings it might have had.

   If you were to compile and run this code now, however, you'd get a segfault. In order to make it work, you'll need to add a structure to your `php_sample.h` file:

```
#if (PHP_MAJOR_VERSION > 5) || (PHP_MAJOR_VERSION == 5 && \
                       PHP_MINOR_VERSION > 0)
static
    ZEND_BEGIN_ARG_INFO_EX(php_sample_retref_arginfo, 0, 1, 0)
    ZEND_END_ARG_INFO ()
#endif /* PHP >= 5.1.0 */
```

Then use that structure when you declare your function in `php_sample_functions`:

```
#if (PHP_MAJOR_VERSION > 5) || (PHP_MAJOR_VERSION == 5 && \
                       PHP_MINOR_VERSION > 0)
    PHP_FE(sample_reference_a, php_sample_retref_arginfo)
#endif /* PHP >= 5.1.0 */
```

This structure, which you'll learn more about later in this chapter, provides vital hints to the Zend Engine function call routine. In this case it tells the ZE that `return_value` will need to be overridden, and that it should populate `return_value_ptr` with the correct address. Without this hint, ZE will simply place NULL in `return_value_ptr`, which would make this particular function crash when it reached `zval_ptr_dtor()`.

> **Note**
>
> Each of these code fragments has been wrapped in an `#if` block to instruct the compiler that support for them should only be enabled if the PHP version is greater than or equal to 5.1. Without these conditional directives, the extension would not be able to compile on PHP4 (because several elements, including `return_value_ptr`, do not exist), and would fail to function properly on PHP 5.0 (where a bug causes reference returns to be copied by value).

Returning Values by Reference

Using the return construct to send values and variable references back from a function is all well and good, but sometimes you want to return multiple values from a function. You could use an array to do this, which we'll explore in Chapter 8, "Working with Arrays and Hashtables," or you can return values back through the parameter stack.

Call-time Pass-by-ref

One of the simpler ways to pass variables by reference is by requiring the calling scope
to include an ampersand (&) with the parameter such as in the following piece of userspace code:

```
function sample_byref_calltime($a) {
    $a .= ` (modified by ref!)';
}
$foo = 'I am a string';
sample_byref_calltime(&$foo);
echo $foo;
```

The ampersand (&) placed in the parameter call causes the actual zval used by $foo,
rather than a copy of its contents, to be sent to the function. This allows the function to
modify the value in place and effectively return information through its passed parameter. If sample_byref_calltime() hadn't been called with the ampersand placed in front
of $foo, the changes made inside the function would not have affected the original
variable.

Repeating this endeavor in C requires nothing particularly special. Create the following function after sample_long() in your sample.c source file:

```
PHP_FUNCTION(sample_byref_calltime)
{
    zval *a;
    int addtl_len = sizeof(" (modified by ref!)") - 1;

    if (zend_parse_parameters(ZEND_NUM_ARGS() TSRMLS_CC, "z", &a) == FAILURE) {
        RETURN_NULL();
    }
    if (!a->is_ref) {
        /* parameter was not passed by reference,
         * leave without doing anything
         */
        return;
    }
    /* Make sure the variable is a string */
    convert_to_string(a);
    /* Enlarge a's buffer to hold the additional data */
    Z_STRVAL_P(a) = erealloc(Z_STRVAL_P(a),
        Z_STRLEN_P(a) + addtl_len + 1);
    memcpy(Z_STRVAL_P(a) + Z_STRLEN_P(a),
    " (modified by ref!)", addtl_len + 1);
    Z_STRLEN_P(a) += addtl_len;
}
```

As always, this function needs to be added to the php_sample_functions structure:

```
    PHP_FE(sample_byref_calltime,          NULL)
```

Compile-time Pass-by-ref

The more common way to pass by reference is by using compile-time pass-by-ref. Here, the parameters to a function are declared to be for reference use only and attempts to pass constants or intermediate values—such as the result of a function call—will result in an error because there is nowhere for the function to store the resulting value back into. A userspace compile-time pass-by-ref function might look something like the following:

```
function sample_byref_compiletime(&$a) {
    $a .= ' (modified by ref!)';
}
$foo = 'I am a string';
sample_byref_compiletime($foo);
echo $foo;
```

As you can see, this varies from the calltime version only in the placement of the referencing ampersand. When looking at this function in C, the implementation in terms of function code is entirely identical. The only true difference is in how it is declared in the `php_sample_functions` block:

```
PHP_FE(sample_byref_compiletime, php_sample_byref_arginfo)
```

where `php_sample_byref_arginfo` is a (verbosely named) constant structure which you'll obviously need to define before this entry will compile.

> **Note**
>
> The check for `is_ref` could actually be left out of the compiletime version because it will always fail—and not exit—but it causes no harm to leave it in for now.

In Zend Engine 1 (PHP4), this will be a simple `char*` list made up of a length byte followed by a set of flags pertaining to each of a function's parameters in turn.

```
static unsigned char php_sample_byref_arginfo[] =
                            { 1, BYREF_FORCE };
```

Here, the 1 indicates that the vector only contains argument info for one parameter. The argument-specific arg info then follows in subsequent elements with the first arg going in the second element as shown. If there had been a second or third argument involved, their flags would have gone in the third and fourth elements respectively and so on. Possible values for a given argument's element are shown in Table 6.2.

Table 6.2 **Zend Engine 1 Arg Info Constants**

Reference Type	Meaning
BYREF_NONE	Pass-by-ref is never allowed on this parameter. Attempts to use call-time pass-by-ref will be ignored and the parameter will be copied instead.

Table 6.2 **Continued**

Reference Type	Meaning
BYREF_FORCE	Arguments are always passed by reference regardless of how the function is called. This is equivalent to using an ampersand in a userspace function parameter declaration.
BYREF_ALLOW	Argument passing by reference is determined by call-time semantics. This is equivalent to ordinary userspace function declaration.
BYREF_FORCE_REST	The current argument and all subsequent arguments will have BYREF_FORCE applied. This flag may only be the last arg info flag in the list. Placing additional flags after BYREF_FORCE_REST will result in undefined behavior.

In Zend Engine 2 (PHP5+), you'll use a much more extensive structure containing information such as minimum and maximum parameter requirements, type hinting, and whether or not to force referencing.

First the arg info struct is declared using one of two macros. The simpler macro, ZEND_BEGIN_ARG_INFO(), takes two parameters:

```
ZEND_BEGIN_ARG_INFO(name, pass_rest_by_reference)
```

name is quite simply how this struct will be referred to within the extension, in this case: php_sample_byref_arginfo.

pass_rest_by_reference takes on the same meaning here as using BYREF_FORCE_REST as the last element of a Zend Engine 1 arg info vector. If this parameter is set to 1, all arguments not explicitly described within the struct will be assumed to be compile-time pass-by-ref arguments.

The alternative begin macro, which introduces two new options not found in the Zend Engine 1 version, is ZEND_BEGIN_ARG_INFO_EX():

```
ZEND_BEGIN_ARG_INFO_EX(name, pass_rest_by_reference, return_reference,
                       required_num_args)
```

name and pass_rest_by_reference have the same meanings here of course. return_reference, as you saw earlier in the chapter, gives a hint to Zend that your function will be overriding return_value_ptr with your own zval.

The final argument, required_num_args, is another shortcut hint to Zend that allows it to skip certain function calls entirely when that function's prototype is known to be incompatible with how its being called.

After you have a suitable begin macro in place, it may be followed by zero or more ZEND_ARG_*INFO elements. The types and usages of these macros are shown in Table 6.3.

Table 6.3   **ZEND_ARG_INFO Family of Macros**

Arg Info macro	Purpose
`ZEND_ARG_PASS_INFO(by_ref)`	`by_ref` here—as in all subsequent macros—is a binary option indicating whether the corresponding parameter should be forced as pass-by-reference. Setting this option to 1 is equivalent to using `BYREF_FORCE` in a Zend Engine 1 vector.
`ZEND_ARG_INFO(by_ref, name)`	This macro provides an additional name attribute used by internally generated error messages and the reflection API. It should be set to something helpful and non-cryptic.
`ZEND_ARG_ARRAY_INFO(by_ref, name, allow_null)` `ZEND_ARG_OBJ_INFO(by_ref, name, classname, allow_null)`	These two macros provide argument type hinting to internal functions specifying that either an array or particular class instance is expected as the parameter. Setting `allow_null` to a non-zero value will allow the calling scope to pass a `NULL` value in place of an array/object.

Lastly, all arg info structs using the Zend Engine 2 macros must terminate their list using `ZEND_END_ARG_INFO()`. For your sample function, you might select a final structure that looks like the following:

```
ZEND_BEGIN_ARG_INFO(php_sample_byref_arginfo, 0)
    ZEND_ARG_PASS_INFO(1)
ZEND_END_ARG_INFO()
```

In order to make extensions that are compatible with both ZE1 and ZE2, it's necessary to use an `#ifdef` statement and define the same `arg_info` structure for both, in this case:

```
#ifdef ZEND_ENGINE_2
static
    ZEND_BEGIN_ARG_INFO(php_sample_byref_arginfo, 0)
        ZEND_ARG_PASS_INFO(1)
    ZEND_END_ARG_INFO()
#else /* ZE 1 */
static unsigned char php_sample_byref_arginfo[] =
                        { 1, BYREF_FORCE };
#endif
```

Now that all the pieces are gathered together, it's time to create an actual compile-time pass-by-reference implementation. First let's put the block defining `php_sample_byref_arginfo` for ZE1 and ZE2 into the header file `php_sample.h`.

Next, you could take two approaches: One approach would be to copy and paste the `PHP_FUNCTION(sample_byref_calltime)` implementation and rename it to `PHP_FUNCTION(sample_byref_compiletime)`, and then add a `PHP_FE(sample_byref_compiletime, php_sample_byref_arginfo)` line to `php_sample_functions`.

This approach is straightforward and probably less prone to confusion when making changes years from now. Because this is just sample code, however, you can play a little looser and avoid code duplication by using `PHP_FALIAS()`, which you saw last chapter.

This time, rather than making a duplicate of `PHP_FUNCTION(sample_byref_calltime)`, add a single line to `php_sample_functions`:

```
PHP_FALIAS(sample_byref_compiletime, sample_byref_calltime,
    php_sample_byref_arginfo)
```

As you'll recall from Chapter 5, this creates a userspace function called `sample_byref_compiletime()` with an internal implementation using `sample_byref_calltime()`'s code. The addition of `php_sample_byref_arginfo` makes this version unique.

Summary

In this chapter you looked at how to return values from internal functions both directly by value, as a reference, and through their parameter stack using references. You also got a first look at argument type hinting using Zend Engine 2's `zend_arg_info` struct.

In the next chapter you'll delve more deeply into accepting parameters both as elementary zvals and using `zend_parse_parameters()`'s powerful type juggling features.

7

Accepting Parameters

WITH A COUPLE OF "SNEAK PREVIEW" EXCEPTIONS, the extension functions you've dealt with so far have been simple, return-only factories. Most functions, however, won't be so single purposed. You usually want to pass in some kind of parameter and receive a meaningful response based on the value and some additional processing.

Automatic Type Conversion with
`zend_parse_parameters()`

As with return values, which you saw last chapter, parameter values are moved around using indirect zval references. The easiest way to get at these zval* values is using the `zend_parse_parameters()` function.

Calls to `zend_parse_parameters()` almost invariably begin with the `ZEND_NUM_ARGS()` macro followed by the ubiquitous `TSRMLS_CC`. `ZEND_NUM_ARGS()`, as its name suggests, returns an `int` representing the number of arguments actually passed to the function. Because of the way `zend_parse_parameters()` works internally, you'll probably never need to inspect this value directly, so just pass it on for now.

The next parameter to `zend_parse_parameters()` is the format parameter, which is made up of a string of letters or character sequences corresponding to the various primitive types supported by the Zend Engine. Table 7.1 shows the basic type characters.

Table 7.1 `zend_parse_parameters()` **Type Specifiers**

Type Specifier	Userspace Datatype
b	Boolean
l	Integer
d	Floating point
s	String
r	Resource

Table 7.1 **Continued**

Type Specifier	Userspace Datatype
a	Array
o	Object instance
O	Object instance of a specified type
z	Non-specific zval
Z	Dereferenced non-specific zval

The remaining parameters to ZPP depend on which specific type you've requested in your format string. For the simpler types, this is a dereferenced C language primitive. For example, a long data type is extracted like such:

```
PHP_FUNCTION(sample_getlong)
{
    long foo;
    if (zend_parse_parameters(ZEND_NUM_ARGS() TSRMLS_CC,
                    "l", &foo) == FAILURE) {
        RETURN_NULL();
    }
    php_printf("The integer value of the parameter you "
            "passed is: %ld\n", foo);
    RETURN_TRUE;
}
```

> **Note**
> Although it's common for integers and longs to have the same data storage size, they cannot always be used interchangeably. Attempting to dereference an int data type into a long* parameter can lead to unexpected results, especially as 64-bit platforms become more prevalent. Always use the appropriate data type(s) as listed in Table 7.2.

Table 7.2 `zend_parse_parameters()` **Data Types**

Type specifier	C datatype(s)
b	zend_bool
l	long
d	double
s	char*, int
r	zval*
a	zval*
o	zval*
O	zval*, zend_class_entry*

Table 7.2   **Continued**

Type specifier	C datatype(s)
z	zval*
Z	zval**

Notice that all the more complex data types actually parse out as simple zvals. For the most part this is due to the same limitation that prevents returning complex data types using RETURN_*() macros: There's really no C-space analog to these structures. What ZPP does do for your function, however, is ensure that the zval* you do receive is of the appropriate type. If necessary, it will even perform implicit conversions such as casting arrays to stdClass objects.

The s and O types are also worth pointing out because they require a pair of parameters for each invocation. You'll see O more closely when you explore the Object data type in Chapters 10, "PHP4 Objects," and 11, "PHP5 Objects." In the case of the s type, let's say you're extending the sample_hello_world() function from Chapter 5, "Your First Extension," to greet a specific person by name:

```
function sample_hello_world($name) {
    echo "Hello $name!\n";
}
```

In C, you'll use the zend_parse_parameters() function to ask for a string:

```
PHP_FUNCTION(sample_hello_world)
{
    char *name;
    int name_len;

    if (zend_parse_parameters(ZEND_NUM_ARGS() TSRMLS_CC, "s",
                    &name, &name_len) == FAILURE) {
        RETURN_NULL();
    }
    php_printf("Hello ");
    PHPWRITE(name, name_len);
    php_printf("!\n");
}
```

> **Tip**
>
> The zend_parse_parameters() function may fail due to the function being passed to too few arguments to satisfy the format string or because one of the arguments passed simply cannot be converted to the requested type. In such a case, it will automatically output an error message so your extension doesn't have to.

To request more than one parameter, extend the format specifier to include additional characters and stack the subsequent arguments onto the zend_parse_parameters() call. Parameters are parsed left to right just as they are in a userspace function declaration:

```
function sample_hello_world($name, $greeting) {
    echo "Hello $greeting $name!\n";
}
sample_hello_world('John Smith', 'Mr.');
Or:
PHP_FUNCTION(sample_hello_world)
{
    char *name;
    int name_len;
    char *greeting;
    int greeting_len;

    if (zend_parse_parameters(ZEND_NUM_ARGS() TSRMLS_CC, "ss",
        &name, &name_len, &greeting, &greeting_len) == FAILURE) {
        RETURN_NULL();
    }
    php_printf("Hello ");
    PHPWRITE(greeting, greeting_len);
    php_printf(" ");
    PHPWRITE(name, name_len);
    php_printf("!\n");
}
```

In addition to the type primitives, an additional three metacharacters exist for modifying how the parameters will be processed. Table 7.3 lists these modifiers.

Table 7.3 `zend_parse_parameters()` **Modifiers**

Type Modifier	Meaning
|	Optional parameters follow. When this is specified, all previous parameters are considered required and all subsequent parameters are considered optional.
!	If a NULL is passed for the parameter corresponding to the preceding argument specifier, the internal variable provided will be set to an actual NULL pointer as opposed to an IS_NULL zval.
/	If the parameter corresponding to the preceding argument specifier is in a copy-on-write reference set, it will be automatically separated into a new zval with is_ref==0, and refcount==1.

Optional Parameters

Taking another look at the revised `sample_hello_world()` example, your next step in building this out might be to make the `$greeting` parameter optional. In PHP:

```
function sample_hello_world($name, $greeting='Mr./Ms.') {
    echo "Hello $greeting $name!\n";
}
```

`sample_hello_world()` can now be called with both parameters or just the name:

```
sample_hello_world('Ginger Rogers','Ms.');
sample_hello_world('Fred Astaire');
```

with the default argument being used when none is explicitly given. In a C implementation, optional parameters are specified in a similar manner.

To accomplish this, use the pipe character (|) in `zend_parse_parameters()`'s format string. Arguments to the left of the pipe will parsed from the call stack—if possible—while any argument on the right that isn't provided will be left unmodified. For example:

```
PHP_FUNCTION(sample_hello_world)
{
    char *name;
    int name_len;
    char *greeting = "Mr./Mrs.";
    int greeting_len = sizeof("Mr./Mrs.") - 1;

    if (zend_parse_parameters(ZEND_NUM_ARGS() TSRMLS_CC, "s|s",
      &name, &name_len, &greeting, &greeting_len) == FAILURE) {
        RETURN_NULL();
    }
    php_printf("Hello ");
    PHPWRITE(greeting, greeting_len);
    php_printf(" ");
    PHPWRITE(name, name_len);
    php_printf("!\n");
}
```

Because optional parameters are not modified from their initial values unless they're provided as arguments, it's important to initialize any parameters to some default value. In most cases this will be NULL/0, though sometimes—as above—another default is sensible.

`IS_NULL` Versus `NULL`

Every zval, even the ultra-simple `IS_NULL` data type, occupies a certain minimal amount of memory overhead. Beyond that, it takes a certain number of clock cycles to allocate that memory space, initialize the values, and then ultimately free it when it's deemed no longer useful.

For many functions, it makes no sense to go through this process only to find out that the parameter was flagged as unimportant by the calling scope through the use of a `NULL` argument. Fortunately `zend_parse_parameters()` allows arguments to be flagged as "NULL permissible" by appending an exclamation point to their format specifier. Consider the following two code fragments, one with the modifier and one without:

```
PHP_FUNCTION(sample_arg_fullnull)
{
    zval *val;
    if (zend_parse_parameters(ZEND_NUM_ARGS() TSRMLS_CC, "z",
                                    &val) == FAILURE) {
        RETURN_NULL();
    }
    if (Z_TYPE_P(val) == IS_NULL) {
        val = php_sample_make_defaultval(TSRMLS_C);
    }
...
PHP_FUNCTION(sample_arg_nullok)
{
    zval *val;
    if (zend_parse_parameters(ZEND_NUM_ARGS() TSRMLS_CC, "z!",
                                    &val) == FAILURE) {
        RETURN_NULL();
    }
    if (!val) {
        val = php_sample_make_defaultval(TSRMLS_C);
    }
...
```

These two versions really aren't so different code wise, though the former uses nominally more processor time. In general, this feature won't be very useful, but it's good to know it's available.

Forced Separation

When a variable is passed into a function, whether by reference or not, its refcount is almost always at least 2; one reference for the variable itself, and another for the copy that was passed into the function. Before making changes to that zval (if acting on the zval directly), it's important to separate it from any non-reference set it may be part of.

This would be a tedious task were it not for the / format specifier, which automatically separates any copy-on-write referenced variable so that your function can do as it pleases. Like the NULL flag, this modifier goes after the type it means to impact. Also like the NULL flag, you won't know you need this feature until you actually have a use for it.

zend_get_arguments()

If you happen to be designing your code to work on very old versions of PHP, or you just have a function that never needs anything other than zval*s, you might consider using the zend_get_parameters() API call.

The zend_get_parameters() call differs from its newer parse counterpart in a few crucial ways. First, it performs no automatic type conversion; instead all arguments are extracted as primitive `zval*` data types. The simplest use of `zend_get_parameters()` might be something like the following:

```
PHP_FUNCTION(sample_onearg)
{
    zval *firstarg;
    if (zend_get_parameters(ZEND_NUM_ARGS(), 1, &firstarg)
                              == FAILURE) {
        php_error_docref(NULL TSRMLS_CC, E_WARNING,
            "Expected at least 1 parameter.");
        RETURN_NULL();
    }
    /* Do something with firstarg... */
}
```

Second, as you can see from the manually applied error message, `zend_get_parameters()` does not output error text on failure. It's also very poor at handling optional parameters. Specifically, if you ask it to fetch four arguments, you had better be certain that at least four arguments were provided or it will return FAILURE.

Lastly, unlike parse, this specific get variant will automatically separate any copy-on-write reference sets. If you still wanted to skip automatic separation, you could use its sibling: `zend_get_parameters_ex()`.

In addition to not separating copy-on-write reference sets, `zend_get_parameters_ex()` differs in that it returns `zval**` pointers rather than simply `zval*`. Though that distinction is probably one you won't know you need until you have cause to use it, its usage is ultimately quite similar:

```
PHP_FUNCTION(sample_onearg)
{
    zval **firstarg;
    if (zend_get_parameters_ex(1, &firstarg) == FAILURE) {
        WRONG_PARAM_COUNT;
    }
    /* Do something with firstarg... */
}
```

> **Note**
>
> Notice that the _ex version does not require the `ZEND_NUM_ARGS()` parameter. This is due to the _ex version being added at a later time when changes to the Zend Engine made this parameter unnecessary.
>
> In this example, you also used the `WRONG_PARAM_COUNT` macro, which handles displaying an `E_WARNING` error message and automatically leaving the function.

Handling Arbitrary Numbers of Arguments

Two more members of the zend_get_parameter family exist for extracting a set of zval* and zval** pointers in situations where either the number of parameters is prohibitively large, or will not actually be known until runtime.

Consider the var_dump() function, which will display the contents of an arbitrary number of variables passed to it:

```
PHP_FUNCTION(var_dump)
{
    int i, argc = ZEND_NUM_ARGS();
    zval ***args;

    args = (zval ***)safe_emalloc(argc, sizeof(zval **), 0);
    if (ZEND_NUM_ARGS() == 0 ||
        zend_get_parameters_array_ex(argc, args) == FAILURE) {
        efree(args);
        WRONG_PARAM_COUNT;
    }
    for (i=0; i<argc; i++) {
        php_var_dump(args[i], 1 TSRMLS_CC);
    }
    efree(args);
}
```

Here, var_dump() pre-allocates a vector of zval** pointers based on the count of parameters passed into the function. It then uses zend_get_parameters_array_ex() to populate that vector in a single shot. As you can probably guess, another version of this function exists as zend_get_parameters_array() with a similar set of differences: auto-separation, zval* instead of zval**, and required ZEND_NUM_ARGS() in the first parameter.

Arg Info and Type-hinting

In the last chapter you were introduced very briefly to the concept of type-hinting using the Zend Engine 2's argument info structure. As a reminder, this feature is unique to ZE2 and is not available in ZE1—which is what PHP4 is built on.

Let's start by recapping ZE2's argument info struct. Every arg info declaration is made up of either a ZEND_BEGIN_ARG_INFO() or ZEND_BEGIN_ARG_INFO_EX() macro, followed by zero or more ZEND_ARG_*INFO() lines, and terminated by a ZEND_END_ARG_INFO() call.

The definitions and basic usage of each of these macro calls can be found near the end of Chapter 6, "Returning Values," in the section on compile-time pass-by-ref.

Assuming you wanted to reimplement the count() function, you might create a simple function like the following:

```
PHP_FUNCTION(sample_count_array)
{
    zval *arr;
    if (zend_parse_parameters(ZEND_NUM_ARGS() TSRMLS_CC, "a",
                                &arr) == FAILURE) {
        RETURN_NULL();
    }
    RETURN_LONG(zend_hash_num_elements(Z_ARRVAL_P(arr)));
}
```

By itself, `zend_parse_parameters()` does an excellent job of ensuring that the variable passed to your function is in fact an array. However, if you needed to use the `zend_get_parameter()` function—or one of its siblings—you would need to build type checking directly into your function. That is, unless you used type hinting! By defining an `arg_info` struct like the following:

```
static
    ZEND_BEGIN_ARG_INFO(php_sample_array_arginfo, 0)
        ZEND_ARG_ARRAY_INFO(0, "arr", 0)
    ZEND_END_ARG_INFO()
```

and using it in your function's entry in `php_sample_functions`:

```
    PHP_FE(sample_count_array, php_sample_array_arginfo)
```

you pass the work of type checking off to the Zend Engine. You've also given your argument a name so that the generated error messages can be more meaningful to script writers attempting to use your API.

Objects, as you probably noticed in Chapter 6 when the arg info structure was first introduced, can also be type hinted using an `ARG_INFO` macro. Simply name the class type as an additional parameter following name:

```
static
    ZEND_BEGIN_ARG_INFO(php_sample_class_arginfo, 0)
        ZEND_ARG_OBJECT_INFO(1, "obj", "stdClass", 0)
    ZEND_END_ARG_INFO()
```

Notice that the first parameter here (`by_ref`) was set to one. Ordinarily this parameter is fairly unimportant to objects because all objects in ZE2 are referenced by default and copies must be explicitly generated through clone. Forcing a clone within a function call can be done, but that's an entirely different route around reference forcing.

The reason you might care about the setting of `by_ref` in a `ZEND_ARG_OBJECT_INFO` line is when the `zend.ze1_compatibility_mode` flag has been set. In this specific case, an object will still be implicitly passed as a copy rather than a reference. Because you'll probably want a true reference when dealing with objects, it will be best to just set this flag and not have to worry about it.

> **Note**
>
> Don't forget about the `allow_null` option for the array and object arg info macros. For more information on allowing NULLs, see the section on compile-time pass-by-ref in the previous chapter.

Of course, using arg info for type hinting is only available with version 2 of the Zend Engine so if you plan to make your extension PHP4-compliant and need to use `zend_get_parameters()`, your only remaining option for type validation is manually examining `Z_TYPE_P(value)` or automatically casting the type with one of the `convert_to_type()` methods you saw in Chapter 2.

Summary

By now you've gotten your hands a little dirty with real, functional code that can communicate with userspace through simple input/output functions. You've explored the zval reference counting system a little more deeply and learned ways to control how and when variables will be passed to your internal function.

In the next chapter you'll explore the array data type and see how its userspace representation maps to its underlying `HashTable`. You'll also take a look at the wide selection of Zend and PHP API functions available for manipulating these complex structures.

8

Working with Arrays and HashTables

IN C, THERE ARE TWO FUNDAMENTALLY DIFFERENT WAYS of storing an arbitrary number of independent data elements in a single structure. Both have their pros and cons.

Vectors Versus Linked Lists

One is usually picked over the other based on the specific type of application being written, how much data it needs to store, and how quickly it needs to be able to retrieve it. For the sake of speaking the same vocabulary, let's look at both these storage mechanisms in brief.

Vectors

A *vector* is a contiguous block of memory that contains successive pieces of data at regular intervals. Easily the most ubiquitous example of a vector is the string variable (`char*` or `char[]`), which contains a sequence of characters (bytes) one after the next.

```
char foo[4] = "bar";
```

Here, `foo[0]` contains the letter 'b'; immediately afterward, you would find the letter 'a' in `foo[1]` and so on ending up with a NULL character '\0' at `foo[3]`.

Almost as common, pointers to other structures are stored in vectors as well such as in the zval vector you saw last chapter while using the `zend_get_parameters_array_ex()` function. There, you saw `var_dump()` declare a `zval***` function variable and then allocate space to store the `zval**` pointers, which would ultimately come from the `zend_get_parameters_ex()` call.

```
zval ***args = safe_emalloc(ZEND_NUM_ARGS(), sizeof(zval**), 0);
```

Similar to accessing characters in strings, the `var_dump()` implementation used `args[i]` to pass individual `zval**` elements, in turn, to the `php_var_dump()` internal function.

The biggest advantage to vectors is the speed with which individual elements can be accessed at runtime. A variable reference such as args[i] is quickly calculated as being the data at the address pointed to by args plus i times the size of args' data type. Storage space for this index structure is allocated and freed in a single, efficient call.

Linked Lists

Another common approach to data storage is the linked list. With a linked list, every data element is a struct with at least two properties: A pointer to the next item in the list, and some piece of actual data. Consider the following hypothetical data structure:

```
typedef struct _namelist namelist;
struct {
    struct namelist *next;
    char *name;
} _namelist;
```

An application using this data struct might have a variable declared as

```
static namelist *people;
```

The first name in the list can be found by checking the name property of the people variable: people->name; the second name is accessed by following the next property: people->next->name, and then people->next->next->name, and so on until next is NULL meaning that no more names exist in the list. More commonly, a loop might be used to iterate through such a list:

```
void name_show(namelist *p)
{
    while (p) {
        printf("Name: %s\n", p->name);
        p = p->next;
    }
}
```

Such lists are very handy for FIFO chains where new data is added to the end of a list as it comes in, leaving another branch or thread to handle consuming the data:

```
static namelist *people = NULL, *last_person = NULL;
void name_add(namelist *person)
{
    person->next = NULL;
    if (!last_person) {
        /* No one in the list yet */
        people = last_person = person;
        return;
    }
    /* Append new person to the end of the list */
    last_person->next = person;
```

```
    /* Update the list tail */
    last_person = person;
}
namelist *name_pop(void)
{
    namelist *first_person = people;
    if (people) {
    people = people->next;
    }
    return first_person;
}
```

New namelist structures can be shifted in and popped out of this list as many times as necessary without having to adjust the structure's size or block copy elements between positions.

The form of the linked list you just saw is singly linked, and while it has some interesting features, it also has some serious weaknesses. Given a pointer to one item in the linked list, it becomes difficult to cut that element out of the chain and ensure that the prior element will be properly linked to the next one.

In order to even know what the prior element was, it's necessary to iterate through the entire list until the element to be removed is found within the next property of a given temp element. On large lists this can present a significant investment in CPU time. A simple and relatively inexpensive solution to this problem is the doubly linked list.

With the doubly linked list, every element gets an additional pointer value indicating the location of the previous element:

```
typedef struct _namelist namelist;
struct {
    namelist *next, *prev;
    char *name;
} _namelist;
```

When an element is added to a doubly linked list, both of these pointers are updated accordingly:

```
void name_add(namelist *person)
{
    person->next =  NULL;
    if (!last_person) {
        /* No one in the list yet */
        people = last_person = person;
        person->prev = NULL;
        return;
    }
    /* Append new person to the end of the list */
    last_person ->next = person;
    person->prev = last_person;
```

```
    /* Update the list tail */
    last_person = person;
}
```

So far you haven't seen any advantage to this, but now imagine you have an arbitrary namelist record from somewhere in the middle of the people list and you want to remove it. In the singly linked list you'd need to do something like the following:

```
void name_remove(namelist *person)
{
    namelist *p;
    if (person == people) {
        /* Happens to be the first person in the list */
        people = person->next;
        if (last_person == person) {
            /* Also happens to be the last person */
            last_person = NULL;
        }
        return;
    }
    /* Search for prior person */
    p = people;
    while (p) {
        if (p->next == person) {
            /* unlink */
            p->next = person->next;
            if (last_person == person) {
                /* This was the last element */
                last_person = p;
            }
            return;
        }
        p = p->next;
    }
    /* Not found in list */
}
```

Now compare that code with the simpler approach found in a doubly linked list:

```
void name_remove(namelist *person)
{
    if (people == person) {
        people = person->next;
    }
    if (last_person == person) {
        last_person = person->prev;
    }
    if (person->prev) {
```

```
        person->prev->next = person->next;
    }
    if (person->next) {
        person->next->prev = person->prev;
    }
}
```

Rather than a long, complicated loop, delinking this element from the list requires only a simple set of reassignments wrapped in conditionals. A reverse of this process also allows elements to be inserted at arbitrary points in the list with the same improved efficiency.

HashTables—The Best of Both Worlds

Although you'll quite likely use vectors or linked lists in a few places in your application, there exists one more type of collection that you'll end up using even more: The HashTable.

A HashTable is a specialized form of a doubly linked list that adds the speed and efficiency of vectors in the form of lookup indices. HashTables are used so heavily throughout the Zend Engine and the PHP Core that an entire subset of the Zend API is devoted to handling these structures.

As you saw in Chapter 2, "Variables from the Inside Out," all userspace variables are stored in HashTables as zval* pointers. In later chapters you'll see how the Zend Engine uses HashTables to store userspace functions, classes, resources, autoglobal labels, and other structures as well.

To refresh from Chapter 2, a Zend Engine HashTable can literally store any piece of data of any size. Functions, for example, are stored as a complete structure. Autoglobals are smaller elements of just a few bytes, whereas other structures such as variables and PHP5 class definitions are simply stored as pointers to other structs located elsewhere in memory.

Further into this chapter you'll look at the function calls that make up the Zend Hash API and how you can use these methods in your extensions.

Zend Hash API

The Zend Hash API is split into a few basic categories and—with a couple exceptions—the functions in these categories will generally return either SUCCESS or FAILURE.

Creation

Every HashTable is initialized by a common constructor:

```
int zend_hash_init(HashTable *ht, uint nSize,
    hash_func_t pHashFunction,
    dtor_func_t pDestructor, zend_bool persistent)
```

ht is a pointer to a HashTable variable either declared as an immediate value, or dynam-ically allocated via emalloc(), pemalloc(), or more commonly ALLOC_HASHTABLE(ht). The ALLOC_HASHTABLE() macro uses pre-sized blocks of memory from a special pool to speed the allocation time required and is generally preferred over
ht = emalloc(sizeof(HashTable));.

nSize should be set to the maximum number of elements that the HashTable is expected to hold. If more that this number of elements are added to the HashTable, it will be able to grow but only at a noticeable cost in processing time as Zend reindexes the entire table for the newly widened structure. If nSize is not a power of 2, it will be automatically enlarged to the next higher power according to the formula

```
nSize = pow(2, ceil(log(nSize, 2)));
```

pHashFunction is a holdover from an earlier version of the Zend Engine and is no longer used so this value should always be set to NULL. In earlier versions of the Zend Engine, this value could be pointed to an alternate hashing algorithm to be used in place of the standard DJBX33A method—a quick, moderately collision-resistant hashing algo-rithm for converting arbitrary string keys into reproducible integer values.

pDestructor is a pointer to a method to be called whenever an element is removed from a HashTable such as when using zend_hash_del() or replacing an item with zend_hash_update(). The prototype for any destructor method *must* be

```
void method_name(void *pElement);
```

where pElement is a pointer to the item being removed from the HashTable.

The final option, persistent, is a simple flag that the engine passes on to the pemalloc() function calls you were introduced to in Chapter 3, "Memory Management." Any HashTables that need to remain available between requests must have this flag set and must have been allocated using pemalloc().

This method can be seen in use at the start of every PHP request cycle as the EG(symbol_table) global is initialized:

```
zend_hash_init(&EG(symbol_table), 50, NULL, ZVAL_PTR_DTOR, 0);
```

As you can see here, when an item is removed from the symbol table—possibly in response to an unset($foo); statement—a pointer to the zval* stored in the HashTable (effectively a zval**) is sent to zval_ptr_dtor(), which is what the ZVAL_PTR_DTOR macro expands out to.

Because 50 is not an exact power of 2, the size of the initial global symbol table will actually be 64—the next higher power of 2.

Population

There are four primary functions for inserting or updating data in HashTables:

```
int zend_hash_add(HashTable *ht, char *arKey, uint nKeyLen,
                  void **pData, uint nDataSize, void *pDest);
```

```
int zend_hash_update(HashTable *ht, char *arKey, uint nKeyLen,
                void *pData, uint nDataSize, void **pDest);
int zend_hash_index_update(HashTable *ht, ulong h,
                void *pData, uint nDataSize, void **pDest);
int zend_hash_next_index_insert(HashTable *ht,
                void *pData, uint nDataSize, void **pDest);
```

The first two functions here are for adding associatively indexed data to a HashTable such as with the statement $foo['bar'] = 'baz'; which in C would look something like:

```
zend_hash_add(fooHashTbl, "bar", sizeof("bar"), &barZval, sizeof(zval*), NULL);
```

The only difference between zend_hash_add() and zend_hash_update() is that zend_hash_add() will fail if the key already exists.

The next two functions deal with numerically indexed HashTables in a similar manner. This time, the distinction between the two lies in whether a specific index is provided, or if the next available index is assigned automatically.

If it's necessary to store the index value of the element being inserted using zend_hash_next_index_insert(), then the zend_hash_next_free_element() function may be used:

```
ulong nextid = zend_hash_next_free_element(ht);
zend_hash_index_update(ht, nextid, &data, sizeof(data), NULL);
```

In the case of each of these insertion and update functions, if a value is passed for pDest, the void* data element that pDest points to will be populated by a pointer to the copied data value. This parameter has the same usage (and result) as the pData parameter passed to the zend_hash_find() function you're about to look at.

Recall

Because there are two distinct organizations to HashTable indices, there must be two methods for extracting them:

```
int zend_hash_find(HashTable *ht, char *arKey, uint nKeyLength,
                                void **pData);
int zend_hash_index_find(HashTable *ht, ulong h, void **pData);
```

As you can guess, the first is for associatively indexed arrays while the second is for numerically indexed ones. Recall from Chapter 2 that when data is added to a HashTable, a new memory block is allocated for it and the data passed in is copied; when the data is extracted back out it is the pointer to that data which is returned. The following code fragment adds data1 to the HashTable, and then extracts it back out such that at the end of the routine, *data2 contains the same contents as *data1 even though the pointers refer to different memory addresses.

```
void hash_sample(HashTable *ht, sample_data *data1)
```

```
{
    sample_data *data2;
    ulong targetID = zend_hash_next_free_element(ht);
    if (zend_hash_index_update(ht, targetID,
            data1, sizeof(sample_data), NULL) == FAILURE) {
        /* Should never happen */
        return;
    }
    if(zend_hash_index_find(ht, targetID, (void **)&data2) == FAILURE) {
        /* Very unlikely since we just added this element */
        return;
    }
    /* data1 != data2, however *data1 == *data2 */
}
```

Often, retrieving the stored data is not as important as knowing that it exists; for this purpose two more functions exist:

```
int zend_hash_exists(HashTable *ht, char *arKey, uint nKeyLen);
int zend_hash_index_exists(HashTable *ht, ulong h);
```

These two methods do no return SUCCESS/FAILURE; rather they return 1 to indicate that the requested key/index exists or 0 to indicate absence. The following code fragment performs roughly the equivalent of isset($foo):

```
if (zend_hash_exists(EG(active_symbol_table),
                        "foo", sizeof("foo"))) {
    /* $foo is set */
} else {
    /* $foo does not exist */
}
```

Quick Population and Recall

```
ulong zend_get_hash_value(char *arKey, uint nKeyLen);
```

When performing multiple operations with the same associative key, it can be useful to precompute the hash using zend_get_hash_value(). The result can then be passed to a collection of "quick" functions that behave exactly like their non-quick counterparts, but use the precomputed hash value rather than recalculating it each time.

```
int zend_hash_quick_add(HashTable *ht,
    char *arKey, uint nKeyLen, ulong hashval,
    void *pData, uint nDataSize, void **pDest);
int zend_hash_quick_update(HashTable *ht,
    char *arKey, uint nKeyLen, ulong hashval,
    void *pData, uint nDataSize, void **pDest);
int zend_hash_quick_find(HashTable *ht,
```

```
    char *arKey, uint nKeyLen, ulong hashval, void **pData);
int zend_hash_quick_exists(HashTable *ht,
    char *arKey, uint nKeyLen, ulong hashval);
```

Surprisingly there is no `zend_hash_quick_del()`. The "quick" hash functions might be used in something like the following code fragment, which copies a specific element from `hta` to `htb`, which are `zval*` HashTables:

```
void php_sample_hash_copy(HashTable *hta, HashTable *htb,
                    char *arKey, uint nKeyLen TSRMLS_DC)
{
    ulong hashval = zend_get_hash_value(arKey, nKeyLen);
    zval **copyval;

    if (zend_hash_quick_find(hta, arKey, nKeyLen,
            hashval, (void**)&copyval) == FAILURE) {
        /* arKey doesn't actually exist */
        return;
    }
    /* The zval* is about to be owned by another hash table */
    (*copyval)->refcount++;
    zend_hash_quick_update(htb, arKey, nKeyLen, hashval,
            copyval, sizeof(zval*), NULL);
}
```

Copying and Merging

The previous task, duplicating an element from one HashTable to another, is extremely common and is often done en masse. To avoid the headache and trouble of repeated recall and population cycles, there exist three helper methods:

```
typedef void (*copy_ctor_func_t)(void *pElement);
void zend_hash_copy(HashTable *target, HashTable *source,
        copy_ctor_func_t pCopyConstructor,
        void *tmp, uint size);
```

Every element in `source` will be copied to `target` and then processed through the `pCopyConstructor` function. For HashTables such as userspace variable arrays, this provides the opportunity to increment the reference count so that when the `zval*` is removed from one or the other HashTable, it's not prematurely destroyed. If the same element already exists in the target HashTable, it is overwritten by the new element. Other existing elements—those not being overwritten—are not implicitly removed.

   `tmp` should be a pointer to an area of scratch memory to be used by the `zend_hash_copy()` function while it's executing. Ever since PHP 4.0.3, however, this temporary space is no longer used. If you know your extension will never be compiled against a version older than 4.0.3, just leave this `NULL`.

`size` is the number of bytes occupied by each member element. In the case of a user-space variable hash, this would be `sizeof(zval*)`.

```
void zend_hash_merge(HashTable *target, HashTable *source,
        copy_ctor_func_t pCopyConstructor,
        void *tmp, uint size, int overwrite);
```

`zend_hash_merge()` differs from `zend_hash_copy()` only in the addition of the overwrite parameter. When set to a non-zero value, `zend_hash_merge()` behaves exactly like `zend_hash_copy()`; when set to zero, it skips any already existing elements.

```
typedef zend_bool (*merge_checker_func_t)(HashTable *target_ht,
    void *source_data, zend_hash_key *hash_key, void *pParam);
void zend_hash_merge_ex(HashTable *target, HashTable *source,
        copy_ctor_func_t pCopyConstructor, uint size,
        merge_checker_func_t pMergeSource, void *pParam);
```

The final form of this group of functions allows for selective copying using a merge checker function. The following example shows `zend_hash_merge_ex()` in use to copy only the associatively indexed members of the source HashTable (which happens to be a userspace variable array):

```
zend_bool associative_only(HashTable *ht, void *pData,
        zend_hash_key *hash_key, void *pParam)
{
    /* True if there's a key, false if there's not */
    return (hash_key->arKey && hash_key->nKeyLength);
}
void merge_associative(HashTable *target, HashTable *source)
{
    zend_hash_merge_ex(target, source, zval_add_ref,
            sizeof(zval*), associative_only, NULL);
}
```

Iteration by Hash Apply

Like in userspace, there's more than one way to iterate a cat—er...array. The first, and generally easiest, method is using a callback system similar in function to the `foreach()` construct in userspace. This two part system involves a callback function you'll write—which acts like the code nest in a `foreach` loop—and a call to one of the three hash application API functions.

```
typedef int (*apply_func_t)(void *pDest TSRMLS_DC);
void zend_hash_apply(HashTable *ht,
        apply_func_t apply_func TSRMLS_DC);
```

This simplest form of the hash apply family simply iterates through `ht` calling `apply_func` for each one with a pointer to the current element passed in `pDest`.

```
typedef int (*apply_func_arg_t)(void *pDest,
                          void *argument TSRMLS_DC);
void zend_hash_apply_with_argument(HashTable *ht,
        apply_func_arg_t apply_func, void *data TSRMLS_DC);
```

In this next hash apply form, an arbitrary argument is passed along with the hash element. This is useful for multipurpose hash apply functions where behavior can be customized depending on an additional parameter.

Each callback function, no matter which iterator function it applies to, expects one of the three possible return values shown in Table 8.1.

Table 8.1   **Hash Apply Callback Return Values**

Constant	Meaning
ZEND_HASH_APPLY_KEEP	Returning this value completes the current loop and continues with the next value in the subject hash table. This is equivalent to issuing `continue;` within a `foreach()` control block.
ZEND_HASH_APPLY_STOP	This return value halts iteration through the subject hash table and is the same as issuing `break;` within a `foreach()` loop.
ZEND_HASH_APPLY_REMOVE	Similar to ZEND_HASH_APPLY_KEEP, this return value will jump to the next iteration of the hash apply loop. However, this return value will also delete the current element from the subject hash.

A simple `foreach()` loop in userspace such as the following:

```
<?php
foreach($arr as $val) {
    echo "The value is: $val\n";
}
?>
```

would translate into the following callback in C:

```
int php_sample_print_zval(zval **val TSRMLS_DC)
{
    /* Duplicate the zval so that
     * the original's contents are not destroyed */
    zval tmpcopy = **val;

    zval_copy_ctor(&tmpcopy);
    /* Reset refcount & Convert */
    INIT_PZVAL(&tmpcopy);
    convert_to_string(&tmpcopy);
    /* Output */
```

```
php_printf("The value is: ");
PHPWRITE(Z_STRVAL(tmpcopy), Z_STRLEN(tmpcopy));
php_printf("\n");
/* Toss out old copy */
zval_dtor(&tmpcopy);
/* continue; */
return ZEND_HASH_APPLY_KEEP;
}
```

which would be iterated using

```
zend_hash_apply(arrht, php_sample_print_zval TSRMLS_CC);
```

> **Note**
> Recall that when variables are stored in a hash table, only a pointer to the zval is actually copied; the
> contents of the zval are never touched by the HashTable itself. Your iterator callback prepares for this
> by declaring itself to accept a zval** even though the function type only calls for a single level of indi-
> rection. Refer to Chapter 2 for more information on why this is done.

```
typedef int (*apply_func_args_t)(void *pDest,
        int num_args, va_list args, zend_hash_key *hash_key);
void zend_hash_apply_with_arguments(HashTable *ht,
        apply_func_args_t apply_func, int numargs, ...);
```

In order to receive the key during loops as well as the value, the third form of
zend_hash_apply() must be used. For example, if you extended this exercise to support
outputting the key:

```php
<?php
foreach($arr as $key => $val) {
    echo "The value of $key is: $val\n";
}
?>
```

then your current iterator callback would have nowhere to get $key from. By switching
to zend_hash_apply_with_arguments(), however, your callback prototype and implementation now becomes

```
int php_sample_print_zval_and_key(zval **val,
        int num_args, va_list args, zend_hash_key *hash_key)
{
    /* Duplicate the zval so that
     * the original's contents are not destroyed */
    zval tmpcopy = **val;
    /* tsrm_ls is needed by output functions */
    TSRMLS_FETCH();
```

```
    zval_copy_ctor(&tmpcopy);
    /* Reset refcount & Convert */
    INIT_PZVAL(&tmpcopy);
    convert_to_string(&tmpcopy);
    /* Output */
    php_printf("The value of ");
    if (hash_key->nKeyLength) {
        /* String Key / Associative */
        PHPWRITE(hash_key->arKey, hash_key->nKeyLength);
    } else {
        /* Numeric Key */
        php_printf("%ld", hash_key->h);
    }
    php_printf(" is: ");
    PHPWRITE(Z_STRVAL(tmpcopy), Z_STRLEN(tmpcopy));
    php_printf("\n");
    /* Toss out old copy */
    zval_dtor(&tmpcopy);
    /* continue; */
    return ZEND_HASH_APPLY_KEEP;
}
```

Which can then be called as:

```
zend_hash_apply_with_arguments(arrht,
                php_sample_print_zval_and_key, 0);
```

> **Note**
>
> This particular example required no arguments to be passed; for information on extracting variable argument lists from `va_list args`, see the POSIX documentation pages for `va_start()`, `va_arg()`, and `va_end()`.
>
> Notice that nKeyLength, rather than arKey, was used to test for whether the key was associative or not. This is because implementation specifics in Zend HashTables can sometimes leave data in the arKey variable. nKeyLength, however, can be safely used even for empty keys (for example, `$foo['']` = "Bar";) because the trailing NULL is included giving the key a length of 1.

Iteration by Move Forward

It's also trivially possible to iterate through a HashTable without using a callback. For this, you'll need to be reminded of an often ignored concept in HashTables: The internal pointer.

In userspace, the functions reset(), key(), current(), next(), prev(), each(), and end() can be used to access elements within an array depending on where an invisible bookmark believes the "current" position to be:

```php
<?php
    $arr = array('a'=>1, 'b'=>2, 'c'=>3);
    reset($arr);
    while (list($key, $val) = each($arr)) {
        /* Do something with $key and $val */
    }
    reset($arr);
    $firstkey = key($arr);
    $firstval = current($arr);
    $bval = next($arr);
    $cval = next($arr);
?>
```

Each of these functions is duplicated by—more to the point, wrapped around—internal
Zend Hash API functions with similar names:

```
/* reset() */
void zend_hash_internal_pointer_reset(HashTable *ht);
/* key() */
int zend_hash_get_current_key(HashTable *ht,
        char **strIdx, unit *strIdxLen,
        ulong *numIdx, zend_bool duplicate);
/* current() */
int zend_hash_get_current_data(HashTable *ht, void **pData);
/* next()/each() */
int zend_hash_move_forward(HashTable *ht);
/* prev() */
int zend_hash_move_backwards(HashTable *ht);
/* end() */
void zend_hash_internal_pointer_end(HashTable *ht);
/* Other... */
int zend_hash_get_current_key_type(HashTable *ht);
int zend_hash_has_more_elements(HashTable *ht);
```

> **Note**
>
> The next(), prev(), and end() userspace statements actually map to their move forward/backward
> statements followed by a call to zend_hash_get_current_data(). each() performs the same
> steps as next(), but calls and returns zend_hash_get_current_key() as well.

Emulating a foreach() loop using iteration by moving forward actually starts to look
more familiar, repeating the print_zval_and_key example from earlier:

```
void php_sample_print_var_hash(HashTable *arrht)
{
```

```
    for(zend_hash_internal_pointer_reset(arrht);
    zend_hash_has_more_elements(arrht) == SUCCESS;
    zend_hash_move_forward(arrht)) {
        char *key;
        uint keylen;
        ulong idx;
        int type;
        zval **ppzval, tmpcopy;

        type = zend_hash_get_current_key_ex(arrht, &key, &keylen,
                                            &idx, 0, NULL);
        if (zend_hash_get_current_data(arrht, (void**)&ppzval) == FAILURE) {
            /* Should never actually fail
             * since the key is known to exist. */
            continue;
        }
        /* Duplicate the zval so that
         * the orignal's contents are not destroyed */
        tmpcopy = **ppzval;
        zval_copy_ctor(&tmpcopy);
        /* Reset refcount & Convert */
        INIT_PZVAL(&tmpcopy);
        convert_to_string(&tmpcopy);
        /* Output */
        php_printf("The value of ");
        if (type == HASH_KEY_IS_STRING) {
            /* String Key / Associative */
            PHPWRITE(key, keylen);
        } else {
            /* Numeric Key */
            php_printf("%ld", idx);
        }
        php_printf(" is: ");
        PHPWRITE(Z_STRVAL(tmpcopy), Z_STRLEN(tmpcopy));
        php_printf("\n");
        /* Toss out old copy */
        zval_dtor(&tmpcopy);
    }
}
```

Most of this code fragment should be immediately familiar to you. The one item that hasn't yet been touched on is zend_hash_get_current_key()'s return value. When called, this function will return one of three constants as listed in Table 8.2.

Table 8.2 **Zend Hash Key Types**

Constant	Meaning
HASH_KEY_IS_STRING	The current element is associatively indexed; therefore, a pointer to the element's key name will be populated into strIdx, and its length will be populated into stdIdxLen. If the duplicate flag is set to a nonzero value, the key will be estrndup()'d before being populated into strIdx. The calling application is expected to free this duplicated string.
HASH_KEY_IS_LONG	The current element is numerically indexed and numIdx will be supplied with the index number.
HASH_KEY_NON_EXISTANT	The internal pointer is past the end of the HashTable's contents. Neither a key nor a data value are available at this position because no more exist.

Preserving the Internal Pointer

When iterating through a HashTable, particularly one containing userspace variables, it's not uncommon to encounter circular references, or at least self-overlapping loops. If one iteration context starts looping through a HashTable and the internal pointer reaches—for example—the halfway mark, a subordinate iterator starts looping through the same HashTable and would obliterate the current internal pointer position, leaving the HashTable at the end when it arrived back at the first loop.

The way this is resolved—both within the zend_hash_apply implementation and within custom move forward uses—is to supply an external pointer in the form of a HashPosition variable.

Each of the zend_hash_*() functions listed previously has a zend_hash_*_ex() counterpart that accepts one additional parameter in the form of a pointer to a HashPostion data type. Because the HashPosition variable is seldom used outside of a short-lived iteration loop, it's sufficient to declare it as an immediate variable. You can then dereference it on usage such as in the following variation on the php_sample_print_var_hash() function you saw earlier:

```
void php_sample_print_var_hash(HashTable *arrht)
{
    HashPosition pos;
    for(zend_hash_internal_pointer_reset_ex(arrht, &pos);
    zend_hash_has_more_elements_ex(arrht, &pos) == SUCCESS;
    zend_hash_move_forward_ex(arrht, &pos)) {
        char *key;
        uint keylen;
        ulong idx;
        int type;
```

```
    zval **ppzval, tmpcopy;

    type = zend_hash_get_current_key_ex(arrht,
                            &key, &keylen,
                            &idx, 0, &pos);
    if (zend_hash_get_current_data_ex(arrht,
                (void**)&ppzval, &pos) == FAILURE) {
        /* Should never actually fail
         * since the key is known to exist. */
        continue;
    }
    /* Duplicate the zval so that
     * the original's contents are not destroyed */
    tmpcopy = **ppzval;
    zval_copy_ctor(&tmpcopy);
    /* Reset refcount & Convert */
    INIT_PZVAL(&tmpcopy);
    convert_to_string(&tmpcopy);
    /* Output */
    php_printf("The value of ");
    if (type == HASH_KEY_IS_STRING) {
        /* String Key / Associative */
        PHPWRITE(key, keylen);
    } else {
        /* Numeric Key */
        php_printf("%ld", idx);
    }
    php_printf(" is: ");
    PHPWRITE(Z_STRVAL(tmpcopy), Z_STRLEN(tmpcopy));
    php_printf("\n");
    /* Toss out old copy */
    zval_dtor(&tmpcopy);
    }
}
```

With these very slight additions, the HashTable's true internal pointer is preserved in whatever state it was initially in on entering the function. When it comes to working with internal pointers of userspace variable HashTables (that is, arrays), this extra step will very likely make the difference between whether the scripter's code works as expected.

Destruction

There are only four destruction functions you need to worry about. The first two are used for removing individual elements from a HashTable:

```
int zend_hash_del(HashTable *ht, char *arKey, uint nKeyLen);
int zend_hash_index_del(HashTable *ht, ulong h);
```

As you can guess, these cover a HashTable's split-personality index design by providing deletion functions for both associative and numerically indexed hash elements. Each version returns either SUCCESS or FAILURE.

Recall that when an item is removed from a HashTable, the HashTable's destructor function is called with a pointer to the item to be removed passed as the only parameter.

```
void zend_hash_clean(HashTable *ht);
```

When completely emptying out a HashTable, the quickest method is to call zend_hash_clean(), which will iterate through every element calling zend_hash_del() on them one at a time.

```
void zend_hash_destroy(HashTable *ht);
```

Usually, when cleaning out a HashTable, you'll want to discard it entirely. Calling zend_hash_destroy() will perform all the actions of a zend_hash_clean(), as well as free additional structures allocated during zend_hash_init().

A full HashTable life cycle might look like the following:

```
int sample_strvec_handler(int argc, char **argv TSRMLS_DC)
{
    HashTable *ht;
    /* Allocate a block of memory
     * for the HashTable structure */
    ALLOC_HASHTABLE(ht);
    /* Initialize its internal state */
    if (zend_hash_init(ht, argc, NULL,
                       ZVAL_PTR_DTOR, 0) == FAILURE) {
        FREE_HASHTABLE(ht);
        return FAILURE;
    }
    /* Populate each string into a zval* */
    while (argc-) {
        zval *value;
        MAKE_STD_ZVAL(value);
        ZVAL_STRING(value, argv[argc], 1);
        argv++;
        if (zend_hash_next_index_insert(ht, (void**)&value,
                           sizeof(zval*)) == FAILURE) {
            /* Silently skip failed additions */
            zval_ptr_dtor(&value);
        }
    }
    /* Do some work */
    process_hashtable(ht);
    /* Destroy the hashtable
     * freeing all zval allocations as necessary */
    zend_hash_destroy(ht);
```

```
/* Free the HashTable itself */
FREE_HASHTABLE(ht);
return SUCCESS;
}
```

Sorting, Comparing, and Going to the Extreme(s)

A couple more callbacks exist in the Zend Hash API. The first handles comparing two elements either from the same HashTable, or from similar positions in different HashTables:

```
typedef int (*compare_func_t)(void *a, void *b TSRMLS_DC);
```

Like the usort() callback in userspace PHP, this function expects you to compare the values of a and b. Using your own criteria for comparison, return either -1 if a is less than b, 1 if b is less than a, or 0 if they are equal.

```
int zend_hash_minmax(HashTable *ht, compare_func_t compar,
                     int flag, void **pData TSRMLS_DC);
```

The simplest API function to use this callback is zend_hash_minmax(), which—as the name implies—will return the highest or lowest valued element from a HashTable based on the ultimate result of multiple calls to the comparison callback. Passing zero for flag will return the minimum value; passing non-zero will return maximum.

The following example sorts the list of registered userspace functions by name and returns the lowest and highest named function (not case-sensitive):

```
int fname_compare(zend_function *a, zend_function *b TSRMLS_DC)
{
    return strcasecmp(a->common.function_name, b->common.function_name);
}
void php_sample_funcname_sort(TSRMLS_D)
{
    zend_function *fe;
    if (zend_hash_minmax(EG(function_table), fname_compare,
                0, (void **)&fe) == SUCCESS) {
        php_printf("Min function: %s\n", fe->common.function_name);
    }
    if (zend_hash_minmax(EG(function_table), fname_compare,
                1, (void **)&fe) == SUCCESS) {
        php_printf("Max function: %s\n", fe->common.function_name);
    }
}
```

The hash comparison function is also used in zend_hash_compare(), which evaluates two hashes against each other as a whole. If hta is found to be "greater" than htb, 1 will be returned. -1 is returned if htb is "greater" than hta, and 0 if they are deemed equal.

```
int zend_hash_compare(HashTable *hta, HashTable *htb,
        compare_func_t compar, zend_bool ordered TSRMLS_DC);
```

This method begins by comparing the number of elements in each HashTable. If one
HashTable contains more elements than the other, it is immediately deemed greater and
the function returns quickly.

Next it starts a loop with the first element of hta. If the ordered flag is set, it com-
pares keys/indices with the first element of htb—string keys are compared first on
length, and then on binary sequence using memcmp(). If the keys are equal, the value of
the element is compared with the first element of htb using the comparison callback
function.

If the ordered flag is not set, the data portion of the first element of hta is compared
against the element with a matching key/index in htb using the comparison callback
function. If no matching element can be found for htb, then hta is considered greater
than htb and 1 is returned.

If at the end of a given loop, hta and htb are still considered equal, comparison con-
tinues with the next element of hta until a difference is found or all elements have been
exhausted, in which case 0 is returned.

The second callback function in this family is the sort function:

```
typedef void (*sort_func_t)(void **Buckets, size_t numBuckets,
            size_t sizBucket, compare_func_t comp TSRMLS_DC);
```

This callback will be triggered once, and receive a vector of all the Buckets (elements)
in the HashTable as a series of pointers. These Buckets may be swapped around within
the vector according to the sort function's own logic with or without the use of the
comparison callback. In practice, sizBucket will always be sizeof(Bucket*).

Unless you plan on implementing your own alternative bubblesort method, you
won't need to implement a sort function yourself. A predefined sort method—
zend_qsort—already exists for use as a callback to zend_hash_sort() leaving you to
implement the comparison function only.

```
int zend_hash_sort(HashTable *ht, sort_func_t sort_func,
        compare_func_t compare_func, int renumber TSRMLS_DC);
```

The final parameter to zend_hash_sort(), when set, will toss out any existing associative keys or index numbers and reindex the array based on the result of the sorting operation. The userspace sort() implementation uses zend_hash_sort() in the following
manner:

```
zend_hash_sort(target_hash, zend_qsort,
                    array_data_compare, 1 TSRMLS_CC);
```

where array_data_compare is a simple compare_func_t implementation that sorts
according to the value of the zval*s in the HashTable.

zval* **Array API**

Ninety-five percent of the HashTables you'll work with in a PHP extension are going to be for the purpose of storing and retrieving userspace variables. In turn, most of your HashTables will themselves be wrapped in zval containers.

Easy Array Creation

To aid the creation and manipulation of these common HashTables, the PHP API exposes a simple set of macros and helper functions starting with array_init(zval *arrval). This function allocates a HashTable, calls zend_hash_init() with the appropriate parameters for a userspace variable hash, and populates the zval* with the newly created structure.

No special destruction function is needed because after the zval looses its last refcount—through calls to zval_dtor()/zval_ptr_dtor(), the engine automatically invokes zend_hash_destroy() and FREE_HASHTABLE().

Combine the array_init() method you just learned about with the techniques for returning values from functions you saw in Chapter 6, "Returning Values":

```
PHP_FUNCTION(sample_array)
{
    array_init(return_value);
}
```

Because return_value is a preallocated zval*, you don't have to do anything more to set it up. And because its only reference is the one you sent it out of the function with, you don't have to worry about cleaning it up either.

Easy Array Population

Just like with any HashTable, you'll populate an array by iteratively adding elements to it. With userspace variables specifically, you get to fall back on the primitive data types you know from C. A triumvirate of functions in the form: add_assoc_*(), add_index_*(), and add_next_index_*() exist for each of the data types you already have ZVAL_*(), RETVAL_*(), and RETURN_*() macros for. For example:

```
add_assoc_long(zval *arrval, char *key, long lval);
add_index_long(zval *arrval, ulong idx, long lval);
add_next_index_long(zval *arrval, long lval);
```

In each case, the array zval* comes first followed by an associative keyname, numeric index, or—for the next_index variety—nothing at all. Lastly comes the data element itself, which will ultimately be wrapped in a newly allocated zval* and added to the array with zend_hash_update(), zend_hash_index_update(), or zend_hash_next_index_insert().

The add_assoc_*() function variants with their prototypes are as follows. In each case assoc may be replaced with index or next_index and the key/index parameter adjusted or removed as appropriate.

```
add_assoc_null(zval *aval, char *key);
add_assoc_bool(zval *aval, char *key, zend_bool bval);
add_assoc_long(zval *aval, char *key, long lval);
add_assoc_double(zval *aval, char *key, double dval);
add_assoc_string(zval *aval, char *key, char *strval, int dup);
add_assoc_stringl(zval *aval, char *key,
                        char *strval, uint strlen, int dup);
add_assoc_zval(zval *aval, char *key, zval *value);
```

The last version of these functions allows you to prepare zvals of any arbitrary type—including resource, object, or array—and add them to your growing array with the same simple ease. Try out a few additions to your sample_array() function:

```
PHP_FUNCTION(sample_array)
{
    zval *subarray;

    array_init(return_value);
    /* Add some scalars */
    add_assoc_long(return_value, "life", 42);
    add_index_bool(return_value, 123, 1);
    add_next_index_double(return_value, 3.1415926535);
    /* Toss in a static string, dup'd by PHP */
    add_next_index_string(return_value, "Foo", 1);
    /* Now a manually dup'd string */
    add_next_index_string(return_value, estrdup("Bar"), 0);

    /* Create a subarray */
    MAKE_STD_ZVAL(subarray);
    array_init(subarray);
    /* Populate it with some numbers */
    add_next_index_long(subarray, 1);
    add_next_index_long(subarray, 20);
    add_next_index_long(subarray, 300);
    /* Place the subarray in the parent */
    add_index_zval(return_value, 444, subarray);
}
```

If you were to var_dump() the array returned by this function you'd get output something like the following:

```
array(6) {
  ["life"]=> int(42)
  [123]=> bool(true)
  [124]=> float(3.1415926535)
  [125]=> string(3) "Foo"
  [126]=> string(3) "Bar"
  [444]=> array(3) {
```

```
    [0]=> int(1)
    [1]=> int(20)
    [2]=> int(300)
  }
}
```

These add_*() functions may also be used for internal public properties by simple objects. Watch for them in Chapter 10, "PHP4 Objects."

Summary

You've just spent a long chapter learning about one of the most prevalent structures in the Zend Engine and PHP Core—second only to the zval* of course. You compared different data storage mechanisms and were introduced to a large swath of the API that you'll use repeatedly.

By now you should have enough tools amassed to implement a fair portion of the standard extension. In the next few chapters you'll round off the remaining zval data types by exploring resources and objects.

9

The Resource Data Type

So FAR, YOU'VE WORKED WITH fairly primitive userspace data types, strings, numbers, and true/false values. Even the arrays you started working with last chapter were just collections of primitive data types.

Complex Structures

Out in the real world, you'll usually have to work with more complex collections of data, often involving pointers to opaque structures. One common example of an opaque structure is the stdio file descriptor that appears even to C code as nothing more than a pointer.

```
#include <stdio.h>
int main(void)
{
    FILE *fd;
    fd = fopen("/home/jdoe/.plan", "r");
    fclose(fd);
    return 0;
}
```

The way the stdio file descriptor is then used—like most file descriptors—is like a book-mark. The calling application—your extension—need only pass this value into the implementation functions such as feof(), fread(), fwrite(), fclose(), and so on. At some point, however, this bookmark must be accessible to userspace code; therefore, it's necessary to be able to represent it within the standard PHP variable, or zval*.

This is where a new data type comes into play. The RESOURCE data type stores a simple integer value within the zval* itself, which is then used as a lookup into an index of registered resources. The resource entry contains information about what internal data type the resource index represents as well as a pointer to the stored resource data.

Defining Resource Types

In order for registered resource entries to understand anything about the resource they contain, it's necessary for that resource type to be declared. Start by adding the following piece of code to `sample.c` right after your existing function implementations:

```
static int le_sample_descriptor;
PHP_MINIT_FUNCTION(sample)
{
    le_sample_descriptor = zend_register_list_destructors_ex(
            NULL, NULL, PHP_SAMPLE_DESCRIPTOR_RES_NAME,
            module_number);
    return SUCCESS;
}
```

Next, scroll down to the bottom of your file and modify the `sample_module_entry` structure replacing the `NULL, /* MINIT */` line. Just as when you added your function list to this structure, you will want to make sure to keep a comma at the end of this line.

```
    PHP_MINIT(sample), /* MINIT */
```

Finally, you'll need to define `PHP_SAMPLE_DESCRIPTOR_RES_NAME` within `php_sample.h` by placing the following line next to your other constant definitions:

```
#define PHP_SAMPLE_DESCRIPTOR_RES_NAME "File Descriptor"
```

`PHP_MINIT_FUNCTION()` represents the first of four special startup and shutdown operations that you were introduced to conceptually in Chapter 1, "The PHP Life Cycle," and which you'll explore in greater depth in Chapter 12, "Startup, Shutdown, and a Few Points in Between," and Chapter 13, "INI Settings."

What's important to know at this juncture is that the `MINIT` method is executed once when your extension is first loaded and before any requests have been received. Here you've used that opportunity to register destructor functions—the NULL values, which you'll change soon enough—for a resource type that will be thereafter known by a unique integer ID.

Registering Resources

Now that the engine is aware that you'll be storing some resource data, it's time to give userspace code a way to generate the actual resources. To do that, implement the following re-creation of the `fopen()` command:

```
PHP_FUNCTION(sample_fopen)
{
    FILE *fp;
    char *filename, *mode;
    int filename_len, mode_len;
    if (zend_parse_parameters(ZEND_NUM_ARGS() TSRMLS_CC, "ss",
                    &filename, &filename_len,
```

```
                          &mode, &mode_len) == FAILURE) {
        RETURN_NULL();
    }
    if (!filename_len || !mode_len) {
        php_error_docref(NULL TSRMLS_CC, E_WARNING,
                "Invalid filename or mode length");
        RETURN_FALSE;
    }
    fp = fopen(filename, mode);
    if (!fp) {
        php_error_docref(NULL TSRMLS_CC, E_WARNING,
                "Unable to open %s using mode %s",
                filename, mode);
        RETURN_FALSE;
    }
    ZEND_REGISTER_RESOURCE(return_value, fp,
                            le_sample_descriptor);
}
```

> **Note**
>
> In order for the compiler to know what FILE* is, you'll need to include stdio.h. This could be placed in
> sample.c, but in preparation for a later part of this chapter, I'll ask you to place it in php_sample.h
> instead.

If you've been paying attention to the previous chapters, you'll recognize everything up to the final line. This one command does the job of storing the fp pointer into that index of resources, associating it with the type declared during MINIT, and storing a lookup key into return_value.

> **Note**
>
> If it's necessary to store more than one pointer value, or store an immediate value, a new memory segment
> must be allocated to store the data, and then a pointer to that memory segment can be registered as a
> resource.

Destroying Resources

At this point you have a method for attaching internal chunks of data to userspace variables. Because most of the data you're likely to attach to a userspace resource variable will need to be cleaned up at some point—by calling fclose() in this case—you'll probably assume you need a matching sample_fclose() function to receive the resource variable and handle destroying and unregistering it.

What would happen if the variable were simply unset() though? Without a reference to the original FILE* pointer, there'd be no way to fclose() it, and it would remain open until the PHP process died. Because a single process serves many requests, this could take a very long time.

The answer comes from those NULL pointers you passed to `zend_register_list_destructors_ex`. As the name implies, you're registering destruction methods. The first pointer refers to a method to be called when the last reference to a registered resource falls out of scope within a request. In practice, this typically means when `unset()` is called on the variable in which the resource was stored.

The second pointer passed into `zend_register_list_destructors_ex` refers to another callback method that is executed for persistent resources when a process or thread shuts down. You'll take a look at persistent resources later in this chapter.

Let's define the first of these destruction methods now. Place the following bit of code above your `PHP_MINIT_FUNCTION` block:

```
static void php_sample_descriptor_dtor(
                  zend_rsrc_list_entry *rsrc TSRMLS_DC)
{
    FILE *fp = (FILE*)rsrc->ptr;
    fclose(fp);
}
```

Next replace the first NULL in `zend_register_list_destructors_ex` with a reference back to `php_sample_descriptor_dtor`:

```
    le_sample_descriptor = zend_register_list_destructors_ex(
            php_sample_descriptor_dtor, NULL,
            PHP_SAMPLE_DESCRIPTOR_RES_NAME, module_number);
```

Now, when a variable is assigned with a registered resource value from `sample_fopen()`, it knows to automatically `fclose()` the `FILE*` pointer when the variable falls out of scope either explicitly through `unset()`, or implicitly at the end of a function. No `sample_fclose()` implementation is even needed!

```
<?php
  $fp = sample_fopen("/home/jdoe/notes.txt", "r");
  unset($fp);
?>
```

When `unset($fp);` is called here, `php_sample_descriptor_dtor` is automatically called by the engine to handle cleanup of the resource.

Decoding Resources

Creating a resource is only the first step because a bookmark is only as useful as its ability to return you to the original page. Here's another new function:

```
PHP_FUNCTION(sample_fwrite)
{
    FILE *fp;
```

```
    zval *file_resource;
    char *data;
    int data_len;
    if (zend_parse_parameters(ZEND_NUM_ARGS() TSRMLS_CC, "rs",
            &file_resource, &data, &data_len) == FAILURE ) {
        RETURN_NULL();
    }
    /* Use the zval* to verify the resource type and
     * retrieve its pointer from the lookup table */
    ZEND_FETCH_RESOURCE(fp, FILE*, &file_resource, -1,
        PHP_SAMPLE_DESCRIPTOR_RES_NAME, le_sample_descriptor);
    /* Write the data, and
     * return the number of bytes which were
     * successfully written to the file */
    RETURN_LONG(fwrite(data, 1, data_len, fp));
}
```

Using the "r" format specifier to zend_parse_parameters() is a relatively new trick, but one that should be understandable from what you read in Chapter 7, "Accepting Parameters." What's truly fresh here is the use of ZEND_FETCH_RESOURCE().

Unfolding the ZEND_FETCH_RESOURCE() macro, one finds the following:

```
#define ZEND_FETCH_RESOURCE(rsrc, rsrc_type, passed_id,
            default_id, resource_type_name, resource_type)
    rsrc = (rsrc_type) zend_fetch_resource(passed_id TSRMLS_CC,
                    default_id, resource_type_name, NULL,
                    1, resource_type);
    ZEND_VERIFY_RESOURCE(rsrc);
```

Or in this case:

```
fp = (FILE*) zend_fetch_resource(&file_descriptor TSRMLS_CC, -1,
                PHP_SAMPLE_DESCRIPTOR_RES_NAME, NULL,
                1, le_sample_descriptor);
if (!fp) {
    RETURN_FALSE;
}
```

Like the zend_hash_find() method you explored in the last chapter, zend_fetch_resource() uses an index into a collection—a HashTable in fact—to pull out previously stored data. Unlike zend_hash_find(), this method performs additional data integrity checking such as ensuring that the entry in the resource table matches the correct resource type.

In this case, you've asked zend_fetch_resource() to match the resource type stored in le_sample_descriptor. If the supplied resource ID does not exist, or is of the incorrect type, then zend_fetch_resource() will return NULL and automatically generate an error.

By including the ZEND_VERIFY_RESOURCE() macro within the ZEND_FETCH_
RESOURCE() macro, function implementations can automatically return, leaving the
extension-specific code to focus on handling the generated resource value when condi-
tions are correct. Now that your function has the original FILE* pointer back, it simply
calls the internal fwrite() method as any normal program would.

> **Tip**
>
> To avoid having zend_fetch_resource() generate an error on failure, simply pass NULL for the
> resource_type_name parameter. Without a meaningful error message to display,
> zend_fetch_resource() will fail silently instead.

Another approach to translating a resource variable ID into a pointer is to use the
zend_list_find() function:

```
PHP_FUNCTION(sample_fwrite)
{
    FILE *fp;
    zval *file_resource;
    char *data;
    int data_len, rsrc_type;
    if (zend_parse_parameters(ZEND_NUM_ARGS() TSRMLS_CC, "rs",
            &file_resource, &data, &data_len) == FAILURE ) {
        RETURN_NULL();
    }
    fp = (FILE*)zend_list_find(Z_RESVAL_P(file_resource),
                                    &rsrc_type);
    if (!fp || rsrc_type != le_sample_descriptor) {
        php_error_docref(NULL TSRMLS_CC, E_WARNING,
                    "Invalid resource provided");
        RETURN_FALSE;
    }
    RETURN_LONG(fwrite(data, 1, data_len, fp));
}
```

Although this method is probably more recognizable to someone with a generic back-
ground in C programming, it is also much more verbose than using
ZEND_FETCH_RESOURCE(). Pick a method that suits your programming style best, but
expect to see the ZEND_FETCH_RESOURCE() macro used predominantly in other extension codes such as those found in the PHP core.

Forcing Destruction

Earlier you saw how using unset() to take a variable out of scope can trigger the
destruction of a resource and cause its underlying resources to be cleaned up by your

registered destruction method. Imagine now that a resource variable were copied into other variables:

```php
<?php
  $fp = sample_fopen("/home/jdoe/world_domination.log", "a");
  $evil_log = $fp;
  unset($fp);
?>
```

This time, $fp wasn't the only reference to the registered resource so it hasn't actually gone out of scope yet and won't be destroyed. This means that $evil_log can still be written to. In order to avoid having to search around for lost, stray references to a resource when you really, truly want it gone, it becomes necessary to have a sample_fclose() implementation after all!:

```c
PHP_FUNCTION(sample_fclose)
{
    FILE *fp;
    zval *file_resource;
    if (zend_parse_parameters(ZEND_NUM_ARGS() TSRMLS_CC, "r",
                        &file_resource) == FAILURE ) {
        RETURN_NULL();
    }
    /* While it's not necessary to actually fetch the
     * FILE* resource, performing the fetch provides
     * an opportunity to verify that we are closing
     * the correct resource type. */
    ZEND_FETCH_RESOURCE(fp, FILE*, &file_resource, -1,
        PHP_SAMPLE_DESCRIPTOR_RES_NAME, le_sample_descriptor);
    /* Force the resource into self-destruct mode */
    zend_hash_index_del(&EG(regular_list),
                    Z_RESVAL_P(file_resource));
    RETURN_TRUE;
}
```

This deletion method reinforced the fact that resource variables are registered within a global HashTable. Removing resource entries from this HashTable is a simple matter of using the resource ID as an index lookup into the regular list. Although other direct HashTable manipulation methods—such as zend_hash_index_find() and zend_hash_next_index_insert()—will work in place of the FETCH and REGISTER macros, such practice is discouraged where possible so that changes in the Zend API don't break existing extensions.

Like userspace variable HashTables (arrays), the EG(regular_list) HashTable has an automatic dtor method that is called whenever an entry is removed or overwritten. This method checks your resource's type, and calls the registered destruction method you provided during your MINIT call to zend_register_list_destructors_ex().

> **Note**
> In many places in the PHP Core and the Zend Engine you'll see zend_list_delete() used in this con-
> text rather than zend_hash_index_del(). The zend_list_delete() form takes into account
> reference counting, which you'll see later in this chapter.

Persistent Resources

The type of complex data structures that are usually stored in resource variables often
require a fair amount of memory allocation, CPU time, or network communication to
initialize. In cases where a script is very likely to need to reestablish these kind of
resources on each invocation such as database links, it becomes useful to preserve the
resource between requests.

Memory Allocation

From your exposure to earlier chapters you know that emalloc() and friends are the
preferred set of functions to use when allocating memory within PHP because they are
capable of garbage collection—should a script have to abruptly exit—in ways that system
malloc() functions simply aren't. If a persistent resource is to stick around between
requests, however, such garbage collection is obviously not a good thing.

Imagine for a moment that it became necessary to store the name of the opened file
along with the FILE* pointer. Now, you'd need to create a custom struct in
php_sample.h to hold this combination of information:

```
typedef struct _php_sample_descriptor_data {
    char *filename;
    FILE *fp;
} php_sample_descriptor_data;
```

And all the functions in sample.c dealing with your file resource would need to be
modified:

```
static void php_sample_descriptor_dtor(
                    zend_rsrc_list_entry *rsrc TSRMLS_DC)
{
    php_sample_descriptor_data *fdata =
                (php_sample_descriptor_data*)rsrc->ptr;
    fclose(fdata->fp);
    efree(fdata->filename);
    efree(fdata);
}
PHP_FUNCTION(sample_fopen)
{
    php_sample_descriptor_data *fdata;
    FILE *fp;
```

```
        char *filename, *mode;
        int filename_len, mode_len;
        if (zend_parse_parameters(ZEND_NUM_ARGS() TSRMLS_CC, "ss",
                            &filename, &filename_len,
                            &mode, &mode_len) == FAILURE) {
            RETURN_NULL();
        }
        if (!filename_len || !mode_len) {
            php_error_docref(NULL TSRMLS_CC, E_WARNING,
                    "Invalid filename or mode length");
            RETURN_FALSE;
        }
        fp = fopen(filename, mode);
        if (!fp) {
            php_error_docref(NULL TSRMLS_CC, E_WARNING,
                    "Unable to open %s using mode %s",
                    filename, mode);
            RETURN_FALSE;
        }
        fdata = emalloc(sizeof(php_sample_descriptor_data));
        fdata->fp = fp;
        fdata->filename = estrndup(filename, filename_len);
        ZEND_REGISTER_RESOURCE(return_value, fdata,
                                    le_sample_descriptor);
}
PHP_FUNCTION(sample_fwrite)
{
        php_sample_descriptor_data *fdata;
        zval *file_resource;
        char *data;
        int data_len;
        if (zend_parse_parameters(ZEND_NUM_ARGS() TSRMLS_CC, "rs",
                &file_resource, &data, &data_len) == FAILURE ) {
            RETURN_NULL();
        }
        ZEND_FETCH_RESOURCE(fdata, php_sample_descriptor_data*,
            &file_resource, -1,
            PHP_SAMPLE_DESCRIPTOR_RES_NAME, le_sample_descriptor);
        RETURN_LONG(fwrite(data, 1, data_len, fdata->fp));
}
```

Note

Technically, sample_fclose() can be left as-is because it doesn't actually deal with the resource data directly. If you're feeling confident, try updating it to use the corrections yourself.

So far, everything is perfectly happy because you're still only registering non-persistent descriptor resources. You could even add a new function at this point to retrieve the original name of the file back out of the resource:

```
PHP_FUNCTION(sample_fname)
{
    php_sample_descriptor_data *fdata;
    zval *file_resource;
    if (zend_parse_parameters(ZEND_NUM_ARGS() TSRMLS_CC, "r",
            &file_resource) == FAILURE ) {
        RETURN_NULL();
    }
    ZEND_FETCH_RESOURCE(fdata, php_sample_descriptor_data*,
        &file_resource, -1,
        PHP_SAMPLE_DESCRIPTOR_RES_NAME, le_sample_descriptor);
    RETURN_STRING(fdata->filename, 1);
}
```

However, soon problems will start to arise with usages such as this as you start to register persistent versions of your descriptor resource.

Delayed Destruction

As you've seen with non-persistent resources, once all the variables holding a resource ID have been unset() or have fallen out of scope, they are removed from EG(regular_list), which is the HashTable containing all per-request registered resources.

Persistent resources, as you'll see later this chapter, are also stored in a second HashTable: EG(persistent_list). Unlike EG(regular_list), the indexes used by this table are associative, and the elements are not automatically removed from the HashTable at the end of a request. Entries in EG(persistent_list) are only removed through manual calls to zend_hash_del()—which you'll see shortly—or when a thread or process completely shuts down (usually when the web server is stopped).

Like the EG(regular_list) HashTable, the EG(persistent_list) HashTable also has its own dtor method. Like the regular list, this method is also a simple wrapper that uses the resource's type to look up a proper destruction method. This time, it takes the destruction method from the second parameter to zend_register_list_destructors_ex(), rather than the first.

In practice, persistent and non-persistent resources are typically registered as two distinct types to avoid having non-persistent destruction code run against a resource that is supposed to be persistent. Depending on your implementation, you may choose to combine non-persistent and persistent destruction methods in a single type. For now, add another static int to the top of sample.c for a new persistent descriptor resource:

```
static int le_sample_descriptor_persist;
```

Then extend your MINIT function with a resource registration that uses a new dtor function aimed specifically at persistently allocated structures:

```
static void php_sample_descriptor_dtor_persistent(
                   zend_rsrc_list_entry *rsrc TSRMLS_DC)
{
    php_sample_descriptor_data *fdata =
               (php_sample_descriptor_data*)rsrc->ptr;
    fclose(fdata->fp);
    pefree(fdata->filename, 1);
    pefree(fdata, 1);
}
PHP_MINIT_FUNCTION(sample)
{
    le_sample_descriptor =     zend_register_list_destructors_ex(
            php_sample_descriptor_dtor, NULL,
            PHP_SAMPLE_DESCRIPTOR_RES_NAME, module_number);
    le_sample_descriptor_persist =
                      zend_register_list_destructors_ex(
            NULL, php_sample_descriptor_dtor_persistent,
            PHP_SAMPLE_DESCRIPTOR_RES_NAME, module_number);
    return SUCCESS;
}
```

By giving these two resource types the same name, their distinction will be transparent to the end user. Internally, only one will have php_sample_descriptor_dtor called on it during request cleanup; the other, as you'll see in a moment, will stick around for up to as long as the web server's process or thread does.

Long Term Registration

Now that a suitable cleanup method is in place, it's time to actually create some usable resource structures. Often this is done using two separate functions that map internally to the same implementation, but since that would only complicate an already muddy topic, you'll accomplish the same feat here by simply accepting a Boolean parameter to sample_fopen():

```
PHP_FUNCTION(sample_fopen)
{
    php_sample_descriptor_data *fdata;
    FILE *fp;
    char *filename, *mode;
    int filename_len, mode_len;
    zend_bool persist = 0;
    if (zend_parse_parameters(ZEND_NUM_ARGS() TSRMLS_CC,"ss|b",
                &filename, &filename_len, &mode, &mode_len,
                &persist) == FAILURE) {
```

```
            RETURN_NULL();
    }
    if (!filename_len || !mode_len) {
        php_error_docref(NULL TSRMLS_CC, E_WARNING,
                "Invalid filename or mode length");
        RETURN_FALSE;
    }
    fp = fopen(filename, mode);
    if (!fp) {
        php_error_docref(NULL TSRMLS_CC, E_WARNING,
                "Unable to open %s using mode %s",
                filename, mode);
        RETURN_FALSE;
    }
    if (!persist) {
        fdata = emalloc(sizeof(php_sample_descriptor_data));
        fdata->filename = estrndup(filename, filename_len);
        fdata->fp = fp;
        ZEND_REGISTER_RESOURCE(return_value, fdata,
                               le_sample_descriptor);
    } else {
        list_entry le;
        char *hash_key;
        int hash_key_len;

        fdata =pemalloc(sizeof(php_sample_descriptor_data),1);
        fdata->filename = pemalloc(filename_len + 1, 1);
        memcpy(data->filename, filename, filename_len + 1);
        fdata->fp = fp;
        ZEND_REGISTER_RESOURCE(return_value, fdata,
                            le_sample_descriptor_persist);

        /* Store a copy in the persistent_list */
        le.type = le_sample_descriptor_persist;
        le.ptr = fdata;
        hash_key_len = spprintf(&hash_key, 0,
                "sample_descriptor:%s:%s", filename, mode);
        zend_hash_update(&EG(persistent_list),
            hash_key, hash_key_len + 1,
            (void*)&le, sizeof(list_entry), NULL);
        efree(hash_key);
    }
}
```

The core portions of this function should be very familiar by now. A file was opened, it's name stored into newly allocated memory, and it was registered into a request-specific resource ID populated into `return_value`. What's new this time is the second portion, but hopefully it's not altogether alien.

Here, you've actually done something very similar to what `ZEND_RESOURCE_REGISTER()` does; however, instead of giving it a numeric index and placing it in the per-request list, you've assigned it an associative key that can be reproduced in a later request and stowed into the persistent list, which isn't automatically purged at the end of every script.

When one of these persistent descriptor resources goes out of scope, `EG(regular_list)`'s `dtor` function will check the registered list destructors for `le_sample_descriptor_persist` and, seeing that it's `NULL`, simply do nothing. This leaves the `FILE*` pointer and the `char*` name string safe for the next request.

When the resource is finally removed from `EG(persistent_list)`, either because the thread/process is shutting down or because your extension has deliberately removed it, the engine will now go looking for a persistent destructor. Because you defined one for this resource type, it will be called and issue the appropriate `pefree()`s to match the earlier `pemalloc()`s.

Reuse

Putting a copy of a resource entry into the `persistent_list` would serve no purpose beyond extending the time that such resources can tie up memory and file locks unless you're somehow able to reuse them on subsequent requests.

Here's where that `hash_key` comes in. When `sample_fopen()` is called, either for persistent or non-persistent use, your function can re-create the `hash_key` using the requested filename and mode and try to find it in the `persistent_list` before going to the trouble of opening the file again:

```
PHP_FUNCTION(sample_fopen)
{
    php_sample_descriptor_data *fdata;
    FILE *fp;
    char *filename, *mode, *hash_key;
    int filename_len, mode_len, hash_key_len;
    zend_bool persist = 0;
    list_entry *existing_file;
    if (zend_parse_parameters(ZEND_NUM_ARGS() TSRMLS_CC,"ss|b",
                &filename, &filename_len, &mode, &mode_len,
                &persist) == FAILURE) {
        RETURN_NULL();
    }
    if (!filename_len || !mode_len) {
        php_error_docref(NULL TSRMLS_CC, E_WARNING,
                "Invalid filename or mode length");
        RETURN_FALSE;
    }
```

```
    /* Try to find an already opened file */
    hash_key_len = spprintf(&hash_key, 0,
            "sample_descriptor:%s:%s", filename, mode);
    if (zend_hash_find(&EG(persistent_list), hash_key,
            hash_key_len + 1, (void **)&existing_file) == SUCCESS) {
        /* There's already a file open, return that! */
        ZEND_REGISTER_RESOURCE(return_value,
            existing_file->ptr,le_sample_descriptor_persist);
        efree(hash_key);
        return;
    }
    fp = fopen(filename, mode);
    if (!fp) {
        php_error_docref(NULL TSRMLS_CC, E_WARNING,
                "Unable to open %s using mode %s",
                filename, mode);
        RETURN_FALSE;
    }
    if (!persist) {
        fdata = emalloc(sizeof(php_sample_descriptor_data));
        fdata->filename = estrndup(filename, filename_len);
        fdata->fp = fp;
        ZEND_REGISTER_RESOURCE(return_value, fdata,
                            le_sample_descriptor);
    } else {
        list_entry le;
        fdata =pemalloc(sizeof(php_sample_descriptor_data),1);
        fdata->filename = pemalloc(filename_len + 1, 1);
        memcpy(data->filename, filename, filename_len + 1);
        fdata->fp = fp;
        ZEND_REGISTER_RESOURCE(return_value, fdata,
                            le_sample_descriptor_persist);
        /* Store a copy in the persistent_list */
        le.type = le_sample_descriptor_persist;
        le.ptr = fdata;
        /* hash_key has already been created by now */
        zend_hash_update(&EG(persistent_list),
            hash_key, hash_key_len + 1,
            (void*)&le, sizeof(list_entry), NULL);
    }
    efree(hash_key);
}
```

Because all extensions use the same persistent HashTable list to store their resources in, it's important that you choose a hash key that is both reproducible and unique. A common convention—as seen in the sample_fopen() function—is to use the extension and resource type names as a prefix, followed by the creation criteria.

Liveness Checking and Early Departure

Although it's safe to assume that once you open a file, you can keep it open indefinitely, other resource types—particularly remote network resources—may have a tendency to become invalidated, especially when they're left unused for long periods between requests.

When recalling a stored persistent resource into active duty, it is therefore important to make sure that it's still usable. If the resource is no longer valid, it must be removed from the persistent list and the function should continue as though no already allocated resource had been found.

The following hypothetical code block performs a liveness check on a socket stored in the persistent list:

```
if (zend_hash_find(&EG(persistent_list), hash_key,
        hash_key_len + 1, (void**)&socket) == SUCCESS) {
    if (php_sample_socket_is_alive(socket->ptr)) {
        ZEND_REGISTER_RESOURCE(return_value,
                    socket->ptr, le_sample_socket);
        return;
    }
    zend_hash_del(&EG(persistent_list),
                        hash_key, hash_key_len + 1);
}
```

As you can see, all that's been done here is to manually remove the list entry from the persistent list during runtime as opposed to engine shutdown (when it would normally be destroyed). This action handles the work of calling the persistent dtor method, which would have been defined by zend_register_list_destructors_ex(). On completion of this code block, the function will be in the same state it would have been if no resource had been found in the persistent list.

Agnostic Retrieval

At this point you can create file descriptor resources, store them persistently, and recall them transparently, but have you tried using a persistent version with your sample_fwite() function? Frustratingly, it doesn't work! Recall how the resource pointer is resolved from its numeric ID:

```
ZEND_FETCH_RESOURCE(fdata, php_sample_descriptor_data*,
    &file_resource, -1, PHP_SAMPLE_DESCRIPTOR_RES_NAME,
    le_sample_descriptor);
```

le_sample_descriptor is explicitly named so that the type can be verified and you can be assured that you're not using a mysql_connection_handle* or some other type when you expect to see, for example, a php_sample_descruptor_data* structure. Mixing and matching types is generally a "bad thing." You know that the same data structure stored in `le_sample_descriptor` resources are also stored in `le_sample_descruotor_persist` resources, so to keep things simple in userspace, it'd be ideal if `sample_fwrite()` could simply accept either type equally.

This is solved by using `ZEND_FETCH_RESOURCE()`'s sibling: `ZEND_FETCH_RESOURCE2()`. The only difference between these two macros is that the latter enables you to specify— that's right—two resource types. In this case you'd change that line to the following:

```
ZEND_FETCH_RESOURCE2(fdata, php_sample_descriptor_data*,
    &file_resource, -1, PHP_SAMPLE_DESCRIPTOR_RES_NAME,
    le_sample_descriptor, le_sample_descriptor_persist);
```

Now, the resource ID contained in `file_resource` can refer to either a persistent or non-persistent Sample Descriptor resource and they will both pass validation checks.

Allowing for more than two resource types requires using the underlying `zend_fetch_resource()` implementation. Recall that the `ZEND_FETCH_RESOURCE()` macro you originally used expands out to

```
fp = (FILE*) zend_fetch_resource(&file_descriptor TSRMLS_CC, -1,
    PHP_SAMPLE_DESCRIPTOR_RES_NAME, NULL,
    1, le_sample_descriptor);
ZEND_VERIFY_RESOURCE(fp);
```

Similarly, the `ZEND_FETCH_RESOURCE2()` macro you were just introduced to also expands to the same underlying function:

```
fp = (FILE*) zend_fetch_resource(&file_descriptor TSRMLS_CC, -1,
    PHP_SAMPLE_DESCRIPTOR_RES_NAME, NULL,
    2, le_sample_descriptor, le_sample_descriptor_persist);
ZEND_VERIFY_RESOURCE(fp);
```

See a pattern? The sixth and subsequent parameters to `zend_fetch_resource()` say "There are N possible resource types I'm willing to match, and here they are…." So to match a third resource type (for example: `le_sample_othertype`), type the following:

```
fp = (FILE*) zend_fetch_resource(&file_descriptor TSRMLS_CC, -1,
    PHP_SAMPLE_DESCRIPTOR_RES_NAME, NULL,
    3, le_sample_descriptor, le_sample_descriptor_persist,
    le_sample_othertype);
ZEND_VERIFY_RESOURCE(fp);
```

And so on and so forth.

The Other `refcounter`

Like userspace variables, registered resources also have reference counters. In this case, the reference counter refers to how many container structures know about the resource ID in question.

You already know by now that when a userspace variable (`zval*`) is of type `IS_RESOURCE`, it doesn't really hold the pointer to any structure; it simply holds a

HashTable index number so that it can look up the pointer from the `EG(regular_list)` HashTable.

When a resource is first created, such as by calling `sample_fopen()`, it's placed into a `zval*` container and its `refcount` is initialized to 1 because it's only held by that one variable.

```
$a = sample_fopen('notes.txt', 'r');
/* var->refcount = 1, rsrc->refcount = 1 */
```

If that variable is then copied to another, you know from Chapter 3, "Memory Management," that no new `zval*` is actually created. Rather, the variables share that `zval*` in a copy-on-write reference set. In this case, the `refcount` for the `zval*` is raised to 2; however, the `refcount` for the resource is still 1 because it is only held by one `zval*`.

```
$b = $a;
/* var->refcount = 2, rsrc->refcount = 1 */
```

When one of these two variables is `unset()`, the `zval*`'s refcount is decremented, but it's not destroyed because the other variable still refers to it.

```
unset($b);
/* var->refcount = 1, rsrc->refcount = 1 */
```

You also know by now that mixing full-reference sets with copy-on-write reference sets will force a variable to separate by copying into a new `zval*`. When this happens, the resource's reference count does get incremented because it's now owned by a second `zval*`.

```
$b = $a;
$c = &$a;
/* bvar->refcount = 1,  bvar->is_ref = 0
   acvar->refcount = 2, acvar->is_ref = 1
   rsrc->refcount = 2 */
```

Now, unsetting `$b` would destroy its `zval*` entirely, bringing the `rsrc->refcount` to 1. Unsetting either `$a` or `$c`—but not both—would not decrease the resource refcount, however, as the `acvar`, `zval*` would still exist. It's not until all three variables (and by extension their two `zval*`s) are `unset()` that the resource's refcount reaches 0 and its destruction method is triggered.

Summary

Using the topics covered in this chapter, you can begin to apply the glue that PHP is so famous for. The resource data type enables your extension to connect abstract concepts like opaque pointers from third-party libraries to the easy-to-use userspace scripting language that makes PHP so powerful.

In the next two chapters you'll delve into the last, but by no means least, data type in the PHP lexicon. You'll start by exploring simple Zend Engine 1–based classes, and move into their more powerful Zend Engine 2 successors.

10

PHP4 Objects

ONCE UPON A TIME, IN A VERSION long long ago, PHP did not support object-oriented programming in any form. With the introduction of the Zend Engine (ZE1) with PHP 4, several new features appeared, including the object data type.

The Evolution of the PHP Object Type

This first incarnation of object-oriented programming (OOP) support covered only the barest implementation of object-related characteristics. In the words of one core developer, "A PHP4 object is just an Array with some functions bolted onto the side." It is this generation of PHP objects that you'll explore now.

With the second major release of the Zend Engine (ZE2) found in PHP5, several new features found their way into PHP's OOP implementation. For example, properties and methods may now be marked with access modifiers to make them inaccessible from outside your class definition, an additional suite of overloading functions are available to define custom behavior for internal language constructs, and interfaces can be used to enforce API standards between multiple class chains. When you reach Chapter 11, "PHP5 Objects," you'll build on the knowledge you gain here by implementing these features in PHP5-specific class definitions.

Implementing Classes

As you start to explore the world of OOP, it's time to shake off some of the baggage you've collected in the chapters leading up to this point. To do that, "reset" back to the skeleton extension you started with in Chapter 5, "Your First Extension."

In order to compile it alongside your earlier incarnation, you can name this version sample2. Place the three files shown in Listings 10.1 through 10.3 in ext/sample2/ off of your PHP source tree.

Listing 10.1   **Configuration File:** `config.m4`

```
PHP_ARG_ENABLE(sample2,
  [Whether to enable the "sample2" extension],
  [ —enable-sample2      Enable "sample2" extension support])

if test $PHP_SAMPLE2 != "no"; then
  PHP_SUBST(SAMPLE2_SHARED_LIBADD)
  PHP_NEW_EXTENSION(sample2, sample2.c, $ext_shared)
fi
```

Listing 10.2   Header: `php_sample2.h`

```
#ifndef PHP_SAMPLE2_H
/* Prevent double inclusion */
#define PHP_SAMPLE2_H

/* Define Extension Properties */
#define PHP_SAMPLE2_EXTNAME    "sample2"
#define PHP_SAMPLE2_EXTVER     "1.0"

/* Import configure options
   when building outside of
   the PHP source tree */
#ifdef HAVE_CONFIG_H
#include "config.h"
#endif

/* Include PHP Standard Header */
#include "php.h"

/* Define the entry point symbol
 * Zend will use when loading this module
 */
extern zend_module_entry sample2_module_entry;
#define phpext_sample2_ptr &sample2_module_entry

#endif /* PHP_SAMPLE2_H */
```

Listing 10.3   **Source Code: sample2.c**

```
#include "php_sample2.h"

static function_entry php_sample2_functions[] = {
    { NULL, NULL, NULL }
```

Listing 10.3   **Continued**

```
};

PHP_MINIT_FUNCTION(sample2)
{
    return SUCCESS;
}

zend_module_entry sample2_module_entry = {
#if ZEND_MODULE_API_NO >= 20010901
    STANDARD_MODULE_HEADER,
#endif
    PHP_SAMPLE2_EXTNAME,
    php_sample2_functions,
    PHP_MINIT(sample2),
    NULL, /* MSHUTDOWN */
    NULL, /* RINIT */
    NULL, /* RSHUTDOWN */
    NULL, /* MINFO */
#if ZEND_MODULE_API_NO >= 20010901
    PHP_SAMPLE2_EXTVER,
#endif
    STANDARD_MODULE_PROPERTIES
};

#ifdef COMPILE_DL_SAMPLE2
ZEND_GET_MODULE(sample2)
#endif
```

Now, as you did in Chapter 5, you can issue `phpize`, `./configure`, and `make` to build your `sample2.so` extension module.

> **Note**
> Like `config.m4`, your prior version of `config.w32` will work here with nothing more than occurrences of sample replaced with `sample2`.

Declaring Class Entries

In userspace, the first step to defining a class is to declare it. For example:

```
<?php
class Sample2_FirstClass {
}
?>
```

As you can no doubt guess, this gets slightly—but only slightly—harder from within an extension. First, you'll need to define a `zend_class_entry` pointer within your source file similar to the `le_sample_descriptor` int you defined last chapter:

```
zend_class_entry *php_sample2_firstclass_entry;
```

Now, you can initialize and register the class within your MINIT method:

```
PHP_MINIT_FUNCTION(sample2)
{
    zend_class_entry ce; /* Temporary Variable */

    /* Register Class */
    INIT_CLASS_ENTRY(ce, "Sample2_FirstClass", NULL);
    php_sample2_firstclass_entry =
        zend_register_internal_class(&ce TSRMLS_CC);

    return SUCCESS;
}
```

Building this extension, and examining the output of `get_declared_classes()`, will show that `Sample2_FirstClass` is now available to userspace scripts.

Defining Method Implementations

At this point, you've only managed to implement `stdClass`, which is, of course, already available. You'll want your class to actually do something now.

To accomplish this, you'll fall back on another concept you picked up back in Chapter 5. Replace the NULL parameter to `INIT_CLASS_ENTRY()` with `php_sample2_firstclass_functions` and define that struct directly above the MINIT method as follows:

```
static function_entry php_sample2_firstclass_functions[] = {
    { NULL, NULL, NULL }
};
```

Look familiar? It should. This is the same structure you've been using to define ordinary procedural functions. You'll even populate this structure in nearly the same manner:

```
PHP_NAMED_FE(method1, PHP_FN(Sample2_FirstClass_method1), NULL)
```

Alternatively, you could have used `PHP_FE(method1, NULL)`. However, as you'll recall from Chapter 5, this expects to find an implementation function named `zif_method1`, which might potentially conflict with another `method1()` implementation elsewhere. In order to namespace the function safely away from any procedural implementations, the class name gets prepended to the method name using drop cap-casing for the class name and camel-casing for the method name.

The `PHP_FALIAS(method1, Sample2_FirstClass_method1, NULL)` form is also acceptable; however, it may be slightly less intuitive when you come back later and wonder why there's no matching `PHP_FE()` line to go with it.

Now that you have a function list attached to your class definition, it's time to declare some methods. Create the following function above the `php_sample2_firstclass_functions` struct:

```
PHP_FUNCTION(Sample2_FirstClass_countProps)
{
    RETURN_LONG(zend_hash_num_elements(Z_OBJPROP_P(getThis())));
}
```

Now add a matching `PHP_NAMED_FE()` entry in the function list itself:

```
static function_entry php_sample2_firstclass_functions[] = {
    PHP_NAMED_FE(countprops,
            PHP_FN(Sample2_FirstClass_countProps), NULL)
    { NULL, NULL, NULL }
};
```

Note

Be sure to notice that the function is named for userspace in all lowercase. The case-folding operations meant to ensure case-insensitivity in method and function names require that internal functions be given all lowercase names.

The only new element here should be `getThis()` which, in all current PHP versions, is actually a macro that resolves to `this_ptr`. `this_ptr`, in turn, carries essentially the same meaning as `$this` within a userspace object method. If no object instance is available, such as when a method is called statically, `getThis()` will return NULL.

Just as the data return semantics in object methods is identical to procedural functions, so is the parameter acceptance and `arg_info` methodology:

```
PHP_FUNCTION(Sample2_FirstClass_sayHello)
{
    char *name;
    int name_len;
    if (zend_parse_parameters(ZEND_NUM_ARGS() TSRMLS_CC, "s",
                        &name, &name_len) == FAILURE) {
        RETURN_NULL();
    }
    php_printf("Hello ");
    PHPWRITE(name, name_len);
    php_printf("!\nYou called an object method!\n");
    RETURN_TRUE;
}
```

Constructors

Your class constructor can simply be implemented as any other ordinary class method, and the same rules will apply to internals as to userspace when it comes to nomenclature. Specifically, you'll want to name your constructor identically to the class name. The other ZE1 magic methods, __sleep() and __wakeup(), can be implemented in this manner as well.

Inheritance

Inheritance between internal objects in PHP4 is sketchy at best and should generally be avoided like dark alleys in a horror flick. If you absolutely must inherit from another object, you'll need to duplicate some ZE1 code:

```
void php_sample2_inherit_from_class(zend_class_entry *ce,
                    zend_class_entry *parent_ce) {
    zend_hash_merge(&ce->function_table,
            &parent_ce->function_table, (void (*)(void *))function_add_ref,
            NULL, sizeof(zval*), 0);
    ce->parent = parent_ce;
    if (!ce->handle_property_get) {
        ce->handle_property_get =
                parent_ce->handle_property_get;
    }
    if (!ce->handle_property_set) {
        ce->handle_property_set =
                parent_ce->handle_property_set;
    }
    if (!ce->handle_function_call) {
        ce->handle_function_call =
                parent_ce->handle_function_call;
    }
    if (!zend_hash_exists(&ce->function_table,
            ce->name, ce->name_length + 1)) {
        zend_function *fe;
        if (zend_hash_find(&parent_ce->function_table,
            parent_ce->name, parent_ce->name_length + 1,
            (void**)fe) == SUCCESS) {
            zend_hash_update(&ce->function_table,
                ce->name, ce->name_length + 1,
                fe, sizeof(zend_function), NULL);
            function_add_ref(fe);
        }
    }
}
```

With this function defined, you can now place a call to it following zend_register_internal_class in your MINIT block:

```
INIT_CLASS_ENTRY(ce, "Sample2_FirstClass", NULL);
/* Assumes php_sample2_ancestor is an already
```

```
 * registered zend_class_entry*
 */
php_sample2_firstclass_entry =
        zend_register_internal_class(&ce TSRMLS_CC);
php_sample2_inherit_from_class(php_sample2_firstclass_entry
                           ,php_sample2_ancestor);
```

Caution

Although this approach to inheritance will work, it should generally be avoided as ZE1 simply wasn't designed to handle internal object inheritance properly. As with most OOP practices in PHP, the ZE2 (PHP5) and its revised object model is strongly encouraged for all but the most simple OOP-related tasks.

Working with Instances

Like other userspace variables, objects are stored in `zval*` containers. In ZE1, the `zval*` contained a `HashTable*` for properties, and a `zend_class_entry*` that points to the class definition. In ZE2, these values have been replaced by a handler table, which you'll delve into next chapter, and a numeric object ID that is used in a similar manner to resource IDs (discussed in Chapter 9, "The Resource Data Type."

This discrepancy between ZE1 objects and ZE2 objects is thankfully hidden from your extension by means of a branch of the `z_*()` macro family you first saw way back in Chapter 2, "Variables from the Inside Out." Table 10.1 lists the two ZE1 macros which, like their non-OOP related cousins, have `_P` and `_PP` counterparts for dealing with one and two levels of indirection respectively.

Table 10.1   **Object Access Macros**

Macro	Purpose
Z_OBJPROP(zv)	Resolves the built-in properties `HashTable*`
Z_OBJCE(zv)	Returns the associated `zend_class_entry*`

Creating Instances

The majority of the time, your extension will not create object instances itself. Rather, a userspace script will invoke the `new` keyword to create an instance and call your class' constructor.

Should you need to create an instance, such as within a factory method, the `object_init_ex(zval *val, zend_class_entry *ce)` function from the ZENDAPI may be used to initialize the object instance into a variable.

Note that the `object_init_ex()` function does *not* invoke the constructor. When instantiating objects from an internal function, the constructor *must* be called manually. The following procedural function replicates the functionality of the `new` keyword.

```
PHP_FUNCTION(sample2_new)
{
    int argc = ZEND_NUM_ARGS();
    zval ***argv = safe_emalloc(sizeof(zval**), argc, 0);
    zend_class_entry *ce;
    if (argc == 0 ||
        zend_get_parameters_array_ex(argc, argv) == FAILURE) {
        efree(argv);
        WRONG_PARAM_COUNT;
    }
    /* First arg is classname */
    SEPARATE_ZVAL(argv[0]);
    convert_to_string(*argv[0]);
    /* class names are stored in lowercase */
    php_strtolower(Z_STRVAL_PP(argv[0]), Z_STRLEN_PP(argv[0]));
    if (zend_hash_find(EG(class_table),
            Z_STRVAL_PP(argv[0]), Z_STRLEN_PP(argv[0]) + 1,
            (void**)&ce) == FAILURE) {
        php_error_docref(NULL TSRMLS_CC, E_WARNING,
            "Class %s does not exist.",
            Z_STRVAL_PP(argv[0]));
        zval_ptr_dtor(argv[0]);
        efree(argv);
        RETURN_FALSE;
    }
    object_init_ex(return_value, ce);
    /* Call the constructor if it has one
     * Additional arguments will be passed through as
     * constructor parameters */
    if (zend_hash_exists(&ce->function_table,
            Z_STRVAL_PP(argv[0]),Z_STRLEN_PP(argv[0]) + 1)) {
        /* Object has constructor */
        zval *ctor, *dummy = NULL;

        /* constructor == classname */
        MAKE_STD_ZVAL(ctor);
        array_init(ctor);
        zval_add_ref(argv[0]);
        add_next_index_zval(ctor, *argv[0]);
        zval_add_ref(argv[0]);
        add_next_index_zval(ctor, *argv[0]);
        if (call_user_function_ex(&ce->function_table,
                NULL, ctor,
                &dummy, /* Don't care about return value */
                argc - 1, argv + 1, /* parameters */
                0, NULL TSRMLS_CC) == FAILURE) {
```

```
        php_error_docref(NULL TSRMLS_CC, E_WARNING,
            "Unable to call constructor");
    }
    if (dummy) {
        zval_ptr_dtor(&dummy);
    }
    zval_ptr_dtor(&ctor);
    }
    zval_ptr_dtor(argv[0]);
    efree(argv);
}
```

Don't forget to add a reference to it in `php_sample2_functions`. That's the list for your extension's procedural functions, not the list for your class' methods. You'll also need to add `#include "ext/standard/php_string.h"` in order to get the prototype for the `php_strtolower()` function.

This function is one of the busiest ones you've implemented yet and several features are likely to be entirely new. The first item, `SEPARATE_ZVAL()`, is actually a macroized version of a process you've already done several times involving `zval_copy_ctor()` to duplicate a value into a temporary structure and avoid modifying the original contents.

`php_strtolower()` is used to convert the class name to lowercase because this is how all class and function names are stored in PHP in order to achieve case-insensitivity for identifiers. This is just one of the many PHPAPI utility functions you can find in Appendix B, "PHPAPI."

`EG(class_table)` is a global registry of all `zend_class_entry` definitions available to the request. Note that in ZE1(PHP4) this HashTable stores `zend_class_entry*` structures at a single level of indirection. In ZE2(PHP5), these are stored at two levels of indirection. This shouldn't be an issue because directly accessing this table is an uncommon task, but you'd do well to be aware of it.

`call_user_function_ex()` is one of a pair of ZENDAPI calls you'll take a look at in Chapter 20, "Advanced Embedding." Here you've shifted forward by one `zval**` on the argument stack retrieved by `zend_get_parameters_array_ex()` in order to pass the remaining arguments on to the constructor untouched.

Accepting Instances

Often you'll need your functions or methods to accept objects from userspace. For this purpose, `zend_parse_parameters()` offers two format specifiers. The first is o (lower-case letter o), which will verify that the argument passed is an object and populate it into the passed `zval**`. A simple usage of this type could be the following userspace function, which returns the name of the class for whatever object it is passed:

```
PHP_FUNCTION(sample2_class_getname)
{
    zval *objvar;
```

```
    zend_class_entry *objce;
    if (zend_parse_parameters(ZEND_NUM_ARGS() TSRMLS_CC, "o",
                               &objvar) == FAILURE) {
        RETURN_NULL();
    }
    objce = Z_OBJCE_P(objvar);
    RETURN_STRINGL(objce->name, objce->name_length, 1);
}
```

The second format specifier used with objects O (capital letter O) allows
zend_parse_parameters() to verify not only the zval* type, but the class type as well.
To do this, calling functions pass a zval** container along with a zend_class_entry*
to validate against as in this implementation, which expects a Sample2_FirstClass
object instance:

```
PHP_FUNCTION(sample2_reload)
{
    zval *objvar;
    if (zend_parse_parameters(ZEND_NUM_ARGS() TSRMLS_CC, "O",
        &objvar, php_sample2_firstclass_entry) == FAILURE) {
        RETURN_NULL();
    }
    /* Call hypothetical "reload" function */
    RETURN_BOOL(php_sample2_fc_reload(objvar TSRMLS_CC));
}
```

Accessing Properties

As you already saw, class methods have access to the current object instances by way of
getThis(). Combining the result of this macro, or any other zval* containing an object
instance with the Z_OBJPROP_P() macro, yields a HashTable* containing the real properties associated with the object.

An object's property list—being a simple HashTable* containing zval*s—is just
another userspace variable array that happens to sit in a special location. Just as you'd use
zend_hash_find(EG(active_symbol_table), ...) to retrieve a variable from the current scope, you'd also fetch and set object properties using the zend_hash API you
learned about in Chapter 8, "Working with Arrays and HashTables."

For example, assuming you have an instance of Sample2_FirstClass in the zval*
variable rcvdclass, the following code block would retrieve the property foo from the
standard properties HashTable*.

```
    zval **fooval;
    if (zend_hash_find(Z_OBJPROP_P(rcvdclass),
            "foo", sizeof("foo"), (void**)&fooval) == FAILURE) {
        /* $rcvdclass->foo doesn't exist */
        return;
    }
```

To add elements to the properties table, simply reverse this process with a call to zend_hash_add(), or use a variant of the add_assoc_*() functions you were introduced to in Chapter 8 for dealing with arrays. Simply replace the word assoc with property when dealing with objects.

The following constructor method provides Sample2_FirstClass instances with a set of predefined default properties:

```
PHP_NAMED_FUNCTION(php_sample2_fc_ctor)
{
    /* For brevity, and to illustrate that arbitrary
     * function names may be used, the implementation
     * name was assigned manually this time */
    zval *objvar = getThis();

    if (!objvar) {
        php_error_docref(NULL TSRMLS_CC, E_WARNING,
                        "Constructor called statically!");
        RETURN_FALSE;
    }

    add_property_long(objvar, "life", 42);
    add_property_double(objvar, "pi", 3.1415926535);
    /* Constructor return values are irrelevant */
}
```

The constructor can then be linked into the object through the php_sample2_firstclass_functions list:

```
PHP_NAMED_FE(sample2_firstclass, php_sample2_fc_ctor, NULL)
```

Summary

Although the functionality provided by ZE1 / PHP4 classes is limited at best, they do have the advantage of being compatible with the widely installed PHP4 base currently in production. The simple techniques covered in this chapter will allow you to write functional, versatile code that compiles and runs today and will continue working tomorrow.

In the next chapter, you'll find out what the buzz surrounding PHP5 is really about and why, if you want OOP functionality, you'll find a reason to upgrade and never look back.

11

PHP5 Objects

Comparing a PHP5 object to its PHP4 ancestor is just plain unfair; however many of the API functions used with PHP5 objects are built to conform to the PHP4 API. If you worked through Chapter 10, "PHP4 Objects," you should find yourself in somewhat familiar territory here. Before you begin this chapter, grab the skeleton files from Chapter 10, renaming `sample2` to `sample3` so that you're starting from a nice clean extension source.

Evolutionary Leaps

There are two key components to a PHP5 object variable. The first is a numeric identifier that, much like the numeric resource IDs found in Chapter 9, "The Resource Data Type," acts as a lookup into a requestwide table of object instances. The elements in this instance table contain a reference to the class entry and the internal properties table as well as other instance-specific information.

The second element within object variables is the handler table, which is able to customize the way the Zend Engine interacts with instances. You'll take a look at handler tables later in the chapter.

zend_class_entry

The class entry is an internal representation of a class definition as you'd declare it in userspace. Just as you saw last chapter, this structure is initialized by a call to `INIT_CLASS_ENTRY()` with the class's name and its function table then registered by `zend_register_internal_class()` during the MINIT phase:

```
zend_class_entry *php_sample3_sc_entry;
#define PHP_SAMPLE3_SC_NAME "Sample3_SecondClass"
static function_entry php_sample3_sc_functions[] = {
    { NULL, NULL, NULL }
};
```

```
PHP_MINIT_FUNCTION(sample3)
{
    zend_class_entry ce;
    INIT_CLASS_ENTRY(ce, PHP_SAMPLE3_SC_NAME,
                          php_sample3_sc_functions);
    php_sample3_sc_entry =
                zend_register_internal_class(&ce TSRMLS_CC);
    return SUCCESS;
}
```

Methods

If you did read the last chapter, you're probably starting to think, "It all looks pretty much the same so far", and so far, you're right. Now that it's time to declare some object methods. However, you'll start to see some very definite, and much welcome, differences.

```
PHP_METHOD(Sample3_SecondClass, helloWorld)
{
    php_printf("Hello World\n");
}
```

The PHP_METHOD() macro, introduced with version 2 of the Zend Engine, wraps itself around the PHP_FUNCTION() macro to combine the classname with the method name just as you did manually for PHP4 method declarations. By using this macro, name-spacing conventions are kept consistent between extensions and your code becomes easier to parse by other maintainers.

Declaration

Defining a method implementation, like any other function, is only useful if it's linked into userspace by way of the class entry's function table. As with the PHP_METHOD() macro used for implementation, there are also new macros for declaration within the function list:

- PHP_ME(classname, methodname, arg_info, flags)

    PHP_ME() adds a classname portion to the PHP_FE() macro from Chapter 5, "Your First Extension," as well as a new parameter at the end that provides access control modifiers such as public, protected, private, static, abstract, and a few other options. To declare the helloWorld method you just defined, you might use an entry like:

    ```
    PHP_ME(Sample3_SecondClass,helloWorld,NULL,ZEND_ACC_PUBLIC)
    ```

- PHP_MALIAS(classname, name, alias, arg_info, flags)

    Just like the PHP_FALIAS() macro, this declaration allows you to assign a new name—given in the name parameter—to an existing method implementation from the same class, specified by alias. For example, to give a duplicate name to your helloWorld method you might use:

```
PHP_MALIAS(Sample3_SecondClass, sayHi, helloWorld,
                          NULL, ZEND_ACC_PUBLIC)
```

- PHP_ABSTRACT_ME(classname, methodname, arg_info)

  Abstract methods in internal classes are just like abstract userspace methods.
  They're used as placeholders for within ancestral classes that expect their descen-
  dants to provide true implementations according to a specific API. You will typically use this macro within *Interfaces*, which are a specialized form of class entry.

- PHP_ME_MAPPING(methodname, functionname, arg_info)

  This last form of method declaration macro is aimed primarily at extensions that
  export a dual OOP/non-OOP interface such as the MySQLi extension where the
  mysqli_query() procedural function and MySQLi::query() method are both
  serviced by the same internal implementation. Assuming you already had a procedural function, such as the sample_hello_world() that you wrote in Chapter 5,
  you would use this declaration macro to alias it to a method in the following manner (note that mapped methods are always public, non-static, non-final):

  ```
  PHP_ME_MAPPING(hello, sample_hello_world, NULL)
  ```

So far, all the method declarations you've seen have used ZEND_ACC_PUBLIC for their
flags parameter. In practice, this value can be made up of any (or none) of the type flags
listed in Table 11.1 Bitwise OR'd with exactly one of the visibility flags listed in Table
11.2, and optionally OR'd with one of the special method flags you'll encounter in the
"Special Methods" section later in this chapter.

Table 11.1 **Method Type Flags**

Type Flag	Meaning
ZEND_ACC_STATIC	Method will be called statically. In practice, this simply means that even if the method is called via an instance, $this—or more accurately: this_ptr—will not be populated with the instance's scope.
ZEND_ACC_ABSTRACT	Method is not a true implementation. The current method should be overridden by a child class before being called directly.
ZEND_ACC_FINAL	Method cannot be overridden by child classes.

Table 11.2 **Method Visibility Flags**

Visibility Flag	Meaning
ZEND_ACC_PUBLIC	Callable from any scope or even outside of an object. This is the same visibility shared by all PHP4 methods.
ZEND_ACC_PROTECTED	Only callable from the class it was defined in, or one of its children or ancestors.
ZEND_ACC_PRIVATE	Only callable from the exact class it was defined by.

For example, because the `Sample3_SecondClass::helloWorld()` method you defined earlier has no need for an object instance, you could change its declaration from a simple `ZEND_ACC_PUBLIC` to `ZEND_ACC_PUBLIC|ZEND_ACC_STATIC` so the engine knows not to bother.

Special Methods

In addition to the ZE1 set of magic methods, ZE2 adds a large family of magic methods listed in Table 11.3 and found in the PHP online manual at http://www.php.net/language.oop5.magic.

Table 11.3 **Zend Engine 2 Magic Methods**

Method	Usage
`__construct(...)`	An alternative to the automatically called object constructor (previously defined as the method who's name matches the classname). If method implementation exist for both `__construct()` and `classname()`, `__construct()` will receive priority and be called during instantiation.
`__destruct()`	When the instance falls completely out of scope—or the request as a whole shuts down—all instances implicit call their `__destruct()` methods to handle any last minute cleanup such as shutting down file and network handles.
`__clone()`	By default, all instances are passed around in true-reference sets. As of PHP5, however, an instance can be explicitly copied using the clone keyword. When clone is called on an object instance, the `__clone()` method is implicitly called to allow an object to duplicate any internal resources as needed.
`__toString()`	When expressing an instance as a textual object, such as when using the echo or print statements, the `__toString()` method is automatically called by the engine. Classes implementing this magic method should return a string containing a representation of the object's current state.
`__get($var)`	If a script requests a property from an object instance that either does not exist in the standard properties table or is declared as non-public, the `__get()` magic method is called with the name of the property passed as the only parameter. Implementations may use their own internal logic to determine the most sensible return value to provide.
`__set($var, $value)`	Like `__get()`, `__set()` provides the opportunity to handle variable assignment when the variable being assigned is not in the standard properties table or is declared

Table 11.3 **Continued**

Method	Usage
	non-public. __set() implementations may choose to implicitly create these variables within the standard properties table, set the values within other storage mechanisms, or simply throw an error and discard the value.
__call($fname, $args)	Calling an undefined method on an object may be handled gracefully through the use of a __call() magic method implementation. This method receives two arguments: The method name being called, and a numerically indexed array containing the arguments passed to that method.
__isset($varname)	As of PHP 5.1.0, the calls to isset($obj->prop) will not only check for the prop property within $obj, they will also call into any defined __isset() method within $obj to dynamically evaluate if attempts to read or write the property would succeed given the dynamic __get() and __set() methods.
__unset($varname)	Like __isset(), PHP 5.1.0 introduced a simple OOP interface to the unset() function for properties that, although they might not exist within an objects standard properties table, might have meaning within the __get() and __set() dynamic property space.

Note

Extra magic method functionality is available through certain interfaces such as the ArrayAccess interface as well as several SPL interfaces.

Within an internal object implementation, each of these special "magic methods" can be implemented as any other method within your object by defining a PHP_ME() line with the right name and a PUBLIC access modifier. For __get(), __set(), __call(), __isset(), and __unset(), which require a precise number of arguments to be passed, you must define an appropriate arg_info struct that states that the method takes exactly 1 or 2 arguments. The following code snippets show arg_info structs and their corresponding PHP_ME() entries for each of the magic methods:

```
static
    ZEND_BEGIN_ARG_INFO_EX(php_sample3_one_arg, 0, 0, 1)
    ZEND_END_ARG_INFO()
static
    ZEND_BEGIN_ARG_INFO_EX(php_sample3_two_args, 0, 0, 2)
    ZEND_END_ARG_INFO()
static function_entry php_sample3_sc_functions[] = {
```

```
PHP_ME(Sample3_SecondClass, __construct, NULL,
                    ZEND_ACC_PUBLIC|ZEND_ACC_CTOR)
PHP_ME(Sample3_SecondClass, __destruct, NULL,
                    ZEND_ACC_PUBLIC|ZEND_ACC_DTOR)
PHP_ME(Sample3_SecondClass, __clone, NULL,
                    ZEND_ACC_PUBLIC|ZEND_ACC_CLONE)
PHP_ME(Sample3_SecondClass, __toString, NULL,
                    ZEND_ACC_PUBLIC)
PHP_ME(Sample3_SecondClass, __get, php_sample3_one_arg,
                    ZEND_ACC_PUBLIC)
PHP_ME(Sample3_SecondClass, __set, php_sample3_two_args,
                    ZEND_ACC_PUBLIC)
PHP_ME(Sample3_SecondClass, __call, php_sample3_two_args,
                    ZEND_ACC_PUBLIC)
PHP_ME(Sample3_SecondClass, __isset, php_sample3_one_arg,
                    ZEND_ACC_PUBLIC)
PHP_ME(Sample3_SecondClass, __unset, php_sample3_one_arg,
                    ZEND_ACC_PUBLIC)
{ NULL, NULL, NULL }
};
```

Notice that __construct, __destruct, and __clone were OR'd with additional constants. These three access modifiers are specific to the methods they're named for and should never be used anywhere else.

Properties

Access control within PHP5 object properties is handled somewhat differently than method visibility. When declaring a public property within the standard property table, you can use the zend_hash_add() or add_property_*() family functions just as you would ordinarily expect to.

For protected and private properties, however, a new Zend API function is required:

```
void zend_mangle_property_name(char **dest, int *dest_length,
                    char *class, int class_length,
                    char *prop, int prop_length,
                    int persistent)
```

This function will allocate a new chunk or memory and construct a string according to the layout: \0classname\0propname. If classname is a specific classname, such as Sample3_SecondClass, the property will have private visibility—It will only be visible from within instances of Sample3_SecondClass objects.

If classname is specified as simply *, the property will have protected visibility and be accessible from any ancestor or descendant of the object instance's class. In practice, properties might be added to an object in the following manner:

```
void php_sample3_addprops(zval *objvar)
{
    char *propname;
    int propname_len;
    /* Public */
    add_property_long(objvar, "Chapter", 11);
    /* Protected */
    zend_mangle_property_name(&propname, &propname_len,
        "*", 1, "Title", sizeof("Title")-1, 0);
    add_property_string_ex(objvar, propname, propname_len,
        "PHP5 Objects", 1 TSRMLS_CC);
    efree(propname);
    /* Private */
    zend_mangle_property_name(&propname, &propname_len,
        "Sample3_SecondClass",sizeof("Sample3_SecondClass")-1,
        "Section", sizeof("Section")-1, 0);
    add_property_string_ex(objvar, propname, propname_len,
        "Properties", 1 TSRMLS_CC);
    efree(propname);
}
```

By using the _ex() version of the add_property_*() family of functions, you're able to explicitly identify the length of the property name string. This is necessary because the NULL bytes in protected and private property names would otherwise fool strlen() into thinking that you'd passed zero-length prop names. Notice also that the _ex() version of the add_property_*() functions require TSRMLS_CC to be explicitly passed. Ordinarily, this would be implicitly passed through macro expansion.

Constants

Declaring class constants is much like declaring object properties. The key difference between the two comes from their persistency because properties can wait until instantiation, which occurs during a request, while constants are tied directly to the class definition and are only declared during the MINIT phase.

Because the standard zval* manipulation macros and functions assume non-persistency, you'll need to write a fair amount of code manually. Consider the following function, which might be called following class registration:

```
void php_sample3_register_constants(zend_class_entry *ce)
{
    zval *constval;

    /* Basic scalar values can use Z_*() to set their value */
    constval = pemalloc(sizeof(zval), 1);
    INIT_PZVAL(constval);
    ZVAL_DOUBLE(constval, 2.7182818284);
```

```
    zend_hash_add(&ce->constants_table, "E", sizeof("E"),
                    (void*)&constval, sizeof(zval*), NULL);

    /* Strings require additional mallocs */
    constval = pemalloc(sizeof(zval), 1);
    INIT_PZVAL(constval);
    Z_TYPE_P(constval) = IS_STRING;
    Z_STRLEN_P(constval) = sizeof("Hello World") - 1;
    Z_STRVAL_P(constval) = pemalloc(Z_STRLEN_P(constval)+1, 1);
    memcpy(Z_STRVAL_P(constval), "Hello World",
                        Z_STRLEN_P(constval) + 1);
    zend_hash_add(&ce->constants_table,
                    "GREETING", sizeof("GREETING"),
                    (void*)&constval, sizeof(zval*), NULL);

    /* Objects, Arrays, and Resources can't be constants */
}
PHP_MINIT_FUNCTION(sample3)
{
    zend_class_entry ce;
    INIT_CLASS_ENTRY(ce, PHP_SAMPLE3_SC_NAME,
                        php_sample3_sc_functions);
    php_sample3_sc_entry =
                zend_register_internal_class(&ce TSRMLS_CC);
    php_sample3_register_constants(php_sample3_sc_entry);
    return SUCCESS;
}
```

Following this addition, these class constants can be accessed without instantiation via `Sample3_SecondClass::E` and `Sample3_SecondClass::GREETING`, respectively.

Interfaces

Declaring an interface is just like declaring any other class with the exception of a couple of steps. The first of these steps is declaring all of its methods as abstract, which can be done through using the `PHP_ABSTRACT_ME()` macro:

```
static function_entry php_sample3_iface_methods[] = {
    PHP_ABSTRACT_ME(Sample3_Interface, workerOne, NULL)
    PHP_ABSTRACT_ME(Sample3_Interface, workerTwo, NULL)
    PHP_ABSTRACT_ME(Sample3_Interface, workerThree, NULL)
    { NULL, NULL, NULL }
};
```

Because these methods are abstract, no implementation methods need exist. You're already prepared for the second step, which is registration. Like registration of a real class, this begins with calls to `INIT_CLASS_ENTRY` and `zend_register_internal_class`.

When the class entry is available, the last step is to mark the class as an interface so that it can be implemented:

```
zend_class_entry *php_sample3_iface_entry;
PHP_MINIT_FUNCTION(sample3)
{
    zend_class_entry ce;
    INIT_CLASS_ENTRY(ce, "Sample3_Interface",
                         php_sample3_iface_methods);
    php_sample3_iface_entry =
                zend_register_internal_class(&ce TSRMLS_CC);
    php_sample3_iface_entry->ce_flags|= ZEND_ACC_INTERFACE;
    ...
```

Implementing Interfaces

Assuming you wanted your `Sample3_SecondClass` class to implement the `Sample3_Interface` interface, you'd need to implement each of the abstract methods listed as part of the interface within your class:

```
PHP_METHOD(Sample3_SecondClass,workerOne)
{
    php_printf("Working Hard.\n");
}
PHP_METHOD(Sample3_SecondClass,workerTwo)
{
    php_printf("Hardly Working.\n");
}
PHP_METHOD(Sample3_SecondClass,workerThree)
{
    php_printf("Going wee-wee-wee all the way home.\n");
}
```

Then declare them in the `php_sample3_sc_functions` list:

```
    PHP_ME(Sample3_SecondClass,workerOne,NULL,ZEND_ACC_PUBLIC)
    PHP_ME(Sample3_SecondClass,workerTwo,NULL,ZEND_ACC_PUBLIC)
    PHP_ME(Sample3_SecondClass,workerThree,NULL,ZEND_ACC_PUBLIC)
```

And finally, declare that your newly registered class implements the `php_sample3_iface_entry` interface:

```
PHP_MINIT_FUNCTION(sample3)
{
    zend_class_entry ce;
    /* Register Interface */
    INIT_CLASS_ENTRY(ce, "Sample3_Interface",
                         php_sample3_iface_methods);
```

```
php_sample3_iface_entry =
            zend_register_internal_class(&ce TSRMLS_CC);
php_sample3_iface_entry->ce_flags|= ZEND_ACC_INTERFACE;
/* Register Class implementing interface */
INIT_CLASS_ENTRY(ce, PHP_SAMPLE3_SC_NAME,
                    php_sample3_sc_functions);
php_sample3_sc_entry =
            zend_register_internal_class(&ce TSRMLS_CC);
php_sample3_register_constants(php_sample3_sc_entry);
zend_class_implements(php_sample3_sc_entry TSRMLS_CC,
            1, php_sample3_iface_entry);
return SUCCESS;
}
```

If `Sample3_SecondClass` implemented other interfaces, such as `ArrayAccess`, its class entries could be added as additional parameters to `zend_class_implements()` by incrementing the one parameter to match the number of interfaces passed.

```
zend_class_implements(php_sample3_sc_entry TSRMLS_CC,
            2, php_sample3_iface_entry, php_other_interface_entry);
```

Handlers

Rather than treat every object instance the same, ZE2 associates a handler table with every object instance. When a particular action is performed against an object, the engine calls into the object's handler table so that any custom action can be performed.

Standard Handlers

By default, every object is assigned handlers from the `std_object_handlers` built-in table. The handler methods and their default behavior—as defined by the corresponding method in `std_object_handlers`—follow:

- `void add_ref(zval *object TSRMLS_DC)`

    Called when the `refcount` of an object value is increased, such as when one variable containing an object is assigned into a new one. The default behavior of both the add and `del_ref` functions is to adjust the internal object store `refcount` appropriately.

- `void del_ref(zval *object TSRMLS_DC)`

    Like `add_ref`, this method is called in response to a change in refcount, usually associated with an `unset()` call against a variable containing an object.

- `zend_object_value clone_obj(zval *object TSRMLS_DC)`

    Used to generate a new object copied from an already instantiated one. The default behavior is to create a new object instance, associate the original's handler table with it, copy the properties table and, if the class entry for the object in question defines a __clone() method, call that to allow the new object to perform additional duplication work.

- `zval *read_property(zval *obj, zval *prop, int type TSRMLS_DC)`

  `void write_property(zval *obj, zval *prop, zval *value TSRMLS_DC)`

  The read and write property methods are called in response to userspace attempts to access $obj->prop for either reading or writing. The default handler will first look for the property in the standard properties table. If the property is not defined, it will call the corresponding __get() or __set() magic method, assuming it's defined.

- `zval **get_property_ptr_ptr(zval *obj, zval *value TSRMLS_DC)`

  get_property_ptr_ptr is a variation of read_property, which is meant to allow the calling scope to directly replace the current zval* with a new one. Default behavior is to return a dereferenced pointer to the property in the standard properties table if it exists. If it doesn't exist yet, and there are no __get()/__set() magic methods, a new variable will be implicitly created and a pointer returned. Having existing __get() or __set() methods will cause this handler to fail, letting the engine fall back on individual calls to read_property and write_property.

- `zval *read_dimension(zval *obj, zval *idx, int type TSRMLS_DC)`

  `void write_dimension(zval *obj, zval *idx, zval *value TSRMLS_DC)`

  The read and write dimension pair are similar to their read and write property counterparts; however, they are triggered in response to attempts to treat an object like an array such as using $obj['idx']. If the object's class does not implement the ArrayAccess interface, the default handler will throw an error; otherwise, it will call magic methods offsetget($idx) or offsetset($idx, $value) as appropriate.

- `zval *get(zval *obj TSRMLS_DC)`

  `void set(zval *obj, zval *value TSRMLS_DC)`

  When setting or retrieving the value of an object, the appropriate get() or set() methods are called on that object. The object itself is passed as a courtesy pointer in the first parameter. For sets, the new value is passed in the second parameter. In practice, these methods are used in pairs for arithmetic operations. There are no default handlers for these operations.

- `int has_property(zval *obj, zval *prop, int chk_type TSRMLS_DC)`

  When isset() is called against an object property, this handler is invoked. By default the standard handler will check for the property named by prop, if it's not found and—as of PHP 5.1.0—if an __isset() method is defined it will call that. The chk_type parameter will be one of three possible values. If the value is 2 the property need only exist to qualify as a success. If the chk_type is 0, it must exist and be of any type except IS_NULL. If the value of chk_type is 1, the value must both exist and evaluate to a non-false value. Note: In PHP 5.0.x, the meaning of chk_type matched has_dimension's version of chk_type.

- `int has_dimension(zval *obj, zval *idx, int chk_type TSRMLS_DC)`

  When `isset()` is called against an object that is being treated like an array, such as `isset($obj['idx'])`, this handler is used. The standard handler, if the object implements the `ArrayAccess` interface, will call the `offsetexists($idx)` method first. If not found, it returns failure in the form of a 0. Otherwise, if `chk_type` is 0 it returns true (1) immediately. A `chk_type` of 1 indicates that it must also check that the value is non-false by invoking the object's `offsetget($idx)` method as well and examining the returned value.

- `void unset_property(zval *obj, zval *prop TSRMLS_DC)`

  `void unset_dimension(zval *obj, zval *idx TSRMLS_DC)`

  These methods are called in response to trying to unset an object property, or off-set of an object being treated as an array respectively. The `unset_property()` handler will either remove the property from the standard properties table (if it exists), or attempt to call any implemented `__unset($prop)` method—as of PHP 5.1.0. `unsset_dimension()` will, if the class implements `ArrayAccess`, invoke the `offsetunset($idx)` method.

- `HashTable *get_properties(zval *object TSRMLS_DC)`

  When an internal function uses the `Z_OBJPROP()` macro to retrieve the standard properties HashTable, it is actually this handler that is invoked. The default handler for PHP object then extracts and returns `Z_OBJ_P(object)->properties`, which is the true standard HashTable.

- `union _zend_function *get_method(zval **obj_ptr,`

    `char *method_name, int methodname_len TSRMLS_DC)`

  This handler does the work of resolving an object's method from its class's `function_table`. If no method exists in the primary `function_table`, the default handler will return a `zend_function*` container pointing at a wrapper for the object's `__call($name, $args)` method.

- `int call_method(char *method, INTERNAL_FUNCTION_PARAMETERS)`

  Functions defined as type `ZEND_OVERLOADED_FUNCTION` are executed by way of the `call_method` handler. By default, this handler is not defined.

- `union _zend_function *get_constructor(zval *obj TSRMLS_DC)`

  Like the `get_method()` handler, this handler returns a reference to the appropriate object method. What makes it special is the manner in which constructors are specially stored within class entries. Overriding this method would be very uncommon.

- `zend_class_entry *get_class_entry(zval *obj TSRMLS_DC)`

  Like `get_constructor()`, this handler will almost never be overridden. Its purpose is to map an object instance back to its original class definition.

- int get_class_name(zval *object, char **name, zend_uint *len,
                    int parent TSRMLS_DC)

  get_class_name() takes get_class_entry() a step further by extracting a duplicated copy of the object's classname or its parent's classname, depending on the value of parent, of course. The copy of the class's name must use non-persistent (emalloc) storage.

- int compare_objects(zval *obj1, zval *obj2 TSRMLS_DC)

  When a comparison operator such as ==, !=, <=, <, >, or >= is used with a pair of objects, the compare_objects handler is called for the object in the left half of the equation. Return values follow the typical 1, 0, -1 format for greater-than, equal, and less-than. By default, objects are compared based on their standard properties HashTable using the array comparison rules you saw in Chapter 8, "Working with Arrays and HashTables."

- int cast_object(zval *src, zval *dst, int type, int should_free
                    TSRMLS_DC)

  Certain attempts to convert an object to another data type will trigger this handler. If should_free is set to a non-zero value, zval_dtor() should be called on dst to free any internal resources first. Either way, the handler should attempt to express the object found in src as the type specified by type in the dst zval*. This handler is not defined by default, but should return SUCESS or FAILURE when it is.

- int count_elements(zval *obj, long *count TSRMLS_DC)

  Objects that define an overloaded dimension should implement this handler, which then populates count with the current number of elements and returns SUCCESS. If the current instance does not actually implement overloaded properties, it might return FAILURE to allow the engine to fall back on examining the standard properties table.

Magic Methods, Part Deux

Using customized versions of the object handlers you saw previously, the same overloading behavior—and more—that is available to userspace through __special() methods can be duplicated on a per class or per object basis by internal classes. Pushing these customized handlers on object instances first requires creating a new handler table. Because you will almost certainly not want to override all handlers, it makes sense to copy the standard handlers to your custom table, and then override the handlers you want to change:

```
static zend_object_handlers php_sample3_obj_handlers;
int php_sample3_has_dimension(zval *obj, zval *idx,
                    int chk_type TSRMLS_DC)
{
```

```
    /* Only used when PHP >= 5.1.0 */
    if (chk_type == 0) {
        /* Remap check type */
        chk_type = 2;
    }
    /* Check type of 1 remains unchanged
     * Use standard has_property method with
     * (un)modified Check Type */
    return php_sample3_obj_handlers.has_property(obj,
                        idx, chk_type TSRMLS_CC);
}
PHP_MINIT_FUNCTION(sample3)
{
    zend_class_entry ce;
    zend_object_handlers *h = &php_sample3_obj_handlers;

    /* Register Interface */
    INIT_CLASS_ENTRY(ce, "Sample3_Interface",
                        php_sample3_iface_methods);
    php_sample3_iface_entry =
                zend_register_internal_class(&ce TSRMLS_CC);
    php_sample3_iface_entry->ce_flags = ZEND_ACC_INTERFACE;
    /* Register SecondClass class */
    INIT_CLASS_ENTRY(ce, PHP_SAMPLE3_SC_NAME,
                        php_sample3_sc_functions);
    php_sample3_sc_entry =
                zend_register_internal_class(&ce TSRMLS_CC);
    php_sample3_register_constants(php_sample3_sc_entry);

    /* Implement AbstractClass interface */
    zend_class_implements(php_sample3_sc_entry TSRMLS_CC,
                1, php_sample3_iface_entry);

    /* Create custom Handler Table */
    php_sample3_obj_handlers = *zend_get_std_object_handlers();

    /* Make $obj['foo'] act like $obj->foo */
    h->read_dimension = h->read_property;
    h->write_dimension = h->write_property;
    h->unset_dimension = h->unset_property;
#if PHP_MAJOR_VERSION > 5 || \
            (PHP_MAJOR_VERSION == 5 && PHP_MINOR_VERSION > 0)
    /* As of PHP 5.1.0 has_property and has_dimension differ
     * In order to make them behave the same we have to
     * wrap the call through a proxy */
    h->has_dimension = php_sample3_has_dimension;
```

```
#else
    /* PHP 5.0.x has_property and has_dimension act the same */
    h->has_dimension = h->has_property;
#endif

    return SUCCESS;
}
```

To apply this handler table to an object you have a couple of choices. The simplest is typically going to be implementing a constructor method and reassigning the variable's handler table at that time:

```
PHP_METHOD(Sample3_SecondClass,__construct)
{
    zval *objptr = getThis();

    if (!objptr) {
        php_error_docref(NULL TSRMLS_CC, E_WARNING,
                    "Constructor called statically!");
        RETURN_FALSE;
    }
    /* Perform usual constructor tasks here... */
    /* Override handler table */
    Z_OBJ_HT_P(objptr) = &php_sample3_obj_handlers;
}
```

When the constructor returns, the object will have a new handler table and exhibit custom behavior. Another, and often more favored, approach is to override the class entry's object creation method:

```
zend_object_value php_sample3_sc_create(zend_class_entry *ce
                                        TSRMLS_DC)
{
    zend_object *object;
    zend_object_value retval;

    /* Reuse Zend's generic object creator */
    retval = zend_objects_new(&object, ce TSRMLS_CC);
    /* When overriding create_object,
     * properties must be manually initialized */
    ALLOC_HASHTABLE(object->properties);
    zend_hash_init(object->properties, 0, NULL,
                                    ZVAL_PTR_DTOR, 0);
    /* Override default handlers */
    retval.handlers = &php_sample3_obj_handlers;
    /* Other object initialization may occur here */
    return retval;
}
```

This can then be attached to the class's entry once it's registered in the MINIT phase:

```
INIT_CLASS_ENTRY(ce, PHP_SAMPLE3_SC_NAME,
                       php_sample3_sc_functions);
php_sample3_sc_entry =
           zend_register_internal_class(&ce TSRMLS_CC);
php_sample3_sc_entry->create_object= php_sample3_sc_create;
php_sample3_register_constants(php_sample3_sc_entry);
zend_class_implements(php_sample3_sc_entry TSRMLS_CC,
           1, php_sample3_iface_entry);
```

The only appreciable difference between these two methods is the timing of their actions. The engine calls create_object as soon as it encounters new Sample3_SecondClass but before even considering the constructor or its arguments. Typically, you should use whichever approach coincides with the method (create_object versus __construct) that you plan to override anyway.

Summary

Without a doubt, the PHP5/ZE2 object model is more complex than its PHP4/ZE1 predecessor. After seeing all of the feature and implementation details in this chapter, you're probably a bit overwhelmed by the volume of it all. Fortunately, the layers that make up OOP within PHP enable you to pick and choose the pieces appropriate to your task and leave the rest alone. Find a good comfort level and start working upwards in complexity; the rest will follow.

Now that all of PHP's internal data types have been covered, it's time to return to an earlier topic: the request life cycle. In the next two chapters, you'll add internal state to your extension through the use of thread-safe globals, define custom ini settings, declare constants, and offer superglobals to userspace scripts using your extension.

12

Startup, Shutdown, and a Few Points in Between

Several times through the course of this book you've used the MINIT function to perform initialization tasks when PHP loads your module's shared object library. In Chapter 1, "The PHP Life Cycle," however, you also learned of three other startup and shutdown routines that are part of every extension—one to balance MINIT, called MSHUTDOWN, and a pair of RINIT/RSHUTDOWN methods that are called at the start and end of every page request.

Cycles

In addition to these four methods, which are linked directly into the module entry structure, there are two more methods used only in threaded environments that handle the startup and shutdown of individual threads and the private storage space they use. To get started, set up a slightly more comprehensive version of the basic extension skeleton using these source files in ext/sample4 under your PHP source tree (see Listings 12.1 through 12.3):

Listing 12.1 `config.m4`

```
PHP_ARG_ENABLE(sample4,
  [Whether to enable the "sample4" extension],
  [  —enable-sample4      Enable "sample4" extension support])

if test $PHP_SAMPLE4 != "no"; then
  PHP_SUBST(SAMPLE4_SHARED_LIBADD)
  PHP_NEW_EXTENSION(sample4, sample4.c, $ext_shared)
fi
```

Listing 12.2 `php_sample4.h`

```
#ifndef PHP_SAMPLE4_H
/* Prevent double inclusion */
#define PHP_SAMPLE4_H

/* Define Extension Properties */
#define PHP_SAMPLE4_EXTNAME    "sample4"
#define PHP_SAMPLE4_EXTVER     "1.0"

/* Import configure options
   when building outside of
   the PHP source tree */
#ifdef HAVE_CONFIG_H
#include "config.h"
#endif

/* Include PHP Standard Header */
#include "php.h"

/* Define the entry point symbol
 * Zend will use when loading this module
 */
extern zend_module_entry sample4_module_entry;
#define phpext_sample4_ptr &sample4_module_entry

#endif /* PHP_SAMPLE4_H */
```

Listing 12.3 `sample4.c`

```
#include "php_sample4.h"
#include "ext/standard/info.h"

static function_entry php_sample4_functions[] = {
    { NULL, NULL, NULL }
};

PHP_MINIT_FUNCTION(sample4)
{
    return SUCCESS;
}

PHP_MSHUTDOWN_FUNCTION(sample4)
{
    return SUCCESS;
}
```

Listing 12.3   **Continued**

```
PHP_RINIT_FUNCTION(sample4)
{
    return SUCCESS;
}


PHP_RSHUTDOWN_FUNCTION(sample4)
{
    return SUCCESS;
}


PHP_MINFO_FUNCTION(sample4)
{
}


zend_module_entry sample4_module_entry = {
#if ZEND_MODULE_API_NO >= 20010901
    STANDARD_MODULE_HEADER,
#endif
    PHP_SAMPLE4_EXTNAME,
    php_sample4_functions,
    PHP_MINIT(sample4),
    PHP_MSHUTDOWN(sample4),
    PHP_RINIT(sample4),
    PHP_RSHUTDOWN(sample4),
    PHP_MINFO(sample4),
#if ZEND_MODULE_API_NO >= 20010901
    PHP_SAMPLE4_EXTVER,
#endif
    STANDARD_MODULE_PROPERTIES
};


#ifdef COMPILE_DL_SAMPLE4
ZEND_GET_MODULE(sample4)
#endif
```

Notice that each startup and shutdown method returns SUCCESS on exit. If any method were to return FAILURE, the module load or request would be aborted by PHP to avoid any serious problems elsewhere in the engine.

Module Cycle

MINIT should be familiar as you've used it several times throughout the previous chapters. It's triggered the first time a module is loaded into a process space, which for single-request SAPIs such as CLI And CGI, or multithreaded SAPIs such as Apache2-worker, is exactly once because no forking is involved.

For multiprocess SAPIs such as Apache1 and Apache2-prefork, multiple web server processes are forked and with them multiple instances of mod_php. Each instance of mod_php must then load its own instance of your extension module meaning that your MINIT method is run multiple times, but still only once per process space.

When a module is unloaded, the MSHUTDOWN method is invoked so that any resources owned by that module, such as persistent memory blocks, may be freed and returned to the operating system.

Enginewide features, such as Class Entries, Resource IDs, Stream wrappers and filters, userspace autoglobals, and php.ini entries are some common examples of resources that get allocated and cleaned up in the Module INIT and SHUTDOWN phases respectively.

Note

In theory, you could skip proper resource cleanup during the MSHUTDOWN phase, opting instead to allow the OS to implicitly free memory and file handles. When using your extension with Apache 1.3 however, you'll discover an interesting quirk as Apache will load mod_php, launching all MINIT methods in the process, and then immediately unload mod_php, trigging the MSHUTDOWN methods, and then load it again. Without a proper MSHUTDOWN phase, resources allocated during the initial MINIT will be leaked and wasted.

Thread Cycle

In multithreaded SAPIs, it's sometimes necessary for each thread to allocate its own independent resources or track its own personal per-request counters. For these special situations there is a per-thread hook that allows for an additional set of startup and shutdown methods to be executed. Typically when a multithreaded SAPI such as Apache2-worker starts up, it will spin a dozen or more threads in order to be able to handle multiple concurrent requests.

Any resources that may be shared between requests, but must not be accessed by multiple threads in the same process space simultaneously, are usually allocated and freed in the thread constructor and destructor methods. Examples might include persistent resources in the EG(persistent_list) HashTable because they often include network or file resources that make assumptions about the consistency of their state from instruction to instruction.

Request Cycle

The last and most transient startup and shutdown cycle occurs with every request, and is where your extension might choose to initialize default userspace variables or initialize internal state tracking information. Because both of these methods are called on every single page request, it's important to keep the processing and memory allocation load to a bare minimum.

Exposing Information Through MINFO

Unless you plan on being the only person to use your extension, and you never plan to change the API at all, you'll probably need your extension to be capable of telling user-space a little bit about itself. For example, are all of its environment and version-specific features available? What versions of external libraries was it compiled against? Is there a website or email address someone using your extension can contact for help?

If you've ever looked at the output of phpinfo() or php -i, you've noticed that all this information is grouped into one well-formatted, easy-to-parse output. Your extension can easily add its own block to this listing by placing a few lines into the MINFO (Module Information) method pointed to by your module entry structure:

```
PHP_MINFO_FUNCTION(sample4)
{
    php_info_print_table_start();
    php_info_print_table_row(2, "Sample4 Module", "enabled");
    php_info_print_table_row(2, "version", PHP_SAMPLE4_EXTVER);
    php_info_print_table_end();
}
```

By using these wrapper functions, your Module Info will be automatically wrapped in HTML tags when being output from a webserver SAPI (such as CGI, IIS, Apache, and so on), or formatted using plaintext and newlines when used with CLI. In order to make the prototypes for these functions available to your extension during build time, #include "ext/standard/info.h" was placed in sample4.c in the listing at the beginning of this chapter.

The following functions make up the php_info_*() family available in this header file:

- char *php_info_html_esc(char *str TSRMLS_DC)

  Serves as a wrapper for php_escape_html_entities() which is the underlying implementation of the userspace htmlentites() function. The string returned by the function is emalloc()'d and must be explicitly efree()'d after use.

- void php_info_print_table_start(void)

  void php_info_print_table_end(void)

  Outputs the opening/closing tags required for table formatting. When HTML output is disabled—such as with the CLI sapi—this outputs a simple newline for start, and nothing for end.

- void php_info_print_table_header(int cols, ...)

  void php_info_print_table_colspan_header(int cols, char *header)

  Outputs a row of table headers. The first version outputs one <th></th> pair per column passed as char* elements in the variable argument list. The colspan version outputs only one <th></th> pair but assigns a colspan attribute to the cell.

- `void php_info_print_table_row(int cols, ...)`

  `void php_info_print_table_row_ex(int cols, char *class, ...)`

  Each of these functions will output a row of data with each variable argument `char*` element wrapped in its own `<td></td>` pair. The difference between the two is that the former will assign a `class="v"` attribute automatically, while the second allows the calling extension to specify an alternative class parameter for custom formatting. On non-HTML formatted output, the distinction between these two disappears as there is no class analog for plaintext output.

- `void php_info_print_box_start(int flag)`

  `void php_info_print_box_end()`

  These methods output the beginning and ending framing for a simple one cell table to impose styled formatting in HTML output. If the value of flag is non-zero then class h is used; otherwise the box is assigned a class of v. Using non-HTML output, a flag value of 0 will result in a newline being output by start; no other output is generated by these methods for non-HTML output.

- `void php_info_print_hr(void)`

  This method will output an `<hr />` tag for HTMLized output, or a series of 31 underscores to represent a horizontal rule bounded by a pair of newlines at the start and end.

The usual `PHPWRITE()` and `php_printf()` functions can be used within the `MINFO` method as well, although when outputting content manually you should always take care to output the correct type of information depending on whether the current SAPI expects plaintext or HTML content. To accomplish this, simply examine the global `sapi_module` struct's `phpinfo_as_text` property:

```
PHP_MINFO_FUNCTION(sample4)
{
    php_info_print_table_start();
    php_info_print_table_row(2, "Sample4 Module", "enabled");
    php_info_print_table_row(2, "version", PHP_SAMPLE4_EXTVER);
    if (sapi_module.phpinfo_as_text) {
        /* No HTML for you */
        php_info_print_table_row(2, "By",
            "Example Technologies\nhttp://www.example.com");
    } else {
        /* HTMLified version */
        php_printf("<tr>"
            "<td class=\"v\">By</td>"
            "<td class=\"v\">"
            "<a href=\"http://www.example.com\""
            " alt=\"Example Technologies\">"
            "<img src=\"http://www.example.com/logo.png\" />"
```

```
            "</a></td></tr>");
    }
    php_info_print_table_end();
}
```

Constants

A more accessible place to expose information to the scripts using your extension is to define constants that can be accessed by scripts at runtime, possibly allowing them to modify their behavior. In userspace, you'd declare a constant using the define() function; in internals, it's very nearly the same and uses the REGISTER_*_CONSTANT() family of macros.

Most constants are ones you'll want to make available in all scripts initialized to the same value. To declare these constants you'll declare them in the MINIT method:

```
PHP_MINIT_FUNCTION(sample4)
{
    REGISTER_STRING_CONSTANT("SAMPLE4_VERSION",
            PHP_SAMPLE4_EXTVER, CONST_CS | CONST_PERSISTENT);

    return SUCCESS;
}
```

The first parameter to this macro is the name of the constant as it will be exported to userspace. In this example, a userspace script will be able to issue echo SAMPLE4_ VERSION; and have 1.0 output. It's important to note here that the REGISTER_*_ CONSTANT() family of macros use a call to sizeof() to determine the constant name's length. This means that only literal values may be used. Attempting to use a char* variable will result in an incorrect string length of sizeof(char*)—usually 4 on 32-bit platforms.

Next comes the constant's value itself. In most cases this is a single parameter of the named type; however, the STRINGL version you'll see in a moment does require a second length parameter. When registering string constants, the string value is not copied into the constant, but merely referenced by it. This means that dynamically created strings need to be allocated in permanent memory and freed during the appropriate shutdown phase.

Finally, in the last parameter you'll pass a bitwise OR combination of two optional flags. Including the CONST_CS flag will specify the constant as being case-sensitive. This is the default for user-defined constants and nearly all the internal constants used by PHP as well. For a few special cases, such as TRUE, FALSE, and NULL, this parameter is omitted enabling them to be resolved in a non–case-sensitive manner.

The second of the two flags for constant registration is the persistency flag. When declaring constants in MINIT, they must be built to persist from request to request. When declared within a request, such as during RINIT, you may—and almost always should— omit this flag, allowing the engine to destroy the constant at the end of the request.

The following prototypes describe the four available constant registration macros. Remember that the name parameter must be a string literal and not a `char*` variable.

```
REGISTER_LONG_CONSTANT(char *name, long lval, int flags)
REGISTER_DOUBLE_CONSTANT(char *name, double dval, int flags)
REGISTER_STRING_CONSTANT(char *name, char *value, int flags)
REGISTER_STRINGL_CONSTANT(char *name,
                    char *value, int value_len, int flags)
```

If the string must be initialized from a variable name, such as within a loop, you can use the underlying function calls to which these macros map:

```
void zend_register_long_constant(char *name, uint name_len,
        long lval, int flags, int module_number TSRMLS_DC)
void zend_register_double_constant(char *name, uint name_len,
        double dval, int flags, int module_number TSRMLS_DC)
void zend_register_string_constant(char *name, uint name_len,
        char *strval, int flags, int module_number TSRMLS_DC)
void zend_register_stringl_constant(char *name, uint name_len,
        char *strval, uint strlen, int flags,
        int module_number TSRMLS_DC)
```

This time, the length of the name parameter can be supplied directly by the calling scope. You'll notice this time that `TSRMLS_CC` must be explicitly passed and that a new parameter has been introduced.

`module_number` is assigned by the engine when your extension is loaded and serves as a clue during module cleanup as your extension is unloaded. You don't need to worry about what the value of this variable is; just pass it. It's supplied in the prototype for all `MINIT` and `RINIT` methods, and is therefore available when you declare your constants. Here's the same constant registration again:

```
PHP_MINIT_FUNCTION(sample4)
{
    register_string_constant("SAMPLE4_VERSION",
        sizeof("SAMPLE4_VERSION"),
        PHP_SAMPLE4_EXTVER,
        CONST_CS | CONST_PERSISTENT,
        module_number TSRMLS_CC);

    return SUCCESS;
}
```

Notice again that when `sizeof()` was used to determine the length of SAMPLE4_VERSION, it was not reduced by one. Constant's names are expected to include their terminating NULL. If you're starting with a `strlen()` determined length, be sure to add one to it so that the terminating NULL is included as well.

With the exception of arrays and objects, the remaining types can also be registered, but because no macros or functions exist in the Zend API to cover these types, you'll have to manually declare the constants. To do this, follow this simple recipe, substituting the appropriate type when you create the `zval*`:

```
void php_sample4_register_boolean_constant(char *name, uint len,
    zend_bool bval, int flags, int module_number TSRMLS_DC)
{
    zend_constant c;

    ZVAL_BOOL(&c.value, bval);
    c.flags = CONST_CS | CONST_PERSISTENT;
    c.name = zend_strndup(name, len - 1);
    c.name_len = len;
    c.module_number = module_number;
    zend_register_constant(&c TSRMLS_CC);
}
```

Extension Globals

If it were possible to guarantee that only one PHP script were ever active in a single process at any given time, your extension could declare any global variables it wanted to and access them with the knowledge that no other script actions will corrupt the values between opcodes. For non-threaded SAPIs, this actually is true because any given process space can only execute one code path at a time.

In the case of threaded SAPIs however, two or more requests could wind up trying to read—or worse write—the same value at once. To combat this problem, the concept of extension globals was introduced to provide a unique bucket of data storage for each extension's data.

Declaring Extension Globals

To request a storage bucket for your extension, you first need to declare all your "global" variables in a unified structure somewhere within your `php_sample4.h` file. For example, if your extension kept track of a counter for the number of times a particular function was called within a request, you might define a structure containing an unsigned long:

```
ZEND_BEGIN_MODULE_GLOBALS(sample4)
    unsigned long counter;
ZEND_END_MODULE_GLOBALS(sample4)
```

The `ZEND_BEGIN_MODULE_GLOBALS` and `ZEND_END_MODULE_GLOBALS` macros provide a consistent framework for defining extension global structs. If you were to look at the expansion of this block, you'd see it was simply:

```
typedef struct _zend_sample4_globals {
    unsigned long counter;
} zend_sample4_globals;
```

Additional members could then be added as you would with any other C struct.
Now that you have a definition for your storage bucket, it's time to declare it within
your extension's `sample4.c` file just after the `#include "php_sample4.h"` statement:

```
ZEND_DECLARE_MODULE_GLOBALS(sample4);
```

Depending on whether thread safety is enabled, this will resolve to one of two forms.
For non–thread-safe builds, such as Apache1, Apache2-prefork, CGI, CLI, and many others, this declares the `zend_sample4_globals` structure as an immediate value within the
true global scope:

```
zend_sample4_globals sample4_globals;
```

This is really no different than any other global scope variable you would declare in any
other single-threaded application. The counter value is accessed directly through
`sample4_globals.counter`. For thread-safe builds, on the other hand, only an integer is
declared, which will later act as a reference to the real data:

```
int sample4_globals_id;
```

Populating this ID means declaring your extension globals to the engine. Using the
information provided, the engine will allocate a block of memory at the spawning of
each new thread for private storage space to be used by the individual requests that
thread services. Add the following block of lines to your `MINIT` function:

```
#ifdef ZTS
    ts_allocate_id(&sample4_globals_id,
                sizeof(zend_sample4_globals),
                NULL, NULL);
#endif
```

Notice that this statement has been wrapped in a set of ifdefs to prevent it from executing when Zend Thread Safety (ZTS) is not enabled. This makes sense because the
`sample4_globals_id` is only declared (or needed) in builds that will be used in a
threaded environment. Non-threaded builds will use the immediate `sample4_globals`
variable declared earlier.

Per-Thread Initializing and Shutdown

In non-threaded builds, only one copy of your `zend_sample4_globals` struct will ever
exist within a given process. To initialize it, you could assign default values or allocate
resources within `MINIT` or `RINIT` and, if necessary, free those resources during `MSHUTDOWN`
or `RSHUTDOWN` as appropriate.

However, for threaded builds, a new structure is allocated every time a new thread is
spun. In practice, this may occur a dozen times during web server startup alone and hundreds—possibly thousands—of times during the lifetime of the webserver process. In
order to know how to initialize and shut down your extension's globals, the engine

requires a set of callbacks to issue. This is where the NULL parameters you passed to
`ts_allocate_id()` earlier come into play; add the following two methods above your
MINIT function:

```
static void php_sample4_globals_ctor(
            zend_sample4_globals *sample4_globals TSRMLS_DC)
{
    /* Initialize a new zend_sample4_globals struct
     * During thread spin-up */
    sample4_globals->counter = 0;
}
static void php_sample4_globals_dtor(
            zend_sample4_globals *sample4_globals TSRMLS_DC)
{
    /* Any resources allocated during initialization
     * May be freed here */
}
```

Then use those functions for startup and shutdown:

```
PHP_MINIT_FUNCTION(sample4)
{
    REGISTER_STRING_CONSTANT("SAMPLE4_VERSION",
            PHP_SAMPLE4_EXTVER, CONST_CS | CONST_PERSISTENT);
#ifdef ZTS
    ts_allocate_id(&sample4_globals_id,
                sizeof(zend_sample4_globals),
                (ts_allocate_ctor)php_sample4_globals_ctor,
                (ts_allocate_dtor)php_sample4_globals_dtor);
#else
    php_sample4_globals_ctor(&sample4_globals TSRMLS_CC);
#endif
    return SUCCESS;
}
PHP_MSHUTDOWN_FUNCTION(sample4)
{
#ifndef ZTS
    php_sample4_globals_dtor(&sample4_globals TSRMLS_CC);
#endif
    return SUCCESS;
}
```

Notice that the `ctor` and `dtor` functions were called manually when ZTS is not
defined. Don't forget that non-threaded builds need initialization and shutdown too!

Note
You might be wondering why TSRMLS_CC was used for the direct calls to php_sampl4_
globals_ctor() and php_sample4_globals_dtor(). If you're thinking "That's completely
unnecessary, those evaluate to nothing at all when ZTS is disabled, and because of the #ifdef directives I
know that ZTS is disabled!", then you're absolutely right. These counterparts to the TSRMLS_DC directives
in the declaration are used purely as a matter of consistency. On the positive side, if the Zend API ever
changes in such a way that these values do become relevant even for non-ZTS builds, your code will be
right and ready to accommodate it.

Accessing Extension Globals

Now that your extension has a set of globals, you can start accessing them in your code.
In non-ZTS mode this is nice and simple; just access the sample4_globals variable in
the process's global scope and use the relevant member such as in the following userspace function which increments the counter you defined earlier and returns its current
value:

```
PHP_FUNCTION(sample4_counter)
{
    RETURN_LONG(++sample4_globals.counter);
}
```

Nice and clean. Unfortunately, this approach won't work with threaded PHP builds. For
these, you'll need to do a lot more work. Here's that function's return statement again,
this time using ZTS semantics:

```
    RETURN_LONG(++TSRMG(sample4_globals_id,
                   zend_sample4_globals*, counter));
```

The TSRMG() macro takes that TSRMLS_CC parameter you've been passing around ad
infinitum to find the current thread's pool of resource structures. From there, it uses the
sample4_globals_id index to map into the specific point in that pool where your
extension's specific global structure is. Finally, it uses the data type to map the element
name to an offset within that structure. Because you typically don't know whether your
extension will be used in ZTS or non-ZTS mode, you'll need to accommodate both. To
do that, you could rewrite the function like so:

```
PHP_FUNCTION(sample4_counter)
{
#ifdef ZTS
    RETURN_LONG(++TSRMG(sample4_globals_id, \
                   zend_sample4_globals*, counter));
#else /* non-ZTS */
    RETURN_LONG(++sample4_globals.counter);
#endif
}
```

Look ugly? It is. Imagine your entire codebase peppered with these `ifdef` directives every time a thread-safe global is accessed. It'd look worse than Perl! This is why all core extensions, as well as those found in PECL, use an extra macro layer to abstract this case out. Drop the following definition into your `php_sample4.h` file:

```
#ifdef ZTS
#include "TSRM.h"
#define SAMPLE4_G(v)     TSRMG(sample4_globals_id,
                             zend_sample4_globals*, v)
#else
#define SAMPLE4_G(v)     (sample4_globals.v)
#endif
```

Then replace your new function definition with this simpler, more legible form:

```
PHP_FUNCTION(sample4_counter)
{
    RETURN_LONG(++SAMPLE4_G(counter));
}
```

Does that macro strike a sense of deja vu? It should. It's the same concept and practice that you've already seen when working with `EG(symbol_table)` and `EG(active_symbol_table)`. While looking through various parts of the PHP source tree and other extensions, you'll come across this kind of macro frequently. A few common global access macros are listed in Table 12.1.

Table 12.1 **Common Global Access Macros**

Accessor Macro	Associated Data
EG()	Executor Globals. This structure is primarily used by the engine internals to track the state of the current request. Information such as symbol tables, function and class tables, constants, and resources can be found here.
CG()	Core Globals. Used primarily by the Zend Engine during script compilation and an assortment of deep-core execution steps. It's rare that your extension will examine these values directly.
PG()	PHP Globals. Most of the "Core" php.ini directives map to one or more elements of the php globals structure. PG(register_globals), PG(safe_mode), and PG(memory_limit) are just a few examples.
FG()	File Globals. Most file I/O—or streams—related global variables are tucked into this structure exported by the standard extension.

Userspace Superglobals

The userspace world has its own, completely unrelated notion of globality. Even here, a kind of "special" global variable exists known commonly as a *superglobal*. These unique types of userspace variables, which include $_GET, $_POST, $_FILE, and several others, may be accessed from the global scope, or within functions or methods as though they were local to that scope.

Because of the way that superglobal variables are resolved, they must be declared prior to script compilation. What this means for ordinary scripts is that they may not declare additional variables as being superglobal. For extensions, however, it's possible to declare the variable name as being a superglobal before any requests have even been received.

A prime example of an extension that declares its own superglobal is ext/session, which uses the $_SESSION superglobal variable to store session information between calls to session_start() and session_write_close()—or the end of the script, whichever comes first. To declare $_SESSION as a superglobal, the sessions extension executes this simple one-time statement within its MINIT method:

```
PHP_MINIT_FUNCTION(session)
{
    zend_register_auto_global("_SESSION",
                        sizeof("_SESSION") - 1,
                        NULL TSRMLS_CC);
    return SUCCESS;
}
```

Notice here that the second parameter, referring to the length of the variable name, uses sizeof()-1 to exclude the terminating NULL. This is an about-face from most of the internal calls you've seen so far, so be careful not to get bit by it when declaring your own variables.

The prototype for the zend_register_auto_global() function in Zend Engine 2 looks like the following:

```
int zend_register_auto_global(char *name, uint name_len,
    zend_auto_global_callback auto_global_callback TSRMLS_DC)
```

In Zend Engine 1, the auto_global_callback parameter did not exist. In order to make your extension compatible with legacy installations of PHP4, you'll need to throw in an #ifdef block like the following MINIT method declaring a $_SAMPLE4 autoglobal:

```
PHP_MINIT_FUNCTION(sample4)
{
    zend_register_auto_global("_SAMPLE4", sizeof("_SAMPLE4") - 1
#ifdef ZEND_ENGINE_2
                        , NULL
#endif
                        TSRMLS_CC);
    return SUCCESS;
}
```

Auto Global Callback

The `auto_global_callback` parameter to ZE2's `zend_register_auto_global` is a
pointer to a custom function that will be triggered any time the engine encounters your
superglobal within a userspace script during the compilation phase. In practice, this
could be used to avoid complex initialization routines unless it's known that the variable
actually will be accessed by the current script. Consider the following setup:

```
zend_bool php_sample4_autoglobal_callback(char *name,
                             uint name_len TSRMLS_DC)
{
    zval *sample4_val;
    int i;

    MAKE_STD_ZVAL(sample4_val);
    array_init(sample4_val);
    for(i = 0; i < 10000; i++) {
        add_next_index_long(sample4_val, i);
    }
    ZEND_SET_SYMBOL(&EG(symbol_table), "_SAMPLE4",
                                    sample4_val);
    return 0;
}
PHP_MINIT_FUNCTION(sample4)
{
    zend_register_auto_global("_SAMPLE4", sizeof("_SAMPLE4") - 1
#ifdef ZEND_ENGINE_2
                        , php_sample4_autoglobal_callback
#endif
                        TSRMLS_CC);
    return SUCCESS;
}
```

The work being done by `php_sample4_autoglobal_callback` represents quite a bit
of memory allocation and CPU time which, if the `$_SAMPLE4` variable were never
accessed, would be completely wasted. In this Zend Engine 2 scenario, however, the
`php_sample4_autoglobal_callback` function is only ever called if the `$_SAMPLE4` variable is accessed at some point within the script being compiled. Notice that the function
returns a zero value once the array is initialized and added to the request's symbol table.
This is to "disarm" the callback for the remainder of the request and ensure that additional uses of the `$_SAMPLE4` variable do not call this function multiple times. If your
extension wanted its callback issued for each time your superglobal variable was encountered, it could simply return a truth (non-zero) value instead thus leaving the superglobal
"armed."

Unfortunately, this design is now broken with respect to PHP4 and Zend Engine 1
because this earlier model did not support autoglobal callbacks. In this case, you'll need

to wastefully initialize the variable at the start of each script whether it uses the variable or not. To do so, simply invoke the callback function you've already written from your RINIT method like so:

```
PHP_RINIT_FUNCTION(sample4)
{
#ifndef ZEND_ENGINE_2
    php_sample4_autoglobal_callback("_SAMPLE4",
                          sizeof("_SAMPLE4") - 1,
                          TSRMLS_CC);
#endif
    return SUCCESS;
}
```

Summary

You encountered several new—yet familiar—concepts through the course of this chapter including the internal notion of a thread-safe global variable, and how to expose user-space utilities such as constants, pre-initialized variables, and superglobal variables. In the next chapter, you'll discover how to declare and resolve php.ini values and even tie them to the internal thread-safe global structures you just set up.

13

INI Settings

LIKE SUPERGLOBALS AND PERSISTENT CONSTANTS, which you saw in the last chapter, php.ini values must be declared within an extensions MINIT code block. Unlike these other features however, the INI option declaration consists of nothing more than one simple line for startup, and another for shutdown:

```
PHP_MINIT_FUNCTION(sample4)
{
    REGISTER_INI_ENTRIES();
    return SUCCESS;
}
PHP_MSHUTDOWN_FUNCTION(sample4)
{
    UNREGISTER_INI_ENTRIES();
    return SUCCESS;
}
```

Declaring and Accessing INI Settings

The INI entries themselves are defined in a completely separate block located elsewhere in the same source file above the MINIT block using the following pair of macros, with one or more entries placed between them:

```
PHP_INI_BEIGN()
PHP_INI_END()
```

These macros function in much the same way as the ZEND_BEGIN_MODULE_GLOBALS() and ZEND_END_MODULE_GLOBALS() macros from last chapter do. Instead of providing a struct typedef however, these frame the declaration of a static data instance. Here's that pair again, expanded out:

```
static zend_ini_entry ini_entries[] = {
{0,0,NULL,0,NULL,NULL,NULL,NULL,NULL,0,NULL,0,0,NULL} };
```

As you can see, this defines a vector of zend_ini_entry values terminated by an empty record. This is the same approach to populating static vectors that you've seen repeatedly in the declaration of function_entry structures.

Simple INI Settings

Now that you have an INI structure for declaring entries, and the mechanisms in place to register and unregister settings with the engine, it's time to actually declare some settings that will be useful to your extension.

Assuming your extension exported a simple greeting function—like the one you first saw back in Chapter 5, "Your First Extension,"—you might decide that you wanted to make that greeting customizable:

```
PHP_FUNCTION(sample4_hello_world)
{
    php_printf("Hello World!\n");
}
```

The most straightforward approach will be to define an INI setting, giving it the default value of "Hello World!" like so:

```
#include "php_ini.h"
PHP_INI_BEGIN()
    PHP_INI_ENTRY("sample4.greeting", "Hello World",
                            PHP_INI_ALL, NULL)
PHP_INI_END()
```

As you can probably guess, the first two parameters to this macro represent the name of the INI setting and its default value respectively. The third parameter determines when the engine will allow the setting to be changed and will be covered in the section on access levels later in this chapter. The last parameter takes a pointer to a callback function that is triggered any time the INI value is changed. You'll see this parameter in detail in the section on modification events.

Now that your INI setting has been declared, you're ready to use it in your greeting function:

```
PHP_FUNCTION(sample4_hello_world)
{
    const char *greeting = INI_STR("sample4.greeting");
    php_printf("%s\n", greeting);
}
```

It's important to note that char* values are considered to be owned by the engine and must not be modified. Because of this, the local variable you populated the INI setting into was declared as const within your function. Not all INI values are string-based of course; additional macros exist for retrieving integer, floating-point, or Boolean values:

```
long lval = INI_INT("sample4.intval");
double dval = INI_FLT("sample4.fltval");
zend_bool bval = INI_BOOL("sample4.boolval");
```

Usually you'll want to know the current value of your INI setting; however, a complementing set of macros exist for each type that reveal the original, unmodified INI setting.

```
const char *strval = INI_ORIG_STR("sample4.stringval");
long lval = INI_ORIG_INT("sample4.intval");
double dval = INI_ORIG_FLT("sample4.fltval");
zend_bool bval = INI_ORIG_BOOL("sample4.boolval");
```

Note

In this example, the name of the INI entry "sample4.greeting" was prefixed with the extension name to help guarantee that it won't collide with other INI settings exported by different extensions. This prefixing is not a requirement for private extensions, but is considered a courtesy for any publicly released extension whether commercial or open source.

Access Levels

A given INI value will always start out with a default value. In many cases, that default value is perfectly reasonable to keep; however, these values often need to be modified for a particular environment, or for a particular action within a script. Such setting modifications can occur at any of three distinct points, as shown in Table 13.1.

Table 13.1

Access Level	Meaning
SYSTEM	Settings placed in the php.ini, or outside of <Directory> and <VirtualHost> directives within Apache's httpd.conf configuration file take effect during the engine startup stage and are considered the setting's "global" value.
PERDIR	Any setting found in a <Directory> or <VirtualHost> block within Apache's httpd.conf, or settings located in .htaccess files—as well as certain other locations not exclusive to Apache—are processed just prior to a given request if that request is within the appropriate directory or virtual host.
USER	Once script execution has begun, the only INI changes left to perform are those in response to calls to the userspace function: ini_set().

Certain settings, such as safe_mode, would be useless if they could be modified at any point in time. For example, a malicious script author could simply disable safe_mode, and then read or modify an otherwise disallowed file.

Similarly, some non-security related settings such as `register_globals` or `magic_quotes_gpc` cannot be effectively changed within a script because the point at which they bear relevance has already passed.

Access to change these settings is controlled through the third parameter to `PHP_INI_ENTRY()`. In your setting declaration, you have `PHP_INI_ALL`, which is defined as a bitwise OR combination of `PHP_INI_SYSTEM | PHP_INI_PERDIR | PHP_INI_USER`.

Settings such as `register_globals` and `magic_quotes_gpc` are, in turn, declared with access values of `PHP_INI_SYSTEM | PHP_INI_PERDIR`. The exclusion of `PHP_INI_USER` results in any call to `ini_set()` for these settings ending in failure.

As you can probably guess by now, settings such as `safe_mode` and `open_basedir` are declared with only `PHP_INI_SYSTEM`. This setting ensures that only the system administrators may modify these values as only they have access to modify `php.ini` or `httpd.conf` values.

Modification Events

Whenever an INI setting is modified, either through the use of the `ini_set()` function or during processing of a `perdir` directive, the engine examines the INI setting for an `OnModify` callback. Modification handlers may be defined using the `ZEND_INI_MH()` macro, and then attached to an INI setting by passing the method name in the `OnModify` parameter:

```
ZEND_INI_MH(php_sample4_modify_greeting)
{
    if (new_value_length == 0) {
        return FAILURE;
    }
    return SUCCESS;
}
PHP_INI_BEGIN()
    PHP_INI_ENTRY("sample4.greeting", "Hello World",
            PHP_INI_ALL, php_sample4_modify_greeting)
PHP_INI_END()
```

By returning `FAILURE` when `new_value_length` is zero, this Modify Handler prohibits setting a blank string as the greeting. The entire prototype generated by using the `ZEND_INI_MH()` macro is as follows (see Table 13.2):

```
int php_sample4_modify_greeting(zend_ini_entry *entry,
    char *new_value, uint new_value_length,
    void *mh_arg1, void *mh_arg2, void *mh_arg3,
    int stage TSRMLS_DC);
```

Table 13.2   **INI Setting Modifier Callback Parameters**

Parameter	Meaning
`entry`	Points to the actual INI setting as stored by the engine. This structure provides information about the current value, original value, owning module, and other details as shown in Listing 13.1.
`new_value`	The value about to be set. If the handler returns `SUCCESS`, this value will be populated into `entry->value` and, if `entry->orig_value` is not yet set, the current value will be rotated into that position and the `entry->modified` flag set. The length of this string is passed in `new_value_length`.
`mh_arg1,2,3`	This triplet of pointers provides access to data pointers initially given in the INI setting's declaration. In practice, these values are used by internal engine processes and you won't need to worry about them.
`stage`	One of five values in the form `ZEND_INI_STAGE_s` where s is `STARTUP`, `SHUTDOWN`, `ACTIVATE`, `DEACTIVATE`, or `RUNTIME`. These constants correspond to `MINIT`, `MSHUTDOWN`, `RINIT`, `RSHUTDOWN`, and active script execution, respectively.

Listing 13.1   **Core structure: zend_ini_entry**

```
struct _zend_ini_entry {
    int module_number;
    int modifiable;
    char *name;
    uint name_length;
    ZEND_INI_MH((*on_modify));
    void *mh_arg1;
    void *mh_arg2;
    void *mh_arg3;

    char *value;
    uint value_length;

    char *orig_value;
    uint orig_value_length;
    int modified;

    void ZEND_INI_DISP(*displayer);
};
```

Displaying INI Settings

In the last chapter, you looked at the `MINFO` method and related infrastructure for displaying information about an extension. Because it's very common for extensions to

export INI entries, a unified macro is exported by the engine that can be placed in
`PHP_MINFO_FUNCTION()` blocks:

```
PHP_MINFO_FUNCTION(sample4)
{
    DISPLAY_INI_ENTRIES();
}
```

This macro takes the INI settings already defined between the `PHP_INI_BEGIN` and
`PHP_INI_END` macros and iteratively displays them in a three column table containing the
INI setting's name, it's original (global) setting, and the current setting as modified by
`PERDIR` directives and calls to `ini_set()`.

By default, all entries are simply output according to their string representation as-is.
Some settings, such as Boolean values and color values for syntax highlighting, have
additional formatting applied during the display process. The way this formatting is
applied is through each INI setting's individual display handler, which is a dynamic
pointer to a callback similar to the `OnModify` handler you already saw.

The display handler is specified using an extended version of the `PHP_INI_ENTRY()`
macro, which accepts one additional parameter. If set to `NULL`, the default handler—
which displays the string value as-is—will be used.

```
PHP_INI_ENTRY_EX("sample4.greeting", "Hello World", PHP_INI_ALL,
    php_sample4_modify_greeting, php_sample4_display_greeting)
```

Obviously, this callback then needs to be defined somewhere prior to the INI setting
declaration. As with the `OnModify` callback, this will be done with a wrapper macro and
just a small amount of handler code:

```
#include "SAPI.h" /* needed for sapi_module */
PHP_INI_DISP(php_sample4_display_greeting)
{
    const char *value = ini_entry->value;

    /* Select the current or original value as appropriate */
    if (type == ZEND_INI_DISPLAY_ORIG &&
        ini_entry->modified) {
        value = ini_entry->orig_value;
    }

    /* Make the greeting bold (when HTML output is enabled) */
    if (sapi_module.phpinfo_as_text) {
        php_printf("%s", value);
    } else {
        php_printf("<b>%s</b>", value);
    }
}
```

Binding to Extension Globals

All INI entries are given storage space within the Zend Engine to track changes within scripts and maintain global settings outside of requests. Within this storage space all INI settings are stored as string values. As you already know, these values can be easily translated to scalar values by using the `INI_INT()`, `INI_FLT()`, and `INI_BOOL()` macros.

This lookup and conversion process is horribly inefficient for two reasons: First, every time an INI value is retrieved, it must be located in a hash table by name. This sort of lookup is all well and good for userspace scripts where a given script is only compiled at runtime, but for compiled machine code source, it's pointless to do this work at runtime.

It's even more inefficient for scalar values where the underlying string value must be reconverted every time the scalar value is requested. Using what you already know, you could declare a thread-safe global as your storage medium, and update it with the address of the new value every time it's changed. Then, any code accessing that INI setting can look up the pointer within your thread-safe globals struct and take advantage of compile-time optimizations.

In `php_sample4.h` add `const char *greeting;` to your `MODULE_GLOBALS` struct, and then update the following two methods in `sample4.c`:

```
ZEND_INI_MH(php_sample4_modify_greeting)
{
    /* Disallow empty greetings */
    if (new_value_length == 0) {
        return FAILURE;
    }
    SAMPLE4_G(greeting) = new_value;
    return SUCCESS;
}
PHP_FUNCTION(sample4_hello_world)
{
    php_printf("%s\n", SAMPLE4_G(greeting));
}
```

Because this is a common approach to optimizing INI access, another pair of macros is exported by the engine that handle binding INI settings to global variables.

```
STD_PHP_INI_ENTRY_EX("sample4.greeting", "Hello World",
    PHP_INI_ALL, OnUpdateStringUnempty, greeting,
    zend_sample4_globals, sample4_globals,
    php_sample4_display_greeting)
```

This entry performs the same work as the entry you just had without requiring an `OnModify` callback. Instead, it uses a general purpose modify callback `OnUpdateStringUnempty` along with information about where the storage space it should use is at. To allow empty greetings, you could simply specify the `OnUpdateString` modifier rather than the `OnUpdateStringUnempty` method.

In a similar way, INI settings may be bound to scalar values such as `long`, `double`, and `zend_bool`. Add three more entries to your `MODULE_GLOBALS` struct in `php_sample4.h`:

```
long mylong;
double mydouble;
zend_bool mybool;
```

Now create INI entries in your `PHP_INI_BEGIN()`/`PHP_INI_END()` block using the `STD_PHP_INI_ENTRY()` macro—which only differs from its `_EX` counterpart in the lack of a displayer method—and bind them to your new values:

```
STD_PHP_INI_ENTRY("sample4.longval", "123",
    PHP_INI_ALL, OnUpdateLong, mylong,
    zend_sample4_globals, sample4_globals)
STD_PHP_INI_ENTRY("sample4.doubleval", "123.456",
    PHP_INI_ALL, OnUpdateDouble, mydouble,
    zend_sample4_globals, sample4_globals)
STD_PHP_INI_ENTRY("sample4.boolval", "1",
    PHP_INI_ALL, OnUpdateBool, mybool,
    zend_sample4_globals, sample4_globals)
```

Note that at this point, if `DISPLAY_INI_ENTRIES()` is called, the Boolean INI setting "`sample4.boolval`"—like other INI settings—will be displayed as its string value; however, the preferred output for Boolean settings is the string "on" or "off." To make sure that these display meaningful values, you could either switch to the `STD_PHP_INI_ENTRY_EX()` macro and create a displayer method, or you could use the alternative macro, which does the work for you:

```
STD_PHP_INI_BOOLEAN("sample4.boolval", "1",
    PHP_INI_ALL, OnUpdateBool, mybool,
    zend_sample4_globals *, sample4_globals)
```

This type-specific macro is unique to Booleans within the INI family of macros and only serves to provide a display handler that translates truth values to "on," and non-truth values of "off."

Summary

In this chapter, you explored the implementation of one of the oldest features in the PHP language, and arguably the greatest obstacle to PHP's otherwise robust portability. With every new INI setting available, the obstacles to writing code that can be run anywhere grow more and more complex. Use these features with discretion and extension will be evermore useful; use them carelessly and its behavior from system to system may become too unpredictable to maintain.

In the next three chapters, you'll delve into the streams API, beginning with use and progressing through the implementation layers into stream and wrapper operations, contexts, and filters.

14

Accessing Streams

ALL FILE I/O HANDLED IN PHP USERSPACE is processed through the PHP streams
layer introduced with PHP 4.3. Internally, extension code might opt to use stdio or
posix file handles to communicate with the local file system or berkeley domain sockets,
or it might call into that same API used by userspace stream I/O.

Streams Overview

Often a direct file descriptor will be less CPU- and memory-intensive than calling
through the streams layer; however, it places all the work of implementing a particular
protocol on you as the extension writer. By hooking into the streams layer, your extension code can transparently use any of the built-in stream wrappers such as HTTP, FTP,
and their SSL-enabled counterparts, as well as the gzip and bzip2 compression wrappers.
By including certain PEAR or PECL modules, your code also has access to other protocols such as SSH2, WebDav, and even Gopher!

This chapter will introduce the basic API for working with streams from the internals. Later on, in Chapter 16, "Diverting the Stream," you'll take a look at more
advanced concepts like applying filters and using context options and parameters.

Opening Streams

Despite being a heavily unified API, there are actually four distinct paths to opening a
stream depending on the type of stream required. Looking at it from a userspace perspective, the four categories are differentiated roughly as follows (function lists are repre-
sentative samples, not comprehensive listings):

```php
<?php
    /* fopen wrappers
     * Functions that operate on files or
     * URIs specifying a remote file-like resource */
    $fp = fopen($url, $mode);
```

```
$data = file_get_contents($url);
file_put_contents($url, $data);
$lines = file($url);

/* Transports
 * Socket-based sequential I/O */
$fp = fsockopen($host, $port);
$fp = stream_socket_client($uri);
$fp = stream_socket_server($uri, $options);

/* Directory streams */
$dir = opendir($url);
$files = scandir($url);
$obj = dir($url);

/* "Special" streams */
$fp = tmpfile();
$fp = popen($cmd);
proc_open($cmd, $pipes);
?>
```

No matter which type of stream you'll be opening, they are all stored in a single common structure: php_stream.

Fopen Wrappers

Let's start by simply re-implementing the fopen() function and proceed from there. By now you should be accustomed to creating an extension skeleton; if not, refer back to Chapter 5, "Your First Extension," for the basic structure:

```
PHP_FUNCTION(sample5_fopen)
{
    php_stream *stream;
    char *path, *mode;
    int path_len, mode_len;
    int options = ENFORCE_SAFE_MODE | REPORT_ERRORS;

    if (zend_parse_parameters(ZEND_NUM_ARGS() TSRMLS_CC, "ss",
            &path, &path_len, &mode, &mode_len) == FAILURE) {
        return;
    }
    stream = php_stream_open_wrapper(path, mode, options, NULL);
    if (!stream) {
        RETURN_FALSE;
    }
    php_stream_to_zval(stream, return_value);
}
```

The purpose of `php_stream_open_wrapper()` should be pretty clear right off the bat. `path` specifies a filename or URL to be opened for reading, writing, or both depending on the value of `mode`.

`options` is a set of zero or more flag bits, in this case set to a fixed pair of values described here:

USE_PATH	Relative paths will be applied to the locations specified in the `.ini` option `include_path`. This option is specified by the built-in `fopen()` function when the third parameter is passed as TRUE.
STREAM_USE_URL	When set, only remote URLs will be opened. Wrappers that are not flagged as remote URLs such as file://, php://, compress.zlib://, and compress.bzip2:// will result in failure.
ENFORCE_SAFE_MODE	Despite the naming of this constant, safe mode checks are only truly enforced if this option is set, and the corresponding `safe_mode ini` directive has been enabled. Excluding this option causes `safe_mode` checks to be skipped regardless of the INI setting.
REPORT_ERRORS	If an error is encountered during the opening of the specified resource, an error will only be generated if this flag is passed.
STREAM_MUST_SEEK	Some streams, such as socket transports, are never seekable; others, such as file handles, are only seekable under certain circumstances. If a calling scope specifies this option and the wrapper determines that it cannot guarantee seekability, it will refuse to open the stream.
STREAM_WILL_CAST	If the calling scope will require the stream to be castable to a stdio or posix file descriptor, it should pass this option to the `open_wrapper` function so that it can fail gracefully before I/O operations have begun.
STREAM_ONLY_GET_HEADERS	Indicates that only metadata will be requested from the stream. In practice this is used by the http wrapper to populate the `$http_response_headers` global variable without actually fetching the contents of the remote file.

STREAM_DISABLE_OPEN_BASEDIR	Like the safe_mode check, this option, even when absent, still requires the open_basedir ini option to be enabled for checks to be performed. Specifying it as an option simply allows the default check to be bypassed.
STREAM_OPEN_PERSISTENT	Instructs the streams layer to allocate all internal structures persistently and register the associated resource in the persistent list.
IGNORE_PATH	If not specified, the default include path will be searched. Most URL wrappers ignore this option.
IGNORE_URL	When provided, only local files will be opened by the streams layer. All is_url wrappers will be ignored.

The final NULL parameter could have been a char** that will be initially set to match path and, if the path points to a plainfiles URL, updated to exclude the file:// portion, leaving a simple filepath to be used by traditional filename operations. This parameter is traditionally used by internal engine processes only.

An extended version of php_stream_open_wrapper() also exists:

```
php_stream *php_stream_open_wrapper_ex(char *path,
        char *mode, int options, char **opened_path,
        php_stream_context *context);
```

This last parameter, context, allows for additional control of, and notification from, the wrapper in use. You'll see this parameter in action in Chapter 16.

Transports

Although transport streams are made up of the same component parts as fopen wrapper streams, they're given their own scheme registry and kept apart from the rest of the crowd. In part, this is because of the difference in how they've been traditionally accessed from userspace; however, there are additional implementation factors that are only relevant to socket-based streams.

From your perspective as an extension developer, the process of opening transports is just the same. Take a look at this re-creation of fsockopen():

```
PHP_FUNCTION(sample5_fsockopen)
{
    php_stream *stream;
    char *host, *transport, *errstr = NULL;
    int host_len, transport_len, implicit_tcp = 1, errcode = 0;
    long port = 0;
    int options = ENFORCE_SAFE_MODE;
```

```
int flags = STREAM_XPORT_CLIENT | STREAM_XPORT_CONNECT;
    if (zend_parse_parameters(ZEND_NUM_ARGS() TSRMLS_CC, "s|l",
                            &host, &host_len, &port) == FAILURE) {
        return;
    }
    if (port) {
        int implicit_tcp = 1;
        if (strstr(host, "://")) {
                /* A protocol was specified,
                 * no need to fall back on tcp:// */
            implicit_tcp = 0;
        }
        transport_len = spprintf(&transport, 0, "%s%s:%d",
                implicit_tcp ? "tcp://" : "", host, port);
    } else {
        /* When port isn't specified
         * we can safely assume that a protocol was
         * (e.g. unix:// or udg://) */
        transport = host;
        transport_len = host_len;
    }
    stream = php_stream_xport_create(transport, transport_len,
                            options, flags,
                            NULL, NULL, NULL, &errstr, &errcode);
    if (transport != host) {
        efree(transport);
    }
    if (errstr) {
        php_error_docref(NULL TSRMLS_CC, E_WARNING, "[%d] %s",
                            errcode, errstr);
        efree(errstr);
    }
    if (!stream) {
        RETURN_FALSE;
    }
    php_stream_to_zval(stream, return_value);
}
```

The basic mechanics of this function are the same. All that has changed is that host and port, being specified in different parameters, must be joined together in order to generate a transport URI. After a meaningful "path" is generated, it's passed into the xport_create() function in the same way as fopen() used the open_wrapper() API call. The full prototype for php_stream_xport_create() is described here:

```
php_stream *php_stream_xport_create(char *xport, int xport_len,
                    int options, int flags,
                    const char *persistent_id,
```

```
                          struct timeval *timeout,
                          php_stream_context *context,
                          char **errstr, int *errcode);
```

The meaning of each of these parameters is as follows:

xport	URI-based transport descriptor. For inet socket-based streams this might be `tcp://127.0.0.1:80`, `udp://10.0.0.1:53`, or `ssl://169.254.13.24:445`. Reasonable values might also be `unix:///path/to/socket` or `udg:///path/to/dgramsocket` for UNIX transports. The `xport_len` allows `xport` to specify a binary safe value by explicitly naming the length of the transport string.
options	This value is made up of a bitwise OR'd combination of the same values used by `php_stream_open_wrapper()` documented earlier in this chapter.
flags	Also a bitwise OR'd combination of either `STREAM_XPORT_CLIENT` or `STREAM_XPORT_SERVER` combined with any number of the remaining `STREAM_XPORT_*` constants defined in the next table.
persistent_id	If this transport should persist between requests, the calling scope can provide a keyname to describe the connection. Specifying this value as `NULL` creates a non-persistent connection; specifying a unique string value will attempt to recover an existing transport from the persistent pool, or create a new persistent stream if one does not exist yet.
timeout	How long a connection attempt should block before timing out and returning failure. A value of `NULL` passed here will use the default timeout as specified in the `php.ini`. This parameter has no meaning for server transports.
errstr	If an error occurs while creating, connecting, binding, or listening for the selected transport, the `char*` value passed by reference here will be populated with a descriptive string reporting the cause of the failure. The value of `errstr` should initially point to `NULL`; if it is populated with a value on return, the calling scope is responsible for freeing the memory associated with this string.
errcode	A numeric error code corresponding to the error message returned via `errstr`.

The `STREAM_XPORT_*` family of constants—for use in the `flags` parameter to `php_stream_xport_create()`—are as follows:

STREAM_XPORT_CLIENT	The local end will be establishing a connection to a remote resource via the transport. This flag is usually accompanied by STREAM_XPORT_CONNECT or STREAM_XPORT_CONNECT_ASYNC.
STREAM_XPORT_SERVER	The local end will accept connections from a remote client via the transport. This flag is usually accompanied by STREAM_XPORT_BIND, and often STREAM_XPORT_LISTEN as well.
STREAM_XPORT_CONNECT	A connection to the remote resource should be established as part of the transport creation process. Omitting this flag when creating a client transport is legal, but requires a separate call to php_stream_xport_connect() in this case.
STREAM_XPORT_CONNECT_ASYNC	Attempt to connect to the remote resource, but do not block.
STREAM_XPORT_BIND	Bind the transport to a local resource. When used with server transports this prepares the transport for accepting connections on a particular port, path, or other specific endpoint identifier.
STREAM_XPORT_LISTEN	Listen for inbound connections on the bound transport endpoint. This is typically used with stream-based transports such as tcp://, ssl://, and unix://.

Directory Access

For fopen wrappers that support directory access, such as file:// and ftp://, a third stream opener function can be used as in this re-creation of opendir():

```
PHP_FUNCTION(sample5_opendir)
{
    php_stream *stream;
    char *path;
    int path_len, options = ENFORCE_SAFE_MODE | REPORT_ERRORS;
    if (zend_parse_parameters(ZEND_NUM_ARGS() TSRMLS_CC, "s",
                                    &path, &path_len) == FAILURE) {
        return;
    }
    stream = php_stream_opendir(path, options, NULL);
    if (!stream) {
        RETURN_FALSE;
```

```
    }
    php_stream_to_zval(stream, return_value);
}
```

Once again, a stream is being opened for a particular path description that may be a simple directory name on the local filesystem, or a URL-formatted resource describing a wrapper that supports directory access. We find the options parameter again, which has its usual meaning, and a third parameter—set to NULL here—for passing a php_stream_context.

After the directory stream is open, it's passed out to userspace just like any other file or transport stream.

Special Streams

A few more specialized stream types exist that don't fit cleanly within the fopen/transport/directory molds. Each of these are generated by their own unique API calls:

```
php_stream *php_stream_fopen_tmpfile(void);
php_stream *php_stream_fopen_temporary_file(const char *dir,
                        const char *pfx, char **opened_path);
```

Create a seekable buffer stream that can be written to and read from. Upon closing, any resources temporarily in use by this stream, including all buffers whether in memory or on disk, will be released. Using the latter function in this pair allows the temporary file to be spooled to a specific location with a specifically formatted name. These internal API calls are shadowed by the userspace tmpfile() function.

```
php_stream *php_stream_fopen_from_fd(int fd,
            const char *mode, const char *persistent_id);
php_stream *php_stream_fopen_from_file(FILE *file,
            const char *mode);
php_stream *php_stream_fopen_from_pipe(FILE *file,
        const char *mode);
```

These three API methods take an already opened FILE* resource or file descriptor ID and wrap it in the appropriate stream operations for use with the Streams API. The fd form will not search for a matching persistent id like the earlier fopen methods you're familiar with, but it will register the produced stream as persistent for later opening.

Accessing Streams

After you have a stream opened up, it's time to start performing I/O operations on it. It doesn't matter what protocol wrapper, transport, or "special" API call was used to create the stream; the set of API calls used to access it will be the same.

Reading

Stream reading—and writing—can be performed using any combination of the following API functions, many of which follow the conventions of their POSIX I/O counterparts:

```
int php_stream_getc(php_stream *stream);
```

Retrieve a single character from the data stream. If no more data is available on the stream, EOF is returned instead.

```
size_t php_stream_read(php_stream *stream, char *buf, size_t count);
```

Read a specific number of bytes from the stream. buf must be preallocated to a size of at least count bytes. The function will return the number of bytes actually populated into buf from the data stream.

> **Note**
>
> php_stream_read() differs from other stream read functions in one surprising way. If the stream in use is not a plain files stream, only one call to the underlying stream implementation's read function will be made, even if more data was requested and more is actually available to return. This is a compromise to let packet-based protocols such as UDP function cleanly without blocking.

```
char *php_stream_get_line(php_stream *stream, char *buf,
                          size_t maxlen, size_t *returned_len);
char *php_stream_gets(php_stream *stream, char *buf,
                          size_t maxlen);
```

This code reads from stream up to a maximum of maxlen characters until a newline is encountered or the end of stream is reached. buf might be either a pointer to a preallocated buffer of at least maxlen bytes, or NULL, in which case a dynamically sized buffer will be created to fit the amount of data actually read from the stream. In either case, a pointer to the buffer is returned on success, or NULL on failure. If returned_len is passed with a non-NULL value, it will be populated according to the amount of data read from stream.

```
char *php_stream_get_record(php_stream *stream,
        size_t maxlen, size_t *returned_len,
        char *delim, size_t delim_len
        TSRMLS_DC);
```

Like php_stream_get_line(), this method will read up to maxlen, EOF, or an end or line marker, whichever comes first. Unlike php_stream_get_line(), however, this method allows the specification of an arbitrary marker to stop reading at.

Reading Directory Entries

Reading a directory entry from a PHP stream is, at the end of the day, identical to reading ordinary data from an ordinary file. The trick is that this data is delivered in fixed block sizes called *dirents*, or Directory Entries. Internally a `php_stream_dirent` structure has the following simple format, which is consistent with the POSIX definition of a `dirent struct`:

```
typedef struct _php_stream_dirent {
    char d_name[MAXPATHLEN];
} php_stream_dirent;
```

In practice you could simply read into this `struct` using the `php_stream_read()` method that you've already seen:

```
{
    struct dirent entry;
    if (php_stream_read(stream, (char*)&entry, sizeof(entry))
                              == sizeof(entry)) {
        /* Successfully read an entry from a dirstream */
        php_printf("File: %s\n", entry.d_name);
    }
}
```

Because reading from directory streams is common, the PHP streams layer exposes an API call to handle the record-size checking and typecasting issues in a single call:

```
php_stream_dirent *php_stream_readdir(php_stream *dirstream,
                      php_stream_dirent *entry);
```

If a directory entry is successfully read, the pointer passed in for `entry` will be returned; otherwise, NULL is used to indicate an error condition. It's important to use this purpose-built method rather than attempting to read directly from the directory stream so that future changes to the streams API won't conflict with your code.

Writing

Similar to reading, writing to a stream simply requires passing a buffer and a buffer length to a stream.

```
size_t php_stream_write(php_stream *stream, char *buf,
                                                size_t count);
size_t php_stream_write_string(php_stream *stream, char *stf);
```

The `write_string` version here is actually a convenience macro that allows writing a simple NULL terminated string without having to explicitly provide the length. The actual number of bytes written on the stream will be returned. Take careful note that if an attempt to write a large amount of data would cause the stream to block—such as with a socket stream—and the stream is marked non-blocking, the actual amount of data written may be less that what was passed into the function.

```
int php_stream_putc(php_stream *stream, int c);
int php_stream_puts(php_string *stream, char *buf);
```

Alternatively, `php_stream_putc()` and `php_stream_puts()` may be used to write a character or string of characters to the stream respectively. Note that `php_stream_puts()` differs from `php_stream_write_string()`—which has a nearly identical prototype—in that a newline character will automatically be written to the stream following the value in `buf`.

```
size_t php_stream_printf(php_stream *stream TSRMLS_DC,
                                    const char *format, ...);
```

Similar to `fprintf()` in form and function, this API call allows easy writing of compound strings without having to create temporary buffers to construct the data in. The one obvious difference to watch out for is the atypical addition of the `TSRMLS_CC` macro needed for thread safety.

Seeking, Telling, and Flushing

File-based streams, as well as a few other stream types, are capable of random access. That is, after reading data in one portion of the stream, the file pointer can be sought backwards or forwards within the data to read another section in a nonlinear order.

If your streams-using code expects the underlying stream to support seeking, it should pass the `STREAM_MUST_SEEK` option during opening. For streams where seekability is available, this will usually—but not always—have no net effect because the stream would have been seekable anyway. For non-seekable streams, such as network I/O or linear access files such as FIFO pipes, this hint allows the calling program a chance to fail more gracefully, before the stream's data has been consumed or acted upon.

After you have a working, seekable stream resource, the following call serves to seek to an arbitrary location:

```
int php_stream_seek(php_stream *stream,off_t offset,int whence);
int php_stream_rewind(php_stream *stream);
```

`offset` is a byte count relative to the stream location indicated by `whence` that can be any of the following three values:

SEEK_SET	`offset` is relative to the beginning of the file. The `php_stream_rewind()` API call is actually a macro that resolves to `php_stream_seek(stream, 0, SEEK_SET)` indicating zero bytes from the beginning of the file. Passing a negative value for `offset` when using SEEK_SET is considered an error and will result in undefined behavior. Seeking past the end of the stream is also undefined but usually results in an error or the file being enlarged to satisfy the offset specified.
SEEK_CUR	`offset` is relative to the current position within the file. Calling `php_stream_seek(stream, offset, SEEK_CUR)` is generally equivalent to `php_stream_seek(stream, php_stream_tell() + offset, SEEK_SET)`.

SEEK_END   offset is relative to the current EOF location. offset values
                                should usually be negative to indicate some position prior to
                                EOF; however, positive values might work for certain stream
                                implementations according to the same semantics as described
                                for SEEK_SET.

```
int php_stream_rewinddir(php_stream *dirstream);
```

When seeking on directory streams, only the php_stream_rewinddir() method should
be used. Using the underlying php_stream_seek() method will result in undefined
behavior. All seek family functions just mentioned return either 0 to indicate success, or
-1 to indicate failure.

```
off_t php_stream_tell(php_stream *stream);
```

As you saw a moment ago, php_stream_tell() will return the current offset from the
beginning of the file in bytes.

```
int php_stream_flush(php_stream *stream);
```

Calling the flush() method will force any data held by internal buffers such as stream
filters to be output to the final resource. Upon closing a stream resource, the flush()
method is called automatically, and most unfiltered stream resources perform no internal
buffering that would require flushing. Explicitly calling this method is therefore uncommon and usually not needed.

```
int php_stream_stat(php_stream *stream,php_stream_statbuf *ssb);
```

Additional information about a stream instance can be obtained using the
php_stream_stat() call, which behaves similarly to the fstat() function. In fact, the
php_stream_statbuf structure currently only contains one element: struct statbuf
sb; therefore, the php_stream_stat() call can be dropped directly in place of a traditional fstat() operation as in the following example, which translates a posix stat operation into a streams compatible one:

```
int php_sample4_fd_is_fifo(int fd)
{
    struct statbuf sb;
    fstat(fd, &sb);
    return S_ISFIFO(sb.st_mode);
}
int php_sample4_stream_is_fifo(php_stream *stream)
{
    php_stream_statbuf ssb;
    php_stream_stat(stream, &ssb);
    return S_ISFIFO(ssb.sb.st_mode);
}
```

Closing

All stream closing is handled through the `php_stream_free()` method, which has the following prototype:

```
int php_stream_free(php_stream *stream, int options);
```

The permitted values for `options` in this method call are a bitwise OR combination of `PHP_STREAM_FREE_f` values, where f is one of the following:

CALL_DTOR	The stream implementation's destructor method should be called. This provides an opportunity for any resources specific to the stream type to be explicitly freed.
RELEASE_STREAM	Free the memory allocated for the `php_stream` structure.
PRESERVE_HANDLE	Instruct the stream's destructor method to not close its underlying descriptor handle.
RSRC_DTOR	Used internally by the streams layer to manage the resource list garbage collection.
PERSISTENT	When used on a persistent stream, actions will be permanent and not localized to the current request.
CLOSE	Combination of CALL_DTOR and RELEASE_STREAM. This is the normal `options` value for closing a non-persistent stream.
CLOSE_CASTED	Combination of CLOSE options plus PRESERVE_HANDLE.
CLOSE_PERSISTENT	Combination of CLOSE options plus the PERSISTENT flag. This is the normal `options` value for closing persistent streams permanently.

In practice, you'll never need to call the `php_stream_free()` method directly. Instead, you'll use one of the following two macros when closing your stream:

```
#define php_stream_close(stream) \
    php_stream_free((stream), PHP_STREAM_FREE_CLOSE)
#define php_stream_pclose(stream) \
    php_stream_free((stream), PHP_STREAM_FREE_CLOSE_PERSISTENT)
```

Exchanging Streams for `zvals`

Because streams are often mapped to `zvals` and vice versa, a set of macros exists to make the operations cleaner, simpler, and more uniform:

```
#define php_stream_to_zval(stream, pzval) \
    ZVAL_RESOURCE((pzval), (stream)->rsrc_id);
```

Notice here that `ZEND_REGISTER_RESOURCE()` was not called. This is because when the stream was opened it was automatically registered as a resource, thus taking advantage of the engine's built-in garbage collection and shutdown system. It's important that you use this macro rather than attempting to manually (re)register the stream as a new resource ID; doing so will ultimately result in the stream being closed twice and the engine crashing.

```
#define php_stream_from_zval(stream, ppzval) \
    ZEND_FETCH_RESOURCE2((stream), php_stream*, (ppzval), \
    -1, "stream", php_file_le_stream(), php_file_le_pstream())
#define php_stream_from_zval_no_verify(stream, ppzval) \
    (stream) = (php_stream*)zend_fetch_resource((ppzval) \
    TSRMLS_CC, -1, "stream", NULL, 2, \
    php_file_le_stream(), php_file_le_pstream())
```

Fetching the `php_stream*` back from a passed-in `zval*` uses a similar macro. As you can see, this macro simply wraps the resource fetching functions that you're already familiar with from Chapter 9, "The Resource Data Type." You'll recall that the `ZEND_FETCH_RESOURCE2()` macro, which is wrapped in the first `php_stream_from_zval()` macro, will throw a warning and attempt to return from a function implementation if the resource type does not match. If you'll be fetching a `php_stream*` from a passed `zval*` but don't want the automatic error handling, be sure to use `php_stream_from_zval_no_verify()` and check the resulting value manually instead.

Static Stream Operations

Some streams-based actions perform atomic operations and don't require an active instance. The following API calls perform these actions using only a URL:

```
int php_stream_stat_path(char *path, php_stream_statbuf *ssb);
```

Like `php_stream_stat()` earlier, this method provides a protocol-independent wrapper around a more familiar posix function—in this case, `stat()`. Note that not all protocols support the notion of stating a URL, and those that do will not always report values for some portions of the `statbuf` structure. Be sure to check the return value of `php_stream_stat_path()` for failure—zero would indicate success—and be aware that unsupported elements will contain the default value of zero.

```
int php_stream_stat_path_ex(char *path, int flags,
        php_stream_statbuf *ssb, php_stream_context *context);
```

This extended version of `php_stream_url_stat()` allows two additional parameters to be passed. The first is `flags`, which specifies any combination of the following `PHP_STREAM_URL_STAT_*` bitmask flags. You'll also notice the addition of a `context` parameter, which appears in several other streams functions. You'll see this soon enough in Chapter 16.

LINK   Ordinarily `php_stream_stat_path()` will follow all symbolic links or
            redirections until it reaches a protocol-defined end resource. Passing
            the `PHP_STREAM_URL_STAT_LINK` flag will cause

`php_stream_stat_path()` to return information about the specific resource requested without following symlinks or redirections.

QUIET   By default, errors encountered during the process of performing a URL stat operation, including file-not-found errors, will be triggered through the PHP error-handling chain. Passing the QUIET flag will ensure that `php_stream_stat_path()` returns without reporting errors.

```
int php_stream_mkdir(char *path, int mode, int options,
                        php_stream_context *context);
int php_stream_rmdir(char *path, int options,
                        php_stream_context *context);
```

Creating and removing directories works just as you'd expect. The options parameter here refers to the same options parameter described earlier for the php_stream_open_ wrapper() method. In the case of php_stream_mkdir(), an additional mode parameter is used to specify the classic octal mode value for read, write, and execute permissions.

Summary

In this chapter you've started to scratch the surface of working with streams-based I/O from an internals perspective. The next chapter will demonstrate how to implement your own protocol wrappers, and even define your own stream type.

15

Implementing Streams

ONE OF THE MOST POWERFUL FEATURES ABOUT PHP streams is their ability to access a multitude of data sources—plainfile, compressed file, clear-channel network, encrypted network, named pipes, and domain sockets to name a few—from a single, unified API at both the userspace and internals layers.

PHP Streams Below the Surface

A given stream instance "knows," for example, that it's a file stream as opposed to a network stream based on the ops element of the php_stream record returned by one of the stream creation functions you used last chapter:

```
typedef struct _php_stream {
    ...
    php_stream_ops *ops;
    ...
} php_stream;
```

The php_stream_ops struct, in turn, is defined as a collection of method pointers and a descriptive label:

```
typedef struct _php_stream_ops {
    size_t (*write)(php_stream *stream, const char *buf,
                        size_t count TSRMLS_DC);
    size_t (*read)(php_stream *stream, char *buf,
                        size_t count TSRMLS_DC);
    int    (*close)(php_stream *stream, int close_handle
                        TSRMLS_DC);
    int    (*flush)(php_stream *stream TSRMLS_DC);

    const char *label;

    int (*seek)(php_stream *stream, off_t offset, int whence,
```

```
                              off_t *newoffset TSRMLS_DC);
      int (*cast)(php_stream *stream, int castas, void **ret
                              TSRMLS_DC);
      int (*stat)(php_stream *stream, php_stream_statbuf *ssb
                              TSRMLS_DC);
      int (*set_option)(php_stream *stream, int option,int value,
                              void *ptrparam TSRMLS_DC);
} php_stream_ops;
```

When a stream access method such as `php_stream_read()` is called, the streams layer actually resolves the corresponding method in the `stream->ops` structure to call that stream type's specific read implementation function. For example, the implementation of the read function in the plainfiles stream ops structure looks like a slightly more complex version of the following:

```
size_t php_stdio_read(php_stream *stream, char *buf,
                              size_t count TSRMLS_DC)
{
    php_stdio_stream_data *data =
                (php_stdio_stream_data*)stream->abstract;
    return read(data->fd, buf, count);
}
```

Whereas `compress.zlib` streams use an ops struct that points at something roughly along the lines of this read method:

```
size_t php_zlib_read(php_stream *stream, char *buf,
                              size_t count TSRMLS_DC)
{
    struct php_gz_stream_data_t *data =
            (struct php_gz_stream_data_t *) stream->abstract;

    return gzread(data->gz_file, buf, count);
}
```

The first thing to notice here is that the method referenced by the ops structure's function pointer often only has to serve as a thin proxy around the underlying data source's true read method. In the case of these two examples, stdio streams find their way to the posix `read()` function, whereas `zlib` streams are routed into a call to libz's `gzread()` method.

You probably also noticed the `stream->abstract` element being used. This is a convenience pointer that stream implementations can use to carry around any relevant bound information. In these cases, pointers to custom structures are used to store the file descriptor used by the underlying read function.

One more thing you might have noticed is that each of the methods in the `php_stream_ops` structure expect an existing stream instance, but how does a given stream get instantiated? How does that abstract element get populated and when is a stream instructed what ops structure it will be using? The answer lies in the name of the first method you used to open a stream last chapter: `php_stream_open_wrapper()`.

When this method is called, the PHP streams layer attempts to determine what protocol is being requested based on the `scheme://` designation used in the passed URL. From there it looks up the corresponding `php_stream_wrapper` entry in PHP's wrapper registry. Each `php_stream_wrapper` structure, in turn, carries its own ops element pointing at a `php_stream_wrapper_ops` struct with the following type definition:

```
typedef struct _php_stream_wrapper_ops {
    php_stream *(*stream_opener)(php_stream_wrapper *wrapper,
                       char *filename, char *mode,
                       int options, char **opened_path,
                       php_stream_context *context
                       STREAMS_DC TSRMLS_DC);
    int (*stream_closer)(php_stream_wrapper *wrapper,
                       php_stream *stream TSRMLS_DC);
    int (*stream_stat)(php_stream_wrapper *wrapper,
                       php_stream *stream,
                       php_stream_statbuf *ssb
                       TSRMLS_DC);
    int (*url_stat)(php_stream_wrapper *wrapper,
                       char *url, int flags,
                       php_stream_statbuf *ssb,
                       php_stream_context *context
                       TSRMLS_DC);
    php_stream *(*dir_opener)(php_stream_wrapper *wrapper,
                       char *filename, char *mode,
                       int options, char **opened_path,
                       php_stream_context *context
                       STREAMS_DC TSRMLS_DC);

    const char *label;

    int (*unlink)(php_stream_wrapper *wrapper, char *url,
                       int options,
                       php_stream_context *context
                       TSRMLS_DC);

    int (*rename)(php_stream_wrapper *wrapper,
                       char *url_from, char *url_to,
                       int options,
                       php_stream_context *context
                       TSRMLS_DC);

    int (*stream_mkdir)(php_stream_wrapper *wrapper,
                       char *url, int mode, int options,
```

```
                        php_stream_context *context
                        TSRMLS_DC);
    int (*stream_rmdir)(php_stream_wrapper *wrapper, char *url,
                        int options,
                        php_stream_context *context
                        TSRMLS_DC);
} php_stream_wrapper_ops;
```

From here, the streams layer calls into `wrapper->ops->stream_opener()`, which performs the wrapper-specific operations to create a stream instance, assign the appropriate `php_stream_ops` structure, and bind any relevant abstract data.

The `dir_opener()` method serves the same basic purpose as `stream_opener()`; however, it's called in response to an API call to `php_stream_opendir()`, and typically binds a different `php_stream_ops` struct to the returned instance. The `stat()` and `close()` methods are duplicated at this layer in order to allow the wrapper to add protocol-specific logic to these operations.

The remaining methods allow static stream operations to be performed without actually creating a stream instance. Recall that their streams API calls don't actually return a `php_stream` object. You'll see them in more detail in just a moment.

> **Note**
>
> Although `url_stat` existed internally as a wrapper ops method when the streams layer was introduced in PHP 4.3, it was not used by the core until PHP 5.0. In addition, the last three methods, `rename()`, `stream_mkdir()`, and `stream_rmdir()`, were not introduced until PHP 5.0 and thus are not part of the wrapper op structure until this version.

Wrapper Operations

With the exception of the `url_stat()` method, each of the wrapper operations located prior to the `const char *label` element are used with active stream instances. The purpose of each of these methods are as follows:

`stream_opener()`	Instantiates a stream instance. This method is called when one of the `fopen()` userspace functions is called. The `php_stream` instance returned by this function is the internal representation of a file handle resource such as what is returned by `fopen()`. All-in-one functions like `file()`, `file_get_contents()`, `file_put_contents()`, `readfile()`, and too many others to enumerate also use this wrapper ops method when a wrapped resource is requested.
`stream_closer()`	Called when a stream instance is shutting down. Any resources allocated by `stream_opener()` should be freed during this phase.

`stream_stat()`	Analogous to the userspace `fstat()` function, this method should fill the `ssb` structure—which in practice only contains a `struct statbuf sb;` element.
`dir_opener()`	Behaves in the same way as `stream_opener()`, except that it's called in response to the `opendir()` family of userspace functions. The underlying stream implementation used by the directory streams follows the same basic rules as file streams; however, a directory stream only needs to return `struct dirent`-sized records containing the filename found in the opened directory.

Static Wrapper Operations

The remainder of the wrapper op methods perform atomic operations on URI paths according to the semantics of their protocol wrapper. Only `url_stat()` and `unlink()` existed in the PHP 4.3 `php_stream_wrapper_ops` structure; the remaining methods were defined in PHP 5.0 and should be excluded through appropriate `#ifdef` blocks.

`url_stat()`	Used by the `stat()` family of functions to return file metadata such as access permissions, size, and type; also used to access, modify, and create dates. Although this function appears in the `php_stream_wrapper_ops` structure all the way back to PHP 4.3 when the streams layer was introduced, it was never executed by the userspace `stat()` functions until PHP 5.0.
`unlink()`	Named according to posix filesystem semantics, an `unlink()` almost always refers to file deletion. If deletion does not make sense for the current wrapper, such as the built-in `http://` wrapper, this method should be defined to NULL, allowing the core to issue an appropriate error message.
`rename()`	When both the `$from` and `$to` parameters to the userspace `rename()` function refer to the same underlying wrapper, PHP will dispatch the rename request to that wrapper's rename method.
`mkdir()` & `rmdir()`	These two methods map directly to their userspace counterparts.

Implementing a Wrapper

To illustrate the internal workings of wrappers and stream operations, you'll be reimplementing the `var://` wrapper described in the PHP manual's `stream_wrapper_register()` page.

This time, start with the following, fully functional, variable stream wrapper implementation. Once built, you can start examining the workings of each individual piece (see Listings 14.1, 14.2, and 14.3).

Listing 14.1 `config.m4`

```
PHP_ARG_ENABLE(varstream,whether to enable varstream support,
[  —enable-varstream       Enable varstream support])

if test "$PHP_VARSTREAM" = "yes"; then
  AC_DEFINE(HAVE_VARSTREAM,1,[Whether you want varstream])
  PHP_NEW_EXTENSION(varstream, varstream.c, $ext_shared)
fi
```

Listing 14.2 `php_varstream.h`

```
#ifdef HAVE_CONFIG_H
#include "config.h"
#endif

#include "php.h"

#define PHP_VARSTREAM_EXTNAME      "varstream"
#define PHP_VARSTREAM_EXTVER       "1.0"

/* Will be registered as var:// */
#define PHP_VARSTREAM_WRAPPER      "var"
#define PHP_VARSTREAM_STREAMTYPE   "varstream"

extern zend_module_entry varstream_module_entry;
#define phpext_varstream_ptr &varstream_module_entry

typedef struct _php_varstream_data {
    off_t position;
    char *varname;
    int varname_len;
} php_varstream_data;
```

Listing 14.3 `varstream.c`

```
#include "php_varstream.h"
#include "ext/standard/url.h"

/* Define the stream operations */

static size_t php_varstream_write(php_stream *stream,
            const char *buf, size_t count TSRMLS_DC)
```

Listing 14.3   **Continued**

```
{
    php_varstream_data *data = stream->abstract;
    zval **var;
    size_t newlen;

    /* Fetch variable */
    if (zend_hash_find(&EG(symbol_table), data->varname,
            data->varname_len + 1,(void**)&var) == FAILURE) {
        /* $var doesn't exist,
         * Simply create it as a string
         * holding the new contents */
        zval *newval;
        MAKE_STD_ZVAL(newval);
        ZVAL_STRINGL(newval, buf, count, 1);
        /* Store new zval* in $var */
        zend_hash_add(&EG(symbol_table), data->varname,
            data->varname_len + 1, (void*)&newval,
            sizeof(zval*), NULL);
        return count;
    }
    /* Make the variable writable if necessary */
    SEPARATE_ZVAL_IF_NOT_REF(var);
    convert_to_string_ex(var);
    if (data->position > Z_STRLEN_PP(var)) {
        data->position = Z_STRLEN_PP(var);
    }
    newlen = data->position + count;
    if (newlen < Z_STRLEN_PP(var)) {
        /* Total length stays the same */
        newlen = Z_STRLEN_PP(var);
    } else if (newlen > Z_STRLEN_PP(var)) {
        /* Resize the buffer to hold new contents */
        Z_STRVAL_PP(var) =erealloc(Z_STRVAL_PP(var),newlen+1);
        /* Update string length */
        Z_STRLEN_PP(var) = newlen;
        /* Make sure string winds up NULL terminated */
        Z_STRVAL_PP(var)[newlen] = 0;
    }
    /* Write new data into $var */
    memcpy(Z_STRVAL_PP(var) + data->position, buf, count);
    data->position += count;

    return count;
}

static size_t php_varstream_read(php_stream *stream,
            char *buf, size_t count TSRMLS_DC)
```

Listing 14.3 **Continued**

```
{
    php_varstream_data *data = stream->abstract;
    zval **var, copyval;
    int got_copied = 0;
    size_t toread = count;

    if (zend_hash_find(&EG(symbol_table), data->varname,
        data->varname_len + 1, (void**)&var) == FAILURE) {
        /* The variable doesn't exist
         * so there's nothing to read,
         * "return" zero bytes */
        return 0;
    }
    copyval = **var;
    if (Z_TYPE(copyval) != IS_STRING) {
        /* Turn non-string type into sensible value */
        zval_copy_ctor(&copyval);
        INIT_PZVAL(&copyval);
        got_copied = 1;
    }
    if (data->position > Z_STRLEN(copyval)) {
        data->position = Z_STRLEN(copyval);
    }
    if ((Z_STRLEN(copyval) - data->position) < toread) {
        /* Don't overrun the available buffer */
        toread = Z_STRLEN(copyval) - data->position;
    }
    /* Populate buffer */
    memcpy(buf, Z_STRVAL(copyval) + data->position, toread);
    data->position += toread;

    /* Free temporary zval if necessary */
    if (got_copied) {
        zval_dtor(&copyval);
    }

    /* Return number of bytes populated into buf */
    return toread;
}

static int php_varstream_closer(php_stream *stream,
                        int close_handle TSRMLS_DC)
{
    php_varstream_data *data = stream->abstract;

    /* Free the internal state structure to avoid leaking */
```

Listing 14.3   **Continued**

```
    efree(data->varname);
    efree(data);

    return 0;
}

static int php_varstream_flush(php_stream *stream TSRMLS_DC)
{
    php_varstream_data *data = stream->abstract;
    zval **var;

    if (zend_hash_find(&EG(symbol_table), data->varname,
                    data->varname_len + 1, (void**)&var)
                    == SUCCESS) {
        if (Z_TYPE_PP(var) == IS_STRING) {
            data->position = Z_STRLEN_PP(var);
        } else {
            zval copyval = **var;
            zval_copy_ctor(&copyval);
            convert_to_string(&copyval);
            data->position = Z_STRLEN(copyval);
            zval_dtor(&copyval);
        }
    } else {
        data->position = 0;
    }

    return 0;
}

static int php_varstream_seek(php_stream *stream, off_t offset,
                    int whence, off_t *newoffset TSRMLS_DC)
{
    php_varstream_data *data = stream->abstract;

    switch (whence) {
        case SEEK_SET:
            data->position = offset;
            break;
        case SEEK_CUR:
            data->position += offset;
            break;
        case SEEK_END:
        {
            zval **var;
```

Listing 14.3 **Continued**

```
            size_t curlen = 0;

            if (zend_hash_find(&EG(symbol_table),
                    data->varname,    data->varname_len + 1,
                    (void**)&var) == SUCCESS) {
                if (Z_TYPE_PP(var) == IS_STRING) {
                    curlen = Z_STRLEN_PP(var);
                } else {
                    zval copyval = **var;
                    zval_copy_ctor(&copyval);
                    convert_to_string(&copyval);
                    curlen = Z_STRLEN(copyval);
                    zval_dtor(&copyval);
                }
            }

            data->position = curlen + offset;
            break;
        }
    }

    /* Prevent seeking prior to the start */
    if (data->position < 0) {
        data->position = 0;
    }

    if (newoffset) {
        *newoffset = data->position;
    }

    return 0;
}

static php_stream_ops php_varstream_ops = {
    php_varstream_write,
    php_varstream_read,
    php_varstream_closer,
    php_varstream_flush,
    PHP_VARSTREAM_STREAMTYPE,
    php_varstream_seek,
    NULL, /* cast */
    NULL, /* stat */
    NULL, /* set_option */
};

/* Define the wrapper operations */
```

Listing 14.3 **Continued**

```
static php_stream *php_varstream_opener(
            php_stream_wrapper *wrapper,
            char *filename, char *mode, int options,
            char **opened_path, php_stream_context *context
            STREAMS_DC TSRMLS_DC)
{
    php_varstream_data *data;
    php_url *url;

    if (options & STREAM_OPEN_PERSISTENT) {
        /* variable streams, by definition, can't be persistent
         * Since their variable disapears
         * at the end of a request */
        php_stream_wrapper_log_error(wrapper, options
            TSRMLS_CC, "Unable to open %s persistently",
                                        filename);
        return NULL;
    }

    url = php_url_parse(filename);
    if (!url) {
        php_stream_wrapper_log_error(wrapper, options
            TSRMLS_CC, "Unexpected error parsing URL");
        return NULL;
    }
    if (!url->host || (url->host[0] == 0) ||
        strcasecmp("var", url->scheme) != 0) {
        /* Bad URL or wrong wrapper */
        php_stream_wrapper_log_error(wrapper, options
            TSRMLS_CC, "Invalid URL, must be in the form: "
                    "var://variablename");
        php_url_free(url);
        return NULL;
    }

    /* Create data struct for protocol information */
    data = emalloc(sizeof(php_varstream_data));
    data->position = 0;
    data->varname_len = strlen(url->host);
    data->varname = estrndup(url->host, data->varname_len + 1);
    php_url_free(url);

    /* Instantiate a stream,
     * assign the appropriate stream ops,
     * and bind the abstract data */
    return php_stream_alloc(&php_varstream_ops, data, 0, mode);
```

Listing 14.3 **Continued**

```
}

static php_stream_wrapper_ops php_varstream_wrapper_ops = {
    php_varstream_opener, /* stream_opener */
    NULL, /* stream_close */
    NULL, /* stream_stat */
    NULL, /* url_stat */
    NULL, /* dir_opener */
    PHP_VARSTREAM_WRAPPER,
    NULL, /* unlink */
#if PHP_MAJOR_VERSION >= 5
    /* PHP >= 5.0 only */
    NULL, /* rename */
    NULL, /* mkdir */
    NULL, /* rmdir */
#endif
};

static php_stream_wrapper php_varstream_wrapper = {
    &php_varstream_wrapper_ops,
    NULL, /* abstract */
    0, /* is_url */
};

PHP_MINIT_FUNCTION(varstream)
{
    /* Register the stream wrapper */
    if (php_register_url_stream_wrapper(PHP_VARSTREAM_WRAPPER,
            &php_varstream_wrapper TSRMLS_CC)==FAILURE) {
        return FAILURE;
    }
    return SUCCESS;
}

PHP_MSHUTDOWN_FUNCTION(varstream)
{
    /* Unregister the stream wrapper */
    if (php_unregister_url_stream_wrapper(PHP_VARSTREAM_WRAPPER
                            TSRMLS_CC) == FAILURE) {
        return FAILURE;
    }
    return SUCCESS;
}

/* Declare the module */
zend_module_entry varstream_module_entry = {
```

Listing 14.3   **Continued**

```
#if ZEND_MODULE_API_NO >= 20010901
    STANDARD_MODULE_HEADER,
#endif
    PHP_VARSTREAM_EXTNAME,
    NULL, /* functions */
    PHP_MINIT(varstream),
    PHP_MSHUTDOWN(varstream),
    NULL, /* RINIT */
    NULL, /* RSHUTDOWN */
    NULL, /* MINFO */
#if ZEND_MODULE_API_NO >= 20010901
    PHP_VARSTREAM_EXTVER,
#endif
    STANDARD_MODULE_PROPERTIES
};

/* Export the shared symbol */
#ifdef COMPILE_DL_VARSTREAM
ZEND_GET_MODULE(varstream)
#endif
```

After building and loading the extension, PHP will be aware of, and ready to dispatch stream requests for, URLs beginning with `var://` mimicking all the behavior found in the matching userspace implementation.

Inside the Implementation

The first thing you'll notice about this extension is that it exports absolutely no user-space functions whatsoever. What is does do is call into a core PHPAPI hook from its MINIT method to associate a scheme name—var in this case—with a short and simple wrapper definition structure.

```
static php_stream_wrapper php_varstream_wrapper = {
    &php_varstream_wrapper_ops,
    NULL, /* abstract */
    0, /* is_url */
}
```

The most important element here is, obviously, the ops element, which provides access to the wrapper-specific stream creation and inspection functions. You can safely ignore the abstract property as it's only used during runtime and exists in the initial declaration as simply a placeholder. The third element, is_url, tells PHP whether or not the allow_url_fopen option in the php.ini should be considered when using this wrapper. If this value is nonzero and allow_url_fopen is set to false, this wrapper will be unavailable to running scripts.

As you already know from earlier in this chapter, calls to userspace functions such as `fopen()` will follow this wrapper through its ops element to `php_varstream_wrapper_ops`, where it can call the stream opener function, `php_varstream_opener`.

The first block of code used by this method checks to see whether a persistent stream has been requested:

```
if (options & STREAM_OPEN_PERSISTENT) {
```

For many wrappers such a request is perfectly valid; however, in this case such behavior simply doesn't make sense. Userspace variables are ephemeral by definition and the relative cheapness of instantiating a varstream makes the advantages of using persistency negligible.

Reporting failure to the streams layer requires nothing more than returning a NULL value from the method rather than a stream instance. As the failure bubbles its way up to userspace, the streams layer will generate a nondescript failure message saying that it was unable to open the URL. To give the developer more detailed information, you'd use the `php_stream_wrapper_log_error()` function prior to returning:

```
php_stream_wrapper_log_error(wrapper, options
    TSRMLS_CC, "Unable to open %s persistently",
                          filename);
return NULL;
```

URL Parsing

The next step in instantiating varstream requires taking the human readable URL, and chunking it up into manageable pieces. Fortunately, the same mechanism used by the userspace `url_parse()` function is available as an internal API call. If the URL can be successfully parsed, a `php_url` structure will be allocated and populated with the appropriate values. If a particular value is not present in the URL, its value will be set to NULL. This structure must be explicitly freed before leaving the `php_varstream_opener` function, or its memory will be leaked.

```
typedef struct php_url {
    /* scheme://user:pass@host:port/path?query#fragment */
    char *scheme;
    char *user;
    char *pass;
    char *host;
    unsigned short port;
    char *path;
    char *query;
    char *fragment;
} php_url;
```

Finally, the varstream wrapper creates a data structure to hold the name of the variable being streamed, and its current location—for read streams. This structure will be used by the stream's read and write functions to locate the variable to act upon, and will be freed during stream shutdown by the `php_varstream_close` method.

opendir()

This example could be extended beyond the basic implementation of reading and writing variable contents. One new feature might be to allow the use of the directory functions to read through the keys in an array. Add the following code prior to your existing `php_varstream_wrapper_ops` structure:

```
static size_t php_varstream_readdir(php_stream *stream,
            char *buf, size_t count TSRMLS_DC)
{
    php_stream_dirent *ent = (php_stream_dirent*)buf;
    php_varstream_dirdata *data = stream->abstract;
    char *key;
    int type, key_len;
    long idx;

    type = zend_hash_get_current_key_ex(Z_ARRVAL_P(data->arr),
                &key, &key_len, &idx, 0, &(data->pos));

    if (type == HASH_KEY_IS_STRING) {
        if (key_len >= sizeof(ent->d_name)) {
            /* truncate long keys to maximum length */
            key_len = sizeof(ent->d_name) - 1;
        }
        memcpy(ent->d_name, key, key_len);
        ent->d_name[key_len] = 0;
    } else if (type == HASH_KEY_IS_LONG) {
        snprintf(ent->d_name, sizeof(ent->d_name), "%ld",idx);
    } else {
        /* No more keys */
        return 0;
    }
    zend_hash_move_forward_ex(Z_ARRVAL_P(data->arr),
                                    &data->pos);
    return sizeof(php_stream_dirent);
}

static int php_varstream_closedir(php_stream *stream,
                        int close_handle TSRMLS_DC)
{
    php_varstream_dirdata *data = stream->abstract;

    zval_ptr_dtor(&(data->arr));
```

```
    efree(data);
    return 0;
}

static int php_varstream_dirseek(php_stream *stream,
                    off_t offset, int whence,
                    off_t *newoffset TSRMLS_DC)
{
    php_varstream_dirdata *data = stream->abstract;

    if (whence == SEEK_SET && offset == 0) {
        /* rewinddir() */
        zend_hash_internal_pointer_reset_ex(
                    Z_ARRVAL_P(data->arr), &(data->pos));
        if (newoffset) {
            *newoffset = 0;
        }
        return 0;
    }
    /* Other types of seeking not supported */
    return -1;
}

static php_stream_ops php_varstream_dirops = {
    NULL, /* write */
    php_varstream_readdir,
    php_varstream_closedir,
    NULL, /* flush */
    PHP_VARSTREAM_DIRSTREAMTYPE,
    php_varstream_dirseek,
    NULL, /* cast */
    NULL, /* stat */
    NULL, /* set_option */
};

static php_stream *php_varstream_opendir(
            php_stream_wrapper *wrapper,
            char *filename, char *mode, int options,
            char **opened_path, php_stream_context *context
            STREAMS_DC TSRMLS_DC)
{
    php_varstream_dirdata *data;
    php_url *url;
    zval **var;

    if (options & STREAM_OPEN_PERSISTENT) {
```

```
        php_stream_wrapper_log_error(wrapper, options
            TSRMLS_CC, "Unable to open %s persistently",
                                        filename);
        return NULL;
    }

    url = php_url_parse(filename);
    if (!url) {
        php_stream_wrapper_log_error(wrapper, options
            TSRMLS_CC, "Unexpected error parsing URL");
        return NULL;
    }
    if (!url->host || (url->host[0] == 0) ||
        strcasecmp("var", url->scheme) != 0) {
        /* Bad URL or wrong wrapper */
        php_stream_wrapper_log_error(wrapper, options
            TSRMLS_CC, "Invalid URL, must be in the form: "
                    "var://variablename");
        php_url_free(url);
        return NULL;
    }

    if (zend_hash_find(&EG(symbol_table), url->host,
        strlen(url->host) + 1, (void**)&var) == FAILURE) {
        php_stream_wrapper_log_error(wrapper, options
            TSRMLS_CC, "Variable $%s not found", url->host);
        php_url_free(url);
        return NULL;
    }

    if (Z_TYPE_PP(var) != IS_ARRAY) {
        php_stream_wrapper_log_error(wrapper, options
            TSRMLS_CC, "$%s is not an array", url->host);
        php_url_free(url);
        return NULL;
    }
    php_url_free(url);

    data = emalloc(sizeof(php_varstream_dirdata));
    if ((*var)->is_ref && (*var)->refcount > 1) {
        /* Make a full copy */
        MAKE_STD_ZVAL(data->arr);
        *(data->arr) = **var;
        zval_copy_ctor(data->arr);
        INIT_PZVAL(data->arr);
    } else {
```

```
    /* Put in copy-on-write set */
    data->arr = *var;
    ZVAL_ADDREF(data->arr);
}
zend_hash_internal_pointer_reset_ex(Z_ARRVAL_P(data->arr),
                                    &data->pos);
return php_stream_alloc(&php_varstream_dirops,data,0,mode);
}
```

Now, replace the NULL entry in your `php_varstream_wrapper_ops` structure for
`dir_opener` with a reference to your `php_varstream_opendir` method. Lastly, add the
new defines and types used in this code block to your `php_varstream.h` file following
the definition of `php_varstream_data`:

```
#define PHP_VARSTREAM_DIRSTREAMTYPE    "varstream directory"
typedef struct _php_varstream_dirdata {
    zval *arr;
    HashPosition pos;
} php_varstream_dirdata;
```

In the `fopen()`-based implementation of your varstream wrapper, you simply referenced
the name of the variable and fetched it from the symbol table each time a read or write
operation was performed. This time, you fetched the variable during the `opendir()`
implementation allowing errors such as the variable not existing or being of the wrong
type to be handled immediately. You also made a point-in-time copy of the array variable, meaning that any changes to the original array will not change the results of subsequent `readdir()` calls. The original approach—storing the variable name—would have
worked just as well; this alternative is simply provided for illustration.

Because directory access is based on *blocks*—directory entries—rather than characters,
a separate set of stream operations is necessary. For this version, `write` has no meaning so
you're able to simply leave it as NULL. `read` is implemented as a method that uses the
`zend_hash_get_current_key_ex()` method to map the array indices to directory
names. And seek focuses on the `SEEK_SET` whence to jump to the start of the array in
response to calls to `rewinddir()`.

Note
In practice, directory streams never use SEEK_SET, SEEK_END, or an offset other than 0. When implementing directory stream operations, however, it's best to design your method with some way to handle
these cases should the streams layer ever change to accommodate the notion of true directory seeking.

Manipulation

Four of the five static wrapper operations handle non-I/O based manipulation of
streamable resources. You've already seen what they are and how their prototypes look;
now it's time to implement them within the framework of the varstream wrapper.

unlink

Add the following function, which allows `unlink()` to behave much like `unset()` when used with the varstream wrapper anywhere above your `wrapper_ops` structure:

```
static int php_varstream_unlink(php_stream_wrapper *wrapper,
                    char *filename, int options,
                    php_stream_context *context
                    TSRMLS_DC)
{
    php_url *url;

    url = php_url_parse(filename);
    if (!url) {
        php_stream_wrapper_log_error(wrapper, options
            TSRMLS_CC, "Unexpected error parsing URL");
        return -1;
    }
    if (!url->host || (url->host[0] == 0) ||
        strcasecmp("var", url->scheme) != 0) {
        /* Bad URL or wrong wrapper */
        php_stream_wrapper_log_error(wrapper, options
            TSRMLS_CC, "Invalid URL, must be in the form: "
                "var://variablename");
        php_url_free(url);
        return -1;
    }

    /* Delete it */
    zend_hash_del(&EG(symbol_table), url->host,
                            strlen(url->host) + 1);
    php_url_free(url);
    return 0;
}
```

The bulk of this function should look familiar as it's taken straight out of `php_varstream_opener`. The only difference is that this time you've passed the variable name to `zend_hash_del` instead.

rename, mkdir, and rmdir

Just for completeness, here are implementations of the `rename`, `mkdir`, and `rmdir` methods:

```
static int php_varstream_rename(php_stream_wrapper *wrapper,
        char *url_from, char *url_to, int options,
        php_stream_context *context TSRMLS_DC)
{
    php_url *from, *to;
```

```
    zval **var;

    from = php_url_parse(url_from);
    if (!from) {
        php_stream_wrapper_log_error(wrapper, options
            TSRMLS_CC, "Unexpected error parsing source");
        return -1;
    }
    if (zend_hash_find(&EG(symbol_table), from->host,
                strlen(from->host) + 1,
                (void**)&var) == FAILURE) {
        php_stream_wrapper_log_error(wrapper, options
            TSRMLS_CC, "$%s does not exist", from->host);
        php_url_free(from);
        return -1;
    }
    to = php_url_parse(url_to);
    if (!to) {
        php_stream_wrapper_log_error(wrapper, options
            TSRMLS_CC, "Unexpected error parsing dest");
        php_url_free(from);
        return -1;
    }
    ZVAL_ADDREF(*var);
    zend_hash_update(&EG(symbol_table), to->host,
                strlen(to->host) + 1, (void*)var,
                sizeof(zval*), NULL);
    zend_hash_del(&EG(symbol_table), from->host,
                strlen(from->host) + 1);
    php_url_free(from);
    php_url_free(to);
    return 0;
}

static int php_varstream_mkdir(php_stream_wrapper *wrapper,
                char *url_from, int mode, int options,
                php_stream_context *context TSRMLS_DC)
{
    php_url *url;

    php_url_parse(url_from);
    if (!url) {
        php_stream_wrapper_log_error(wrapper, options
            TSRMLS_CC, "Unexpected error parsing URL");
        return -1;
    }
```

```
    if (zend_hash_exists(&EG(symbol_table), url->host,
                strlen(url->host) + 1)) {
        php_stream_wrapper_log_error(wrapper, options
            TSRMLS_CC, "$%s already exists", url->host);
        php_url_free(url);
        return -1;
    }
    /* EG(uninitialized_zval_ptr) is a general purpose
     * IS_NULL zval* with an unlimited refcount */
    zend_hash_add(&EG(symbol_table), url->host,
            strlen(url->host) + 1,
            (void*)&EG(uninitialized_zval_ptr),
            sizeof(zval*), NULL);
    php_url_free(url);
    return 0;
}


static int php_varstream_rmdir(php_stream_wrapper *wrapper,
                char *url, int options,
                php_stream_context *context TSRMLS_DC)
{
    /* Act just like unlink() */
    wrapper->wops->unlink(wrapper, url, options,
                            context TSRMLS_CC);
}
```

Inspection

Not all stream operations involve resource manipulation. Occasionally it's just a good
idea to see what an active stream is doing at the moment, or to check on a potentially
openable resource to see how it will react.

Both of the stream and wrapper ops functions in this section work with the same data
structure: php_stream_statbuf, which is made up of a single element: the standard
POSIX struct statbuf. When either method is called, it should attempt to fill as many
of the statbuf elements as possible while leaving the unknown elements alone.

stat

If set, wrapper->ops->stream_stat() will be called when information about an active
stream instance is requested. If not, the corresponding stream->ops->stat() method
will be called instead. Whichever method is invoked, it should make every effort to populate as much meaningful information about the stream instance into the statbuf structure ssb->sb. In ordinary file I/O parlance, these calls correspond to the fstat() stdio
call.

`url_stat`

`wrapper->ops->url_stat()` is called outside of a stream instance to retrieve metadata about a streamable resource. Typically, any symbolic links—or redirections—should be followed until a real resource is found and stat information for that resource returned according to the same semantics as the `stat()` syscall. The `flags` parameter to `url_stat` allows this, and other behavior, to be modified according to the `PHP_STREAM_URL_STAT_*` family of constants:

LINK   Do not follow symlinks and redirects. Rather, report information about the first node encountered whether it is a link or real resource.

QUIET   Do not report errors. Note that this is the inverse of the `REPORT_ERRORS` logic found in many other streams functions.

Summary

Exposing streamable resources, whether remote network I/O or local data sources, allows your extension to hook into the core data manipulation functions and avoid reimplementing the tedious work of descriptor management and I/O buffering. This makes it more useful, and more powerful when placed in a userspace setting.

The next chapter will finish up the streams layer by taking a look at filters and contexts that can be used to alter the default behavior of streams, and even modify data en route.

16

Diverting the Stream

ONE OFTEN UNDERSOLD PHP FEATURE is the stream context. These optional arguments—available even from userspace on most stream creation–related functions—serve as a generalized framework for passing additional information into or out of a given wrapper or stream implementation.

Contexts

Every stream context contains two intrinsic types of information. The first, and most commonly used, is the context option. These values, arranged into a two-level nested array within contexts, are typically used to change how a stream wrapper initializes. The other type, context parameters, are meant to be wrapper agnostic and currently provide a means for event notification within the streams layer to bubble up to a piece of streams-using code.

```
php_stream_context *php_stream_context_alloc(void);
```

Creating a context uses this simple API call, which allocates some storage space and initializes the HashTables that will hold the context's options and parameters. It is also automatically registered as a resource and is therefore implicitly cleaned up on request shutdown.

Setting Options

The internal API for setting context options shadows the userspace APIs almost identically:

```
int php_stream_context_set_option(php_stream_context *context,
          const char *wrappername, const char *optionname,
          zval *optionvalue);
```

All that really differs from the userspace proto:

```
bool stream_context_set_option(resource $context,
            string $wrapper, string $optionname,
            mixed $value);
```

is the specific data types, which differ between userspace and internals out of necessity. As an example, a piece of internals code might use the two API calls just covered to make an HTTP request using the built-in wrapper, while overriding the user_agent setting with a context option.

```
php_stream *php_sample6_get_homepage(
                            const char *alt_user_agent)
{
    php_stream_context *context;
    zval tmpval;

    context = php_stream_context_alloc();
    ZVAL_STRING(&tmpval, alt_user_agent, 0);
    php_stream_context_set_option(context, "http",
                                "user_agent", &tmpval);
    return php_stream_open_wrapper_ex("http://www.php.net",
                "rb", REPORT_ERRORS | ENFORCE_SAFE_MODE,
                NULL, context);
}
```

> **Note**
>
> Notice that `tmpval` wasn't allocated any permanent storage, and the string it was populated with wasn't duplicated. `php_stream_context_set_option` automatically makes a duplicate of both the passed `zval` and all of its contents.

Retrieving Options

The API call to retrieve a context option mirrors its setting counterpart with an extra hint of déjà vu.

```
int php_stream_context_get_option(php_stream_context *context,
            const char *wrappername, const char *optionname,
            zval ***optionvalue);
```

Recall that context options are stored in a set of nested HashTables and that when retrieving values from a `HashTable`, the normal approach is to pass a pointer to a `zval**` into `zend_hash_find()`. Well, because `php_stream_context_get_option()` is a specialized proxy for `zend_hash_find()`, it only stands to reason that the semantics would be the same.

Here's a simplified look at one of the built-in http wrapper's uses of `php_stream_` `context_get_option` showing how the `user_agent` setting is applied to a specific request:

```
zval **ua_zval;
char *user_agent = "PHP/5.1.0";
if (context &&
    php_stream_context_get_option(context, "http",
                "user_agent", &ua_zval) == SUCCESS &&
                Z_TYPE_PP(ua_zval) == IS_STRING) {
    user_agent = Z_STRVAL_PP(ua_zval);
}
```

In this case, non-string values are simply thrown out because it doesn't make sense to use a number for a user agent string. Other context options, such as `max_redirects`, do take numeric values, and because it's not uncommon to find a numeric value stored in a string zval, it might be necessary to perform a type conversion to use the otherwise legitimate setting.

Unfortunately, these variables are owned by the context so they can't be simply converted immediately; instead they must be separated—as you did in prior chapters—and then converted, and finally destroyed if necessary:

```
long max_redirects = 20;
zval **tmpzval;
if (context &&
    php_stream_context_get_option(context, "http",
            "max_redirects", &tmpzval) == SUCCESS) {
    if (Z_TYPE_PP(tmpzval) == IS_LONG) {
        max_redirects = Z_LVAL_PP(tmpzval);
    } else {
        zval copyval = **tmpzval;
        zval_copy_ctor(&copyval);
        convert_to_long(&copyval);
        max_redirects = Z_LVAL(copyval);
        zval_dtor(&copyval);
    }
}
```

> **Note**
>
> In practice, the `zval_dtor()` in this example would not be necessary. `IS_LONG` variables do not use any additional storage beyond the `zval` container itself and thus a `zval_dtor()` is a non-op. It's included in this example for completeness as it is necessary—and vital—for String, Array, Object, Resource, and potentially other data types in the future.

Parameters

Although the userspace API presents context parameters as a unified looking construct similar to context options, they are actually declared as independent members of the php_stream_context struct within the language internals.

At present, only one context parameter is supported: notifier. This element of the php_stream_context struct can optionally point to a php_stream_notifier struct that has the following members:

```
typedef struct {
    php_stream_notification_func func;
    void (*dtor)(php_stream_notifier *notifier);
    void *ptr;
    int mask;
    size_t progress, progress_max;
} php_stream_notifier;
```

When a php_stream_notifier struct is assigned to context->notifier, it provides—at minimum—a callback func that is triggered on special stream events shown in Table 16.1 as PHP_STREAM_NOTIFY_* codes. A given event will also bear one of the PHP_STREAM_NOTIFY_SEVERITY_* levels shown in Table 16.2.

A convenience pointer *ptr is provided for notifier implementations to carry around additional data. If that pointer refers to space that must be freed when the context is destructed, a dtor method may be specified and will be called when the last reference to the context falls out of scope.

The mask element allows event triggers to be limited to specific severity levels. If an event occurs at a severity level not included in mask, the notifier function will not be triggered.

The last two elements—progress and progress_max—can be populated by the stream implementation; however, notifier functions should avoid using either of these values until they have received at least one PHP_STREAM_NOTIFY_PROGRESS or PHP_STREAM_NOTIFY_FILE_SIZE_IS event respectively.

The following example conforms to the prototype for the php_stream_notification_func callback:

```
void php_sample6_notifier(php_stream_context *context,
        int notifycode, int severity, char *xmsg, int xcode,
        size_t bytes_sofar, size_t bytes_max,
        void *ptr TSRMLS_DC)
{
    if (notifycode != PHP_STREAM_NOTIFY_FAILURE) {
        /* Ignore all other notifications */
        return;
    }
    if (severity == PHP_STREAM_NOTIFY_SEVERITY_ERR) {
        /* Dispatch to crisis handler */
```

```
        php_sample6_theskyisfalling(context, xcode, xmsg);
        return;
    } else if (severity == PHP_STREAM_NOTIFY_SEVERITY_WARN) {
        /* Log the potential problem */
        php_sample6_logstrangeevent(context, xcode, xmsg);
        return;
    }
}
```

Table 16.1 **Notification Codes**

PHP_STREAM_NOTIFY_* Codes	Meaning
RESOLVE	A host address resolution has completed. Most socket-based wrappers perform this lookup just prior to connection.
CONNECT	A socket stream connection to a remote resource has completed.
AUTH_REQUIRED	The requested resource is unavailable due to access controls and insufficient authorization.
MIME_TYPE_IS	The mime-type of the remote resource is now available.
FILE_SIZE_IS	The size of the remote resource is now available.
REDIRECTED	The original URL request resulted in a redirect to another location.
PROGRESS	The progress and (possibly) progress_max elements of the php_stream_notifier struct have been updated as a result of addition data having been transferred.
COMPLETED	There is no more data available on the stream.
FAILURE	The URL resource request was unsuccessful or could not complete.
AUTH_RESULT	The remote system has processed authentication credentials—possibly successfully.

Table 16.2 **Severity Codes**

PHP_STREAM_NOTIFY_SEVERITY_* Levels	Meaning
INFO	Informational update. Equivalent to an E_NOTICE error.
WARN	Minor error condition. Equivalent to an E_WARNING error.
ERR	Sever error condition. Equivalent to an E_ERROR error.

The Default Context

As of PHP 5.0, when a userspace stream creation function is called without a context parameter, the requestwide default context is used instead. This context variable is stored in the File Globals structure as FG(default_context) and may be accessed identically to any other php_stream_context variable. When performing stream creation for a user-space script, it's generally preferable to allow the user to specify a context or at least fall back on the default context. Decoding a userspace zval* into a php_stream_context can be accomplished by using the php_stream_context_from_zval() macro as in the following example adapted from Chapter 14, "Accessing Streams":

```
PHP_FUNCTION(sample6_fopen)
{
    php_stream *stream;
    char *path, *mode;
    int path_len, mode_len;
    int options = ENFORCE_SAFE_MODE | REPORT_ERRORS;
    zend_bool use_include_path = 0;
    zval *zcontext = NULL;
    php_stream_context *context;

    if (zend_parse_parameters(ZEND_NUM_ARGS() TSRMLS_CC,
            "ss|br", &path, &path_len, &mode, &mode_len,
                &use_include_path, &zcontext) == FAILURE) {
        return;
    }
    context = php_stream_context_from_zval(zcontext, 0);
    if (use_include_path) {
        options |= PHP_FILE_USE_INCLUDE_PATH;
    }
    stream = php_stream_open_wrapper_ex(path, mode, options,
                                    NULL, context);
    if (!stream) {
        RETURN_FALSE;
    }
    php_stream_to_zval(stream, return_value);
}
```

If zcontext contains a userspace context resource, its associated pointer will be populated into context as with any ZEND_FETCH_RESOURCE() call. On the other hand, if zcontext is NULL and the second parameter to php_stream_context_from_zval() is set to a nonzero value, the result of the macro will simply be NULL. When set to zero—as in this example and nearly all the core stream creation userspace functions—the value of FG(default_context) will be used (and initialized if appropriate) instead.

Filters

Filters apply an extra stage of transformation to stream contents during read and write operations. Note that while stream filters existed in PHP as far back as version 4.3, the design of the stream filter API changed dramatically with PHP 5.0. The contents of this chapter refer specifically to the PHP5 generation of stream filters.

Applying Existing Filters to Streams

Applying a filter to an open stream is just a few lines of code:

```
php_stream *php_sample6_fopen_read_ucase(const char *path
                                         TSRMLS_DC) {
    php_stream_filter *filter;
    php_stream *stream;

    stream = php_stream_open_wrapper_ex(path, "r",
                    REPORT_ERRORS | ENFORCE_SAFE_MODE,
                    NULL, FG(default_context));
    if (!stream) {
        return NULL;
    }

    filter = php_stream_filter_create("string.toupper", NULL,
                                      0 TSRMLS_CC);
    if (!filter) {
        php_stream_close(stream);
        return NULL;
    }
    php_stream_filter_append(&stream->readfilters, filter);

    return stream;
}
```

First, a look at the API functions just introduced along with one of their siblings:

```
php_stream_filter *php_stream_filter_create(
                const char *filtername, zval *filterparams,
                int persistent TSRMLS_DC);
void php_stream_filter_prepend(php_stream_filter_chain *chain,
                php_stream_filter *filter);
void php_stream_filter_append(php_stream_filter_chain *chain,
                php_stream_filter *filter);
```

The filterparams parameter to php_stream_filter_create() holds the same meaning as its counterpart in the userspace stream_filter_append() and stream_filter_prepend() functions. Note that any zval* data passed into php_stream_filter_create() does not become "owned" by the filter; it just borrows it during filter creation so anything allocated to be passed in must be destroyed by the calling scope.

If the filter will be applied to a persistent stream, the persistent flag must be set to a nonzero value. If you're not sure about the stream you'll be applying a filter to, just use the `php_stream_is_persistent()` macro, which simply takes a `php_stream*` variable as its only argument.

As you saw in the earlier example, stream filtering is split into two separate chains. One is used for writing—which is wound through in response to a `php_stream_write()` call just prior to issuing the `stream->ops->write()` call. The other one is used for reading—which processes all data received from `stream->ops->read()` actions within the streams layer.

In this example you used `&stream->readfilters` to denote the read chain. If you wanted to apply a filter to the write chain instead, you'd simply use `&stream->writefilters`.

Defining a Filter Implementation

Registering a filter implementation follows the same basic rules as registering a wrapper. The first step in introducing PHP to your filter comes in the MINIT phase, matched with a balancing removal in the MSHUTDOWN phase. Here's the prototype for the API calls you'll use, along with a sample usage registering two filter factories:

```
int php_stream_filter_register_factory(
        const char *filterpattern,
        php_stream_filter_factory *factory TSRMLS_DC);
int php_stream_filter_unregister_factory(
        const char *filterpattern TSRMLS_DC);

PHP_MINIT_FUNCTION(sample6)
{
    php_stream_filter_register_factory("sample6",
        &php_sample6_sample6_factory TSRMLS_CC);
    php_stream_filter_register_factory("sample.*",
        &php_sample6_samples_factory TSRMLS_CC);
    return SUCCESS;
}
PHP_MSHUTDOWN_FUNCTION(sample6)
{
    php_stream_filter_unregister_factory("sample6" TSRMLS_CC);
    php_stream_filter_unregister_factory("sample.*"
                                    TSRMLS_CC);
    return SUCCESS;
}
```

The first filter factory registered here declares a specific filter name, `sample6`; the second takes advantage of some rudimentary pattern matching built into the streams layer. To illustrate, each of the following lines of userspace code would attempt to instantiate the `php_sample6_samples_factory` despite being called by different names:

```
<?php
    stream_filter_append(STDERR, 'sample.one');
    stream_filter_append(STDERR, 'sample.3');
    stream_filter_append(STDERR, 'sample.filter.thingymabob');
    stream_filter_append(STDERR, 'sample.whatever');
?>
```

The definition of php_sample6_samples_factory might look like the following block
of code, which you can place anywhere above your MINIT block:

```
#include "ext/standard/php_string.h"
typedef struct {
    char is_persistent;
    char *tr_from;
    char *tr_to;
    int tr_len;
} php_sample6_filter_data;

static php_stream_filter_status_t php_sample6_filter(
    php_stream *stream, php_stream_filter *thisfilter,
    php_stream_bucket_brigade *buckets_in,
    php_stream_bucket_brigade *buckets_out,
    size_t *bytes_consumed, int flags TSRMLS_DC)
{
    php_sample6_filter_data *data = thisfilter->abstract;
    php_stream_bucket *bucket;
    size_t consumed = 0;

    while (buckets_in->head) {
        bucket = php_stream_bucket_make_writeable(
                            buckets_in->head TSRMLS_CC);
        php_strtr(bucket->buf, bucket->buflen, data->tr_from,
                            data->tr_to, data->tr_len);
        consumed += bucket->buflen;
        php_stream_bucket_append(buckets_out, bucket TSRMLS_CC);
    }
    if (bytes_consumed) {
        *bytes_consumed = consumed;
    }
    return PSFS_PASS_ON;
}

static void php_sample6_filter_dtor(
        php_stream_filter *thisfilter TSRMLS_DC)
{
    php_sample6_filter_data *data = thisfilter->abstract;
    pefree(data, data->is_persistent);
```

```
}

static php_stream_filter_ops php_sample6_filter_ops = {
    php_sample6_filter,
    php_sample6_filter_dtor,
    "sample.*",
};

#define PHP_SAMPLE6_ALPHA_UCASE "ABCDEFGHIJKLMNOPQRSTUVWXYZ"
#define PHP_SAMPLE6_ALPHA_LCASE "abcdefghijklmnopqrstuvwxyz"
#define PHP_SAMPLE6_ROT13_UCASE "NOPQRSTUVWXYZABCDEFGHIJKLM"
#define PHP_SAMPLE6_ROT13_LCASE "nopqrstuvwxyzabcdefghijklm"

static php_stream_filter *php_sample6_filter_create(
    const char *name, zval *param, int persistent TSRMLS_DC)
{
    php_sample6_filter_data *data;
    char *subname;

    if (strlen(name) < sizeof("sample.") ||
        strncmp(name, "sample.", sizeof("sample.") - 1)) {
        /* Misfired filter creation */
        return NULL;
    }

    /* Prepare filter data storage */
    data = pemalloc(sizeof(php_sample6_filter_data),
                    persistent);
    if (!data) {
        /* Persistent mallocs might return NULL */
        return NULL;
    }
    /* Remember if allocation was persistent or not */
    data->is_persistent = persistent;

    /* Focus on the specific subfilter being requested */
    subname = name + sizeof("sample.") - 1;

    if (strcmp(subname, "ucase") == 0) {
        data->tr_from = PHP_SAMPLE6_ALPHA_LCASE;
        data->tr_to = PHP_SAMPLE6_ALPHA_UCASE;
    } else if (strcmp(subname, "lcase") == 0) {
        data->tr_from = PHP_SAMPLE6_ALPHA_UCASE;
        data->tr_to = PHP_SAMPLE6_ALPHA_LCASE;
    } else if (strcmp(subname, "rot13") == 0) {
        data->tr_from = PHP_SAMPLE6_ALPHA_LCASE
                        PHP_SAMPLE6_ALPHA_UCASE;
```

```
            data->tr_to = PHP_SAMPLE6_ROT13_LCASE
                          PHP_SAMPLE6_ROT13_UCASE;
        } else {
            /* Unrecognized filter name */
            pefree(data, persistent);
            return NULL;
        }
        /* Save having to compute this every time */
        data->tr_len = strlen(data->tr_from);

        return php_stream_filter_alloc(&php_sample6_filter_ops,
                                       data, persistent);
}

static php_stream_filter_factory
                      php_sample6_samples_factory = {
    php_sample6_filter_create
};
```

Being familiar with implementing stream wrappers from the last chapter, you'll probably recognize the basic structure at work here. A factory method (`php_sample6_samples_filter_create`) is invoked to allocate a filter instance and assign a set of operations and abstract data to it. In this case, your factor assigns the same `ops` struct to all filter types, but initializes the data structure differently.

The calling scope will take this allocated filter and assign it to a stream's readfilters chain, or its writefilters chain. Then, when a stream read or write call is issued, the filter chain places the data in one or more `php_stream_bucket` structures and passes these buckets in brigade fashion through the attached filters.

Here, your filter implementation, in the form of `php_sample6_filter`, plucks the buckets of data of the input brigade, performs a string translate according to the character sets defined in `php_sample6_filter_create`, and pushes the modified bucket onto the output brigade.

Because this filter implementation doesn't perform any internal buffering and there's precious little that can go wrong, it always returns an exit code of `PSFS_PASS_ON`, which tells the streams layer that at least some data was deposited into the output brigade by the filter. When a filter that does perform internal buffering consumes all the input data without producing output, it is expected to return `PSFS_FEED_ME` to indicate that filter cycling can stop until more input data is available. If a filter encounters a critical error, it should return `PSFS_ERR_FATAL`, which will instruct the streams layer that the filter chain is no longer in a stable state. This results in the stream being closed.

The API functions available for manipulating buckets and bucket brigades are listed here:

```
php_stream_bucket *php_stream_bucket_new(php_stream *stream,
                    char *buf, size_t buflen, int own_buf,
                    int buf_persistent TSRMLS_DC);
```

Create a `php_stream_bucket` for placing on an output brigade. If `own_buf` is set to a nonzero value, the streams layer can—and most likely will—modify its contents or free the allocated memory at some point in time. A nonzero value for `buf_persistent` indicates whether the memory used by `buf` was allocated persistently:

```
int php_stream_bucket_split(php_stream_bucket *in,
        php_stream_bucket **left, php_stream_bucket **right,
        size_t length TSRMLS_DC);
```

This method splits the contents of bucket `in` into two separate bucket objects. The bucket produced and populated into `left` will contain the first `length` characters from `in`, whereas the bucket populated into `right` will contain all remaining characters.

```
void php_stream_bucket_delref(php_stream_bucket *bucket
                                        TSRMLS_DC);
void php_stream_bucket_addref(php_stream_bucket *bucket);
```

Buckets use the same type of reference counting system as zvals and resources. Typically, a bucket will only be owned by one context—the brigade to which it is attached.

```
void php_stream_bucket_prepend(
                php_stream_bucket_brigade *brigade,
                php_stream_bucket *bucket TSRMLS_DC);
void php_stream_bucket_append(
        php_stream_bucket_brigade *brigade,
        php_stream_bucket *bucket TSRMLS_DC);
```

These two methods act as the workhorses of the filter subsystem, attaching buckets to brigades at the beginning (prepend) or end (append).

```
void php_stream_bucket_unlink(php_stream_bucket *bucket
                                        TSRMLS_DC);
```

During the process of applying filter logic, old buckets must be consumed by removing (unlinking) them from their input brigades using this function.

```
php_stream_bucket *php_stream_bucket_make_writeable(
        php_stream_bucket *bucket TSRMLS_DC);
```

Removes a bucket from its attached brigade and, if necessary, duplicates its internal buffer to gain ownership of `bucket->buf`, thus making its contents modifiable. In some cases, such as when the input bucket has a refcount greater than 1, the bucket returned will be a different instance than the bucket passed in. Always be sure to use the returned bucket rather than trusting that the passed-in bucket will be the one returned.

Summary

Filters and contexts allow generic stream types to be modified without requiring direct code changes, or INI settings that would affect an entire request. Using the techniques covered in this chapter, you'll be able to make your own wrapper implementations more useful and alter the data produced by other wrappers as well.

As you move on, we'll be leaving the workings of the PHPAPI behind and returning to the mechanics of the PHP build system to produce more complicated extensions that link into other applications, but find easier ways to generate them using collections of tools to handle the tedious work.

17

Configuration and Linking

ALL OF THE SAMPLE CODE YOU'VE SEEN so far has been self-contained C versions of code you could have already written in PHP userspace. If the project you've got in mind is anything like most PHP extensions, however, you're going to want to link against at least one external library.

Autoconf

In a simple application, you'd probably just add something to your Makefile's CFLAGS and LDFLAGS lines like of the following:

```
CFLAGS = ${CFLAGS} -I/usr/local/foobar/include
LDFLAGS = ${LDFLAGS} -lfoobar -L/usr/local/foobar/lib
```

Anyone else building your application who doesn't have libfoobar, or has it installed in another location, would get treated to a cryptic error message and left to his own devices to determine what went wrong.

Most OSS applications developed in the past decade or so—PHP included—take advantage of a utility called autoconf to generate a complicated configure script from a set of simple macros. This generated script then does the work of looking for where those dependent libraries and their headers are installed. Based on this information, a package can customize that build line, or provide meaningful error messages before compilation time has been wasted on a configuration that won't work.

In building PHP extensions, whether or not you plan to release them to the public, you'll take advantage of this same autoconf mechanism. Even if you're already familiar with autoconf, take a minute to read through this chapter as PHP includes several custom macros not found in the usual autoconf setup.

Unlike traditional autoconf setups, where a central configure.in file at the base of the package contains all configuration macros, PHP only uses configure.in to manage the coordination of several smaller config.m4 scripts located throughout the source tree, including one for every extension, SAPI, the Core itself, and the Zend Engine.

You've already seen a very simple version of this `config.m4` script in previous chapters. In the coming pages, you'll add additional `autoconf` syntax to this file, allowing more configuration time information to be collected by your extension.

Looking for Libraries

The most common use for `config.m4` scripts is to check if dependent libraries have been installed. Extensions such as MySQL, LDAP, GMP, and others are designed to be a simple glue layer between the world of PHP userspace and the C libraries that implement their functionality. If these dependent libraries aren't installed, or if the installed version is too old, either compilation would fail, or the resulting binary would be unable to run.

Scanning for Headers

The simplest step in searching for a dependent library is to look for the include files that your script will use when linking against it. Listing 17.1 attempts to find `zlib.h` in a number of common locations.

Listing 17.1   **A** `config.m4` **File That Checks for** `libz`

```
PHP_ARG_WITH(zlib,[for zlib Support]
[  —with-zlib              Include ZLIB Support])

if test "$PHP_ZLIB" != "no"; then
  for i in /usr /usr/local /opt; do
    if test -f $i/include/zlib/zlib.h; then
      ZLIB_DIR=$i
    fi
  done

  if test -z "$ZLIB_DIR"; then
    AC_MSG_ERROR([zlib not installed (http://www.zlib.org)])
  fi

  PHP_ADD_LIBRARY_WITH_PATH(z,$ZLIB_DIR/lib, ZLIB_SHARED_LIBADD)
  PHP_ADD_INCLUDE($ZLIB_DIR/include)

  AC_MSG_RESULT([found in $ZLIB_DIR])
  AC_DEFINE(HAVE_ZLIB,1,[libz found and included])

  PHP_NEW_EXTENSION(zlib, zlib.c, $ext_shared)
  PHP_SUBST(ZLIB_SHARED_LIBADD)
fi
```

This `config.m4` file is noticeably larger than those you've worked with up till now. Fortunately, the syntax is fairly straightforward and even familiar if you've done bourne shell scripting.

The file begins with the `PHP_ARG_WITH()` macro that was first mentioned in Chapter 5, "Your First Extension." This macro behaves the same way as the `PHP_ARG_ENABLE()` macro you've been using except that the resulting `./configure` option becomes `—with-extname` / `—without-extname` rather than `—enable-extname` / `—disable-extname`.

Recall that these macros are functionally identical, and differ only to provide a hint to the end user of your package. You're free to choose either one for any private extension you create. However, if you plan to release it to the public you should bear in mind that PHP's formal coding standards dictate enable/disable for use with extensions that do not link against external libraries, and with/without for extensions that do.

Because this hypothetical extension will be linking against the zlib library, your `config.m4` script begins by trying to find the `zlib.h` header that will be included by the extensions source code files. This is accomplished by checking a few standard locations—`/usr`, `/usr/local`, and `/opt`—for any file named `zlib.h` located two folders below these locations in `include/zlib`.

If it finds `zlib.h`, it places the base path into a temporary variable: `ZLIB_DIR`. Once the loop completes, the `config.m4` script checks that `ZLIB_DIR` actually contains something—indicating that it found `zlib.h` somewhere. If it doesn't, a meaningful error is produced letting the user know why `./configure` can't continue.

At this point, the script assumes that if the header file exists, the corresponding library must be there as well so it uses the next two lines to modify the build environment, ultimately adding `-lz -L$ZLIB_DIR/lib` to `LDFLAGS` and `-I$ZLIB_DIR/include` to `CFLAGS`.

Finally, a confirmation message is output stating that a zlib installation was found, and what location will be used during compilation. The remaining lines should already be familiar from your earlier work with `config.m4`. Declare a `#define` for `config.h`, declare an extension and specify its source files, and identify a variable substitution to finish tying it to the build system.

Testing for Functionality

So far, this `config.m4` example only looks for the necessary header files. Although this is sufficient for compilation, it doesn't ensure that the resulting binary will link properly because it's possible that the matching library file doesn't exist, or—more likely—is the wrong version.

The simplest way to test for the presence of `libz.so`—the library file that corresponds to `zlib.h`—might be to simply test that the file exists:

```
if ! test -f $ZLIB_DIR/lib/libz.so; then
  AC_MSG_ERROR([zlib.h found, but libz.so not present!])
fi
```

Of course, that only covers half of the question. What if, for example, another identically named library was installed, but it's incompatible with the library you're looking for? The best way to test that your extension will successfully compile against this found library will be to actually compile something against it. The way you'll do this is through a new config.m4 macro placed right before the call to PHP_ADD_LIBRARY_WITH_PATH:

```
PHP_CHECK_LIBRARY(z, deflateInit,,[
  AC_MSG_ERROR([Invalid zlib extension, gzInit() not found])
],-L$ZLIB_DIR/lib)
```

This utility macro will expand out to an entire program that ./configure will attempt to compile. If compilation succeeds, it means that the symbol defined by the second parameter was found in the library named by the first parameter. On success, any auto-conf script located in the third parameter would be executed; on failure, the autoconf script located in the fourth parameter is run. In this example, the third (success) parameter was left empty because no news is good news. The fifth and final parameter is used to specify additional compiler and linker flags, in this case, a -L indicating an additional location to look for libraries.

Optional Functionality

So now you've got a bead on a matching set of library and header files, but depending on what version of that library is installed, you may want to include or exclude addition-al functionality. Because these kinds of version changes often involve the introduction or removal of a particular procedure entry point, you can reuse the PHP_CHECK_LIBRARY() macro you just used to get a finer grain read on the library's capabilities.

```
PHP_CHECK_LIBRARY(z, gzgets,[
  AC_DEFINE(HAVE_ZLIB_GETS,1,[Having gzgets indicates zlib >= 1.0.9])
],[
  AC_MSG_WARN([zlib < 1.0.9 installed, gzgets() will not be available])
],-L$ZLIB_DIR/lib)
```

Testing Actual Behavior

It might not be enough to simply know that a symbol exists and that your code will compile successfully; some libraries have bugs in specific versions that can only be spot-ted—and subsequently worked around—by running some test code against them.

The AC_TRY_RUN() macro will compile a small source file to an executable program and let it run. Depending on the return code, which is passed up through ./configure, your script can then set optional #define statements or just bail out with a message requesting an upgrade if the bug cannot be worked around. Consider the following excerpt from ext/standard/config.m4:

```
AC_TRY_RUN([
#include <math.h>
```

```
double somefn(double n) {
  return floor(n*pow(10,2) + 0.5);
}
int main() {
  return somefn(0.045)/10.0 != 0.5;
}
],[
  PHP_ROUND_FUZZ=0.5
  AC_MSG_RESULT(yes)
],[
  PHP_ROUND_FUZZ=0.50000000001
  AC_MSG_RESULT(no)
],[
  PHP_ROUND_FUZZ=0.50000000001
  AC_MSG_RESULT(cross compile)
])
AC_DEFINE_UNQUOTED(PHP_ROUND_FUZZ, $PHP_ROUND_FUZZ,
                  [Is double precision imprecise?])
```

As you can see, the first parameter to AC_TRY_RUN() is a block of literal C code that will
be compiled and executed. If the exit code of this block is zero, the autoconf script
located in the second parameter will be executed, in this case indicating that round()
functions as expected and splits on precisely 0.5.

  If the code block returns a nonzero value, the autoconf script located in the third
parameter will be executed instead. The fourth and final parameter is a default used
when PHP is being cross-compiled. In this case, any attempts to run sample code will be
pointless because the target platform is different from the platform on which the extension will be compiled.

Enforcing Module Dependencies

As of PHP 5.1, interdependencies between extensions can be enforced. Because extensions can be either built statically into PHP or loaded dynamically as shared objects, it's
necessary to enforce the dependencies in two locations.

Configuretime Module Dependency

  The first location is within the config.m4 file you've been looking so closely at during the course of this chapter. Here, you'll use the
PHP_ADD_EXTENSION_DEP(extname,depname[,optional]) macro to indicate that the
extname extension depends on the depname extension. When extname is built statically
into PHP, the ./configure script will use this line to determine that depname must be
initialized first. The optional parameter is a flag to indicate that depname should be
loaded before extname if its also being built statically, but that it's not a required dependency.

An example of this macro in use can be found in PDO drivers—such as
pdo_mysql—which are predictably dependent on the PDO extension:

```
ifdef([PHP_ADD_EXTENDION_DEP],
[
  PHP_ADD_EXTENSION_DEP(pdo_mysql, pdo)
])
```

Notice that the PHP_ADD_EXTENSION_DEP() macro was wrapped in an ifdef() construct. This is because PDO and its drivers are meant to compile on any version of PHP
greater than or equal to 5.0, yet the PHP_ADD_EXTENSION_DEP() macro does not exist
until version 5.1.0.

Runtime Module Dependency

The next location where you'll need to register dependencies is within the zend_
module_entry structure itself. Consider the zend_module_entry structure you declared
in Chapter 5:

```
zend_module_entry sample_module_entry = {
#if ZEND_MODULE_API_NO >= 20010901
    STANDARD_MODULE_HEADER,
#endif
    PHP_SAMPLE_EXTNAME,
    php_sample_functions,
    NULL, /* MINIT */
    NULL, /* MSHUTDOWN */
    NULL, /* RINIT */
    NULL, /* RSHUTDOWN */
    NULL, /* MINFO */
#if ZEND_MODULE_API_NO >= 20010901
    PHP_SAMPLE_EXTVER,
#endif
    STANDARD_MODULE_PROPERTIES
};
```

Adding runtime module dependency information means making a minor change to the
STANDARD_MODULE_HEADER section.

```
zend_module_entry sample_module_entry = {
#if ZEND_MODULE_API_NO >= 220050617
    STANDARD_MODULE_HEADER_EX, NULL,
    php_sample_deps,
#elif ZEND_MODULE_API_NO >= 20010901
    STANDARD_MODULE_HEADER,
#endif
    PHP_SAMPLE_EXTNAME,
    php_sample_functions,
```

```
    NULL, /* MINIT */
    NULL, /* MSHUTDOWN */
    NULL, /* RINIT */
    NULL, /* RSHUTDOWN */
    NULL, /* MINFO */
#if ZEND_MODULE_API_NO >= 20010901
    PHP_SAMPLE_EXTVER,
#endif
    STANDARD_MODULE_PROPERTIES
};
```

Now, if the ZEND_MODULE_API_NO is high enough—indicating one of the beta releases of PHP 5.1.0 or later—STANDARD_MODULE_PROPERTIES will be replaced with a slightly more complex structure containing a reference to module dependency information.

This target structure would then be defined above your zend_module_entry struct as something like the following:

```
#if ZEND_MODULE_API_NO >= 220050617
static zend_module_dep php_sample_deps[] = {
    ZEND_MODULE_REQUIRED("zlib")
    {NULL,NULL,NULL}
};
#endif
```

Just like a zend_function_entry vector, this list can take as many entries as necessary checking each dependency in order. If an attempt is made to load a module with an unmet dependency, Zend will abort the load reporting the name of the unmet dependency so that the end user can resolve it by loading the other module first.

Speaking the Windows Dialect

Everything you've seen so far—with the exception of the runtime dependency section—has been based around the UNIX build system's config.m4 file. Although most of the concepts surrounding config.m4 syntax are directly mappable to the config.w32 file, the actual syntax used requires that a few concepts be reworked to fit this unique environment.

The first and most prevalent difference between these two styles is that config.m4 is based on bourne shell scripting whereas the config.w32 file for Windows is executed by the Windows scripting host as JScript code.

The remainder of this chapter lists the macros you've already seen plus a few more along with their config.w32 counterparts and a brief description of their use.

```
PHP_ARG_WITH(argname,description,helptext)
ARG_WITH(argname,helptext,default)
```

As you can see, the win32 variant has a noticeably different prototype. Unlike the m4 version, where the default is implied by how the value is tested later in the script, the default is explicitly set here and the descriptive text is completely omitted.

```
PHP_ARG_ENABLE(argname,description,helptext)
ARG_ENABLE(argname,helptext,default)
```

The `ENABLE` macro follows the same exceptions as its `WITH` counterpart.

```
PHP_CHECK_LIBRARY(library,symbol,success,failure,flags)
CHECK_LIB(library,symbol,path,common)
```

The win32 version of this macro-based action returns a true or false value depending on whether `symbol` is not found in the `library` located in `path`. If common is specified—with the common name for the package that contains this library—additional search paths containing this name will be scanned as well. Config files using `CHECK_LIB` should test the return value and take action using a more traditional if/then/else construct.

```
AC_DEFINE(name,value,comment)
AC_DEFINE(name,value,comment)
```

This macro has the same name and definitions in `config.w32` parlance as `config.m4`.

```
AD_DEFINE_UNQUOTED(name,value,comment)
DEFINE(name,value)
```

The `UNQUOTED` variant of `AC_DEFINE` varies in that the contents of `name` and `value` are used in their literal form in the resulting `config.h` file. In the case of `config.w32`'s variant—`DEFINE`—no comment is allowed because defines are included in a different fashion.

```
PHP_ADD_EXTENSION_DEP(extname,depname,optional)
ADD_EXTENSION_DEP(extname,depname,optional)
```

The only difference between the `config.m4` and `config.w32` versions of this macro are the name.

```
PHP_NEW_EXTENSION(extname,sources[,shared[,sapi[,cflags[,cxx]]]])
EXTENSION(extname,sources[,shared[,cflags[,dllname[,objdir]]]])
```

In both cases, a new PHP extension named `extname` is declared using the source files specified in `sources`. `shared` may be either *shared* or *yes* to indicate that the extension will be compiled as a dynamically loadable module. Typically this value is passed with as the `$ext_shared` variable, which is automatically provided by `./configure` / `./configure.js` if the extension is included as `--enable-extname=shared`. `sapi` may be optionally set to `cli` to indicate that the module is only built for the `CLI` or `CGI` sapis. The `cflags` parameter can contain additional compiler settings to be passed to `CC` when the objects are being built. By default, the Windows DLL will be named `php_extname.dll` unless an alternative is specified in the `dllname` parameter. All source files are compiled using the `Visual C++` compiler under Windows; however, UNIX builds will use `CC` (typically `gcc`) to build files unless the `cxx` parameter is set to a truth value. Under Windows, `objdir` may be specified to place intermediate object files in a specific temporary folder.

```
AC_MSG_ERROR(message)
ERROR(message)
```

These macros will output an error `message` and halt the configuration process. Use this anytime your configuration script encounters a condition that can't be worked around by gracefully degrading its compile options.

```
AC_MSG_WARNING(message)
WARNING(message)
```

Like the error macros, these constructs will output a `message` during configuration. In this case, the message is a warning, and configuration will continue without stopping.

Summary

If your extension will be built under unknown or uncontrolled environments, it will be crucial to make it intelligent enough to adapt to those strange surroundings. Using the powerful scripting capabilities offered by PHP's UNIX and Windows build systems, you should be able to detect trouble and lead that unknown administrator to a solution before she needs to call for help.

Now that you've got a foundation in building up extensions from scratch and interfacing with the PHP api, you're ready to take the drudgery out of extension development by using some of the handy tools developed for PHP over the years to make prototyping new extensions quick and relatively painless.

18

Extension Generators

AS YOU'VE NO DOUBT NOTICED, EVERY PHP extension contains a few very common—and frankly boring—structures and files. When starting a new extension, it would make sense to begin with these common structures already in place and only have to worry about filling in the functional bits. To that end, there's a very simple, very practical shell script included with the standard PHP distribution.

ext_skel

Navigate to the `ext/` folder under your PHP source tree and execute the following command:

```
jdoe@devbox:/home/jdoe/cvs/php-src/ext/$ ./ext_skel —extname=sample7
```

After a few moments and a little bit of text, you'll receive some instructions along the lines of the following:

```
To use your new extension, you will have to execute the following steps:

1.  $ cd ..
2.  $ vi ext/sample7/config.m4
3.  $ ./buildconf
4.  $ ./configure —[with|enable]-sample7
5.  $ make
6.  $ ./php -f ext/sample7/sample7.php
7.  $ vi ext/sample7/sample7.c
8.  $ make

Repeat steps 3-6 until you are satisfied with ext/sample7/config.m4 and
step 6 confirms that your module is compiled into PHP. Then, start writing
code and repeat the last two steps as often as necessary.
```

Looking in `ext/sample7` at this point, you'll see a verbosely commented version of the files you first put together in Chapter 5, "Your First Extension." As it stands you won't be able to compile your extension just yet; however, with just a little bit of work massaging `config.m4` as the instructions state, you should be off and running with an extension that accomplishes nearly as much as you originally wrote in Chapter 5.

Generating Function Prototypes

If you're writing an extension to wrap a third-party library, you already have a machine readable version of what the functions need to look like and what their basic behavior needs to be. By passing one extra parameter to `./ext_skel`, it will automatically scan your header file and create simple `PHP_FUNCTION()` blocks to accommodate the interface. Try it out by instructing `./ext_skel` to parse the `zlib` headers:

```
jdoe@devbox:/home/jdoe/cvs/php-src/ext/$ ./ext_skel —extname=sample8 \
—proto=/usr/local/include/zlib/zlib.h
```

Glancing inside `ext/sample8/sample8.c` now, you'll find more than a dozen `PHP_FUNCTION()` declarations, one for each `zlib` function. Notice, however, that the skeleton generation process issued some warning messages about unknown resource types. You'll need to pay particular attention to these functions and apply some of the experience you gained in Chapter 9, "The Resource Data Type," in order to link the internal complex structures to userspace accessible variables.

PECL_Gen

A more complete but complex code generator, `PECL_Gen`, is available from PECL (http://pecl.php.net) and can be installed with the usual `pear install PECL_Gen` command.

Once installed, it can be run identically to `ext_skel`, taking the same input arguments and producing roughly the same output, or if a complete XML definition file is provided, it will produce a more robust and complete ready-to-compile extension. `PECL_Gen` doesn't save you from writing the core functionality of your extension; rather, it provides an alternative form to express your code prior to being generated into an extension.

specfile.xml

The simplest extension definition file might look like Listing 18.1.

Listing 18.1 **A Minimal** `specfile.xml`

```
<?xml version="1.0" encoding="utf-8">
<extension name="sample9">
 <functions>
  <function name="sample9_hello_world" role="public">
   <code>
<![CDATA[
```

Listing 18.1   **Continued**

```
    php_printf("Hello World!");
]]>
   </code>
  </function>
 </functions>
</extension>
```

By running this file through the PECL-Gen command:

```
jdoe@devbox:/home/jdoe/cvs/php-src/ext/$ pecl-gen specfile.xml
```

a full set of files will be produced to generate an extension named sample9, which exports a userspace function, sample9_hello_world().

About the Extension

In addition to the functional files you're already familiar with, PECL_Gen also builds a package.xml file that can be used by the pear installer. Having this file will be useful if you plan to release packages in the PECL repository, or if you just want to use the pear packaging system to deliver your content.

Either way, you can specify most of the package.xml file's elements as part of your PECL_Gen specfile.

```
<extension name="sample9">
 <summary>Extension 9 generated by PECL_Gen</summary>
 <description>Another sample of PHP Extension Writing</description>
 <maintainers>
  <maintainer>
   <name>John D. Bookreader</name>
   <email>jdb@example.com</email>
   <role>lead</role>
  </maintainer>
 </maintainers>
 <release>
  <version>0.1</version>
  <date>2006-01-01</date>
  <state>beta</state>
  <notes>Initial Release</notes>
 </release>
 ...
</extension>
```

This information will be translated into the final package.xml file when PECL_Gen creates the rest of your extension.

Dependencies

As you saw in Chapter 17, "Configuration and Linking," dependencies can be scanned for in `config.m4` and `config.w32` files. `PECL_Gen` is able to craft these scanning steps using the `<deps>` section to declare various types of dependencies. By default, dependencies listed under the `<deps>` tag apply to both UNIX and win32 builds unless the `platform` attribute is specified listing one of these targets.

```
<extension name="sample9">
 ...
 <deps platform="unix">
 <!- UNIX specific dependencies ->
 </deps>
 <deps platform="win32">
 <!- Win32 specific dependencies ->
 </deps>
 <deps platform="all">
 <!- Dependencies that apply to all platforms ->
 </deps>
</extension>
```

—with

Ordinarily, an extension will be configured to use the —enable-extname style configuration option. By adding one or more `<with>` tags to the `<deps>` block, not only is the configuration option changed to —with-extname, but required headers can be scanned for as well:

```
<deps platform="unix">
 <with defaults="/usr:/usr/local:/opt"
       testfile="include/zlib/zlib.h">zlib headers</with>
</deps>
```

Libraries

Required libraries are also listed under the `<deps>` section using the `<lib>` tag.

```
<deps platform="all">
 <lib name="ssleay" platform="win32"/>
 <lib name="crypto" platform="unix"/>
 <lib name="z" platform="unix" function="inflate"/>
</deps>
```

In the first two examples here, only the presence of the library was checked for; in the third example, the library was actually loaded and scanned to be sure the `inflate()` function was defined.

> **Note**
> Despite the fact that the `<deps>` tag has already named the target platform, the `<lib>` tag also has a
> platform attribute that can override the `<deps>` tag's platform setting. Be careful when mixing and
> matching these!

`<header>`

Additional include files needed by your code can be appended to a list of `#include`
directives by specifying the `<header>` tag within a `<deps>` block. To force a specific
header to be included first, add the `prepend="yes"` parameter to your `<header>` tag.
Like the `<lib>` dependency, `<header>` can be restricted on a per-platform basis:

```
<deps>
 <header name="sys/types.h" platform="unix" prepend="yes"/>
 <header name="zlib/zlib.h"/>
</deps>
```

Constants

Userspace constants are declared using one or more `<constant>` tags within the
`<constants>` block. Each tag requires a `name` and `value` attribute as well as a `type`
attribute that must be equal to one of the following: `int`, `float`, or `string`.

```
<example name="sample9">
 <constants>
  <constant name="SAMPLE9_APINO" type="int" value="20060101"/>
  <constant name="SAMPLE9_VERSION" type="float" value="1.0"/>
  <constant name="SAMPLE9_AUTHOR" type="string" value="John Doe"/>
 </constants>
 ...
</example>
```

Globals

Per thread globals are declared in nearly the same way. The only difference is that the
`type` parameter is specified using its C language prototype rather than a PHP userspace
descriptor. Once declared and built, globals are accessed through the usual `EXTNAME_`
`G(globalname)` macro syntax discussed in Chapter 12, "Startup, Shutdown, and a Few
Points in Between" In this case, the `value` attribute represents the default value held by
that variable at the start of a request. Note that the default should only be specified in
`specfile.xml` for simple scalar numerics. Strings and other complex structures should
be manually set in `RINIT`.

```
<example name="example9">
 <globals>
```

```
 <global name="greeting" type="char *"/>
 <global name="greeting_was_issued" type="zend_bool" value="1"/>
 </globals>
 ...
</example>
```

INI Options

To bind a thread-safe global to a `php.ini` setting, use the `<phpini>` tag rather than `<global>`. This tag requires two additional parameters: `onupdate="updatemethod"` to indicate how INI changes should be processed, and `access="mode"` where mode is one of `all`, `user`, `perdir`, or `system` and carries the same meanings as they did in Chapter 13, "INI Settings."

```
<example name="sample9">
 <globals>
  <!— Defines sample9.mysetting —>
  <phpini name="mysetting" type="int" value="42"
          onupdate="OnUpdateLong" access="all"/>
 </globals>
</example>
```

Functions

You already saw the most basic kind of function declaration; however, the `<function>` tag in a `PECL_Gen` specfile actually supports two different types of functions.

Both versions support a `<summary>` and `<description>` attribute that you've already used at the `<extension>` level; however, the only required element for each type is the `<code>` tag, which contains literal C code that will be placed in your source file.

```
<extension name="sample9">
 <functions>
  <!— Function definitions go here —>
 </functions>
</extension>
```

role="public"

As you might expect, any function declared with a public role will be wrapped in the appropriate `PHP_FUNCTION()` header and curly braces with matching entries going into the extension's function entry vector.

In addition to the tags supported by other functions, public types also allow a `<proto>` tag to be specified. This tag should be formatted to match the prototypes shown in the PHP online manual so they can be parsed by documentation generators.

```
<functions>
 <function role="public" name="sample9_greet_me">
  <summary>Greet a person by name</summary>
  <description>Accept a name parameter as a string and say
   hello to that person.  Returns TRUE.</description>
  <proto>bool sample9_greet_me(string name)</proto>
  <code>
<![CDATA[
    char *name;
    int name_len;

    if (zend_parse_parameters(ZEND_NUM_ARGS() TSRMLS_CC, "s",
                              &name, &name_len) == FAILURE) {
        return;
    }

    php_printf("Hello ");
    PHPWRITE(name, name_len);
    php_printf("!\n");
    RETURN_TRUE;
]]>
  </code>
 </function>
</functions>
```

role="internal"

Internal functions cover the five `zend_module_entry` functions: `MINIT`, `MSHUTDOWN`, `RINIT`, `RSHUTDOWN`, and `MINFO`. Specifying a name other than one of these five is an error and will not be processed by the `pecl-gen` command.

```
<functions>
 <function role="internal" name="MINFO">
  <code>
<![CDATA[
    php_info_print_table_start();
    php_info_print_table_header(2, "Column1", "Column2");
    php_info_print_table_end();
]]>
  </code>
 </function>
</functions>
```

Custom Code

Any other program code that needs to exist in your extension can be included using the `<code>` tag. To place the arbitrary code in your target `extname.c` file, use `role="code"`;

otherwise, use `role="header"` to place the code in the target `php_extname.h` file. By default, code will be placed near the bottom of the code or header file unless `position="top"` is specified.

```
<example name="sample9">
  <code name="php_sample9_data" role="header" position="bottom">
<![CDATA[
typedef struct _php_sample9_data {
  long val;
} php_sample9_data;
]]>
  </code>
  <code name="php_sample9_data_ctor" role="code" position="top">
<![CDATA[
static php_sample9_data *php_sample9_data_ctor(long value)
{
    php_sample9_data *ret;
    ret = emalloc(sizeof(php_sample9_data));
    ret->val = value;
    return ret;
}
]]>
  </code>
  ...
</example>
```

Summary

Using the tools covered in this chapter, you're ready to develop PHP extensions quickly and bring your code to production with fewer bugs than writing everything by hand. Now it's time to turn towards embedding PHP into other projects. In the coming chapters you'll take control of the PHP environment and leverage the power of the Zend Engine to add scripting capabilities to your existing applications, making them more versatile and more useful to your customers.

19

Setting Up a Host Environment

Now that you've explored the world of the PHPAPI and are comfortable working with zvals and extending the language with internal hooks and bindings, it's time to turn the tables and really use the language for what it does best: interpreting script code.

The Embed SAPI

Recall from the Introduction that PHP is built out of a system of layers. At the highest layer are all the extensions that provide the userspace library of functions and classes. Meanwhile, the bottom is occupied by the Server API (SAPI) layer, which acts as an interface to web servers such as Apache and IIS as well as the command line interface (CLI).

Among the many SAPI implementations is a special type known as *Embed*—short for embeddable. When this SAPI implementation is built, a library object is created that contains all the PHP and Zend API functions and variables you've come to know, along with an extra set of helper functions and macros to make interfacing from an external program simple.

Generating the library and header files of the Embed SAPI is performed just like any other SAPI compilation. Just pass —enable-embed to the ./configure command and build as usual. As before, it will be helpful to use —enable-debug in case errors pop up and need to be tracked down.

You'll also want to keep —enable-maintainer-zts turned on both for the familiar reason that it will help you notice coding mistakes, but also for another reason. Imagine for a moment that you have more than one application that will be using the PHP Embed library to perform scripting tasks; one of these is a simple, short-lived application with no use for threading and so would want ZTS turned off for efficiency.

Now imagine that the second application does use threading and that, like a web server, each thread needs to track its own request context. If ZTS is turned off, only the first application will be able to use the library; however, with ZTS enabled, both applications can take advantage of the same shared object in their own process space.

You could, of course, build both versions and simply give them different names, but that tends to be more problematic than does simply accepting the minor slowdown that including ZTS support when it's not needed.

By default, the embed library will be built as a shared object libphp5.so—or dynamic link library under Windows—however, it might be built as a static library using the optional static keyword: –enable-embed=static.

Building a static version of the Embed SAPI avoids the ZTS versus non-ZTS problem, as well as the potential situation of having multiple PHP versions on a single system. On the downside, it does mean that your resulting application binary will be significantly larger—bearing the full weight of the Zend Engine and PHP framework—so consider your choices with as much or more care as you would other, smaller libraries.

Whichever build type you choose, once you issue make install, libphp5 will be copied to lib/ under your ./configure selected EPREFIX root. An additional header file named php_embed.h will also be placed into EPREFIX/include/php/sapi/embed next to several other important headers that you'll need as you compile programs that use the PHP Embed library.

Building and Compiling a Host Application

By itself, a library is just a collection of code with no purpose. In order to "make it go," you'll need something to embed PHP into. To begin, let's put together a very simple wrapper application that starts up the Zend Engine and initializes PHP to handle a request, and then reverses the process to unwind the stack and clean up resources (see Listing 19.1).

Listing 19.1 **A Simple** embed1.c **Application**

```
#include <sapi/embed/php_embed.h>

int main(int argc, char *argv[])
{
    PHP_EMBED_START_BLOCK(argc,argv)
    PHP_EMBED_END_BLOCK()

    return 0;
}
```

Because so many header files are involved, building actually requires a longer command than this simple code snippet would suggest. If you used a different EPREFIX location than the default (/usr/local), be sure to substitute that location in the following example:

```
$ gcc -o embed1 embed1.c \
    -I/usr/local/include/php/ \
    -I/usr/local/include/php/main \
```

```
-I/usr/local/include/php/Zend \
-I/usr/local/include/php/TSRM \
-L/usr/local/lib -lphp5
```

Because this command will become a hassle to type over and over again, you might prefer to use a simple Makefile instead (see Listing 19.2).

Listing 19.2   **Reducing the Work with a Makefile**

```
CC = gcc
CFLAGS = -c -I/usr/local/include/php/ \
           -I/usr/local/include/php/main \
           -I/usr/local/include/php/Zend \
           -I/usr/local/include/php/TSRM \
           -Wall -g
LDFLAGS = -L/usr/local/lib -lphp5

all: embed1.c
    $(CC) -o embed1.o embed1.c $(CFLAGS)
    $(CC) -o embed1 embed1.o $(LDFLAGS)
```

> **Note**
>
> This `Makefile` differs from the earlier command provided in a few important ways. First, it enables compile-time warnings with the `-Wall` switch, and adds debugging information with `-g`. It also splits the compilation and linking stages into two separate pieces to make it easier to add more source files later on. Feel free to reorganize this `Makefile` to suit your personal tastes; just be sure to use tabs for indentation here, not spaces.

Now, as you make changes to your `embed1.c` source file, you'll be able to rebuild the `embed1` executable with just a simple `make` command.

Re-creating CLI by Wrapping Embed

Now that PHP is accessible from your application, it's time to make it do something. The remainder of this chapter centers around re-creating portions of the CLI SAPI's behavior within the framework of this test application.

Easily, the most basic functionality of the CLI binary is the ability to name a script on the command line and have it interpreted by PHP. Implement that in your application by replacing `embed1.c` with the code in Listing 19.3.

Listing 19.3   `embed1.c`

```
#include <stdio.h>
#include <sapi/embed/php_embed.h>

int main(int argc, char *argv[])
```

Listing 19.3   **Continued**

```
{
    zend_file_handle script;

    /* Basic parameter checking */
    if (argc <= 1) {
        fprintf(stderr, "Usage: embed1 filename.php <arguments>\n");
        return -1;
    }

    /* Set up a File Handle structure */
    script.type = ZEND_HANDLE_FP;
    script.filename = argv[1];
    script.opened_path = NULL;
    script.free_filename = 0;
    if (!(script.handle.fp = fopen(script.filename, "rb"))) {
        fprintf(stderr, "Unable to open: %s\n", argv[1]);
        return -1;
    }

    /* Ignore argv[0] when passing to PHP */
    argc--;
    argv++;

    PHP_EMBED_START_BLOCK(argc,argv)
        php_execute_script(&script TSRMLS_CC);
    PHP_EMBED_END_BLOCK()

    return 0;
}
```

Of course, you'll need a file to test this out with, make a short PHP script—anything you like—in a file called test.php, and then execute it using your embed1 binary:

```
$ ./embed1 test.php
```

If you pass additional arguments onto the command line, you'll see that they reach your script in the $_SERVER['argc'] and $_SERVER['argv'] variables.

> **Note**
>
> You might have noticed that the code placed between PHP_EMBED_START_BLOCK() and
> PHP_EMBED_END_BLOCK() was indented. This is a subtle homage to the fact that these macros form a
> C block scope. That is, the PHP_EMBED_START_BLOCK() contains an opening curly brace { with a
> matching closing curly brace } that is hidden within PHP_EMBED_END_BLOCK(). What's important
> about this is that these macros can't be buried in separate utility startup/shutdown functions. You'll see this
> problem resolved in the next chapter.

Reusing Old Tricks

After the `PHP_EMBED_START_BLOCK()` has been called, your application is positioned at the start of a PHP request cycle, just after the completion of `RINIT` callbacks. At this point you could issue `php_execute_script()` commands such as you did earlier, or any other valid PHP/Zend API instruction you might find in a `PHP_FUNCTION()` or `RINIT()` block.

Setting Initial Variables

Chapter 2, "Variables from the Inside Out," introduced the concept of manipulating the symbol table, then Chapters 5–18 showed you how to use those techniques with internal functions called by userspace scripts. Nothing has changed as a result of the process being turned around; your wrapper application can still manipulate the symbol table even though no userspace script is active. Try replacing your current `PHP_EMBED_START_BLOCK()`/`PHP_EMBED_END_BLOCK()` group with the following listing:

```
PHP_EMBED_START_BLOCK(argc,argv)
    zval *type;

    /* $type = "Embedded"; */
    ALLOC_INIT_ZVAL(type);
    ZVAL_STRING(type, "Embedded", 1);
    ZEND_SET_SYMBOL(&EG(symbol_table), "type", type);

    php_execute_script(&script TSRMLS_CC);
PHP_EMBED_END_BLOCK()
```

Now rebuild `embed1` with `make` and try it out with the following simple test script:

```
<?php
    var_dump($type);
?>
```

This simple concept can be easily extended to fill in the `$_SERVER` superglobal array—which is of course, where this type of information belongs.

```
PHP_EMBED_START_BLOCK(argc,argv)
    zval **SERVER, *type;

    /* Fetch $_SERVER from the global scope */
    zend_hash_find(&EG(symbol_table), "_SERVER", sizeof("_SERVER"),
                                        (void**)&SERVER);

    /* $_SERVER['SAPI_TYPE'] = "Embedded"; */
    ALLOC_INIT_ZVAL(type);
    ZVAL_STRING(type, "Embedded", 1);
```

```
    ZEND_SET_SYMBOL(Z_ARRVAL_PP(SERVER), "SAPI_TYPE", type);

    php_execute_script(&script TSRMLS_CC);
PHP_EMBED_END_BLOCK()
```

Overriding INI options

In Chapter 13, "INI Settings," as part of the topic on INI modification handlers, you
looked briefly at the topic of INI stages. The PHP_EMBED_START_BLOCK() macro being
used in these examples places all of your code squarely in the RUNTIME stage. What this
means in practice is that it's simply too late to modify certain settings such as
register_globals and magic_quotes_gpc.

Having access to the internals is not without its benefit however. So-called "adminis-
trative settings" such as safe_mode can be turned on or off even at this late stage by
using the zend_alter_ini_entry() command described in the following prototype:

```
int zend_alter_ini_entry(char *name, uint name_length,
                         char *new_value, uint new_value_length,
                         int modify_type, int stage);
```

name, new_value, and their corresponding length parameters are exactly what you'd
expect them to be: Change the INI setting described by name to new_value. Note that
name_length includes the trailing null byte, whereas new_value_length does not; however, both strings must be null terminated.

modify_type is meant to provide simplified access control checking. Recall that every
INI setting is given a modifiable attribute comprised of a combination of the
PHP_INI_SYSTEM, PHP_INI_PERDIR, or PHP_INI_USER constants. When using
zend_alter_ini_entry() to modify an INI setting, the modify_type parameter must
contain at least one flag in common with the INI setting's modifiable attribute.

The userspace ini_set() function takes advantage of this built-in feature by passing
PHP_INI_USER, meaning only INI settings with a modifiable attribute containing the
PHP_INI_USER flag can be changed using this function. When using this API call from
your embedded application, you can short-circuit this access control system by passing
the PHP_INI_ALL flag instead, which contains a combination of all INI access levels.

stage must correspond to the current state of the Zend Engine; for these simple
embed examples, this is always PHP_INI_STAGE_RUNTIME. If this were an extension or a
more sophisticated embedding application—which you'll get into soon enough—this
value might be PHP_INI_STAGE_STARTUP or PHP_INI_STAGE_ACTIVE instead.

Extend your current embed1.c source file by enforcing safe_mode at the start before
executing the script file:

```
PHP_EMBED_START_BLOCK(argc,argv)
    zval **SERVER, *type;

    /* Ensure that safe_mode is always enabled
```

```
     * regardless of php.ini settings */
    zend_alter_ini_entry("safe_mode", sizeof("safe_mode"),
                         "1", sizeof("1") - 1,
                         PHP_INI_ALL, PHP_INI_STAGE_RUNTIME);

    /* Fetch $_SERVER from the global scope */
    zend_hash_find(&EG(symbol_table), "_SERVER", sizeof("_SERVER"),
                                          (void**)&SERVER);

    /* $_SERVER['SAPI_TYPE'] = "Embedded"; */
    ALLOC_INIT_ZVAL(type);
    ZVAL_STRING(type, "Embedded", 1);
    ZEND_SET_SYMBOL(Z_ARRVAL_PP(SERVER), "SAPI_TYPE", type);

    php_execute_script(&script TSRMLS_CC);
PHP_EMBED_END_BLOCK()
```

Declaring Additional Superglobals

In Chapter 12, "Startup, Shutdown, and a Few Points in Between," you were told that userspace autoglobals, also known as *superglobals*, could only be declared during the startup (MINIT) phase. Meanwhile, the embedding method described in this chapter jumps straight through startup and activation into the runtime stage. As with INI overrides, that doesn't mean it's entirely too late.

The reality of superglobal declaration is that it merely needs to come before script compilation, and it should only happen once during the lifetime of the PHP process. Under normal circumstances in an extension, MINIT is the only place where this can be guaranteed.

Because your wrapper application is now the one in control however, it's possible to guarantee both of these points are respected merely by declaring the userspace autoglobal prior to the php_execute_script() command—which is where the script source file is actually compiled. Try it out by declaring $_EMBED as a superglobal and initializing it to some default value:

```
PHP_EMBED_START_BLOCK(argc,argv)
    zval *EMBED, *foo;

    /* Create $_EMBED as an array in the global scope */
    ALLOC_INIT_ZVAL(EMBED);
    array_init(EMBED);
    ZEND_SET_SYMBOL(&EG(symbol_table), "_EMBED", EMBED);

    /* $_EMBED['foo'] = "Bar"; */
    ALLOC_INIT_ZVAL(foo);
    ZVAL_STRING(foo, "Bar", 1);
```

```
        ZEND_SET_SYMBOL(Z_ARRVAL_P(EMBED), "foo", foo);


        /* Declare $_EMBED as a superglobal */
        zend_register_auto_global("_EMBED", sizeof("_EMBED") - 1
#ifdef ZEND_ENGINE_2
                                , NULL TSRMLS_CC);
#if PHP_MAJOR_VERSION > 5 || (PHP_MAJOR_VERSION == 5 && PHP_MINOR_VERSION > 0)
        /* PHP >= 5.1 requires the arming function to be manually disabled */
        zend_auto_global_disable_jit("_EMBED", sizeof("_EMBED") - 1 TSRMLS_CC);
#endif

#else
                            TSRMLS_CC);
#endif
        php_execute_script(&script TSRMLS_CC);
    PHP_EMBED_END_BLOCK()
```

Remember, Zend Engine 2 (PHP 5.0 and later) uses a different prototype for
`zend_register_auto_global()` so you need the `#ifdef` shown previously to maintain
PHP4 compatibility. If you don't care about maintaining compatibility with older versions of PHP, you can leave these directives out and have cleaner code at the end of
the day.

Summary

As you can see, embedding the full force of the Zend Engine and PHP language into
your application actually requires less work than extending it with new functionality.
Because they both share the same basic API, learning to do one makes the other instantly accessible.

Through this chapter you explored the simplest form of embedding script code by
taking advantage of the all-in-one macros `PHP_EMBED_START_BLOCK()` and `PHP_EMBED_
END_BLOCK()`. In the next chapter, you'll peel back the layers of these macros to integrate
PHP more seamlessly with your host application.

20

Advanced Embedding

PHP's EMBEDED SAPI CAN PROVIDE MORE THAN just a means to synchronously load and execute script files. By understanding how the pieces of PHP's execution model fit together, it's possible to slide in and out of PHP's environment during a given request, and even give a script the power to call back into your host application. This chapter will cover the means to take advantage of the I/O hooks provided by the SAPI layer, and expand on the execution model you've already started to explore as part of previous topics.

Calling Back into PHP

In addition to loading external scripts, as you saw in the last chapter, your PHP embedding application can also execute smaller snippets of arbitrary code using the underlying function that implements the familiar userspace eval() command.

```
int zend_eval_string(char *str, zval *retval_ptr,
                     char *string_name TSRMLS_DC)
```

Here, str is the actual PHP script code to be executed, whereas string_name is an arbitrary description to associate with the execution. If an error occurs, PHP will report this description as the "filename" in the error output. retval_ptr, as you might guess, will be populated with any return value generated by the passed code. Try it out by creating a new project from Listing 20.1.

Listing 20.1   embed2.c—**Running Arbitrary PHP Code**

```
#include <sapi/embed/php_embed.h>

int main(int argc, char *argv[])
{
    PHP_EMBED_START_BLOCK(argc, argv)
        zend_eval_string("echo 'Hello World!';", NULL,
                         "Simple Hello World App" TSRMLS_CC);
```

Listing 20.1   **Continued**

```
    PHP_EMBED_END_BLOCK()
    return 0;
}
```

Now build this using the command or `Makefile` shown in Chapter 19, "Setting Up a Host Environment," with `embed1` replaced by `embed2`.

Alternatives to Script File Inclusion

Predictably, this makes compiling and executing external script files far easier than the method given previously because your application can simply replace its more complicated sequence of open/prepare/execute with this simpler, more functional design:

```
#include <sapi/embed/php_embed.h>

int main(int argc, char *argv[])
{
    char *filename;

    if (argc <= 1) {
        fprintf(stderr, "Usage: embed1 filename.php <arguments>\n");
        return -1;
    }
    filename = argv[1];

    /* Ignore argv[0] when passing to PHP */
    argc--;
    argv++;

    PHP_EMBED_START_BLOCK(argc,argv)
        char *include_script;

        spprintf(&include_script, 0, "include '%s';", filename);
        zend_eval_string(include_script, NULL, filename TSRMLS_CC);
        efree(include_script);
    PHP_EMBED_END_BLOCK()

    return 0;
}
```

> **Note**
>
> This particular method suffers from the disadvantage that if the filename contains a single quote, a parse error will result—at best. Fortunately this can be solved by using the `php_addslashes()` API call found in `ext/standard/php_string.h`. Take some time to look through this file and the API reference in the appendices as you'll find many features that can save you from reinventing the wheel later on.

Calling Userspace Functions

As you saw with loading and executing script files, there are two ways to call a userspace function from internals. The most obvious at this point would probably be to reuse `zend_eval_string()`, combining the function name and all its parameters into one monolithic string, and then collecting the return value:

```
PHP_EMBED_START_BLOCK(argc,argv)
  char *command;
  zval retval;

  spprintf(&command, 0, "return nl2br('%s');", paramin);
  zend_eval_string(command, &retval, "nl2br() execution");
  efree(command);
  paramout = Z_STRVAL(retval);
PHP_EMBED_END_BLOCK()
```

Just like the include variant a moment ago, this method has a fatal flaw: If bad data is given by `paramin`, the function will fail at best, or cause unexpected results at worst. The solution is to avoid compiling a runtime snippet of code at all, and call the function directly using the `call_user_function()` API method instead:

```
int call_user_function(HashTable *function_table, zval **object_pp,
                        zval *function_name, zval *retval_ptr,
                        zend_uint param_count, zval *params[] TSRMLS_DC);
```

In practice, `function_table` will always be `EG(function_table)` when called from outside the engine. If calling an object or class method, `object_pp` can be an `IS_OJBECT` zval for calling an instance method, or an `IS_STRING` value for making a static class call. `function_name` is typically an `IS_STRING` value containing the name of the function to be called, but can be an `IS_ARRAY` containing an object or classname in element 0, and a method name in element 1.

The result of the function call will be populated into the zval pointer passed in `retval_ptr`. `param_count` and `params` act like the functions argc/argv data. That is, `params[0]` contains the first parameter to pass, and `params[param_count-1]` contains the last parameter to be passed.

This method can now be used to replace the prior example:

```
PHP_EMBED_START_BLOCK(argc, argv)
  zval *args[1];
  zval retval, str, funcname;

  ZVAL_STRING(&funcname, "nl2br", 0);
  args[0] = &str;
  ZVAL_STRINGL(args[0], paramin, paramin_len, 0);
  call_user_function(EG(function_table), NULL, &funcname,
                     &retval, 1, args TSRMLS_CC);
```

```
    paramout = Z_STRVAL(retval);
  PHP_EMBED_END_BLOCK()
```

Although the code listing here has actually become longer, the work being done has decreased dramatically because no intermediate code has to be compiled, the data being passed doesn't need to be duplicated, and each argument is already in a Zend-compatible structure. Also, remember that the original example was prone to potential errors if a string containing a quote was used. This version has no such drawback.

Dealing with Errors

When a serious error occurs, such as a script parse error, PHP will go into bailout mode. In the case of the simple embed examples you've seen so far, that means jumping directly to the PHP_EMBED_END_BLOCK() macro and bypassing any remaining code within the block. Because the purpose of most applications that embed the PHP interpreter is not strictly about executing PHP code, it makes sense to avoid having a PHP script bailout kill the entire application.

One approach might be to confine all executions to very small START/END blocks, so that a given bailout only bails out on the current chuck. The disadvantage to this is that each START/END block functions as its own isolated PHP request. Thus a pair of START/END blocks, as shown here, will not share a common scope, even though the legal syntax of each should allow one block to work with the other:

```
int main(int argc, char *argv[])
{
    PHP_EMBED_START_BLOCK(argc, argv)
        zend_eval_string("$a = 1;", NULL, "Script Block 1");
    PHP_EMBED_END_BLOCK()
    PHP_EMBED_START_BLOCK(argc, argv)
        /* Will display "NULL",
         * since variable $a isn't defined in this request */
        zend_eval_string("var_dump($a);", NULL, "Script Block 2");
    PHP_EMBED_END_BLOCK()
    return 0;
}
```

Another way to isolate these two zend_eval_string() calls is through the use of some Zend-specific pseudolanguage constructs: zend_try, zend_catch, and zend_end_try. Using these constructs, your application can set up a temporary override for the bailout target and deal with these serious errors in a sane manner. Consider the following variation of the prior example:

```
int main(int argc, char *argv[])
{
    PHP_EMBED_START_BLOCK(argc, argv)
        zend_try {
```

```
            /* Try to execute something that will fail */
            zend_eval_string("$1a = 1;", NULL, "Script Block 1a");
        } zend_catch {
            /* There was an error!
             * Try a different line instead */
            zend_eval_string("$a = 1;", NULL, "Script Block 1");
        } zend_end_try();
        /* Will display "NULL",
         * since variable $a isn't defined in this request */
        zend_eval_string("var_dump($a);", NULL, "Script Block 2");
    PHP_EMBED_END_BLOCK()
    return 0;
}
```

In the second version of this code sample, the parse error that occurs within the
zend_try block only bails out as far as the zend_catch block where it's handled by
using a good piece of code instead. The same block could be applied to the var_dump()
section later on as well; go ahead and try that out for yourself.

Initializing PHP

So far, you've seen the PHP_EMBED_START_BLOCK() and PHP_EMBED_END_BLOCK() macros
used to start up, execute, and shut down a PHP request in a nice tight, atomic package.
The advantage to this is that any serious errors will result in PHP bailing out only as far
as the PHP_EMBED_END_BLOCK() macro for its current scope. By keeping all your code
executions to small blocks located between these macros, a PHP error should be completely unable to take down your entire application.

As you just learned, the major disadvantage to this nice little theory is that each time
you establish a new START/END block, you effectively create a new request with a fresh
symbol table and you lose any sense of persistency.

The means by which to get the best of both worlds—error isolation and persistency—is to disassemble the START and END macros into their component pieces. Listing
20.2 shows the embed2.c program from the start of this chapter again, this time split into
bite-sized pieces.

Listing 20.2   embed3.c—**Manually Initializing and Shutting Down**

```
#include <sapi/embed/php_embed.h>

int main(int argc, char *argv[])
{
#ifdef ZTS
    void ***tsrm_ls;
#endif

    php_embed_init(argc, argv PTSRMLS_CC);
```

Listing 20.2 **Continued**

```
    zend_first_try {
        zend_eval_string("echo 'Hello World!';", NULL,
                         "Embed 2 Eval'd string" TSRMLS_CC);
    } zend_end_try();
    php_embed_shutdown(TSRMLS_C);

    return 0;
}
```

The same code is being executed as before, only this time you can see the open and close braces that have locked you into being unable to separate the START and END blocks. By placing php_embed_init() at the start of your application and php_emebd_shutdown() at the end, you gain the persistency of a single request for the life of your application while being able to use the zend_first_try { } zend_end_try(); construct to catch any fatal errors that would otherwise cause your entire wrapper app to bail out to the PHP_EMBED_END_BLOCK() macro at the end of your app.

> **Note**
>
> Notice that this time, zend_first_try was used rather than zend_try. It's important to use zend_first_try in the outermost try/catch block because zend_first_try performs a few extra steps that must not be stacked within each other.

To see this approach used in a more "real-world" environment, abstract out the startup and shutdown process as in the following variation of the script execution program you wrote earlier this chapter (see Listing 20.3).

Listing 20.3   embed4.c—**Abstracting Startup and Shutdown**

```
#include <sapi/embed/php_embed.h>
#ifdef ZTS
    void ***tsrm_ls;
#endif
static void startup_php(void)
{
    /* Create "dummy" argc/argv to hide the arguments
     * meant for our actual application */
    int argc = 1;
    char *argv[2] = { "embed4", NULL };
    php_embed_init(argc, argv PTSRMLS_CC);
}
static void shutdown_php(void)
{
```

Listing 20.3   **Continued**

```
    php_embed_shutdown(TSRMLS_C);
}
static void execute_php(char *filename)
{
    zend_first_try {
        char *include_script;
        spprintf(&include_script, 0, "include '%s';", filename);
        zend_eval_string(include_script, NULL, filename TSRMLS_CC);
        efree(include_script);
    } zend_end_try();
}

int main(int argc, char *argv[])
{

    if (argc <= 1) {
        printf("Usage: embed4 scriptfile");
        return -1;
    }
    startup_php();
    execute_php(argv[1]);
    shutdown_php();
    return 0;
}
```

Similar concepts can be applied to handling arbitrary code execution and other tasks. Just be sure to use `zend_first_try` for your outermost container, and `zend_try` for any blocks inside that container.

Overriding `INI_SYSTEM` and `INI_PERDIR` Options

In the last chapter, you used `zend_alter_ini_setting()` to modify some PHP INI options. Because sapi/embed thrusts your script directly into runtime mode, most of the more important INI options are unmodifiable after control has been returned to your application. To change these values, it's necessary to be able to execute code after the main engine startup so that space for these variables is available, yet before the request startup.

One approach might be to copy and paste the contents of `php_embed_init()` into your application, make the necessary changes in your local copy, and then use that method instead. Of course, this approach presents some problems.

First and foremost, you've effectively forked a portion of code someone else was already busily putting the work in on maintaining. Now, instead of just maintaining your application, you've got to keep up with a random bit of forked code someone else wrote as well. Fortunately, there are a few much simpler methods.

Overriding the Default `php.ini` File

Because embed is a sapi just like any other PHP sapi implementation, it's hooked into the engine by way of a `sapi_module_struct`. The embed SAPI declares and populates an instance of this structure that your application has access to even before calling `php_embed_init()`.

In this structure is a simple `char*` field named `php_ini_path_override`. To request that embed—and by extension PHP and Zend—use your alternate file, just populate this field with a `NULL`-terminated string prior to calling `php_embed_init()` as in the following modified `startup_php()` function in `embed4.c`.

```
static void startup_php(void)
{
    /* Create "dummy" argc/argv to hide the arguments
     * meant for our actual application */
    int argc = 1;
    char *argv[2] = { "embed4", NULL };

    php_embed_module.php_ini_path_override = "/etc/php_embed4.ini";
    php_embed_init(argc, argv PTSRMLS_CC);
}
```

This allows each application using the embed library to remain customizable, without imposing their configurations on each other. Conversely, if you'd rather prevent your application from using `php.ini` at all, simply set the `php_ini_ignore` field in `php_embed_module` and all settings will default to their built-in values unless specifically modified by your application.

Overriding Embed Startup

The `sapi_module_struct` also contains several callback functions, four of which are of interest for periodically taking back control during PHP startup and shutdown.

```
/* From main/SAPI.h */
typedef struct _sapi_module_struct {
    ...
    int (*startup)(struct _sapi_module_struct *sapi_module);
    int (*shutdown)(struct _sapi_module_struct *sapi_module);
    int (*activate)(TSRMLS_D);
    int (*deactivate)(TSRMLS_D);
    ...
} sapi_module_struct;
```

Do these method names ring a bell? They should—they correspond to an extension's `MINIT`, `MSHUTDOWN`, `RINIT`, and `RSHUTDOWN` methods and trigger during the same cycles as they do for extensions. To take advantage of these hooks, modify `startup_php()` in `embed4` to the following version along with the additional code provided:

```
static int (*original_embed_startup)(struct _sapi_module_struct *sapi_module);

static int embed4_startup_callback(struct _sapi_module_struct *sapi_module)
{
    /* Call original startup callback first,
     * otherwise the environment won't be ready */
    if (original_embed_startup(sapi_module) == FAILURE) {
        /* Application failure handling may occur here */
        return FAILURE;
    }
    /* Calling the original embed_startup actually places us
     * in the ACTIVATE stage rather than the STARTUP stage, but
     * we can still alter most INI_SYSTEM and INI_PERDIR entries anyhow
     */
    zend_alter_ini_entry("max_execution_time", sizeof("max_execution_time"),
                "15", sizeof("15") - 1, PHP_INI_SYSTEM, PHP_INI_STAGE_ACTIVATE);
    zend_alter_ini_entry("safe_mode", sizeof("safe_mode"),
                "1", sizeof("1") - 1, PHP_INI_SYSTEM, PHP_INI_STAGE_ACTIVATE);
    return SUCCESS;
}

static void startup_php(void)
{
    /* Create "dummy" argc/argv to hide the arguments
     * meant for our actual application */
    int argc = 1;
    char *argv[2] = { "embed4", NULL };

    /* Override the standard startup method with our own
     * but save the original so that it can still be invoked. */
    original_embed_startup = php_embed_module.startup;
    php_embed_module.startup = embed4_startup_callback;

    php_embed_init(argc, argv PTSRMLS_CC);
}
```

Using options like safe_mode, open_basedir, and others will help limit what individuals scripting behavior into your application can do and should help ensure a safer, more reliable application.

Capturing Output

Unless you're developing an incredibly simple console application, you probably don't want output generated by PHP script code to simply spill out onto the active terminal. Catching this output can be performed in a similar manner to the technique you just used to override the startup handler.

Hiding out in the `sapi_module_struct` are a few more useful callbacks:

```
typedef struct _sapi_module_struct {
    ...
    int (*ub_write)(const char *str, unsigned int str_length TSRMLS_DC);
    void (*flush)(void *server_context);
    void (*sapi_error)(int type, const char *error_msg, ...);
    void (*log_message)(char *message);
    ...
} sapi_module_struct;
```

Standard Out: `ub_write`

Any output produced by userspace `echo` and `print` statements, as well as any other internally generated output issued via `php_printf()` or `PHPWRITE()`, ultimately winds up being sent to the active SAPI's `ub_write()` method. By default, the embed SAPI shuttles this data directly to the `stdout` pipe with no regard for your application's output strategy.

Imagine for a moment that your application wants all PHP output sent to a separate console window; you might implement a callback similar to the following hypothetical block of code:

```
static int embed4_ub_write(const char *str, unsigned int str_length TSRMLS_DC)
{
    output_string_to_window(CONSOLE_WINDOW_ID, str, str_length);
    return str_length;
}
```

To make this method the output handler for PHP-generated content, you'll need to make the appropriate modification to the `php_embed_module` struct just prior to calling `php_embed_init()`:

```
php_embed_module.ub_write = embed4_ub_write;
```

> **Note**
> Even if you decide your application has no need for PHP-generated output, you must set `ub_write` to a valid callback. Setting it to a value of `NULL` will crash the engine and take your application with it.

Buffering Output: Flush

Because it might be optimal for your application to buffer output generated by PHP, the SAPI layer provides a callback to inform your application "It's important for you to send your buffered data NOW!" Your application isn't obligated to heed this advice; however, because this signal is usually generated for a very good reason (such as the end of a request), it probably wouldn't hurt to listen.

The following pair of callback buffers output in 256 byte increments, optionally flushing when ordered to by the engine:

```c
char buffer[256];
int buffer_pos = 0;
static int embed4_ubwrite(const char *str, unsigned int str_length TSRMLS_DC)
{
    char *s = str;
    char *d = buffer + buffer_pos;
    int consumed = 0;
    /* Finish prior block */
    if (str_length < (256 - buffer_pos)) {
        /* Add to buffer and exit */
        memcpy(d, s, str_length);
        buffer_pos += str_length;
        return str_length;
    }
    consumed = 256 - buffer_pos;
    memcpy(d, s, consumed);
    embed4_output_chunk(buffer, 256);
    str_length -= consumed;
    s += consumed;
    /* Consume whole passed blocks */
    while (str_length >= 256) {
        embed4_output_chunk(s, 256);
        s += 256;
        consumed += 256;
    }
    /* Buffer remaining  partial */
    memcpy(buffer, s, str_length);
    buffer_pos = str_length;
    consumed += str_length;
    return consumed;
}
static void embed4_flush(void *server_context)
{
    if (buffer_pos > 0) {
        /* Output an unfinished block */
        embed4_output_chunk(buffer, buffer_pos);
        buffer_pos = 0;
    }
}
```

Add the appropriate lines to startup_php() and this rudimentary buffering mechanism is ready to go:

```c
php_embed_module.ub_write = embed4_ub_write;
php_embed_module.flush = embed4_flush;
```

Standard Error: `log_message`

The `log_message` callback is activated by the default PHP error handler when an error has occurred during startup or script execution and the `log_errors` INI setting has been enabled. The default PHP error handler takes care of formatting these error messages into tidy, human readable content before handing if off to the display, or in this case, the `log_message` callback.

The first thing you'll notice about the `log_message` callback is that it does not contain a length parameter and is thus not binary safe. That is, it will only ever contain a single NULL character, located at the end of the string.

For error reporting uses this is almost never a problem; in fact, it's helpful as more assumptions can be made about what can be done with the error message. By default, sapi/embed will send such error messages to the standard error pipe via this simple built-in callback:

```
static void php_embed_log_message(char *message)
{
    fprintf (stderr, "%s\n", message);
}
```

If you'd rather send these messages to a logfile, you might replace this version with something like the following:

```
static void embed4_log_message(char *message)
{
    FILE *log;
    log = fopen("/var/log/embed4.log", "a");
    fprintf (log, "%s\n", message);
    fclose(log);
}
```

Special Errors: `sapi_error`

A few case-specific errors belong solely to the SAPI and bypass the main PHP error handler. These errors generally revolve around inappropriate use of the `header()` function—something your non–web-based application shouldn't have to worry about—and poorly formatted HTTP file uploads—even less of an issue for a console application.

Because these cases are so far removed from what you'll likely be doing with sapi/embed, it will probably be best to leave this callback alone. However, if you insist on catching each type of error at its source, just implement the callback proto already provided, and override it prior to calling `php_embed_init()`.

Extending and Embedding at Once

Running PHP code within your application is all well and good, but at this point, the PHP execution environment is still an isolated orphan of functionality hastily tagged onto the side of your main app, with no real means of interacting with it on a substantive level.

By now you should be familiar with developing a PHP extension and the parts that go into building and enabling such an extension. Well, you're embedding now so you can throw half of that out. Planting extension code into an embedded application actually requires less glue than a standalone extension. Start off with a nice fresh embed project as shown in Listing 20.4.

Listing 20.4   embed5.c—**Extending and Embedding PHP**

```c
#include <sapi/embed/php_embed.h>
#ifdef ZTS
    void ***tsrm_ls;
#endif
/* Extension bits */
zend_module_entry php_mymod_module_entry = {
    STANDARD_MODULE_HEADER,
    "mymod", /* extension name */
    NULL, /* function entries */
    NULL, /* MINIT */
    NULL, /* MSHUTDOWN */
    NULL, /* RINIT */
    NULL, /* RSHUTDOWN */
    NULL, /* MINFO */
    "1.0", /* version */
    STANDARD_MODULE_PROPERTIES
};
/* Embedded bits */
static void startup_php(void)
{
    int argc = 1;
    char *argv[2] = { "embed5", NULL };
    php_embed_init(argc, argv PTSRMLS_CC);
    zend_startup_module(&php_mymod_module_entry);
}
static void execute_php(char *filename)
{
    zend_first_try {
        char *include_script;
        spprintf(&include_script, 0, "include '%s';", filename);
        zend_eval_string(include_script, NULL, filename TSRMLS_CC);
        efree(include_script);
    } zend_end_try();
]
int main(int argc, char *argv[])
```

Listing 20.4   **Continued**

```
{

    if (argc <= 1) {
        printf("Usage: embed4 scriptfile");
        return -1;
    }
    startup_php();
    execute_php(argv[1]);
    php_embed_shutdown(TSRMLS_CC);
    return 0;
}
```

And that's it! From here you can define a `function_entry` vector, startup and shutdown methods, declare classes, whatever you want. It's as if you're loading an extension library using the userspace `dl()` command; Zend automatically handles all the sticky bits and gets your module registered and ready to use with that one command.

Summary

In this chapter you took the simple embedding examples from the last chapter and expanded them to the point where you can handle dropping PHP into most any non-threaded application. Now that you've got the basics of extending, embedding, and working with zvals, class entries, resources, and hash tables, you're ready to apply that to a real project.

In the remaining appendices, you'll find a catalog of the many API functions exported by PHP, Zend, and other extensions. You'll see a collection of common use code snippets and a directory of just a few of the hundreds of open source PECL projects that will serve as reference for your future projects.

Zend API Reference

AT THE CORE OF THE ZEND ENGINE ARE TWO FUNDAMENTAL SETS of APIs. The first is instruction processing, which includes script tokenization, compilation, and execution, as well as generating and handling function calls and object instantiation and destruction. The second set of APIs revolves around the manipulation of variables, or as you've come to know them, zvals. In this appendix you'll look at the functions and macros exported by the Zend Engine that simplify these operations and make them nearly consistent across all versions of PHP.

Parameter Retrieval

```
int zend_get_parameters(int ht, int param_count, ...);
int zend_get_parameters_ex(int param_count, ...);
int zend_get_parameters_array(int ht, int param_count, zval **argument_array);
int zend_get_parameters_array_ex(int param_count, zval ***argument_array);
```

Maps the current function call's argument stack into zval* values—_ex variants map to an additional level of indirection: zval**. See also: Chapter 7, "Accepting Parameters."

Argument	Purpose
ht	Deprecated. This parameter is always ignored by these methods.
param_count	The number of zval* or zval** containers passed as either individual parameters or vector units.
...	Variable argument list expecting param_count instances of references to the desired data type; that is, zval**, or zval*** for the _ex version.
argument_array	Vector containing sufficient space to store param_count zval* or zval** elements.

```
int zend_copy_parameters_array(int param_count, zval *argument_array
TSRMLS_DC);
```

Maps the current function call's argument stack into a pre-initialized `Array` variable suitable for exporting to userspace. Each value's `refcount` is implicitly increased as a result of being placed in `argument_array`.

Argument	Purpose
param_count	Number of parameters to copy from the stack to the target array. This value must be equal to or less than the actual number of parameters available.
argument_array	Target `zval*` to copy parameters into. `argument_array` must be allocated and initialized as an array (for example, using `array_init()`) prior to being used in this function).

```
int ZEND_NUM_ARGS(void);
```

Returns the number of arguments waiting on the current function call's parameter stack.

```
int zend_parse_parameters(int num_args TSRMLS_DC, char *type_spec, ...);
int zend_parse_parameters_ex(int flags, int num_args TSRMLS_DC,
                             char *type_spec, ...);
int zend_parse_method_parameters(int num_args TSRMLS_DC,
                             zval *this_ptr, char *type_spec, ...);
int zend_parse_method_parameters_ex(int flags, int num_args TSRMLS_DC,
                             zval *this_ptr, char *type_spec, ...);
```

Maps the current function call's argument stack into native C data types converting where possible. Provides automatic userspace error reporting on failure.

Arguments	Purpose
num_args	The number of arguments actually waiting on the stack. This should always be populated using the `ZEND_NUM_ARGS()` macro.
type_spec	Argument type specifier. Arguments processed will be validated against these types and converted if necessary. Refer to Chapter 7 for details on this field.
...	Dereferenced native C data types to be populated with values parsed from the argument stack. See Chapter 7.
flags	A bitmask field currently allowing only one possible value—`ZEND_PARSE_PARAMS_QUIET`—which suppresses warning and failure messages.
this_ptr	A `zval*` containing the current object instance such as returned by `getThis()`.

Classes

```
void INIT_CLASS_ENTRY(zend_class_entry ce, char *classname,
                      zend_function_entry *functions);
void INIT_OVERLOADED_CLASS_ENTRY(zend_class_entry ce, char *classname,
        zend_function_entry *functions, zend_function *handle_fcall,
        zend_function *handle_propget, zend_function *handle_propset);
void INIT_OVERLOADED_CLASS_ENTRY_EX(zend_class_entry ce, char *classname,
        zend_function_entry *functions, zend_function *handle_fcall,
        zend_function *handle_propget, zend_function *handle_propset,
        zend_function *handle_propunset, zend_function *handle_propisset);
```

This triplet of macros initializes a zend_class_entry structure using the properties given. Note that although ce is passed as an immediate value, these are macro structures and thus can and do modify the calling value.

Argument	Purpose
ce	A temporary storage unit for holding initialization values. When zend_register_internal_class() is called later, this value will no longer be relevant.
classname	NULL-terminated character string containing the userspace visible name of the class.
functions	A NULL-terminated vector of zend_function_entry elements as used with zend_module_entry structures.
handle_fcall handle_propget handle_propset handle_propunset handle_propisset	Series of "magic methods" corresponding to __call(), __get(), __set(), __unset(), and __isset() respectively.

```
void zend_class_implements(zend_class_entry *ce TSRMLS_DC,
                      int num_interfaces, ...);
```

Marks a class as implementing one or more interfaces.

Argument	Purpose
ce	Class entry implementing the interfaces listed
num_interfaces	The number of interfaces that follow, passed as zend_class_entry*
...	num_interfaces instances of zend_class_entry* pointers

```
zend_class_entry *zend_register_internal_class(
                   zend_class_entry *ce  TSRMLS_DC);
zend_class_entry *zend_register_internal_class_ex(zend_class_entry *ce,
                   zend_class_entry *parent_ce, char *parent_name TSRMLS_DC);
zend_class_entry *zend_register_internal_interface(
                   zend_class_entry *ce TSRMLS_DC);
```

Registers a zend_class_entry previously initialized using the INIT_CLASS_ENTRY
family of macros. The _ex variant of this method allows for inheritance at time of registration.

Argument	Purpose
ce	The previously initialized class entry being registered
parent_ce	The already registered class entry of this class's parent
parent_name	Name of the parent class used in error reporting should parent_ce->name be unavailable

```
int zend_lookup_class(char *name, int name_len,
                   zend_class_entry ***ppce TSRMLS_DC);
int zend_lookup_class_ex(char *name, int name_len, int use_autoload,
                   zend_class_entry ***ppce TSRMLS_DC);
zend_class_entry *zend_fetch_class(char * name, uint name_len,
                   int fetch_type TSRMLS_DC);
```

Locates a class entry by name. zend_fetch_class() returns the class entry directly,
whereas the other two methods return a zend_class_entry** container by reference.

Argument	Purpose
name	NULL-terminated name of class to look for. Does not need to be lowercased prior to calling this function.
name_len	Length of class name excluding the trailing NULL.
use_autoload	Set to nonzero if the __autoload() mechanism should be used.
ppce	Pointer to a zend_class_entry** variable to store the class definition in.

Properties

```
int zend_declare_property(zend_class_entry *ce, char *name, int name_length,
                   zval *value, int access_type TSRMLS_DC);
int zend_declare_property_ex(zend_class_entry *ce, char *name, int name_length,
                   zval *value, int access_type,
                   char *doc_comment, int doc_comment_len TSRMLS_DC);
```

```
int zend_declare_property_null(zend_class_entry *ce,
                    char *name, int name_length, int access_type TSRMLS_DC);
int zend_declare_property_bool(zend_class_entry *ce,
                    char *name, int name_length, long value,
                    int access_type TSRMLS_DC);
int zend_declare_property_long(zend_class_entry *ce,
                    char *name, int name_length, long value,
                    int access_type TSRMLS_DC);
int zend_declare_property_double(zend_class_entry *ce,
                    char *name, int name_length, double value,
                    int access_type TSRMLS_DC);
int zend_declare_property_string(zend_class_entry *ce,
                    char *name, int name_length, char *value,
                    int access_type TSRMLS_DC);
int zend_declare_property_stringl(zend_class_entry *ce,
                    char *name, int name_length,
                    char *value, int value_len,
                    int access_type TSRMLS_DC);
```

Declares a default property for a class definition. These methods should be called during class declaration time (such as the MINIT phase).

Argument	Purpose
ce	The zend_class_entry* being modified.
name	NULL-terminated property name.
name_length	Length of property name excluding the trailing NULL byte.
value	Type-specific value—depends on method being used. Note that when declaring a property from a zval, the zval must be persistently allocated.
value_len	Unique to the stringl variant of these methods; specifies the length of the string pointed to by value excluding the trailing NULL.
access_type	One of ZEND_ACC_PUBLIC, ZEND_ACC_PROTECTED, or ZEND_ACC_PRIVATE. To declare a static property rather than a standard one, combine the value of ZEND_ACC_STATIC using a bitwise OR.

```
int zend_declare_class_constant(zend_class_entry *ce,
                    char *name, size_t name_length,
                    zval *value TSRMLS_DC);
int zend_declare_class_constant_long(zend_class_entry *ce,
                    char *name, size_t name_length,
                    long value TSRMLS_DC);
```

```
int zend_declare_class_constant_bool(zend_class_entry *ce,
                      char *name, size_t name_length,
                      zend_bool value TSRMLS_DC);
int zend_declare_class_constant_double(zend_class_entry *ce,
                      char *name, size_t name_length,
                      double value TSRMLS_DC);
int zend_declare_class_constant_string(zend_class_entry *ce,
                      char *name, size_t name_length,
                      char *value TSRMLS_DC);
int zend_declare_class_constant_stringl(zend_class_entry *ce,
                      char *name, size_t name_length,
                      char *value, size_t value_len TSRMLS_DC);
```

Declares a class constant for ce with the provided name and value.

Argument	Purpose
ce	The zend_class_entry* being modified.
name	NULL-terminated constant name.
name_length	Length of property name excluding the trailing NULL byte.
value	Type-specific value—depends on method being used. Note that when declaring a property from a zval, the zval must be persistently allocated.
value_len	Unique to the stringl variant of these methods, specifies the length of the string pointed to by value excluding the trailing NULL.

```
void zend_update_property(zend_class_entry *scope, zval *object,
                      char *name, int name_length,
                      zval *value TSRMLS_DC);
void zend_update_property_null(zend_class_entry *scope, zval *object,
                      char *name, int name_length TSRMLS_DC);
void zend_update_property_bool(zend_class_entry *scope, zval *object,
                      char *name, int name_length, long value TSRMLS_DC);
void zend_update_property_long(zend_class_entry *scope, zval *object,
                      char *name, int name_length, long value TSRMLS_DC);
void zend_update_property_double(zend_class_entry *scope, zval *object,
                      char *name, int name_length, double value TSRMLS_DC);
void zend_update_property_string(zend_class_entry *scope, zval *object,
                      char *name, int name_length, char *value TSRMLS_DC);
void zend_update_property_stringl(zend_class_entry *scope, zval *object,
                      char *name, int name_length,
                      char *value, int value_len TSRMLS_DC);
int zend_update_static_property(zend_class_entry *scope,
                      char *name, int name_length,
                      zval *value TSRMLS_DC);
```

```
int zend_update_static_property_null(zend_class_entry *scope,
                    char *name, int name_length TSRMLS_DC);
int zend_update_static_property_bool(zend_class_entry *scope,
                    char *name, int name_length,
                    long value TSRMLS_DC);
int zend_update_static_property_long(zend_class_entry *scope,
                    char *name, int name_length,
                    long value TSRMLS_DC);
int zend_update_static_property_double(zend_class_entry *scope,
                    char *name, int name_length,
                    double value TSRMLS_DC);
int zend_update_static_property_string(zend_class_entry *scope,
                    char *name, int name_length,
                    char *value TSRMLS_DC);
int zend_update_static_property_stringl(zend_class_entry *scope,
                    char *name, int name_length,
                    char *value, int value_len TSRMLS_DC);
```

Sets a standard or static property of an instantiated object. The nonstatic methods invoke the `write_property` handler enabling the consistent use of overloading.

Argument	Purpose
scope	Active scope at the time of method call to enforce PPP (Public/Protected/Private) restrictions.
object	When updating a nonstatic property, this refers to the instance being updated.
name	NULL-terminated property name.
name_length	Length of property name excluding the trailing NULL byte.
value	Type-specific value—depends on method being used.
value_len	Unique to the `stringl` variant of these methods; specifies the length of the string pointed to by `value` excluding the trailing NULL.

```
zval *zend_read_property(zend_class_entry *scope, zval *object,
                    char *name, int name_length,
                    zend_bool silent TSRMLS_DC);
zval *zend_read_static_property(zend_class_entry *scope,
                    char *name, int name_length,
                    zend_bool silent TSRMLS_DC);
```

Reads a property from a given class or object instance. The nonstatic version invokes the object's `read_property` handler to allow proper handling of overloaded objects.

Argument	Purpose
scope	Active scope at the time of method call to enforce PPP (Public/Protected/Private) restrictions.
object	When fetching a nonstatic property, this refers to the instance being updated.
name	NULL-terminated property name.
name_length	Length of property name excluding the trailing NULL byte.
silent	When set to a nonzero value, no "undefined property" errors will be reported. Note: Instances with no read_property handler defined will report an error regardless of the silent argument.

```
int add_property_long_ex(zval *object, char *key, uint key_len,
                long l TSRMLS_DC);
int add_property_null_ex(zval *object, char *key, uint key_len TSRMLS_DC);
int add_property_bool_ex(zval *object, char *key, uint key_len,
                int value TSRMLS_DC);
int add_property_resource_ex(zval *object, char *key, uint key_len,
                long value TSRMLS_DC);
int add_property_double_ex(zval *object, char *key, uint key_len,
                double value TSRMLS_DC);
int add_property_string_ex(zval *object, char *key, uint key_len,
                char *str, int dup TSRMLS_DC);
int add_property_stringl_ex(zval *object, char *key, uint key_len,
                char *value, uint value_len, int dup TSRMLS_DC);
int add_property_zval_ex(zval *object, char *key, uint key_len,
                zval *value TSRMLS_DC);
```

Adds a property to an instantiated object.

Argument	Purpose
object	Object instance being updated.
key	Either an ordinary NULL-terminated string (for public properties), or a specially formatted string as returned by zend_mangle_property_name().
ken_len	Length of key including the trailing NULL byte. Note: A non-_ex version of these functions also exists that excludes the last NULL from this length parameter.
value	Type-specific value—depends on method being used.
value_len	Unique to the stringl variant of these methods; specifies the length of the string pointed to by value excluding the trailing NULL.

Arguments	Purpose
dup	Set to 0 if the string is in an `emalloc`'d buffer that can be given to the engine. Set to nonzero to force duplication of the string.

```
void zend_mangle_property_name(char **dest, int *dest_len,
                  char *scope, int scope_len,
                  char *propname, int propname_len, int internal);
```

Encodes a property name with scope visibility information.

Argument	Purpose
dest	Populated by reference with newly allocated memory containing mangled property name.
dest_len	Length of mangled property name including the trailing NULL byte.
scope	To encode the property name for PRIVATE access, specify the NULL-terminated name of the "owning" class here. PROTECTED properties should use a scope of *. PUBLIC properties should not use this function.
scope_len	Length of scope string excluding the trailing NULL byte. For example, PROTECTED scope will always have a length of 1.
propname	NULL-terminated name of actual property as it will appear in userspace.
propname_len	Length of property name excluding the trailing NULL.
internal	When set to 0, per-request memory allocation will be used; otherwise, persistent allocation will be performed. Either way, it is the calling scope's responsibility to free this memory.

Objects

```
int object_init(zval *arg);
int object_init_ex(zval *arg, zend_class_entry *ce);
int object_and_properties_init(zval *arg, zend_class_entry *ce,
                  HashTable *properties TSRMLS_DC);
```

Instantiates a new object.

Argument	Purpose
arg	Preallocated zval* variable to be initialized as an object.
ce	Class entry of the object to instantiate. object_init() will automatically assign the call entry corresponding to the built-in stdClass.
properties	Initial properties to be copied into the new object in lieu of that class's default properties.

```
zend_object *zend_objects_get_address(zval *object TSRMLS_DC);
void *zend_object_store_get_object(zval *object TSRMLS_DC);
```

These functions are identical in all but the typecast in their return value. They retrieve a pointer to the zend_object* struct (or custom structure containing a zend_object in the first element) that corresponds to the passed object zval.

Argument	Purpose
object	Object instance

```
zend_class_entry *Z_OBJCE_P(zval *object)
zend_class_entry *zend_get_class_entry(zval *object TSRMLS_DC);
int zend_get_object_classname(zval *object,
                    char **name, zend_uint *name_len TSRMLS_DC);
```

Retrieves the class entry or name for a given object.

Argument	Purpose
object	Object instance.
name	On return, populated with a pointer to a NULL-terminated string containing the classname associated with object. The memory location return remains the property of the class entry and should not be freed by the calling scope.
name_len	Returned as the length of the string pointed to by name.

```
zend_object_handlers *zend_get_std_object_handlers();
```

Returns a const (unmodifiable) structure containing the standard object handlers used by userspace class definitions and instances of stdClass.

Exceptions

```
zval * zend_throw_exception(zend_class_entry *exception_ce,
                    char *message, long code TSRMLS_DC);
zval * zend_throw_exception_ex(zend_class_entry *exception_ce,
                    long code TSRMLS_DC, char *format, ...);
```

```
zval * zend_throw_error_exception(zend_class_entry *exception_ce,
                       char *message, long code, int severity TSRMLS_DC);
void zend_throw_exception_object(zval *exception_obj TSRMLS_DC);
```

Throws an exception similar to calling using the `throw` keyword from userspace. Calling this function from internals does not immediately resume script execution at the next catch block, meaning that additional post-throw processing might be done. After your internal function returns control to the executor however, the catch will be processed.

Argument	Purpose
exception_ce	Type of exception to throw given as a class entry. Typically this will be passed using one of `zend_exception_get_default()` or `zend_get_error_exception()`.
exception_obj	A prepared exception object descended from the `Exception` class.
code	Numeric exception code; returned by `$e->getCode();`.
severity	Specific to the error exception class; returned by its `$e->getSeverity();` method.
message	Simple `NULL`-terminated message.
format	`sprintf`-style format argument used with subsequent variable argument list.
...	Variable argument list containing data corresponding to the `sprintf` style format specifier.

```
zend_class_entry *zend_exception_get_default(void);
zend_class_entry *zend_get_error_exception(void);
```

Returns the class entries for exception classes defined by the engine. `ErrorException` is a child of the default `Exception` class used by `zend_throw_error_exception()`.

Execution

```
zend_bool zend_make_callable(zval *callable, char **callable_name TSRMLS_DC);
zend_bool zend_is_callable(zval *callable, uint check_flags,
                   char **call_name);
zend_bool zend_is_callable_ex(zval *callable, uint check_flags,
                   char **call_name, int *call_name_len,
                   zend_class_entry **ce_ptr, zend_function **fptr_ptr,
                   zval ***zobj_ptr_ptr TSRMLS_DC);
```

Checks whether the named function is callable. Returns 0 if callable, nonzero if otherwise.

Argument	Purpose
callable	Universal callback value. Might be a simple string identifying a normal function, or an array containing an object/class and a method name.
check_flags	Either or none of the following values: IS_CALLABLE_CHECK_SYNTAX_ONLY, IS_CALLABLE_CHECK_IS_STATIC.
call_name	If not passed as NULL, populated with a human readable representation of the call syntax that would be used. Helpful for error messages.
call_name_len	Length of the formatted call_name string.
ce_ptr	When specified using array syntax, this value is populated with the discovered class entry.
fptr_ptr	Populated with a pointer to the zend_function* of the discovered function or method.
zobj_ptr_ptr	When specified using array syntax, this value is populated with the discovered object instance.

```
int call_user_function(HashTable *function_table, zval **object_pp,
                zval *function_name, zval *retval_ptr,
                zend_uint param_count, zval *params[] TSRMLS_DC);
int call_user_function_ex(HashTable *function_table, zval **object_pp,
                zval *function_name, zval **retval_ptr_ptr,
                zend_uint param_count, zval **params[],
                int no_separation, HashTable *symbol_table TSRMLS_DC);
```

Calls a userspace or internal function by its userspace name. The function's return value will be either copied into retval_ptr or referenced into retval_ptr_ptr. Returns SUCCESS or FAILURE.

Argument	Purpose
function_table	Default function table to look for the named function in. Typically this will be EG(function_table).
object_pp	Object instance or classname to perform a method call.
function_name	Universal callback value. Either String or Array as described for zend_is_callable().
retval_ptr(_ptr)	Populated with the result of the called function.
param_count	Number of parameters to expect in the params vector.
params	Vector of param_count elements of single or double dereferenced zvals.

Arguments	Purpose
`no_separation`	When set to 1, attempts to separate the passed argument will result in a call FAILURE.
`symbol_table`	Prebuilt symbol table to be given to function being called. Note: On completion of this function the symbol table will be destroyed.

```
int zend_eval_string(char *str, zval *retval_ptr, char *string_name TSRMLS_DC);
int zend_eval_string_ex(char *str, zval *retval_ptr, char *string_name,
                int handle_exceptns TSRMLS_DC);
```

Evaluates an arbitrary string of PHP code as with the userspace function `eval()`.

Argument	Purpose
`str`	PHP code string to process.
`retval_ptr`	Populated with the return value if one is produced.
`string_name`	Descriptive string used for error responding.
`handle_exceptns`	If set to true, any exceptions will be automatically re-thrown and a result code of FAILURE returned.

```
int zend_execute_scripts(int type TSRMLS_DC, zval **retval, int count, ...);
```

Executes one or more script files referred to by prepared `zend_file_handle` structures. This method is similar to the `php_execute_script()` function used in Chapter 19, "Setting Up a Host Environment." That shouldn't be any surprise because it's the underlying function call that `php_execute_script()` uses. The primary difference between these two is that the PHPAPI version handles additional INI setting such as `auto_prepend_file` and `auto_append_file`.

Argument	Purpose
`type`	Inclusion type. One of ZEND_INCLUDE, ZEND_REQUIRE, ZEND_INCLUDE_ONCE, or ZEND_REQUIRE_ONCE.
`retval`	Populated on completion with the final return value produced by the series of scripts.
`count`	Number of `zend_file_handle` structs that can be expected in the following variable argument list.
`...`	List of `count` occurrences of `zend_file_handle*` variables to be processed.

```
void zend_set_timeout(long seconds);
void zend_unset_timeout(TSRMLS_D);
```

Control script execution timeouts as with the userspace set_time_limit() function.

INI Settings

```
int zend_alter_ini_entry(char *name, uint name_length,
                    char *value, uint value_length,
                    int modify_type, int stage);
int zend_restore_ini_entry(char *name, uint name_length, int stage);
```

Changes or restores an INI setting.

Argument	Purpose
name	NULL-terminated name of INI entry being modified.
name_length	Length of name including the trailing NULL byte.
value	New value as a text string, regardless of what the ultimate storage type is. NULL-terminated as always.
value_length	Length of value excluding the trailing NULL byte.
modify_type	Calling scope's declared access level; must contain the same level as the option being modified but can include other levels as well: PHP_INI_SYSTEM, PHP_INI_PERDIR, PHP_INI_USER.
stage	Current execution stage of the Zend Engine. One of: PHP_INI_STAGE_STARTUP, PHP_INI_STAGE_ACTIVATE, PHP_INI_STAGE_RUNTIME, PHP_INI_STAGE_DEACTIVATE, PHP_INI_STAGE_SHUTDOWN.

```
long zend_ini_long(char *name, uint name_length, int orig);
double zend_ini_double(char *name, uint name_length, int orig);
char *zend_ini_string(char *name, uint name_length, int orig);
```

Fetches and converts an INI value. These API functions also come wrapped in macros such as INI_STR() or INI_ORIG_LONG(); refer to Chapter 13, "INI Settings," for more information.

Argument	Purpose
name	NULL-terminated name of INI option to look up.
length	Length of name including trailing NULL byte.
orig	When set to zero, the current INI setting—which might have been overridden—will be returned. Otherwise, the original, unmodified setting will be returned.

Array Manipulation

```
int array_init(zval *arg);
```

Initializes an array into the preallocated variable arg.

```
int add_assoc_null(zval *arg, char *key);
int add_assoc_bool(zval *arg, char *key, int val);
int add_assoc_long(zval *arg, char *key, long val);
int add_assoc_double(zval *arg, char *key, double val);
int add_assoc_resource(zval *arg, char *key, int val);
int add_assoc_string(zval *arg, char *key, char *val, int dup);
int add_assoc_stringl(zval *arg, char *key, char *val, uint len, int dup);
int add_assoc_zval(zval *arg, char *key, zval *val);
int add_index_null(zval *arg, ulong idx);
int add_index_bool(zval *arg, ulong idx, int val);
int add_index_long(zval *arg, ulong idx, long val);
int add_index_resource(zval *arg, ulong idx, int val);
int add_index_double(zval *arg, ulong idx, double val);
int add_index_string(zval *arg, ulong idx, char *val, int dup);
int add_index_stringl(zval *arg, ulong idx, char *val, uint len, int dup);
int add_index_zval(zval *arg, ulong index, zval *val);
int add_next_index_null(zval *arg);
int add_next_index_bool(zval *arg, int val);
int add_next_index_long(zval *arg, long val);
int add_next_index_resource(zval *arg, int val);
int add_next_index_double(zval *arg, double val);
int add_next_index_string(zval *arg, char *val, int dup);
int add_next_index_stringl(zval *arg, char *val, uint len, int dup);
int add_next_index_zval(zval *arg, zval *val);
```

Adds an element to an Array variable as a specific index, key location, or at the next successive index position.

Argument	Purpose
arg	Preinitialized Array zval to be extended.
index / key	Numeric or associative position in the array to place the new element.
val	Type-specific data to be wrapped in a zval (if necessary) and placed into the array's HashTable. Note that a raw zval's refcount is not automatically incremented by these functions.
len	String-specific length specifier.
dup	String-specific duplication flag, if the passed string cannot be owned by the engine as-is.

Hash Tables

```
int zend_hash_init(HashTable *ht, uint nSize, hash_func_t pHashFunction,
                   dtor_func_t pDestructor, zend_bool persistent);
int zend_hash_init_ex(HashTable *ht, uint nSize, hash_func_t pHashFunction,
                      dtor_func_t pDestructor, zend_bool persistent,
                      zend_bool bApplyProtection);
```

Creates a raw HashTable. The array_init() and zval_ptr_dtor() methods should be preferred for these tasks when possible.

Argument	Purpose
ht	HashTable object being initialized, destroyed, or cleaned.
nSize	Nominal count of elements the HashTable is expected to hold. Increasing this number will require more memory, however making it too small will encourage costly rein-dexing operations. Note that this value is automatically rounded up to the next higher power of 2.
pHashFunction	Deprecated. Older versions of the Zend Engine allowed the hashing function to be overridden. Current versions force DJBX33A.
pDestructor	Function called automatically whenever an element is removed from the HashTable or replaced.
persistent	When set to a nonzero value, persistent memory allocators will be used rather than the per-request emalloc() family.
bApplyProtection	When set to a nonzero value, attempts to traverse the HashTable iteratively will be throttled to a maximum number of recursions.

```
int zend_hash_add(HashTable *ht, char *arKey, uint nKeyLength,
                  void *pData, uint nDataSize, void **pDest);
int zend_hash_update(HashTable *ht, char *arKey, uint nKeyLength,
                     void *pData, uint nDataSize, void **pDest);
int zend_hash_quick_add(HashTable *ht, char *arKey, uint nKeyLength,
                        ulong hash_value, void *pData, uint nDataSize,
                        void **pDest);
int zend_hash_quick_update(HashTable *ht, char *arKey, uint nKeyLength,
                           ulong hash_value, void *pData, uint nDataSize,
                           void **pDest);
int zend_hash_index_update(HashTable *ht, ulong index,
                           void *pData, uint nDataSize, void **pDest);
int zend_hash_next_insert(HashTable *ht, void *pData, uint nDataSize,
                          void **pDest);
```

Argument	Purpose
ht	HashTable being modified.
arKey	NULL-terminated associative key string.
nKeyLength	Length of arKey including trailing NULL byte.
index	Numeric hash index.
hash_value	Precomputed associative key hash value.
pData	Pointer to data to be stored.
nDataSize	Size of the data being stored in bytes.
pDest	If requested, populated with a pointer to where the duplicate of the data pointed to by pData resides within the HashTable. Allows for modifying in place.

```
void zend_hash_clean(HashTable *ht);
void zend_hash_destroy(HashTable *ht);
void zend_hash_graceful_destroy(HashTable *ht);
void zend_hash_graceful_reverse_destroy(HashTable *ht);
```

zend_hash_clean() will merely empty a HashTable's contents while the destroy variants will deallocate all internal structures and leave the HashTable unusable. A graceful shutdown takes slightly longer; however, it keeps the HashTable in a consistent state to allow access and modifications to be made during destruction.

```
void zend_hash_apply(HashTable *ht, apply_func_t apply_func TSRMLS_DC);
void zend_hash_apply_with_argument(HashTable *ht,
                apply_func_arg_t apply_func, void *arg TSRMLS_DC);
void zend_hash_apply_with_arguments(HashTable *ht,
                apply_func_args_t apply_func, int, ...);
void zend_hash_reverse_apply(HashTable *ht, apply_func_t apply_func TSRMLS_DC);
```

Iterates through a HashTable calling an apply function for each element while passing optional parameters.

Argument	Purpose
ht	HashTable to traverse.
apply_func	Callback function conforming to the appropriate prototype; refer to Chapter 8, "Working with Arrays and HashTables," for more information.
arg	Generic pointer argument for single arg passing.
arg_count	Number of arguments that will follow in the variable argument list.
...	Variable argument list containing arg_count arguments for the apply function.

```
void zend_hash_internal_pointer_reset_ex(HashTable *ht, HashPosition *pos);
int zend_hash_move_forward_ex(HashTable *ht, HashPosition *pos);
int zend_hash_move_backwards_ex(HashTable *ht, HashPosition *pos);
void zend_hash_internal_pointer_end_ex(HashTable *ht, HashPosition *pos);
```

Manually traverses a `HashTable` using a `HashPosition` indicator.

Argument	Meaning
ht	`HashTable` being traversed.
pos	Ephemeral position indicator. This value will be automatically initialized by `zend_hash_internal_pointer_reset_ex()`, and does not need to be destroyed.

```
int zend_hash_get_current_key_type_ex(HashTable *ht, HashPosition *pos);
```

Determines the key type at the `HashTable` position indicated by `pos`. Returns one of three values: `HASH_KEY_IS_LONG`, `HASH_KEY_IS_STRING`, or `HASH_KEY_NON_EXISTANT`.

```
int zend_hash_get_current_key_ex(HashTable *ht,
                    char **str_index, uint *str_length, ulong *num_index,
                    zend_bool duplicate, HashPosition *pos);
int zend_hash_get_current_data_ex(HashTable *ht, void **pData,
                    HashPosition *pos);
```

Inspects the key and data elements at the current `HashTable` position. Data variant returns `SUCCESS` or `FAILURE`, key variant returns key type as described under `zend_hash_get_current_key_type_ex()`.

Argument	Purpose
ht	`HashTable` being examined.
str_index	Populated with associative key name.
str_length	Populated with length of associative key. This value will include the trailing `NULL` byte.
num_index	Populated with numeric key index.
duplicate	Set to a nonzero value if the key name should be duplicated before being returned to the calling scope, in which case the calling scope is required to free the duplicate copy at the appropriate time.
pData	Populated with a pointer to the data as held in the `HashTable`'s internal storage. This value can be modified directly, passively inspected, or copied into a local structure.
pos	Current `HashTable` traversal position.

```
int zend_hash_exists(HashTable *ht, char *arKey, uint nKeyLength);
int zend_hash_quick_exists(HashTable *ht, char *arKey, uint nKeyLength, ulong
hash_value);
int zend_hash_index_exists(HashTable *ht, ulong index);
```

Determines whether a given position in a HashTable is occupied. Returns 1 if the index or key exists, and 0 if it doesn't.

Argument	Purpose
ht	HashTable being examined
arKey	Associative key name
nKeyLength	Length of key name including trailing NULL byte
hash_value	Precomputed key hash, as returned by zend_get_hash_value()
index	Numeric key index

```
int zend_hash_find(HashTable *ht, char *arKey, uint nKeyLength, void **pData);
int zend_hash_quick_find(HashTable *ht, char *arKey, uint nKeyLength,
                    ulong hash_value, void **pData);
int zend_hash_index_find(HashTable *ht, ulong index, void **pData);
```

Fetches a data element from a HashTable by key or index.

Argument	Purpose
ht	HashTable being examined
arKey	Associative key name
nKeyLength	Length of key name including trailing NULL byte
hash_value	Pre-computed key hash, as returned by zend_get_hash_value()
index	Numeric key index

```
int zend_hash_update_current_key_ex(HashTable *ht, int key_type,
                    char *str_index, uint str_length,
                    ulong num_index, HashPosition *pos);
```

Changes the key or index associated with the current data bucket. May also change a given HashTable position from indexed to associative or vice versa.

Argument	Purpose
ht	HashTable being modified
key_type	New key type: HASH_KEY_IS_LONG, or HASH_KEY_IS_STRING

Arguments	Purpose
str_index	Associative key value—only used with HASH_KEY_IS_STRING
str_length	Length of associative key value
index	Numeric index—only used with HASH_KEY_IS_LONG
pos	Current HashTable traversal position

```
int zend_hash_del(HashTable *ht, char *arKey, uint nKeyLength);
int zend_hash_index_del(HashTable *ht, ulong index);
```

Deletes an element from a HashTable by index or associative key.

Argument	Purpose
ht	HashTable being modified
arKey	NULL-terminated associative key
nKeyLength	Length of arKey including the terminating NULL byte
index	Numeric index value

```
void zend_hash_copy(HashTable *dst, HashTable *src,
                    copy_ctor_func_t pCopyConstructor,
                    void *tmp, uint size);
void zend_hash_merge(HashTable *dst, HashTable *src,
                    copy_ctor_func_t pCopyConstructor,
                    void *tmp, uint size, int overwrite);
void zend_hash_merge_ex(HashTable *dst, HashTable *src,
                    copy_ctor_func_t pCopyConstructor,
                    uint size, merge_checker_func_t pMergeSource,
                    void *pParam);
```

Copies elements from src to dst using the pCopyConstructor method to perform additional resource duplication if needed. With zend_hash_copy(), every element in src will be copied to dst. zend_hash_merge() behaves the same way unless the value of overwrite is set to zero, in which case existing keys/indexes will remain unchanged. zend_hash_merge_ex() uses a callback method to determine on an individual basis if an element should or should not be replaced. Refer to Chapter 8, "Working with Arrays and HashTables" for more information.

Argument	Purpose
dst	Destination HashTable.
src	Source HashTable.
tmp	Temporary holder variable with enough space to store any one element from src. Note: Unused since PHP version 4.0.3.

Arguments	Purpose
size	Size of member elements.
pCopyConstructor	Callback used to duplicate element subdata.
pMergeChecker	Callback to compare source and dest keys and values to determine if they should be replaced.
pParam	Arbitrary parameter to pass along to pMergeChecker function.
overwrite	Set to a nonzero value to make zend_hash_merge() behave like zend_hash_copy().

```
int zend_hash_sort(HashTable *ht, sort_func_t sort_func,
                    compare_func_t compare_func, int renumber TSRMLS_DC);
int zend_hash_compare(HashTable *ht, HashTable *ht2,
                    compare_func_t compare_func, zend_bool ordered TSRMLS_DC);
```

Sorts a given HashTable or compare it to another one. For examples of using these API calls, refer to Chapter 8.

Argument	Purpose
ht	Main HashTable being sorted or compared.
ht2	Secondary HashTable being compared to.
sort_func	Callback to method that will handle the actual sort operation.
compare_func	Callback to compare an individual element of ht to an individual element of ht2.
renumber	Set to nonzero if numeric indexes should be renumbered from zero as they are sorted.
ordered	Set to nonzero to compare based on order within the HashTable rather than intrinsic index or key value.

```
int zend_hash_num_elements(HashTable *ht);
ulong zend_hash_next_free_element(HashTable *ht);
int zend_hash_minmax(HashTable *ht, compare_func_t compare_func,
                    int findmax, void **pData TSRMLS_DC);
```

Returns the number of elements, the next assignable index number, and the lowest/highest valued data in a HashTable respectively.

Argument	Purpose
ht	HashTable being inspected.
compare_func	Comparison function for determining the greatest/least value.

Arguments	Purpose
findmax	Set to nonzero to find the maximum value, or zero to find the minimum value.
pData	Populated with the minimum/maximum value as determined by compare_func.

```
ulong zend_hash_func(char *arKey, uint nKeyLength);
ulong zend_get_hash_value(char *arKey, uint nKeyLength);
```

Identical functions meant to return a hash value based on arKey and nKeyLength using the built-in DJBX33A hashing function.

Resources/Lists

```
int zend_register_list_destructors(void (*ld)(void *),
                    void (*pld)(void *), int module_number);
int zend_register_list_destructors_ex(rsrc_dtor_func_t ld,
                    rsrc_dtor_func_t pld, char *type_name,
                    int module_number);
```

Registers a list entry and associate destructors with it. When an entry using the associated list type is removed from EG(reuglar_list), the non-persistent ld destructor function will be called. When such a persistent entry is removed, the pld destructor will be called instead.

Argument	Purpose
ld	Non-persistent destructor method.
pld	Persistent destructor method.
type_name	Descriptive name for the resource type.
module_number	Hint to the engine on who owns this resource type. Should be passed unmodified from an MINIT method.

```
int zend_list_insert(void *ptr, int type);
int zend_register_resource(zval *result, void *ptr, int type);
```

Places a resource pointer into the EG(regular_list) HashTable and returns a numeric resource ID. zend_register_resource() goes an extra step further and populates that resource ID into a ZVAL for passing back to userspace code.

Argument	Purpose
ptr	Arbitrary pointer resource to store
type	Registered type to associate with the resource and use for later destruction
result	zval to populate with the resource ID

```
int zend_list_addref(int id);
int zend_list_delete(int id);
```

Increases or decreases a given resource ID's reference count. Note that
zend_list_delete() does not hard delete the resource, it only decreases the refcount
and deletes in the event that refcount reaches zero.

```
void *zend_list_find(int id, int *type);
void *zend_fetch_resource(zval **zval_id TSRMLS_DC, int id,
                    char *type_name, int *type, int num_types, ...);
```

Retrieves a resource from EG(regular_list) using the passed id or zval_id. The
resource will be returned as a pointer or NULL if no matching resource can be found.

Argument	Purpose
id	Numeric resource ID to locate.
zval_id	If id is passed as –1, look for the resource ID encoded into this zval.
type	Populated with the numeric resource type located.
type_name	Populated with the textual name of the resource type located.
num_types	Number of valid resource types to match against this resource.
...	List of expected resource types. If the located resource does not match one of these types, it will not be considered a match.

```
int zend_fetch_list_dtor_id(char *type_name);
```

Returns the numeric resource type based on the requested type name.

```
char *zend_rsrc_list_get_rsrc_type(int resource TSRMLS_DC);
```

Returns the type name of the specified resource ID.

Linked Lists

```
void zend_llist_init(zend_llist *list, size_t size,
                    llist_dtor_func_t dtor, unsigned char persistent);
```

Initializes a preallocated linked list structure. Zend-linked lists are doubly linked and hold
only identical sized values.

Argument	Purpose
list	Linked list structure being initialized
size	Size of each individual element in bytes
dtor	Destructor callback function
persistent	Use persistent allocation functions if set

```
void zend_llist_clean(zend_llist *l);
void zend_llist_destroy(zend_llist *l);
```

Removes all elements from a linked list. Because a Zend-linked list contains no allocated internal structures, the only practical difference between these is that zend_llist_clean() leaves the list in a reusable state.

```
void zend_llist_add_element(zend_llist *l, void *element);
void zend_llist_prepend_element(zend_llist *l, void *element);
```

Adds an element to a linked list at the end (add_element) or beginning (prepend_element). The size of the data pointed to by element must match the size given during initialization.

```
void zend_llist_copy(zend_llist *dst, zend_llist *src);
```

Copies all elements from src linked list to dst linked list.

```
void zend_llist_del_element(zend_llist *l, void *data,
                    int (*compare)(void *element, void *data));
```

Removes elements from the linked list based on the results of the passed compare callback. If the element should be removed, compare should return 0; otherwise it will remain.

```
void *zend_llist_remove_tail(zend_llist *l);
```

Pops an element off the end of a linked list and returns the pointer to it.

```
void zend_llist_sort(zend_llist *l, llist_compare_func_t compare TSRMLS_DC);
```

Sorts a linked list using the passed compare callback to determine relative greatness.

```
void zend_llist_apply(zend_llist *l, llist_apply_func_t func TSRMLS_DC);
void zend_llist_apply_with_del(zend_llist *l, int (*func)(void *data));
void zend_llist_apply_with_argument(zend_llist *l,
                    llist_apply_with_arg_func_t func, void *arg TSRMLS_DC);
void zend_llist_apply_with_arguments(zend_llist *l,
                    llist_apply_with_args_func_t func TSRMLS_DC,
                    int num_args, ...);
```

Iterates through a linked list, passing each element to the apply function; similar to HashTables as discussed in Chapter 8.

```
void *zend_llist_get_first_ex(zend_llist *l, zend_llist_position *pos);
void *zend_llist_get_last_ex(zend_llist *l, zend_llist_position *pos);
void *zend_llist_get_next_ex(zend_llist *l, zend_llist_position *pos);
void *zend_llist_get_prev_ex(zend_llist *l, zend_llist_position *pos);
```

Manually steps through a linked list, returning each element as a pointer using the same semantics as the Zend hash iterators found in Chapter 8.

```
int zend_llist_count(zend_llist *l);
```

Returns the number of elements in a Zend-linked list.

Memory

```
void *emalloc(size_t size);
void *safe_emalloc(size_t nmemb, size_t size, size_t offset);
void *ecalloc(size_t nmemb, size_t siz);
void *erealloc(void *ptr, size_t size, int allow_failure);
void *pemalloc(size_t size, int persistent);
void *safe_pemalloc(size_t nmemb, size_t size, size_t offset, int persistent);
vpod *pecalloc(size_t nmemb, size_t siz, int persistent);
void *perealloc(void *ptr, size_t size, int allow_failure);
```

Allocates memory of size or ((nmemb*size)+offset) as appropriate. The meaning of these functions generally map to their ANSI-C equivalents. Any p* variant will conditionally allocate persistent memory. If the persistent flag is set to 0, or the non p* family of allocators is used, any memory allocated will be automatically freed at the end of a request.

Argument	Purpose
ptr	Already allocated pointer to be reallocated to a new size.
size	Number of bytes to allocate.
nmemb	Used with calloc and the safe_* family of allocators. Multiplied by size to allocate multiple contiguous blocks of equal size.
offset	Added to size*nmemb calculation to allocate additional "odd" bytes.
allow_failure	Ordinarily a failure in the underlying realloc() function will cause erealloc() to force the engine into bailout mode and end any running script. Setting this flag will allow a erealloc to fail quietly, returning NULL.
persistent	When set, the normal system allocation functions will be used rather than the per-request allocators.

```
char *estrdup(const char *s);
char *estrndup(const char *s, unsigned int length);
char *pestrdup(const char *s, persistent);
char *zend_strndup(const char *s, unsigned int length);
```

Duplicates a string of data ending with (but including) the first NULL byte or at length number of characters. Unlike most memory-related functions, the persistent version of estrndup() is named zend_strndup() and does not have a flag to interactively disable persistency.

Argument	Purpose
s	String to duplicate.
length	Length of data to be duplicated, if known.
persistent	When set, the normal system allocation functions will be used rather than the per-request allocators.

```
void efree(void *ptr);
void pefree(void *ptr, int persistent);
```

Frees a previously allocated block of memory. If that memory was allocated persistently, it must be freed the same way and vice versa. Using a persistent free on a non-persistent block of memory or the other way around will lead to corruption and a likely segfault.

```
int zend_set_memory_limit(unsigned int memory_limit);
```

Alters the php.ini specified memory limit. If memory limits aren't actually enabled, this function will return FAILURE.

Constants

```
int zend_get_constant(char *name, uint name_len, zval *result TSRMLS_DC);
```

Looks up the value of a registered constant. If found, the value will be copied into result and the function will return 0 indicating success.

Argument	Purpose
name	NULL-terminated name of constant to fetch. May also be in the form CLASSNAME::CONSTANT to fetch class constants.
name_len	Length of constant name not including the terminating NULL byte.
result	Preallocated zval container to populate a copy of the constant into.

```
void zend_register_long_constant(char *name, uint name_len, long value,
                    int flags, int module_number TSRMLS_DC);
void zend_register_double_constant(char *name, uint name_len, double value,
                    int flags, int module_number TSRMLS_DC);
void zend_register_string_constant(char *name, uint name_len, char *value,
                    int flags, int module_number TSRMLS_DC);
void zend_register_stringl_constant(char *name, uint name_len,
                    char *value, uint value_len,
                    int flags, int module_number TSRMLS_DC);
int zend_register_constant(zend_constant *c TSRMLS_DC);
```

Registers a constant of the specified type with the value passed. Constants of certain other types (not including Arrays and Objects) can also be registered by manually constructing a `zend_constant` and passing it to `zend_register_constant()`.

Argument	Purpose
name	NULL-terminated name of constant to register.
name_len	Length of constant name including the trailing NULL byte.
value	Value to initialize the constant with.
value_len	Specific to strings, length of the string value not including the trailing NULL byte.
flags	Any combination of CONST_CS and/or CONST_PERSISTENT.
module_number	Passed unmodified from MINIT or RINIT.
c	Initialized zend_constant structure. Refer to Chapter 12, "Startup, Shutdown, and a Few Points in Between" for more information.

Variables

```
void zval_add_ref(zval **ppzval);
```

Increases the `refcount` of `ppzval`. This function is identical to the command: `(*ppzval)->refcount++;` Like the other accessor functions and macros, its use is encouraged over direct access of the zvals in order to ensure maximum forward compatibility.

```
void zval_copy_ctor(zval *zvalue);
```

Duplicates all of a zval's internal structures. This command typically follows copying one zval's contents into another. Refer to Chapter 8 for a detailed use of this API call.

```
void zval_ptr_dtor(zval **zval_ptr);
```

Decreases a zval's `refcount` by one. If the `refcount` reaches zero, the internal structures of the zval are destroyed by automatically calling through to `zval_dtor(*zval_ptr);`.

After the internal structures are destroyed, `efree(*zval_ptr);` is called to destroy the zval container as well.

```
void zval_dtor(zval *zvalue);
```

Frees all of a zval's associated internal structures regardless of `refcount`. For example, an `IS_STRING` variable would have `efree(Z_STRVAL_P(zvalue));` called.

```
char *zend_zval_type_name(zval *arg);
```

Translates a zval's numeric type identifier into a human readable name. For example, if arg is an `IS_LONG` zval, this function will return "`integer`".

```
int zend_is_true(zval *arg);
```

Tests the passed `arg` for truthness. As in, if this variable were used in a userspace conditional statement, would it yield a net result of `TRUE` or `FALSE`? False values may occur from `IS_NULL` variables as well as literal Boolean `FALSE` values, or numeric values of `0` or `0.0`. Empty strings, empty arrays, and a few specially designed objects can also result in a net-false value.

```
int zend_register_auto_global(char *name, uint name_len,
                   zend_auto_global_callback callback TSRMLS_DC);
```

Register an auto (super) global variable. Any variable named here will automatically resolve itself to the global scope as if it were accessed as `$GLOBALS['name']`.

Argument	Purpose
name	NULL-terminated, case-sensitive variable name to be auto-globalled.
name_len	Length of name excluding the trailing NULL.
callback	Compiler hook to execute additional code when an auto-global variable is used in a compiled script. Refer to Chapter 12 for more information.

Miscellaneous API Function

```
char *get_zend_version(void);
```

Reports a textual string representing the current Zend Engine version. This string remains owned by the engine and must not be freed by the calling scope.

```
char *zend_get_module_version(char *module_name);
```

Reports the extension-specific version associated with the named module. The string reported by this API call comes directly from the `zend_module_entry` struct declared by the named extension. Returns `NULL` if the named extension is not loaded.

```
int zend_disable_function(char *function_name,
                   uint function_name_length TSRMLS_DC);
int zend_disable_class(char *class_name, uint class_name_length TSRMLS_DC);
```

Typically called by the engine itself, these API calls replace an existing function handler with a stub definition designed to report a fatal error. These API calls should only be made during the Startup (MINIT) phase of execution.

```
void zend_qsort(void *base, size_t nmemb, size_t size,
                   compare_func_t compare TSRMLS_DC);
```

A generic qsort algorithm meant to be used with the Hash and Linked List sorting functions, but can also be used separately.

Argument	Purpose
base	Location of vector containing nmemb members of size bytes.
nmemb	The number of elements in the vector pointed to by base.
size	The size of each individual element to be sorted.
compare	A comparison callback used to determine which of two given elements is greater than the other.

```
void zend_bailout(void);
```

End the current zend_try block immediately (typically this is the active script/request). The CPU will make an immediate longjmp() to the nearest zend_catch or zend_end_try block.

Summary

Although the preceding list of API calls might seem extensive, it pales in comparison to the number of wrapper macros, overridable callbacks, and other gems that can be found in the Zend Engine. Many of these wrapper macros have been covered in earlier chapters, such as the variable manipulating ZVAL_*() family, and the TSRM accessing *G() family. Spend some time looking through the source and other extensions and you're sure to find a few more hidden treasures.

In Appendix B, "PHPAPI," you'll round out the core API reference with a listing of functions found in the PHP core and throughout its extensions (standard, optional, and PECL).

B

PHPAPI

THE PHP CORE AND EXTENSION LAYERS EXPORT A WIDE RANGE of functions meant to provide access to the SAPI, TSRM, and Engine layers as well as address common needs for the web-based environment common to most implementations of PHP. These API calls cover topics such as simple string manipulation, access to file and console I/O, and request resource management. In this appendix you'll see the extensive catalog of core API methods, its equally massive streams layer sibling, and the standard portion of the extension APIs.

Core PHP

API functions within the PHP Core are always available without the need for additional include files. Some of these methods provide unique functionality, while others simply serve as PHPized mappings to underlying Zend API functions.

Output

```
int php_printf(const char *format, ...);
int php_write(void *buf, uint size TSRMLS_DC);
int PHPWRITE(void *buf, uint size);
void php_html_puts(const char *buf, uint size TSRMLS_DC)
```

Generates output. These three methods—PHPWRITE() being identical to php_write()—pump data into the current output buffer. The last version of these methods, php_html_puts(), performs additional work by escaping HTML entities and encoding other special characters such as tabs and newlines to ensure that non-HTML formatted data looks consistent when used with HTML-driven SAPIs.

Argument	Purpose
buf	Pointer to arbitrary data to be output
size	Length of data pointed to by buf measured in bytes
format	sprintf() style formatting string

Arguments	Purpose
. . .	Type-specific arguments corresponding to the `format` specifier

```
int php_start_ob_buffer(zval *output_handler, uint chunk_size,
                    zend_bool erase TSRMLS_DC);
int php_start_ob_buffer_named(const char *handler_name,
                    uint chunk_size, zend_bool erase TSRMLS_DC);
```

Initializes a new output buffer. Note that output buffers can be stacked; therefore any data produced by this new output buffer will be re-buffered by any previously initialized output buffer. These methods have the same meaning and use as their userspace counterpart: `ob_start()`.

Argument	Purpose
output_handler	Universal callback value. Name of the function or method to be invoked with a single IS_STRING parameter when output is generated for this buffer. This callback function does not need to handle the actual work of buffering; it's just an opportunity to modify content prior to display. The callback should return an IS_STRING value.
chunk_size	Size of buffer chucks to use, in bytes.
erase	Set to a nonzero value if the buffers should be erased as they are consumed.
handler_name	`php_start_ob_buffer_named()` is a convenience wrapper that loads handler_name into a zval and then dispatches to `php_start_ob_buffer()` with all other arguments unmodified.

```
void php_end_ob_buffer(zend_bool send_buffer,
                    zend_bool just_flush TSRMLS_DC);
```

Terminates or flushes the active output buffer. Despite the name, this function will not necessarily bring the current output buffer to an end.

Argument	Purpose
send_buffer	Pass the contents of the current buffer to the next buffer down, ultimately resulting in output.
just_flush	If set to a nonzero value, the current output buffer will remain in place ready to process additional data; otherwise it will terminate and the next lower output buffer will become active.

```
void php_end_ob_buffers(zend_bool send_buffer TSRMLS_DC);
```

Ends all output buffering, optionally discarding still-buffered data on the way if
send_buffer is set to zero. When this method has finished, no output buffer will be
active and all further output will go directly to the SAPI's output mechanism.

```
int php_ob_get_buffer(zval *p TSRMLS_DC);
int php_ob_get_length(zval *p TSRMLS_DC);
```

Copies the contents of the currently buffered data—or length thereof—into an allocated,
but uninitialized zval. Note that this operation does not consume the contents of the
buffer; it simply makes a passive copy.

```
void php_start_implicit_flush(TSRMLS_D);
void php_end_implicit_flush(TSRMLS_D);
```

Toggles implicit flush mode. Calling php_start_implicit_flush() is equivalent to setting implicit_flush in php.ini.

```
const char *php_get_output_start_filename(TSRMLS_D);
int php_get_output_start_lineno(TSRMLS_D);
```

Retrieves the filename and line number where the current request began outputting
non-header data. This is typically used in error messages when attempting to use the
userspace header() function after already starting body output, but might be invoked by
extensions or SAPIs to perform other tasks

Error Reporting

```
void php_set_error_handling(error_handling_t error_handling,
                    zend_class_entry *exception_class TSRMLS_DC)
```

Switches the current error handling mode. By default, all internally generated errors are
raised as traditional, non-exception errors. Calling this method with EH_THROW will cause
noncritical errors (E_CORE_ERROR, E_COMPILE_ERROR, E_PARSE) and nontrivial errors
(E_NOTICE, E_USER_NOTICE), to be thrown as instances of the specified exception class
instead.

Argument	Purpose
error_handling	One of the three error handling constants: EH_NORMAL, EH_SUPRESS, or EH_THROW.
exception_class	Specific exception class to instantiate as an error exception when a throwable error occurs. Typically zend_get_error_exception().

```
void php_log_err(char *log_message TSRMLS_DC);
```

Sends an error message to the PHP error logging facility. This message will be appended to the logfile specified in `php.ini`, or shuttled to the SAPI's `log_message` callback as discussed in Chapter 20, "Advanced Embedding."

```
void php_error(int type, const char *format, ...);
void php_error_docref(const char *docref TSRMLS_DC,
                      int type, const char *format, ...);
void php_error_docref0(const char *docref TSRMLS_DC,
                       int type, const char *format, ...);
void php_error_docref1(const char *docref TSRMLS_DC, const char *param1,
                       int type, const char *format, ...);
void php_error_docref2(const char *docref TSRMLS_DC,
                       const char *param1, const char *param2,
                       int type, const char *format, ...);
void php_verror(const char *docref, const char *params,
                int type, const char *format, va_list args TSRMLS_DC) ;
```

Produces a standard PHP error message. Note that all forms of this method ultimately dispatch via `php_verror()`.

Arguments	Purpose
docref	Manual section fragment, or full URL where help on the error topic can be found. For example, if the error being thrown relates to the core function `mysql_connect()`, specify a docref of `function.mysql-connect`. For third-party extensions, use a complete URL such as http://myext.example.com/doc/myext_foo.html.
params	Comma-separated list of parameters as they were passed to the function. Take care not to reveal sensitive information as the error might be displayed in a browser.
param1,param2	In methods that expect these parameters, they will be concatenated together with a comma to form a single parameter list that is then passed on to `php_verror()` as the params argument.
type	Type of error being raised. Can be any of the `E_*` constants. Typically set to one of: `E_ERROR`, `E_WARNING`, or `E_NOTICE`.
format	`sprintf()` style format specifier.
...	Variable argument list corresponding to the type specifiers given by format.
args	Compiled variable argument object as produced by `va_start()`.

Startup, Shutdown, and Execution

```
int php_request_startup(TSRMLS_D);
void php_request_shutdown(void *dummy);
```

Startup or shutdown a script request. This will almost exclusively be done by a SAPI or host application using the embed SAPI. The dummy parameter is completely unused and might be passed a NULL value.

```
int php_register_extensions(zend_module_entry **list, int count TSRMLS_DC);
int php_register_extension(zend_module_entry *ptr);
```

Registers one or more additional extensions manually.

Argument	Purpose
count	Number of extensions to register
list	Vector of count extension entries
ptr	Pointer to a single zend_module_entry struct, provided as a convenience wrapper for initializing a single extension at a time

```
int php_execute_script(zend_file_handle *primary_file TSRMLS_DC);
int php_lint_script(zend_file_handle *file TSRMLS_DC);
```

Compiles and (optionally) execute a script file. Both methods process the named script through the lexer to produce tokens, and assemble those tokens into opcodes using the parser. Only php_execute_script() however, dispatches the compiled opcodes to the executor. Refer to Chapter 19, "Setting Up a Host Environment," for details on how to populate a zend_file_handle structure.

> **Note**
> As a side effect of compilation, any functions or classes contained in the target file will be loaded into the current process space, even if the compiled file is not executed. Appendix C, "Extending and Embedding Cookbook," shows an example of how to overcome this typically undesired behavior.

Safe Mode and Open Basedir

```
char *php_get_current_user(void);
```

Resolves the name of the owner of the currently running script.

```
int php_checkuid(const char *filename, char *fopen_mode, int check_mode);
int php_checkuid_ex(const char *filename, char *fopen_mode,
                    int check_mode, int flags);
```

Applies safe_mode restrictions to the named file to ensure that the owner of the currently running script has the rights to access the filename.

Argument	Purpose
filename	Filename to check safe_mode access right to
fopen_mode	How the calling scope plans to subsequently open the file, if other access checks succeed
check_mode	Exactly one of the following: CHECKUID_DISALLOW_FILE_NOT_EXISTS, CHECKUID_ALLOW_FILE_NOT_EXISTS, CHECKUID_CHECK_FILE_AND_DIR, CHECKUID_ALLOW_ONLY_DIR, CHECKUID_CHECK_MODE_PARAM, or CHECKUID_ALLOW_ONLY_FILE
flags	Can optionally be set to CHECKUID_NO_ERRORS to prevent the raising of php_error() messages

```
int php_check_open_basedir(const char *path TSRMLS_DC);
int php_check_open_basedir_ex(const char *path, int warn TSRMLS_DC);
```

Checks that the file referred to by path is within the allowed path specified by the php.ini option open_basedir. If warn is set to a nonzero value, a php_error() will be raised in the event that path is not within an allowed base directory. php_check_open_basedir() is a convenience wrapper for calling php_check_open_basedir_ex() with warn set to 1. These methods return zero if the file is in a permissible location, or non-zero if access is prohibited by php.ini settings.

String Formatting

```
int spprintf( char **pbuf, size_t max_len, const char *format, ...);
int vspprintf(char **pbuf, size_t max_len, const char *format, va_list ap);
```

Similar to snprintf() and vsnprintf(), with the exception that these methods handle allocating a non-persistent buffer of an appropriate size. Remember to either assign these strings to a zval, or manually free them using PHP's efree() deallocator in order to avoid leaks. Refer to the string handling section in the Extension APIs later in this chapter for more string manipulation functions.

Reentrancy Safety

```
struct tm *php_localtime_r(const time_t *const timep, struct tm *p_tm);
char *php_ctime_r(const time_t *clock, char *buf);
char *php_asctime_r(const struct tm *tm, char *buf);
struct tm *php_gmtime_r(const time_t *const timep, struct tm *p_tm);
int php_rand_r(unsigned int *seed);
char *php_strtok_r(char *s, const char *delim, char **last);
```

These functions follow the prototype of their POSIX counterparts with added reentrancy safety. Use of these variants is always recommended in the interest of maintaining thread safety. Refer to their man pages for the meaning and purpose of their fields.

Miscellaneous

```
int php_register_info_logo(char *logo_string, char *mimetype,
                    unsigned char *data, int size);
int php_unregister_info_logo(char *logo_string);
```

These two methods allow an extension or SAPI to declare a logo or "Easter egg" content. When a PHP page is requested from a server that has the expose_php option enabled, where the query string is =logo_string, the content pointed to by data will be served up rather than the otherwise requested page. This is the mechanism used by the PHP Credits page (logo_string=PHPB8B5F2A0-3C92-11d3-A3A9-4C7B08C10000), the Easter Egg image (logo_string=PHPE9568F36-D428-11d2-A769-00AA001ACF42), and a collection of other embedded content.

Argument	Purpose
logo_string	Unique label for this special content. Traditionally, this is a GUID, though any unique string will work.
mimetype	Mime-type string to be sent as a header when outputting data.
data	The arbitrary data associated with logo_string. Note that data is not copied by the registration process, only the pointer to its location; therefore this pointer must remain valid until PHP shuts down or the logo_string identifier is unregistered.
size	Size of content pointed to by data in bytes.

```
void php_add_tick_function(void (*func)(int));
void php_remove_tick_function(void (*func)(int));
```

Adds or removes a tick function to be used with the userspace directive declare(ticks=count). Note that multiple tick handlers can be registered and will be called in the order they were added.

Streams API

The streams layer is easily the largest piece of PHP's core API. To help navigate through the sheer volume of method calls, this section of the appendix will attempt to break them down into functional groupings covering creation, access, manipulation, and destruction.

Stream Creation and Destruction

```
php_stream *php_stream_alloc(php_stream_ops *ops, void *abstract,
                    const char *persistent_id, const char *mode);
```

Allocates a PHP Stream instance associated with the identified stream ops. This method is typically used by stream or wrapper implementations; refer to Chapter 15.

Argument	Purpose
ops	Structure containing a list of callback operations for performing read, write, flush, close, and other operations.
abstract	Attaches an arbitrary data structure to the stream instance, typically referring to the underlying data resource.
persistent_id	Unique identifier for this stream resource used for retrieving persistent stream instances.
mode	fopen mode to associate with this stream instance (such as r, w, a, r+, and so on).

```
int php_stream_from_persistent_id(const char *persistent_id,
                    php_stream **stream TSRMLS_DC);
```

Recovers a stream instance based on its persistent ID (as provided to php_stream_alloc()).

```
int php_stream_free(php_stream *stream, int close_options);
int php_stream_close(php_stream *stream);
int php_stream_pclose(php_stream *stream);
```

Closes a stream and free the resources associated with it. close_options can be any combination of the following flags. php_stream_close() calls php_stream_free() with close_options set to PHP_STREAM_FREE_CLOSE, while php_stream_pclose() calls it with PHP_STREAM_FREE_CLOSE_PERSISTENT.

close_options Flags	Description
PHP_STREAM_FREE_CALL_DTOR	Call the stream's ops->close() method
PHP_STREAM_FREE_RELEASE_STREAM	Free memory allocated to store the stream instance
PHP_STREAM_FREE_PRESERVE_HANDLE	Passed to ops->close() to instruct it not to close the underlying handle
PHP_STREAM_FREE_RSRC_DTOR	Used internally by the streams layer to avoid recursion when destroying the stream's associated resource
PHP_STREAM_FREE_PERSISTENT	Explicitly close an otherwise persistent stream instance

close_options Flags	Description
PHP_STREAM_FREE_CLOSE	Combination of PHP_STREAM_FREE_CALL_DTOR and PHP_STREAM_FREE_RELEASE_STREAM
PHP_STREAM_FREE_CLOSE_CASTED	Combination of PHP_STREAM_FREE_CLOSE and PHP_STREAM_FREE_PRESERVE_HANDLE
PHP_STREAM_FREE_CLOSE_PERSISTENT	Combination of PHP_STREAM_FREE_CLOSE and PHP_STREAM_FREE_PERSISTENT

```
php_stream_wrapper *php_stream_locate_url_wrapper(const char *path,
                char **path_for_open, int options TSRMLS_DC);
```

Retrieves the currently registered wrapper struct associated with a given URI. Typically path_for_open will simply be populated with the value of path; however, when file-based URIs are given, the leading file:// scheme identifier will be automatically stripped so that calls to the underlying open() syscall will function normally.

Argument	Purpose
path	Full URI of resource to be mapped to its wrapper structure.
path_for_open	Populated with (possibly) modified version of path to use in actual open call.
options	Bitmask flag containing zero or more of the following options: IGNORE_URL, STREAM_LOCATE_WRAPPERS_ONLY, and REPORT_ERRORS. Refer to Chapter 14 for explanations of these flags.

```
php_stream *php_stream_open_wrapper(char *path, char *mode,
                int options, char **opened_path);
php_stream *php_stream_open_wrapper_ex(char *path, char *mode,
                int options, char **opened_path,
                php_stream_context *context);
FILE *php_stream_open_wrapper_as_file(char *path, char *mode,
                int options, char **opened_path);
```

Creates a stream instance or stdio file pointer from the given path. The php_stream_open_wrapper() variant functions identically to the extended version with a value of NULL passed for context. If php_stream_open_wrapper_as_file() is called for a protocol that does not support casting to FILE*, the streams layer will raise an error, close the intermediate stream, and return NULL.

Argument	Purpose
path	URI pointing to location of resource to be opened.
mode	Access mode to apply to file being opened (such as r, w+, a, and so on).
options	Zero or more of the stream open options described in Chapter 14.
opened_path	Populated with the actual location of the opened resource. Due to symlinks and redirects, this will commonly be different from the actual path requested.
context	Stream context to be used while opening or accessing the stream.

Stream I/O

```
size_t php_stream_read(php_stream *stream, char *buf, size_t maxlen);
char *php_stream_get_record(php_stream *stream, size_t maxlen,
                      size_t *returned_len, char *delim,
                      size_t delim_len TSRMLS_DC);
char *php_stream_get_line(php_stream *stream, char *buf, size_t maxlen,
                      size_t *returned_len);
char *php_stream_gets(php_stream *stream, char *buf, size_t maxlen);
int php_stream_getc(php_stream *stream);
```

Reads data from a stream instance. php_stream_read() reads raw bytes with no regard to their content and only attempts one read call to the underlying transport. This means that, depending on the underlying implementation's semantics, fewer than maxlen bytes can be returned even if more data is currently available. Conversely, the three line-oriented data retrieval operations (get_record, get_line, and gets) perform a greedy read, buffering up as much of the stream's data as necessary to either locate an end of line sequence, or fill the provided buffer to maxlen bytes. php_stream_getc() will read a single byte from the stream.

Argument	Purpose
stream	Stream instance to read from.
buf	Buffer to store results to. For methods that return char*, if buf is passed as NULL, a buffer of appropriate size will be emalloc'd to the appropriate size.
maxlen	Maximum number of bytes to read from the stream.
delim	"End of line" delimiter. Sequence at which to stop reading from the stream. Does not require a terminating NULL byte.

Arguments	Purpose
delim_len	Length of delimiter string, not including any optional terminating NULL characters.
returned_len	Length of string returned by methods otherwise returning a char* buffer.

```
size_t php_stream_write(php_stream *stream, const char *buf, size_t count)
size_t php_stream_write_string(php_stream *stream, const char *buf);
int php_stream_puts(php_stream *stream, char *buf);
size_t php_stream_printf(php_stream *stream TSRMLS_DC, const char *fmt, ...);
int php_stream_putc(php_stream *stream, int c);
```

Writes data to a stream instance. php_stream_puts() differs from php_stream_write() by appending an additional newline character after writing the contents of buf. The putc and puts varieties return 1 on success or 0 on failure while the remaining versions return the number of bytes actually written on the stream—which may be fewer that the number of bytes requested to write.

Argument	Purpose
stream	Stream to write data to
buf	Buffer containing data to be written to stream
count	Number of bytes of data contained in buf
c	Single character to write to stream
fmt	sprintf() style format specifier
...	Variable argument list corresponding to fmt specifier

```
int php_stream_eof(php_stream *stream);
```

Returns a nonzero value if the stream's file pointer has reached the end of file.

```
int php_stream_flush(php_stream *stream, int closing);
```

Instructs the underlying stream implementation to flush any internally buffered data to the target resource.

```
size_t php_stream_copy_to_stream(php_stream *src,
                    php_stream *dest, size_t maxlen);
```

Reads remaining content—up to maxlen bytes—from src stream and write it out to dest stream.

```
size_t php_stream_copy_to_mem(php_stream *src, char **buffer,
                  size_t maxlen, int persistent);
```

Reads remaining content—up to `maxlen` bytes—from `src` stream and place it into a newly allocated `buffer`. If `persistent` is nonzero, permanent memory allocators will be used; otherwise, non-persistent memory will be allocated for `buffer`.

```
size_t php_stream_passthru(php_stream * src);
```

Reads remaining content from `src` stream and output it to the browser, command line, or other appropriate target.

```
char *php_stream_mmap_range(php_stream *stream, size_t offset,
                  size_t length, php_stream_mmap_operation_t mode,
                  size_t *mapped_len);
int php_stream_mmap_unmap(php_stream *stream TSRMLS_DC);
int php_stream_mmap_supported(php_stream *stream);
int php_stream_mmap_possible(php_stream *stream);
```

Maps or unmaps a portion of a stream's contents to memory. Note that PHP imposes an artificial limit of 2MB on memory mapping operations. The functions returning integers yield zero for failure or to indicate a negative response, or nonzero otherwise. `php_stream_mmap_range()` returns a pointer to the mem-mapped range on success, or `NULL` on failure.

Argument	Purpose
stream	Stream to map
offset	Beginning offset in the stream's contents from which to map
length	Number of bytes to map; use `PHP_STREAM_COPY_ALL` to map all of the remaining data (however much is available)
mode	Set to `PHP_STREAM_MMAP_MAP_RANGE`; other values are used internally by the streams layer
mapped_len	Populated with the actual number of bytes mapped to the pointer returned by this method

Stream Manipulation

```
int php_stream_seek(php_stream *stream, off_t offset, int whence);
int php_stream_rewind(php_stream *stream);
off_t php_stream_tell(php_stream *stream);
```

Moves the file pointer within a seekable stream (`seek`) or report its current position (`tell`). `php_stream_rewind()` is provided as a convenience macro mapping to `php_stream_seek(stream,0,SEEK_SET);`.

Argument	Purpose
stream	Stream to seek or report the location on
offset	Position to seek to relative to the whence
whence	One of SEEK_SET (relative to beginning of stream), SEEK_CUR (relative to current position), or SEEK_END (relative to end of file)

```
int php_stream_stat(php_stream *stream, php_stream_statbuf *ssb);
int php_stream_stat_path(char *path, int flags, php_stream_statbuf *ssb,
                  php_stream_context *context);
```

Reports fstat() or stat() style information from an open stream or URI path respectively.

Argument	Purpose
stream	Active stream instance to retrieve fstat() information from.
path	URL to a local or remote file resource to retrieve stat() data from.
flags	If set to PHP_STREAM_URL_STAT_LINK, only the immediate resource pointed to by path will be inspected. If this flag is not set, symlinks will be followed to a real resource.
ssb	Stat buffer to populate filestat information into.
context	Stream context to apply when attempting to locate the local or remote resource.

```
int php_stream_set_option(php_stream *stream, int option,
                  int value, void *ptrparam);
int php_stream_truncate_set_size(php_stream *stream, size_t newsize);
```

Performs an ioctl() style operation on PHP stream. php_stream_truncate_set_size() is a convenience wrapper for php_stream_set_option(stream, PHP_STREAM_OPTION_TRUNCATE_API, PHP_STREAM_TRUNCATE_SET_SIZE, &newsize);, which instructs the underlying stream implementation to change the size of its associated file resource.

The full list of options is a topic unto itself and is beyond the scope of this book. Refer to the source code of stream implementations such as main/streams/plain_wrapper.c and main/streams/xp_socket.c to see the implementation side of these controls.

```
int php_stream_can_cast(php_stream *stream, int castas);
int php_stream_cast(php_stream *stream, int castas, void **ret, int show_err);
```

Exposes a stream as a more fundamental system type such as a file descriptor or filestream object. castas must be passed as exactly one of the type flags: PHP_STREAM_AS_STDIO, PHP_STREAM_AS_FD, PHP_STREAM_AS_SOCKETD, or PHP_STREAM_AS_FD_FOR_SELECT optionally combined via bitwise OR with PHP_STREAM_CAST_RELEASE, which will invalidate future uses of the owning stream object. To test if a stream can be cast without actually performing the operation, call php_stream_can_cast() instead. Both methods return SUCCESS or FAILURE.

Argument	Purpose
stream	Stream to be cast.
castas	Type of resource to cast the stream to.
ret	Pointer to a local variable to store the casted stream to.
show_err	Set to a nonzero value to raise php_errors()s if the cast encounters errors.

```
int php_stream_make_seekable(php_stream *origstream,
                    php_stream **newstream, int flags);
```

If origstream is already seekable, and flags does not contain PHP_STREAM_FORCE_CONVERSION, newstream will simply be set to origstream and this method will return PHP_STREAM_UNCHANGED. Otherwise, a new temporary stream will be created and the remaining contents of origstream will be copied to newstream. Note that any content already read from origstream will not become available as a result of calling this method. If the method succeeds, origstream will be closed and the call will return PHP_STREAM_RELEASED. Should it fail, it will return PHP_STREAM_FAILURE to indicate the temporary stream could not be created, or PHP_STREAM_CRITICAL to indicate that the contents of origstream could not be copied to newstream. Note that a copy failure might result in some or all data from origstream being lost. In addition to PHP_STREAM_FORCE_CONVERSION, flags can also be combined with PHP_STREAM_PREFER_STDIO, which will create a STDIO tempfile rather than a temporary file descriptor.

Directory Access

```
int php_stream_mkdir(char *path, int mode, int options,
                    php_stream_context *context);
int php_stream_rmdir(char *path, int options,
                    php_stream_context *context);
```

Creates a new directory or remove one. The criteria and method for creating or removing a directory is wrapper-specific; however, all wrappers implementing the mkdir() method are expected to respect the PHP_STREAM_MKDIR_RECURSIVE option. Note that there are no `options` flags actually defined for `php_stream_rmdir()`. This argument exists purely for forward compatibility.

Argument	Purpose
path	URI describing directory to be created or removed.
mode	POSIX access mode to apply to the newly created directory.
options	`Bitmask` flag argument with—currently—one option: `PHP_STREAM_MKDIR_RECURSIVE`, which applies only to the `mkdir()` variant of these methods. When used, any nonexisting parent directories required by the given `path` will be implicitly created as well.
context	Stream context to apply to wrapper execution.

```
php_stream *php_stream_opendir(char *path, int options,
                    php_stream_context *context);
php_stream_dirent *php_stream_readdir(php_stream *stream,
                    php_stream_dirent *ent);
int php_stream_rewinddir(php_stream *stream);
int php_stream_close(php_stream *stream);
```

Opens, iteratively reads entries from, and closes a directory resource. Directory entries are read in block increments of equal size. The contents of a directory entry can be accessed via `ent->d_name`.

Argument	Purpose
path	URI pointing to directory to be examined.
options	Optional parameters to pass during stream creation. Refer to Chapter 14 for a listing of these options and what they do.
context	Stream context to apply while opening this directory resource.
stream	Active directory stream instance to read from, rewind, or close.
ent	Directory entry buffer that will be populated with the next directory entry name.

```
int php_stream_scandir(char *path, char **namelist[],
                    php_stream_context *context,
                    int (*compare) (const char **a, const char **b));
int php_stream_dirent_alphasort(const char **a, const char **b);
int php_stream_dirent_alphasortr(const char **a, const char **b);
```

`php_stream_scandir()` will read all entries within a given directory into a vector of `char*` strings. If a `compare` function—such as one of the `alphasort` methods shown—is provided, the entries will be sorted after being read. Space for the `namelist` vector and each individual entry will be automatically allocated by the `php_stream_scandir()` method using nonpersistent storage and must be manually freed after use. For example, a `namelist` containing 10 entries will have 11 distinct allocations—one for the vector itself, and another for the individual strings within that vector.

Argument	Purpose
path	URI pointing to the directory to scan for entries.
namelist	Passed as a pointer to local `char**` storage. This will be modified by reference by the `scandir` method.
context	Stream context to use while scanning the directory.
compare	Comparison function to use for sorting. Can be either of the `alphasort` methods given previously, or any callback that accepts two elements as its input and returns -1, 0, or 1 to indicate less-than, equal, or greater-than, respectively.

Internal/Userspace Conversion

```
int php_file_le_stream(void);
int php_file_le_pstream(void);
int php_file_le_stream_filter(void);
int php_le_stream_context(void);
```

Returns list entry type IDs for standard streams, persistent streams, filters, and contexts. These values correspond to the values assigned by `zend_register_list_destructors()` and are used by helper macros such as `php_stream_from_zval()`.

```
void php_stream_to_zval(php_stream *stream, zval *zstream);
void php_stream_from_zval(php_stream *stream, zval *zstream);
void php_stream_from_zval_no_verify(php_stream *stream, zval *zstream);
```

These helper macros encode an allocated stream to a userspace zval, or decode it back again. Note that these are macros and not regular functions, therefore the `stream` variable passed to the `php_stream_from_zval*()`; functions is modified in place. The `php_stream_from_zval()` macro, unique among the rest, will produce `php_error()` warnings if the `zstream` value passed is not a valid PHP Stream resource. Refer back to Chapter 9, "The Resource Data Type," for more information on registering and retrieving resource values.

Contexts

```
php_stream_context *php_stream_context_alloc(void);
void php_stream_context_free(php_stream_context *context);
```

Allocates or frees a stream context. Refer to Chapter 16, "Diverting the Stream," for a more complete explanation of the usage of stream contexts.

```
int php_stream_context_set_option(php_stream_context *context,
                const char *wrappername, const char *optionname,
                zval *optionvalue);
int php_stream_context_get_option(php_stream_context *context,
                const char *wrappername, const char *optionname,
                zval ***optionvalue);
```

Sets or retrieves a context option. Context options are stored in a two-dimensional array of zval* values. The name of the base wrapper defines the first dimension, whereas a wrapper-specific option name defines the second. Wrappers that serve double duty, such as http and https, typically use only one wrapper name (in this case, http) for storing their context options.

Argument	Purpose
context	Context container to set or retrieve options on.
wrappername	Name of the base wrapper for which this option applies.
optionname	Wrapper-specific option name to get or set.
optionvalue	Depending on the specific method called, either a zval* value to store into the context option, or pointer to a local zval** variable to fetch a previously stored value back into. Note that when storing a value it is explicitly separated (copied) by the streams layer, detaching it from the calling scope's ownership.

```
php_stream_context *php_stream_context_set(php_stream *stream,
php_stream_context *context);
```

Associates a context with an already active stream instance. Because most context options take effect when the stream is opened, this action will typically have much less impact than specifying the context to the stream creation method.

Notifiers

```
php_stream_notifier *php_stream_notification_alloc(void);
void php_stream_notification_free(php_stream_notifier *notifier);
void php_stream_notification_notify(php_stream_context *context,
                int notifycode, int severity, char *xmsg,
                int xcode, size_t bytes_sofar, size_t bytes_max,
                void * ptr TSRMLS_DC);
```

Refer to Chapter 16 for details on the use of these methods.

Filters

```
php_stream_filter *php_stream_filter_create(const char *filtername,
                    zval *filterparams, int persistent TSRMLS_DC);
```

Instantiates a filter using the filter-specific parameters provided. When instantiating a filter object to be placed on a persistent stream, the `persistent` flag must be set. This can usually be accomplished by using the `php_stream_is_persistent()` method.

Argument	Purpose
filtername	Name of the filter to instantiate.
filterparams	Optional `zval*` containing filter-specific parameters. Refer to documentation for the filter being instantiated for the types and values accepted.
persistent	Binary flag indicating whether the filter will be placed on a persistent stream.

```
php_stream_filter *php_stream_filter_alloc(php_stream_filter_ops *fops,
                    void *abstract, int persistent);
void php_stream_filter_free(php_stream_filter *filter TSRMLS_DC);
```

Allocates or frees a filter structure. `php_stream_filter_alloc()` is typically used by filter implementations during instantiation. The free method will automatically call the filter's `dtor` method to clean up any internal resources.

Argument	Purpose
fops	Filter ops structure containing callbacks to use with this filter instance.
abstract	Arbitrary data pointer to associate with the filter instance.
persistent	Flag indicating whether the filter will be placed on a persistent stream.

```
void php_stream_filter_prepend(php_stream_filter_chain *chain,
                    php_stream_filter *filter);
void php_stream_filter_append(php_stream_filter_chain *chain,
                    php_stream_filter *filter);
int php_stream_filter_flush(php_stream_filter *filter, int finish);
php_stream_filter *php_stream_filter_remove(php_stream_filter *filter,
                    int call_free TSRMLS_DC);
```

Adds a filter to the beginning or end of a stream's filter stack, flushes its internal buffers, or removes a filter from an active stream. Typically a filter will be flushed prior to removing it so that internally buffered data can be passed to later filters or the read-buffer/write-op as appropriate.

Argument	Purpose
chain	Filter chain to add the named `filter` to. Typically one of `stream->readfilters` or `stream->writefilters`.
filter	Filter instance to add, flush, or remove.
finish	When set to a nonzero value, the filter is instructed to flush as much data from its internal buffers as possible. Otherwise, the filter can choose to only flush the current block of data while retaining some for the next cycle.
call_free	Automatically call `php_stream_filter_free()` after removing it from its stream's filter chain.

```
int php_stream_filter_register_factory(const char *filterpattern,
                    php_stream_filter_factory *factory TSRMLS_DC);
int php_stream_filter_unregister_factory(
                    const char *filterpattern TSRMLS_DC);
int php_stream_filter_register_factory_volatile(const char *filterpattern,
                    php_stream_filter_factory *factory TSRMLS_DC);
int php_stream_filter_unregister_factory_volatile(
                    const char *filterpattern TSRMLS_DC);
```

Registers or unregisters a stream filter. The `volatile` variant of these methods allows wrappers to be overridden for the life of a single request only, whereas the nonvolatile versions handle permanent registrations and unregistrations. As with wrappers, volatile filters should be registered and unregistered during request phases—ACTIVATE, RUNTIME, DEACTIVATE—only, permanent filters, likewise, should only be registered and unregistered during the STARTUP and SHUTDOWN phases.

Buckets

```
php_stream_bucket *php_stream_bucket_new(php_stream *stream,
                    char *buf, size_t buflen, int own_buf,
                    int buf_persistent TSRMLS_DC);
```

Instantiates a bucket object to place on a filter brigade. Refer to Chapter 16 for information on using buckets with custom filter implementations.

Argument	Purpose
stream	Reference to the stream this bucket will ultimately be associated with.
buf	Data buffer to assign to this bucket.
buflen	Length of `buf` in bytes.

Arguments	Purpose
own_buf	Set to a nonzero value if buf can be safely altered or freed by another filter or the streams layer. If this and buf_persistent are set to 0, and the target stream is not persistent, buf will be automatically copied so that the bucket owns a modifiable buffer.
buf_persistent	Set to a nonzero value if the passed buf data will remain available and unchanged for the life of the current request.

```
void php_stream_bucket_delref(php_stream_bucket *bucket TSRMLS_DC);
```

Reduce the internal refcount of the named bucket. In practice, buckets rarely exceed a refcount of one, so this call usually destroys the bucket completely.

```
int php_stream_bucket_split(php_stream_bucket *in, php_stream_bucket **left,
                php_stream_bucket **right, size_t length TSRMLS_DC);
```

Divides the contents of a bucket into two new buckets. The in bucket is consumed and delref'd in the process of splitting with length bytes of buffer data placed in the new bucket populated into left, and any remaining data placed in the new bucket populated into right.

```
void php_stream_bucket_prepend(php_stream_bucket_brigade *brigade,
                php_stream_bucket *bucket TSRMLS_DC);
void php_stream_bucket_append(php_stream_bucket_brigade *brigade,
                php_stream_bucket *bucket TSRMLS_DC);
void php_stream_bucket_unlink(php_stream_bucket *bucket TSRMLS_DC);
```

Adds or removes a bucket to/from a bucket brigade.

```
php_stream_bucket *php_stream_bucket_make_writeable(php_stream_bucket *bucket
                TSRMLS_DC);
```

Ensures that the data contained in a bucket can be safely modified by the calling scope. If necessary, the bucket will duplicate the contents of its internal buffer in order to make it writeable.

Plainfiles and Standard I/O

```
php_stream *php_stream_fopen(const char *filename,
                const char *mode, char **opened_path);
php_stream *php_stream_fopen_with_path(char *filename, char *mode,
                char *include_path, char **opened_path);
```

Local filesystem variant of the php_stream_open_wrapper() method. This version will not dispatch to any stream wrappers other than the plainfiles wrapper, and does not provide a means to specify a context parameter. Neither versions of this method use the php.ini include_path value; however, the _with_path() variant does allow an include_path set to be specified.

```
php_stream *php_stream_fopen_from_file(FILE *file, const char *mode);
php_stream *php_stream_fopen_from_fd(int fd, const char *mode,
                    const char *persistent_id);
php_stream *php_stream_sock_open_from_socket(php_socket_t socket,
                    const char *persistent_id);
php_stream *php_stream_fopen_from_pipe(FILE *file, const char *mode);
```

Casts an already opened file descriptor or stdio file pointer to a PHP stream.

Argument	Purpose
file / fd	Existing file descriptor or stdio file pointer to wrap in a PHP stream
mode	fopen mode to associate with the stream
persistent_id	Persistent ID to assign to the stream

```
php_stream *php_stream_temp_create(int mode, size_t max_memory_usage);
php_stream *php_stream_temp_open(int mode, size_t max_memory_usage,
                    char *buf, size_t length);
```

Creates a temporary stream suitable for reading and writing. When the stream is closed, any contents within the stream as well as secondary resources are discarded. Initially, temporary data is stored in RAM; however, if the size of the stored data grows beyond max_memory_usage, the contents of the memory stream will be written to a temporary file on disk and all further interim storage will take place there.

Argument	Purpose
mode	One of: TEMP_STREAM_DEFAULT, TEMP_STREAM_READONLY, or TEMP_STREAM_TAKE_BUFFER.
max_memory_usage	Maximum amount of memory to allocate for temporary data storage. Once this limit is exceeded, a temp file will be used as the storage medium instead.
buf	Initial buffer to create the temporary stream with.
length	Size of buf in bytes.

```
char *expand_filepath(const char *filepath, char *real_path TSRMLS_DC);
```

Resolves symlinks and parent references in the provided filepath to its real target. This method provides a thread-safe replacement to the standard realpath() method.

Transports

```
php_stream *php_stream_xport_create(const char *name, long namelen,
                    int options, int flags, const char *persistent_id,
                    struct timeval *timeout, php_stream_context *context,
                    char **error_string, int *error_code);
```

Instantiates a socket transport stream. Depending on the passed `flags`, this can be a client or server socket, which may or may not immediately connect or start listening.

Argument	Purpose
name	Transport URI. If no protocol specifier is given, `tcp://` is assumed for backward compatibility with the userspace `fsockopen()` command.
namelen	Length of a `name` argument, not including its trailing NULL.
options	The same options parameter used with `php_stream_open_wrapper()`.
flags	Bitwise OR combination of the STREAM_XPORT flags.
persistent_id	Persistent ID associated with this transport. If available, and the socket is still live, the existing stream will be reused rather than opening a new one.
timeout	Maximum time to block while performing a synchronous connection.
context	Optional stream context.
error_string	Populated with a descriptive error if one occurs.
error_code	Populated with a numeric error code if one occurs.

The `flags` parameter can consist of either STREAM_XPORT_CLIENT or STREAM_XPORT_SERVER. A client transport can optionally specify either STREAM_XPORT_CONNECT or STREAM_XPORT_CONNECT_ASYNC. Server transports can specify STREAM_XPORT_BIND and STREAM_XPORT_LISTEN.

Flag	Meaning
STREAM_XPORT_CLIENT	Create a client-style transport.
STREAM_XPORT_SERVER	Create a server-style transport.
STREAM_XPORT_CONNECT	Immediately connect to the specified resource using a blocking (synchronous) call.
STREAM_XPORT_BIND	Bind to the specified local resource.
STREAM_XPORT_LISTEN	Listen for inbound connections on the transport socket. Typically requires the inclusion of STREAM_XPORT_BIND. By default, a backlog of five connections will be queued.
STREAM_XPORT_CONNECT_ASYNC	Begin connecting to the specified resource asynchronously.

```
int php_stream_xport_connect(php_stream *stream, const char *name, long namelen,
                int asynchronous, struct timeval *timeout,
                char **error_text, int *error_code TSRMLS_DC);
```

Connects a transport stream to the specified resource.

Argument	Purpose
stream	Transport stream to connect to the specified resource
name	Transport protocol–specific resource specified to connect to
namelen	Length of resource specifier
asynchronous	Set to a nonzero value to connect asynchronously
timeout	Maximum length of time to wait for a successful connection
error_text	Populated with descriptive error message on failure
error_code	Populated with numeric error code

```
int php_stream_xport_bind(php_stream *stream, const char *name, long namelen,
                char **error_text TSRMLS_DC);
```

Binds the established stream to a local resource. This can be used for binding server sockets or for source-binding clients prior to connection.

Argument	Purpose
stream	Transport stream to bind to a local resource
name	String describing the local resource to bind to
namelen	Length of name excluding its trailing NULL byte
error_test	Populated with textual error message if the bind was unsuccessful

```
int php_stream_xport_listen(php_stream *stream, int backlog,
                char **error_text TSRMLS_DC);
```

Begins listening on the previously bound transport socket.

Argument	Meaning
stream	Transport stream to bind to a local resource
backlog	Number of unaccepted connections to queue before rejecting additional connection attempts
error_test	Populated with textual error message if the bind was unsuccessful

```
int php_stream_xport_accept(php_stream *stream, php_stream **client,
                            char **textaddr, int *textaddrlen,
                            void **addr, socklen_t *addrlen,
                            struct timeval *time_out, char **error_text TSRMLS_DC);
```

Accepts a queued connection on a transport socket previously instructed to listen. If no connections are currently queued, this method will block for the period specified by time_out.

Argument	Purpose
stream	Server transport stream previously bound and instructed to listen. Connections will be accepted from this transport's backlog.
client	Populated with newly created transport stream using accepted connection.
textaddr	Populated with textual representation of addr.
textaddrlen	Populated with length of textaddr.
addr	Populated with transport-specific address structure.
addrlen	Populated with length of transport-specific address structure.
time_out	Maximum length of time to wait for an inbound connection. NULL to wait indefinitely.
error_text	Populated with textual error message if one occurs.

```
int php_stream_xport_get_name(php_stream *stream, int want_peer,
                              char **textaddr, int *textaddrlen,
                              void **addr, socklen_t *addrlen TSRMLS_DC);
```

Probes the local or remote transport end-point (socket) name.

Argument	Purpose
stream	Connected transport stream
want_peer	Set to nonzero to retrieve the remote end-point's information
textaddr	Populated with textual representation of address information
textaddrlen	Populated with length of textaddr
addr	Populated with transport protocol–specific address information
addrlen	Populated with length of addr

```
int php_stream_xport_sendto(php_stream *stream, const char *buf, size_t buflen,
                    long flags, void *addr, socklen_t addrlen TSRMLS_DC);
int php_stream_xport_recvfrom(php_stream *stream, char *buf, size_t buflen,
                    long flags, void **addr, socklen_t *addrlen,
                    char **textaddr, int *textaddrlen TSRMLS_DC);
```

Connectionless send and receive methods.

Argument	Meaning
stream	Transport stream to use for sending or receiving.
buf	Data to be sent or buffer to populate received data into.
buflen	Length of data to send or length of buffer to receive data into.
flags	Can optionally be set to STREAM_OOB to send or receive out-of-band data. When receiving, can also be set to or combined with STREAM_PEEK to inspect data without consuming it.
addr	When sending: protocol-specific address record to send to. When receiving: populated with protocol-specific source address record.
addrlen	Length of addr in bytes.
textaddr	Populated with textual representation of source address.
textaddrlen	Populated with length of textaddr.

```
int php_stream_xport_crypto_setup(php_stream *stream,
                    php_stream_xport_crypt_method_t crypto_method,
                    php_stream *session_stream TSRMLS_DC);

int php_stream_xport_crypto_enable(php_stream *stream, int activate TSRMLS_DC);
```

Sets up and activates/deactivates encryption on the specified transport stream. In practice only the SSL/TLS crypto methods are implemented and these are only typically used with the TCP transport.

Argument	Purpose
stream	Transport stream to setup cryptography on.
crypto_method	One of: STREAM_CRYPTO_METHOD_SSLv2_CLIENT, STREAM_CRYPTO_METHOD_SSLv3_CLIENT, STREAM_CRYPTO_METHOD_SSLv23_CLIENT, STREAM_CRYPTO_METHOD_TLS_CLIENT, STREAM_CRYPTO_METHOD_SSLv2_SERVER, STREAM_CRYPTO_METHOD_SSLv3_SERVER, STREAM_CRYPTO_METHOD_SSLv23_SERVER, or STREAM_CRYPTO_METHOD_TLS_SERVER.

Arguments	Purpose
session_stream	If provided, the new crypto setup will inherit session parameters from a previously crypto-enabled transport stream.
activate	When set to a nonzero value, the crypto-layer will be enabled; when set to zero, it will be turned off.

```
int php_stream_xport_register(char *protocol,
                    php_stream_transport_factory factory TSRMLS_DC);
typedef php_stream *(*php_stream_transport_factory)(
                    const char *proto, long protolen,
                    char *resourcename, long resourcenamelen,
                    const char *persistent_id, int options, int flags,
                    struct timeval *timeout, php_stream_context *context
                    STREAMS_DC TSRMLS_DC);
int php_stream_xport_unregister(char *protocol TSRMLS_DC);
```

Registers or unregisters a stream transport factory. Transport factory methods follow the same pattern as stream protocol wrapper opener functions. Refer to Chapter 15 for an overview of stream creation methods.

Argument	Purpose
protocol	Name of protocol to register or unregister.
factory	Factory method called when a transport of the specified protocol is instantiated.
proto	Name of transport protocol being instantiated.
protolen	Length of proto.
resourcename	Protocol-specific URI indicating resource to connect to.
resourcenamelen	Length of resourcename.
persistent_id	Persistent ID associated with the transport stream being instantiated.
options	Option values as passed to php_stream_xport_create().
flags	Flag values as passed to php_stream_xport_create().
timeout	Default timeout value for transport.
context	Optional context parameter to be associated with the stream.

```
HashTable *php_stream_xport_get_hash(void);
```

Returns a pointer to the internal transport registry hash.

```
int php_network_parse_network_address_with_port(const char *addr, long addrlen,
                    struct sockaddr *sa, socklen_t *sl TSRMLS_DC);
```

Parses an `inet` family transport URI into its component parts. If the host portion of the URI is hostname it will be automatically resolved to its IP address. The appropriate address family, address, and port data are loaded into the `sa sockaddr` structure and its final size is populated into `sl`.

Miscellaneous

```
int php_register_url_stream_wrapper(char *protocol,
                    php_stream_wrapper *wrapper TSRMLS_DC);
int php_unregister_url_stream_wrapper(char *protocol TSRMLS_DC);
int php_register_url_stream_wrapper_volatile(char *protocol,
                    php_stream_wrapper *wrapper TSRMLS_DC);
int php_unregister_url_stream_wrapper_volatile(char *protocol TSRMLS_DC);
```

Registers or unregisters a stream protocol wrapper. The `volatile` variant of these methods allows wrappers to be overridden for the life of a single request only, whereas the nonvolatile versions handle permanent registrations and unregistrations. Needless to say, volatile wrappers should be registered and unregistered during request phases— `ACTIVATE`, `RUNTIME`, `DEACTIVATE`—only, permanent wrappers, by contrast, should only be registered and unregistered during the `STARTUP` and `SHUTDOWN` phases. Refer to Chapter 15 for more information.

```
void php_stream_wrapper_log_error(php_stream_wrapper *wrapper,
                    int options TSRMLS_DC, const char *format, ...);
```

Reports a stream error via the wrapper subsystem. This method is typically called from wrapper operations such as `stream_open`. Refer to Chapter 15 for more information on reporting wrapper errors.

Argument	Purpose
wrapper	Reference to the currently active wrapper.
options	Typically passed through from the parameter stack. If the REPORT_ERRORS flag is set, the error message will be dispatched via PHP's normal error handling mechanism with php_error(). If it's not set, the message will be appended to the current wrappers error log.
format	sprintf() style format specifier.
...	Variable argument list corresponding to format.

```
HashTable *php_stream_get_url_stream_wrappers_hash(void);
HashTable *php_stream_get_url_stream_wrappers_hash_global(void);
HashTable *php_get_stream_filters_hash(void);
HashTable *php_get_stream_filters_hash_global(void);
```

Returns a reference to the internal registry of wrappers and filters. The _global() variants of these methods contain the persistent wrapper and filter definitions while the non _global() versions return this list as it has been modified by volatile registrations.

```
int php_stream_is(php_stream *stream, php_stream_ops *ops);
```

Returns nonzero if stream implements the named stream ops.

```
int php_stream_is_persistent(php_stream *stream);
```

Returns a nonzero value if the named stream instance is meant to be persistent between requests.

```
int php_is_url(char *path);
```

Returns a nonzero value if the named path specifies a network-based resource.

```
char *php_strip_url_passwd(char *path);
```

Strips the password from a standard formatted URL. Note that this method modifies the provided path in place; therefore, the value provided must be owned by the calling process and be modifiable.

Extension APIs

Several PHP extensions, the standard extension chief among them, export additional PHP API methods that can be used from other extensions by including the appropriate header file. The most useful of these API methods are shown in the following sections along with the requisite header file that must be included in order to use them.

ext/standard/base64.h

```
char *php_base64_encode(const unsigned char *data, int datalen,
                        int *base64len);
```

Base64 encodes the binary safe string contained in data. Returns a nonpersistently allocated ASCII string containing base64 data approximately 1.33 times as long as the original input.

Argument	Purpose
data	Points to buffer containing binary string to be encoded
datalen	Length of data buffer
base64len	Populated with length of returned base64 data string

```
char *php_base64_decode(const unsigned char *base64, int base64len,
                        int *datalen);
```

Decodes a base64-encoded string to its original binary contents. Returns a nonpersistently allocated buffer containing an octet stream approximately 0.75 times as long as the base64 input.

Argument	Purpose
base64	Points to buffer containing base64 data. Any non-base64 characters in the buffer will be ignored.
base64len	Length of base64 buffer.
datalen	Populated with length of binary data string returned.

ext/standard/exec.h

```
char *php_escape_shell_cmd(char *);
```

```
char *php_escape_shell_arg(char *);
```

These methods provide the internal implementations of the userspace
escapeshellcmd() and escapeshellarg() methods. Each returns a nonpersistently
allocated buffer containing the modified string.

ext/standard/file.h

```
int php_copy_file(char *src, char *dest TSRMLS_DC);
```

Copies the contents of src to dest. This method is the underlying internal implementation of the userspace copy() call.

ext/standard/flock_compat.h

```
int php_flock(int fd, int operation);
```

Creates or clears a file lock on an open descriptor. operation can be exactly one of the
following modes listed; optionally combined via bitwise OR with LOCK_NB to prevent
blocking during a file lock.

Operation	Meaning
LOCK_SH	Shared locking to allow mutual read access
LOCK_EX	Exclusive locking to prevent access from other processes
LOCK_UN	Discontinue blocking

ext/standard/head.h

```
int php_setcookie(char *name, int name_len, char *value, int value_len,
                  time_t expires, char *path, int path_len,
                  char *domain, int domain_len, int secure,
                  int url_encode TSRMLS_DC);
```

Sends a cookie. This method is the internal implementation of the userspace
set_cookie() function. value can be passed as NULL to send a request to clear the
cookie. path and/or domain can be passed as NULL to prevent their use in the generated
cookie header.

Argument	Purpose
name	NULL-terminated cookie name.
name_len	Length of name excluding trailing NULL.
value	NULL-terminated contents to set cookie to.
value_len	Length of value excluding trailing NULL.
expires	UNIX timestamp value for when the cookie is set to expire.
path	If provided, the browser will be instructed to only provide the cookie when a page under the specified path is requested.
path_len	Length of path excluding trailing NULL.
domain	If provided, the browser will be instructed to only provide the cookie for the specific hostname or subdomain named; subject to domain security restrictions defined by the HTTP protocol.
domain_len	Length of domain excluding trailing NULL.
secure	When set to a nonzero value, the browser will be instructed to send the cookie data only when performing requests over a secured connection (https).
url_encode	When set to a nonzero value, the contents of value will be automatically URL-encoded prior to being sent to the browser.

ext/standard/html.h

```
char *php_escape_html_entities(unsigned char *old, int oldlen, int *newlen,
                    int all, int quote_style, char *hint_charset TSRMLS_DC);
char *php_unescape_html_entities(unsigned char *old, int oldlen, int *newlen,
                    int all, int quote_style, char *hint_charset TSRMLS_DC);
```

Transforms an input string by interpolating certain characters to the HTML entities and
vice versa. PHP will attempt to determine the appropriate character set if possible; a hint
can be provided in the final parameter.

Argument	Purpose
old	Source string to transform.
oldlen	Length of source string.
newlen	Populated with length of newly allocated NULL-terminated string, not including the trailing NULL.
all	When set to a nonzero value, transforms charset-specific entities as well as general HTML entities.
quote_style	One of: ENT_NOQUOTE to avoid transforming quote-type entities, ENT_QUOTES to enforce transforming quote entities, or ENT_COMPAT to transform double quotes only, but leave single quotes alone.
hint_charset	Character set to assume source or target text is encoded in when transforming all entities.

ext/standard/info.h

```
void php_print_info(int flag TSRMLS_DC);
```

Outputs PHP Core, Zend Engine, and/or Extension information. This method is the internal implementation of the userspace phpinfo() function. flag can be any combination of the following constants combined together using bitwise OR, or simple PHP_INFO_ALL to display everything.

Constant	Meaning
PHP_INFO_GENERAL	Preamble including API version numbers, ./configure line, registered stream components, and Zend attribution
PHP_INFO_CREDITS	Listing of notable PHP Engine, Core, and Extension developers
PHP_INFO_CONFIGURATION	Displays current and global values for core php.ini settings
PHP_INFO_MODULES	Displays MINFO sections for all loaded modules
PHP_INFO_ENVIRONMENT	Dumps contents of $_ENV environment variable
PHP_INFO_VARIABLES	Dumps contents of GPCS variables
PHP_INFO_LICENSE	Displays PHP license information

```
void php_print_info_htmlhead(TSRMLS_D);
```

```
void php_info_print_style(TSRMLS_D);
```

Outputs component pieces of HTML headers used by `php_print_info()`. These methods are typically called implicitly by `php_print_info()` and not by other scopes.

```
char *php_info_html_esc(char *string TSRMLS_DC);
```

Convenience wrapper for `php_escape_html_entities(string, strlen(string), &dummy, 0, ENT_QUOTES, NULL TSRMLS_CC);`.

```
void php_info_print_table_start(void);
```

```
void php_info_print_table_end(void);
```

Outputs the beginning and end of a table header. If the current SAPI does not use HTML output, it will automatically reduce the output to simple linefeed sequences as appropriate.

```
void php_info_print_table_header(int num_cols, ...);
```

```
void php_info_print_table_colspan_header(int num_cols, char *header);
```

Outputs a table heading, applying HTML formatting if desired by the active SAPI. The colspan variant will output a single header cell spanning `num_cols`, whereas the other version accept `num_cols` instances of `char*` strings to be placed in consecutive columns.

```
void php_info_print_table_row_ex(int num_cols, const char *class, ...);
```

```
void php_info_print_table_row(int num_cols, ...);
```

Outputs a table row, applying HTML formatting if desired by the active SAPI. Excepts `num_cols` instances of `char*` strings in the variable argument list. In HTML output mode, each cell will be assigned the `class` attribute for CSS formatting. The non-ex variant of this method is assigned a default classname of `v`.

```
void php_info_print_box_start(int flag);
```

```
void php_info_print_box_end(void);
```

These methods form a single cell table frame around any content output between them. If `flag` is set to a nonzero value, the row will be assigned a class of `h` (for header); otherwise, it will be assigned a class of `v` (for value).

```
void php_info_print_hr(void);
```

Outputs a horizontal rule in HTML mode or a series of underscores in non-HTML mode.

```
char *php_logo_guid(void);
```

Returns the GUID identifier for the standard PHP logo.

ext/standard/php_filestat.h

```
void php_stat(const char *filename, php_stat_len filename_length,
                    int type, zval *return_value TSRMLS_DC);
```

States the specified NULL-terminated filename or URL wrapper path and populates the results into the preallocated return_value. The specific contents of return_value depend on the requested stat type.

Type	Return Value
FS_PERMS	IS_LONG, POSIX file access permissions.
FS_INODE	IS_LONG, inode index on owning disk.
FS_SIZE	IS_LONG, size of named file.
FS_OWNER	IS_LONG, Numeric UID of file owner.
FS_GROUP	IS_LONG, Numeric GID of file owner.
FS_ATIME	IS_LONG, UNIX timestamp of last access.
FS_MTIME	IS_LONG, UNIX timestamp of last modification.
FS_CTIME	IS_LONG, UNIX timestamp of last change (typically refers to change in inode data, not file contents).
FS_TYPE	IS_STRING, one of: fifo, char, dir, block, file, socket, or unknown.
FS_IS_R	IS_BOOL, true if the file is readable.
FS_IS_W	IS_BOOL, true if the file is writable.
FS_IS_X	IS_BOOL, true if the file is executable.
FS_IS_FILE	IS_BOOL, true if filename is a regular file.
FS_IS_DIR	IS_BOOL, true if filename is a directory.
FS_IS_LINK	IS_BOOL, true if filename is a symbolic link.
FS_EXISTS	IS_BOOL, true if filename exists on the filesystem.
FS_LSTAT	IS_ARRAY, each of the above elements as read from the immediate resource (not following symbolic links). Also includes remote device number, block size, and block count if available.
FS_STAT	IS_ARRAY, identical to FS_LSTAT except that all symbolic links are followed to a terminating resource.

ext/standard/php_http.h

```
int php_url_encode_hash_ex(HashTable *ht, smart_str *formstr,
                    const char *num_prefix, int num_prefix_len,
                    const char *key_prefix, int key_prefix_len,
```

```
        const char *key_suffix, int key_suffix_len,
        zval *type, char *arg_sep TSRMLS_DC);
```

Translates an array's contents into a URL-encoded string. This method is the internal implementation of the userspace `http_build_query()` function. Most parameters to this function are used by the function itself to make recursive calls for nested arrays.

Argument	Purpose
ht	HashTable to encode to a URL-encoded string.
formstr	Empty smart string object to append ht's elements to.
num_prefix	Optional string to prepend to numerically indexed entries in order to form valid variable names.
num_prefix_len	Length of num_prefix.
key_prefix	Internally used variable wrapper prefix. Typically passed as NULL to an initial invocation.
key_prefix_len	Length of key_prefix.
key_suffix	Internally used variable wrapper suffix. Typically passed as NULL to an initial invocation.
key_suffix_len	Length of key_suffix.
type	If ht comes from an object's properties table, the object's zval* should be passed here to handle access checks for private and protected properties.
arg_sep	Delimiter to use when separating multiple HashTable elements. If passed as NULL, the php.ini value arg_separator.output will be used instead.

ext/standard/php_mail.h

```
int php_mail(char *to, char *subject, char *message, char *headers,
        char *extra_cmd TSRMLS_DC);
```

Sends an email. This method is the internal implementation of the userspace `mail()` function.

Argument	Purpose
to	Recipient(s) email address. Multiple email addresses can be combined in a comma delimited list.
subject	Email subject line.
message	Message body contents.
headers	Additional headers to use when sending this email.
extra_cmd	Optional arguments to pass to the sendmail-compatible wrapper specified by the php.ini setting sendmail_path.

ext/standard/php_math.h

```
char *_php_math_number_format(double num, int dec, char dec_point,
                    char thousand_sep);
```

Formats a floating point number according to the same rules used by the userspace number_format() function.

Argument	Purpose
num	Number to format
dec	Number of places after the decimal point to express
dec_point	Character to use for decimal separator
thousand_sep	Character to use for thousands separator

ext/standard/php_rand.h

```
void php_srand(long seed TSRMLS_DC);
void php_mt_srand(php_uint32 seed TSRMLS_DC);
```

Seeds the system or Mersenne-Twister random number generators. The seed value itself should have some degree of indeterminacy and can be generated using the built-in macro GENERATE_SEED().

```
long php_rand(TSRMLS_D);
php_uint32 php_mt_rand(TSRMLS_D);
```

Generates a random number using the system or Mersenne-Twister random number generators.

ext/standard/php_string.h

```
char *php_strtoupper(char *s, size_t len);
```

```
char *php_strtolower(char *s, size_t len);
```

Transforms the provided string to upper- or lowercase. Note that these methods modify the provided string in place without allocating new storage.

```
char *php_addslashes(char *str, int length, int *new_length,
                    int freeit TSRMLS_DC);
char *php_addslashes_ex(char *str, int length, int *new_length,
                    int freeit, int ignore_sybase TSRMLS_DC);
```

Adds backslash escaping to single quotes, double quotes, NULLs, and backslash characters unless ignore_sybase is set to zero, and the php.ini option magic_quotes_sybase is enabled, in which case only NULL characters and single quotes are escaped. The non-ex variant of this method is equivalent to calling the ex version with ignore_sybase set to zero.

Argument	Purpose
str	String to be escaped.
length	Length of str.
new_length	Populated with the new, escaped string length.
freeit	When set to a nonzero value, str will be automatically freed just prior to the method returning.
ignore_sybase	When set to a nonzero value, the php.ini setting magic_quotes_sybase will be ignored.

```
void php_stripslashes(char *str, int *length TSRMLS_DC);
```

Reverses the effects of php_addslashes(). Note that unlike php_addslashes(), this method modifies the value of str in place.

```
char *php_addcslashes(char *str, int length, int *new_length,
                      int freeit, char *what, int wlength TSRMLS_DC);
void php_stripcslashes(char *str, int *length);
```

Like php_addslashes() and php_stripslashes() except that these versions will escape any of the characters listed in what. Control characters (ordinal value less than 32) will be replaced with common sequences where possible (such as \r, \n, \t, and so on); the remaining control characters and all extended ASCII values (ordinal value greater than 127) will be encoded as octal values. All other characters are escaped using simple backslash-character sequences.

Argument	Purpose
str	String to be escaped or unescaped.
length	Length of str.
new_length	Populated with the new, escaped string length.
freeit	When set to a nonzero value, str will be automatically freed just prior to the method returning.
what	List of characters to escape.
wlength	Length of character list.

```
char *php_str_to_str(char *haystack, int keystack_len,
                     char *needle, int needle_len,
                     char *str, int str_len, int *new_length);
char *php_str_to_str_ex(char *haystack, int keystack_len,
                        char *needle, int needle_len,
                        char *str, int str_len, int *new_length,
                        int case_sensitivity, int *replace_count);
```

Replaces all occurrences of `needle` in `haystack` with `str`. The non-ex variant of this method defaults to a case-sensitive search and replace. Returns a newly allocated non-persistent string.

Argument	Purpose
haystack	Original string to search and replace.
haystack_len	Length of haystack.
needle	String to search haystack for.
needle_len	Length of needle.
str	Replacement string to populate into haystack.
str_len	Length of str.
new_length	Populated with the length of the resulting string.
case_sensitivity	Set to a nonzero value to perform a case-sensitive search and replace. Zero to ignore case.
replace_count	Populated with the number of occurrences of needle that were replaced in haystack.

```
int php_char_to_str(char *haystack, uint haystack_len,
                    char needle,
                    char *str, int str_len, zval *result);
int php_char_to_str_ex(char *haystack, uint heystack_len,
                    char needle,
                    char *str, int str_len, zval *result,
                    int case_sensitivity, int *replace_count);
```

Identical to their `php_str_to_str()` counterparts, these methods replace a single character needle with a replacement string placing the result into a preallocated `zval*` container.

```
char *php_strtr(char *str, int len, char *str_from, char *str_to, int trlen);
```

Modifies `str` in place (without duplication), replacing any occurrence of a character also found in `str_from` with its corresponding index in `str_to`. This is the internal implementation of the userspace `strtr()` function.

Argument	Purpose
str	String to be modified.
len	Length of str.
str_from	List of characters to search str for.
str_to	Pair-indexed character list to replace into str.
trlen	Length of both str_from and str_to. Note that these two strings must be of identical length.

```
char *php_trim(char *str, int len, char *what, int what_len,
                    zval *return_value, int mode TSRMLS_DC);
```

Trims whitespace or other unimportant characters from the beginning or end of a string. Any character contained in the what parameter can be trimmed for the purpose of this operation. If NULL is passed for what, the default set of characters—space, newline, carriage return, tab, or vertical tab—are used instead.

Argument	Purpose
str	String to be trimmed.
len	Length of string to be trimmed.
what	List of characters to trim, or NULL to use default character list.
what_len	Length of what.
return_value	If NULL, the result will be duplicated and returned by the function. If passed a pointer to a zval, that structure will be populated as an IS_STRING variable using the resulting string and an empty string will be returned instead.
mode	One of either: 1 (trim the beginning of the string), 2 (trim the end of the string), or 3 (trim both ends).

```
size_t php_strip_tags(char *buf, int len, int *state, char *allow, int allow_len);
```

Removes HTML and PHP tags from the provided string. Note that buf is modified in place. The string to be modified can be stripped in multiple phases by maintaining a state value between calls. Refer to the implementation of the userspace function fgetss() for an example of this pointer in use.

Argument	Purpose
buf	String to process for disallowed tags
len	Length of buf
state	State value populated with the strip-tag's parser's internal state between calls
allow	List of allowable tags, following the convention used by the userspace strip_tags() function
allow_len	Length of allow

```
size_t php_strspn(char *s1, char *s2, char *s1_end, char *s2_end);
size_t php_strcspn(char *s1, char *s2, char *s1_end, char *s2_end);
```

`php_strspn()` locates the first segment in s1 containing characters also found in s2. Returns the number of s2 characters found in that sequence. `php_strcspn()` performs the opposite task by locating the first segment in s1, which does not contain characters found in the class defined by s2. These methods are the internal implementations of the userspace `strspn()` and `strcspn()` functions, respectively.

Argument	Purpose
s1	Start of string to search
s2	Start of string defining character class
s1_end	End of string to search
s2_end	End of string defining character class

```
void php_implode(zval *delim, zval *arr, zval *return_value);
void php_explode(zval *delim, zval *str, zval *return_value, int limit);
```

Implodes an array into a delimited string, or explodes a delimited string to an array. Note that the type of arr must be IS_ARRAY, and the type of str must be IS_STRING. delim will be automatically typecasted to a string value regardless of its input type.

Argument	Purpose
delim	Delimiter string to apply
arr	IS_ARRAY variable to be imploded
str	IS_STRING variable to be exploded
return_value	Populated with an IS_STRING or IS_ARRAY variable as appropriate
limit	Maximum number of array elements to extract from the input string

```
char *php_stristr(unsigned char *haystack, unsigned char *needle,
                  size_t haystack_len, size_t needle_len);
```

Non–case-sensitive counterpart to the system `strstr()` call.

Argument	Purpose
haystack	String to search for needle
needle	String to search for in haystack
haystack_len	Length of haystack
needle_len	Length of needle

```
void php_basename(char *str, size_t len, char *sfx, size_t sfx_len,
                  char **ret, size_t *ret_len TSRMLS_DC);
size_t php_dirname(char *str, size_t len);
```

Segregates the basename (pathless filename) from the dirname (directory path without filename). php_basename() will duplicate the located base filename into new storage; conversely php_dirname() will return the length of the directory portion of the string without modifying the contents.

Argument	Purpose
str	Path and filename string to parse
len	Length of str
sfx	Expected filename suffix to strip, if present
sfx_len	Length of sfx string
ret	Populated with newly allocated result string
ret_len	Populated with length of result string

```
int strnatcmp_ex(char const *a, size_t a_len, char const *b,
                 size_t b_len, int fold_case);
```

Performs a "natural" string comparison. Natural comparisons differ from strcmp() style comparisons by ignoring leading whitespace and sorting numeric strings according to integer value rather than ASCII value.

Argument	Purpose
a	One of two strings to compare
a_len	Length of a string
b	Second of two strings to compare
b_len	Length of b string
fold_case	When set to a nonzero value, the strings will be compared in a non–case-sensitive manner

ext/standard/php_smart_str.h

```
typedef struct {
    char *c;
    size_t len;
    size_t a;
} smart_str;
```

Smart strings grow dynamically as content is added. A new smart string can be initialized by simply setting its string member (c) to NULL. Examples of using the smart string library can be found in Appendix C.

```
void smart_str_appendc(smart_str *str, char ch);
void smart_str_appends(smart_str *str, char *buf);
void smart_str_appendl(smart_str *str, char *buf, int buflen);
void smart_str_appends(smart_str *str, smart_str *appe);
```

Appends a character, string, or other smart string to an initialized smart string. If the internal string member is not yet allocated it will be allocated to the appropriate size. If it's already allocated, size is not large enough to hold the new appendage; it will be increased. Smart strings are always slightly overallocated (by up to 128 bytes) to avoid frequent realloc calls.

```
void smart_str_append_long(smart_str *str, long val);
void smart_str_append_off_t(smart_str *str, off_t val);
void smart_str_append_unsigned(smart_str *str, unsigned long val);
```

Append a numeric value to a previously initialized smart string. Numbers are always expressed as decimal integers. To append any other type of number, use a local buffer with `sprintf()` and then append the resulting string.

```
void smart_str_0(smart_str *str);
```

NULL terminates a smart string. The contents of a smart string can be accessed at any time via `str->c` and `str->len`; however, `str->str` is only NULL-terminated following the use of this call and should not be used with `strlen()` or other methods that expect a NULL-terminated string until then.

```
void smart_str_free(smart_str *str);
```

Frees the internal buffer (`str->c`) used by the smart string.

ext/standard/php_uuencode.h

```
int php_uudecode(char *src, int src_len, char **dest);
int php_uuencode(char *src, int src_len, char **dest);
```

UU-encode or decode a string value. Each method returns the length of the newly allocated string and populates the string pointer into `dest`.

Argument	Purpose
src	String to be encoded or decoded
src_len	Length of string to be encoded or decoded
dest	Populated with newly allocated string pointer

ext/standard/php_var.h

```
void php_var_serialize(smart_str *buf, zval **struc,
                       php_serialize_data_t *var_hash TSRMLS_DC);
void PHP_VAR_SERIALIZE_INIT(php_serialize_data_t var_hash);
void PHP_VAR_SERIALIZE_DESTROY(php_serialize_data_t var_hash);
```

Serializes a PHP variable to a simple string value. `php_var_serialize()` uses a special interim storage variable, `var_hash`, to manage references and reduce overhead. Call the `PHP_VAR_SERIALIZE_INIT()` macro prior to serialization, and `PHP_VAR_SERIALIZE_DESTROY()` afterwards.

Argument	Purpose
buf	Destination smart string buffer
struct	PHP variable to be serialized
var_hash	Interim serialization storage variable

```
int php_var_unserialize(zval **rval, const unsigned char **str,
                        const unsigned char *str_end,
                        php_unserialize_data_t *var_hash TSRMLS_DC);
void PHP_VAR_UNSERIALIZE_INIT(php_unserialize_data_t var_hash);
void PHP_VAR_UNSERIALIZE_DESTROY(php_unserialize_data_t var_hash);
```

Unserializes a simple string value to a PHP variable. `php_var_unserialize()` uses a special interim storage variable, `var_hash`, to manage references and reduce overhead. Call the `PHP_VAR_UNSERIALIZE_INIT()` macro prior to deserialization, and `PHP_VAR_UNSERIALIZE_DESTROY()` afterwards.

Argument	Purpose
rval	Destination zval to store resulting data into.
str	Start of serialized string. Will be updated as the string is unserialized and can be used for indicating where an error occurred.
str_end	End of serialized string.
var_hash	Interim deserialization storage variable.

```
void php_var_export(zval **struc, int level TSRMLS_DC);
void php_var_dump(zval **struc, int level TSRMLS_DC);
void php_debug_zval_dump(zval **struc, int level TSRMLS_DC);
```

Outputs the contents of a PHP variable with varying degrees of detail. The `level` parameter is used internally to create progressively indented output and should generally be set to `0` for initial invocation.

ext/standard/php_versioning.h

```
int php_version_compare(const char *v1, const char *v2);
```

Specialized variant of strcmp() designed to compare version strings. This method is the internal implementation of the userspace version_compare() function.

ext/standard/reg.h

```
char *php_reg_replace(const char *pattern, const char *replace,
                      const char *string, int icase, int extended);
```

Performs a regular expression replacement. This is the internal implementation of the userspace ereg_replace() and eregi_replace() functions.

Argument	Purpose
pattern	Regular expression pattern to match
replace	String to replace matched pattern with
string	String to search for pattern and replace with string
icase	Set to a nonzero value to use non–case-sensitive matching during replacement
extended	Set to a nonzero value to perform an extended regular expression replacement

ext/standard/md5.h

```
void PHP_MD5Init(PHP_MD5_CTX *context);
void PHP_MD5Update(PHP_MD5_CTX *context,
                   const unsigned char *buf, unsigned int buf_len);
void PHP_MD5Final(unsigned char output[16], PHP_MD5_CTX *context);
```

Initializes, updates, and finalizes an MD5 digest operation. Refer to Appendix C for an example of using PHP's hashing algorithms.

Argument	Purpose
context	Local digest state context variable.
buf	Data buffer to be processed into the current hashing context.
buf_len	Length of buf.
output	Local storage space to populate with final result of hashing operation.

```
void make_digest(char md5str[33], unsigned char digest[16]);
```

Transforms a raw binary MD5 digest result into human readable hexadecimal characters. `md5str` must include space for the terminating NULL byte.

ext/standard/sha1.h

```
void PHP_SHA1Init(PHP_SHA1_CTX *context);
void PHP_SHA1Update(PHP_SHA1_CTX *context,
                    const unsigned char *buf, unsigned int buf_len);
void PHP_SHA1Final(unsigned char output[20], PHP_SHA1_CTX *context);
```

Initializes, updates, and finalizes an SHA1 digest operation. Refer to Appendix C for an example of using PHP's hashing algorithms. The meaning of these parameters is consistent with the MD5 operations.

ext/standard/url.h

```
php_url *php_url_parse(char const *str);
php_url *php_url_parse_ex(char const *str, int length);
typedef struct php_url {
    /* scheme://user:pass@host:port/path?query#fragment */
    char *scheme;
    char *user;
    char *pass;
    char *host;
    unsigned short port;
    char *path;
    char *query;
    char *fragment;
} php_url;
void php_url_free(php_url *url);
```

Parses a URL into its component pieces. The first form of this method expects a NULL terminated string, whereas the ex version allows a binary safe string containing NULL bytes by accepting an explicit `length` argument. `php_url` structure members can be used as immutable strings or numeric values, and must be explicitly freed by `php_url_free()`. Refer to Chapter 15 for an example of these methods in use.

```
char *php_url_encode(char const *s, int len, int *new_length);
char *php_raw_url_encode(char const *s, int len, int *new_length);
```

Encodes all characters within source string s except for alphanumerics, underscores, hyphens, and dots to their `%xx` mappings. Unlike its "raw" counterpart, `php_url_encode()` escapes spaces to + rather than `%20`. Returns a newly allocated NULL-terminated string. Because preexisting NULL bytes are escaped to `%00`, the new string is inherently binary safe; however, its known length can be retrieved using `new_length`.

```
int php_url_decode(char *str, int len);
int php_raw_url_decode(char *str, int len);
```

Decodes a previously URL-encoded string. Any `%xx` sequence in `str` will be mapped to its normal 8-bit representation. Like the encoding methods, `php_url_decode()` gives special meaning to the + symbol, converting it to a space.

Summary

The PHP Core and its library of extensions contains other, less commonly used or less frequently available API calls than those listed here. If you need a bit of functionality that's already being performed by a core function or some extension, refer to its header files and see if it's not also exported to internals-space for use by extensions or embed wrappers like your project.

Appendix D, "Additional Resources," will highlight just these types of "How'd they do that?" approaches to learning by example. First though, you'll take a look at a set of boiler plate templates for doing the most common tasks that you can freely modify and use in your own projects.

C

Extending and Embedding Cookbook

LIKE A WELL APPOINTED KITCHEN, PHP OFFERS THE ENVIRONMENT and ingredients necessary to create any masterpiece that accomplished chefs puts their mind to. As anyone who has spent time over a stove knows, however, it's not enough to simply toss some ingredients into a blender at random and pop the resulting glop into the microwave. An enjoyable meal, much like a usable extension, requires a recipe. In the preceding chapters, you learned the basic skills you need to create some of these recipes from scratch, but there's no reason to start from square one on most tasks. This appendix offers some examples of common use code that you can reuse in your own extension or embedding projects.

Skeletons

The examples provided in this section serve as a starting point for building or laying out larger extensions. By filling in your own code in the noted places, you can focus on the functional bits rather than worrying about formatting and other boring make-work.

All templates provided here—unless otherwise noted—are neutrally named cookbook and should be changed to a more appropriate name when you implement them. In all instances, assume casing to be significant—for example, cookbook is not the same as COOKBOOK.

> **Note**
> The material covered in this section is just a consolidated rehash of the core material covered in the body of this book. If you already feel familiar with it, skip down to the Code Pantry later in this appendix.

Minimal Extension

If you've been through more than a little of the book, this framework will look instantly familiar. It's the first extension you saw in Chapter 5, aptly named "Your First Extension."

The three files shown in Listings C.1, C.2, and C.3 represent the absolute least amount of code and configuration data necessary to build a loadable PHP extension. Refer back to Chapter 5 for a refresher on how to build this as a loadable module.

Listing C.1   `config.m4`—**A Simple Configuration Script**

```
PHP_ARG_ENABLE(cookbook,
  [Whether to enable the "cookbook" extension],
  [  —enable-cookbook         Enable "cookbook" extension support])

if test $PHP_COOKBOOK != "no"; then
  PHP_SUBST(COOKBOOK_SHARED_LIBADD)
  PHP_NEW_EXTENSION(cookbook, cookbook.c, $ext_shared)
fi
```

Listing C.2   `php_cookbook.h`—**A Simple Header File**

```
#ifndef PHP_COOKBOOK_H
#define PHP_COOKBOOK_H
#define PHP_COOKBOOK_EXTNAME     "cookbook"
/* The value of this constant may be arbitrarily chosen by you.
   PHP does not actually use this value internally; however it
   makes sense to incrementally increase it with each release. */
#define PHP_COOKBOOK_EXTVER      "1.0"
#ifdef HAVE_CONFIG_H
#include "config.h"
#endif
#include "php.h"
extern zend_module_entry cookbook_module_entry;
#define phpext_cookbook_ptr &cookbook_module_entry
#endif
```

Listing C.3   `cookbook.c`—**A Simple Extension Source File**

```
#include "php_cookbook.h"
zend_module_entry cookbook_module_entry = {
#if ZEND_MODULE_API_NO >= 20010901
    STANDARD_MODULE_HEADER,
#endif
    PHP_COOKBOOK_EXTNAME,
    NULL, /* Functions */
```

Listing C.3   **Continued**

```
    NULL, /* MINIT */
    NULL, /* MSHUTDOWN */
    NULL, /* RINIT */
    NULL, /* RSHUTDOWN */
    NULL, /* MINFO */
#if ZEND_MODULE_API_NO >= 20010901
    PHP_COOKBOOK_EXTVER,
#endif
    STANDARD_MODULE_PROPERTIES
};
#ifdef COMPILE_DL_COOKBOOK
ZEND_GET_MODULE(cookbook)
#endif
```

Extension Life Cycle Methods

Chapter 1, "The PHP Life Cycle," and many of the following chapters discussed the five phases engaged by PHP during the course of its execution: Startup, Activation, Runtime, Deactivation, and Shutdown.

During all but the Runtime phase, PHP activates an appropriate callback found in the `zend_module_entry` structure. Each of these methods can be left NULL and unused as in the minimal skeleton shown previously, or implemented independently using the appropriate naming and prototype macros. Under ordinary circumstances each method should return the SUCCESS constant. If a callback is unable to perform a vital task, it must return FAILURE so that PHP can raise the proper error and exit if necessary.

Add any or all of these functions as needed to any of the source files in your project—providing they are visible to your `zend_module_entry` structure. Listing C.4 shows a set of minimal implementations for these callbacks.

Listing C.4   **Declaring Life Cycle Callbacks**

```
PHP_MINIT_FUNCTION(cookbook)
{
    /* Code placed here will be executed during the Startup phase
       Startup occurs when the PHP interpreter is first being initialized
       prior to entering any Activation phases
       The M in MINIT is for "Module" (a.k.a. Extension) Initialization */
    return SUCCESS;
}
PHP_RINIT_FUNCTION(cookbook)
{
    /* Code placed here will be executed during the Activation phase(s)
       Activation occurs just prior to the execution of each script request.
       The R in RINIT is for "Request" Initialization */
```

Listing C.4 **Continued**

```
    return SUCCESS;
}
PHP_RSHUTDOWN_FUNCTION(cookbook)
{
    /* Code placed here will be executed during the Deactivation phase(s)
       Deactivation occurs just after completion of a given script request. */
    return SUCCESS;
}
PHP_MSHUTDOWN_FUNCTION(cookbook)
{
    /* Code placed here will be executed during the Shutdown phase
       Shutdown occurs after all requests have been processed and the SAPI
       is proceeding to unload. */
    return SUCCESS;
}
```

For each callback function added, replace the corresponding NULL entry (denoted by comments in Listing C.3) with the matching use macro (see Listing C.5).

Listing C.5 **Adding Callback Macros to** zend_module_entry

```
zend_module_entry cookbook_module_entry = {
#if ZEND_MODULE_API_NO >= 20010901
    STANDARD_MODULE_HEADER,
#endif
    PHP_COOKBOOK_EXTNAME,
    NULL, /* Functions */
    PHP_MINIT(cookbook), /* MINIT */
    PHP_MSHUTDOWN(cookbook), /* MSHUTDOWN */
    PHP_RINIT(cookbook), /* RINIT */
    PHP_RSHUTDOWN(cookbook), /* RSHUTDOWN */
    NULL, /* MINFO */
#if ZEND_MODULE_API_NO >= 20010901
    PHP_COOKBOOK_EXTVER,
#endif
    STANDARD_MODULE_PROPERTIES
};
```

Declaring Module Info

To add extension-specific information to output generated by phpinfo();, add an MINFO callback function to your source file and place a matching macro into your zend_module_entry structure (see Listing C.6). Unlike the life cycle functions, the MINFO callback does not expect a return value.

Listing C.6   **Declaring Module Information**

```
PHP_MINFO_FUNCTION(cookbook)
{
    /* The following example will display a simple 2x2 table
       Refer to Chapter 12, "Startup, Shutdown, and a Few Points in Between"
       For more information on generating MINFO output */
    php_info_print_table_start();
    php_info_print_table_row(2, "Cookbook Module", "enabled");
    php_info_print_table_row(2, "version", PHP_COOKBOOK_EXTVER);
    php_info_print_table_end();
}
```

As with the life cycle callbacks, replace the NULL entry in your zend_module_entry structure corresponding to MINFO with: PHP_MINFO(cookbook).

Adding Functions

Internal implementations of userspace functions are declared to the engine using a vector of zend_function_entry structures as described in Chapter 5, "Your First Extension." Place the structure shown in Listing C.7 just above your zend_module_entry struct.

Listing C.7   **Empty Function Entry List**

```
zend_function_entry php_cookbook_functions[] = {
    /* Function entry macros such as
       PHP_FE(), PHP_FALIAS, and PHP_NAMED_FE() go here */
    { NULL, NULL, NULL }
};
```

Now link that new structure into your module entry by replacing the NULL corresponding to the functions list with php_cookbook_functions.

After the zend_function_entry structure is in place, define actual function implementations using PHP_FUNCTION() macros such as shown in Listing C.8.

Listing C.8   **Empty Function Declaration**

```
PHP_FUNCTION(cookbook_dosomething)
{
    /* Code to be executed when cookbook_dosomething()
       is called from userspace goes here */
}
```

Now place a matching entry into your zend_function_entry structure prior to the terminating NULL entry: PHP_FE(cookbook_dosomething, NULL).

Adding Resources

PHP uses the resource data type to store opaque or complex data types that don't or can't map to PHP userspace data (see Listing C.9). These types are declared in the MINIT callback of an extension, which is called during the Startup phase. Refer to Chapter 9, "The Resource Data Type," for a detailed explanation of their use.

Listing C.9 **Declaring a Resource Type**

```
/* List Entry type IDs are registered in a common pool shared by all threads
   And therefore can be stored in a true-global scope */
int le_cookbook_type;

/* The name of your resource type may be arbitrarily assigned and
   does not necessarily have to be unique,
   although good practices dictate it should be. */
#define PHP_COOKBOOK_RESOURCE_NAME   "Cookbook Resource"

/* Don't forget: Since MINIT is being used,
   it must be referenced from the zend_module_entry structure */
PHP_MINIT_FUNCTION(cookbook)
{
    le_cookbook_type = zend_register_list_destructors_ex(
                    NULL, /* Non-persistent destructor */
                    NULL, /* Persistent destructor */
                    PHP_COOKBOOK_RESOURCE_NAME, module_number);
    return SUCCESS;
}
```

When a resource variable is implicitly freed during the Deactivation phase or during the course of a request because it has been unset() or has fallen out of scope, its nonpersistent destructor is called. For persistent resources, explained in Chapter 9, the persistent destructor will also be called when the resource is removed from the persistent list, typically in response to an explicit close or shut down command.

The prototypes for both destructors are identical (see Listing C.10):

Listing C.10 **Resource Destructor Callbacks**

```
void php_cookbook_resource_dtor(zend_rsrc_list_entry *rsrc TSRMLS_DC)
{
    /* The registered data to be destructed can be found in rsrc->ptr */
}
```

Once defined, the name of the destructor callback (php_cookbook_resource_dtor) can be added to the zend_register_list_destructors_ex() call in place of either or both of the NULL placeholders as appropriate.

Adding Objects

The simplest useful object declaration begins with a few lines in the MINIT callback and a declaration of at least one method (see Listing C.11).

Listing C.11   **Adding Objects**

```
PHP_METHOD(Cookbook_Class,__construct)
{
    /* Code added here will be executed in response to calling
       Cookbook_Class::__construct(), including in response to
       new Cookbook_Class() which implicitly calls the constructor */
}

zend_function_entry php_cookbook_methods[] = {
    /* Refer to Chapter 11, "PHP5 Objects," for the meaning of
       the ZEND_ACC_* constants */
    PHP_ME(Cookbook_Class,__construct, NULL, ZEND_ACC_PUBLIC | ZEND_ACC_CTOR)
    { NULL, NULL, NULL }
};

/* Don't forget: Because MINIT is being used,
   it must be referenced from the zend_module_entry structure */
PHP_MINIT_FUNCITON(cookbook)
{
    zend_class_entry ce;
    INIT_CLASS_ENTRY(ce, "Cookbook_Class", php_cookbook_methods);
    zend_register_internal_class(&ce TSRMLS_CC);

    return SUCCESS;
}
```

Code Pantry

The remaining examples in this appendix deal with solving real-world problems with short, reusable code-snippets. In most cases they won't be ready to run out of the box, but can be placed within a large project with relative ease.

Calling Back Into Userspace

Occasionally an internal function chooses to make a portion of its functionality customizable at the userspace level. This is typically done by allowing the userspace script to set a callback in one function call, and then using that callback identifier in another. The example in Listing C.12 focuses on the somewhat trickier aspect of using a callback name and calling back into userspace using the call_user_function() API method described in Chapter 20, "Advanced Embedding."

Listing C.12   **Calling Userspace Functions**

```
PHP_FUNCTION(cookbook_call_foo)
{
    zval fname, params[2];
    ZVAL_STRING(&fname, "foo", 1);
    ZVAL_STRING(&params[0], "bar", 1);
    ZVAL_STRING(&params[1], "baz", 1);
    /* Call:  foo("bar", "baz") */
    if (call_user_function(EG(function_table), NULL,
                      &fname, return_value, 2, &params TSRMLS_CC) == FAILURE) {
        php_error_docref(NULL TSRMLS_CC, E_WARNING,
                      "Unable to call foo(), is it defined?");
        RETVAL_FALSE;
        goto cleanup;
    }
    /* Call succeeded,
       return_value will already have been set
       because it was passed through to foo(),
       all that's left is to clean up */
cleanup:
    zval_dtor(&fname);
    zval_dtor(&params[0]);
    zval_dtor(&params[1]);
}
```

Evaluating and Executing Code

The userspace eval() function maps directly to an internal call by nearly the same name. Although the actual implementation used by the Zend Engine looks very different, your extension or embed environment can replicate this function with the function shown in Listing C.13.

Listing C.13   **Reinventing** eval()

```
PHP_FUNCTION(cookbook_eval)
{
    char *code;
    int code_len;

    if (zend_parse_parameters(ZEND_NUM_ARGS() TSRMLS_CC, "s",
                    &code, &code_len) == FAILURE) {
        return;
    }

    if (zend_eval_string(code, return_value, "Cookbook eval'd code") == FAILURE) {
```

Listing C.13   **Continued**

```
        php_error_docref(NULL TSRMLS_CC, E_WARNING, "Error executing provided
code");
        RETVAL_FALSE;
    }
}
```

Testing and Linking External Libraries

Asking PHP to link an additional external library requires nothing more than a single line. However, it's important to do some work to ensure that the library will function properly both during compilation and during execution. The config.m4 shown in Listing C.14 will search for and link a theoretical libexample library.

Listing C.14   **Testing and Linking**

```
PHP_ARG_WITH(cookbook,
  [Whether to enable the "cookbook" extension],
  [ —enable-cookbook[=DIR]  Enable "cookbook" extension using libexample])

if test $PHP_COOKBOOK != "no"; then
  AC_MSG_CHECKING([for libexample headers])
  dnl Look in a couple default locations and whatever is passed to ./configure
  dnl Note, lines beginning with "dnl" are config.m4 comments
  for i in /usr /usr/local $PHP_COOKBOOK; do
    if test -r $i/include/example.h; then
      EXAMPLE_DIR=$i
      AC_MSG_RESULT(found in $i)
    fi
  done
  if test -z "$EXAMPLE_DIR"; then
    dnl This will cancel configuration if the required headers aren't found
    AC_MSG_ERROR([example.h not found])
  fi

  dnl Make sure the library module exists as well
  dnl and that it contains an expected symbol
  PHP_CHECK_LIBRARY(example, example_sort_function,
  [
    PHP_ADD_LIBRARY_WITH_PATH(example, $EXAMPLE_DIR/lib, COOKBOOK_SHARED_LIBADD)
    AC_DEFINE(HAVE_LIBEXAMPLE, 1, [Have libexample])
  ],[
    AC_MSG_ERROR([libexample not found])
  ],[
    -L$EXAMPLE_DIR/lib
```

Listing C.14   **Continued**

```
  ])
  PHP_SUBST(COOKBOOK_SHARED_LIBADD)
  PHP_NEW_EXTENSION(cookbook, cookbook.c, $ext_shared)
fi
```

Mapping Arrays to String Vectors

Because PHP is a glue language, one of the most common tasks is taking userspace data, formatting it for use by an external library, and then processing the results in the opposite direction. The short function shown in Listing C.15, which assumes the third-party library has already been linked using the configure steps outlined in Chapter 17, "Configuration and Linking," accepts a number, a string, and an array of values. The simpler number and string values are passed on relatively unchanged; however, the array is remapped to a string vector more commonly accepted by library functions.

Listing C.15   **External Function Calls**

```
/* Include the third-party library's header file */
#include <example.h>
PHP_FUNCTION(cookbook_sort_strings)
{
    /* Input parameters */
    long lparam;
    char *sparam;
    int sparam_len;
    zval *arr_data;
    /* Intermediate values */
    char **str_vector;
    int str_count, str_index = 0;
    HashPosition pos;
    zval **current;
    int result;

    if (zend_parse_parameters(ZEND_NUM_ARGS() TSRMLS_CC, "lsa", &lparam,
                    &sparam, &sparam_len, &arr_data) == FAILURE) {
        return;
    }

    /* Transform arr_data into a string vector */
    str_count = zend_hash_num_elements(Z_ARRVAL_P(arr_data));
    str_vector = ecalloc(str_count + 1, sizeof(char*));
    for(zend_hash_internal_pointer_reset_ex(Z_ARRVAL_P(arr_data), &pos);
        zend_hash_get_current_data_ex(Z_ARRVAL_P(arr_data),
                                (void**)&current, &pos) == SUCCESS;
```

Listing C.15   **Continued**

```
        zend_hash_move_forward_ex(Z_ARRVAL_P(arr_data), &pos)) {
        zval duplicate = **current;
        /* Make a copy of the current zval's contents so that it can be safely
            converted to a string type and repopulated into a new zval later */
        zval_copy_ctor(&duplicate);
        convert_to_string(&duplicate);
        str_vector[str_index++] = Z_STRVAL(duplicate);
    }

    /* Call the third-party library's method, in this case
     * a sort function that will not change the contents of
     * the string vector's entries, only rearrange them. */
    result = example_sort_function(lparam, sparam, str_count, str_vector);
    if (result < 0) {
        /* An error occurred */
        /* Free individual string elements */
        while (str_index--) {
            if (str_vector[str_index]) {
                efree(str_vector[str_index]);
            }
        }
        /* Free vector container */
        efree(str_vector);
        /* Raise an error */
        php_error_docref(NULL TSRMLS_CC, E_WARNING,
                    "Unable to perform sort operation, "
                    "libexample returned %d", result);
        RETURN_FALSE;
    }
    /* Store resulting strings back into an array of zvals and
        return it to the application */
    array_init(return_value);
    while (str_index--) {
        if (str_vector[str_index]) {
            add_next_index_string(return_value, str_vector[str_index], 0);
        }
    }
}
```

Accessing Streams

Listing C.16 shows basic `fopen`/`fread`/`fwrite`/`fclose` functionality from within a single function. For a more detailed analysis of streams access, refer to Chapter 14, "Accessing Streams."

Listing C.16   **Reading and Writing Stream Contents**

```c
#include <ctype.h>
/* Forces the first character in a file to be uppercase */
PHP_FUNCTION(cookbook_ucfirst)
{
    char *filename, c;
    int filename_len;
    php_stream *stream;
    int options = ENFORCE_SAFE_MODE | REPORT_ERRORS;
    if (zend_parse_parameters(ZEND_NUM_ARGS() TSRMLS_CC, "s",
                    &filename, &filename_len) == FAILURE) {
        return;
    }
    stream = php_stream_open_wrapper(filename, "r+", options, NULL);
    if (!stream) {
        /* Stream already reported why the file couldn't be opened */
        RETURN_FALSE;
    }
    /* Get a character */
    c = php_stream_getc(stream);
    if (c < 'a' || c > 'z') {
        /* Nothing to do, it's not lowercase */
        php_stream_close(stream);
        RETURN_TRUE;
    }
    php_stream_rewind(stream);
    php_stream_putc(stream, toupper(c));
    php_stream_close(stream);
    RETURN_TRUE;
}
```

Accessing Transports

Transports are just specialized types of streams for communicating with socket-style resources such as network endpoints. Listing C.17 shows basic fsockopen/fwrite/stream_get_contents functionality for requesting data from a whois server. For a more detailed analysis of stream transports, refer to Chapter 14.

Listing C.17   **Accessing Transports**

```c
/* Forces the first character in a file to be uppercase */
PHP_FUNCTION(cookbook_whois)
{
    char *host, *query, *xport, *contents;
    int host_len, query_len, xport_len, contents_len;
```

Listing C.17   **Continued**

```
php_stream *stream;
int options = ENFORCE_SAFE_MODE | REPORT_ERRORS;
int flags = STREAM_XPORT_CLIENT | STREAM_XPORT_CONNECT;
if (zend_parse_parameters(ZEND_NUM_ARGS() TSRMLS_CC, "ss",
                  &host, &host_len, &query, &query_len) == FAILURE) {
    return;
}
xport_len = spprintf(&xport, 0, "tcp://%s:43", host);
stream = php_stream_xport_create(xport, xport_len, options, flags,
                             NULL, NULL, NULL, NULL, NULL);
efree(xport);
if (!stream) {
    /* Stream already reported why the file couldn't be opened */
    RETURN_FALSE;
}
/* Send Query */
php_stream_write(stream, query, query_len);
php_stream_write(stream, "\r\n", 2);
/* Fetch results */
contents_len = php_stream_copy_to_mem(stream, &contents,
                                 PHP_STREAM_COPY_ALL, 0);
php_stream_close(stream);
if (contents_len < 0) {
    /* An error occurred */
    RETURN_FALSE;
} else if (contents_len == 0) {
    /* No data */
    RETURN_EMPTY_STRING();
} else {
    /* Send the WHOIS response back to the user */
    RETURN_STRINGL(contents, contents_len, 0);
}
}
```

Computing a Message Digest

Message digests are calculated by initializing a digest context, pumping data into the context, and then finalizing the context into a digest block. The function shown in Listing C.18 duplicates the functionality of the userspace md5() function.

Listing C.18   **Computing a Message Digest**

```
#include "ext/standard/md5.h"
PHP_FUNCTION(cookbook_md5)
{
```

Listing C.18 **Continued**

```
    char *message;
    int message_len;
    zend_bool raw_output = 0;
    PHP_MD5_CTX context;
    char digest[16];

    if (zend_parse_parameters(ZEND_NUM_ARGS() TSRMLS_CC, "s|b",
                    &message, &message_len, &raw_output) == FAILURE) {
        return;
    }

    PHP_MD5Init(&context);
    PHP_MD5Update(&context, message, message_len);
    PHP_MD5Final(digest, &context);

    if (raw_output) {
        RETURN_STRINGL(digest, 16, 1);
    } else {
        char hexdigest[33];

        make_digest(hexdigest, digest);
        RETURN_STRINGL(hexdigest, 32, 1);
    }
}
```

Calculating an SHA1 digest can be done by replacing instances of MD5 with SHA1 in Listing C.18. Note that the `make_digest()` method is specific to MD5-sized digests so you'll need to translate the longer SHA1 digest manually.

Summary

Programming languages are famous for the rigidity of their syntax and the consistency of their interpretation. Often this is frustrating to the new developer who is unfamiliar with the idioms and quirks of a language, or in complicated environments like the PHP internals that effectively alter the dialect of their parent language simply by the mass of their infrastructure. By using simple, well tested templates such as the ones found in this appendix, you can focus on becoming more familiar with the truly interesting parts of the API and avoid that unwelcome initial frustration.

In the final appendix of this title, you'll look at how to move beyond the limits of this book by incorporating the work of open source developers and getting answers to those questions that just couldn't fit within these few hundred pages.

D

Additional Resources

WHEN ATTEMPTING TO SOLVE A NEW PROBLEM, IT'S BEST to ask: "Is this really new?" Chances are, someone out there has done something similar, and released her code for public consumption. Therefore, it's worth engaging the use of your favorite search engine to find out if there's an existing implementation you can borrow from, and adapt to your needs. After all, why reinvent the wheel when someone else has already figured out they should be round?

Open Source Projects

When borrowing implementations from other developers, be sure to check that the code in question has been licensed in such a way as to allow you to reuse the work. Some licenses permit wholesale inclusion of another person's implementation without attribution, while others go so far as to enforce strict limitations on your larger work even though it may only include a small piece of imported code. Read all license documentation carefully, and when in doubt contact the original author for permission.

The PHP Source Tree

Although it should go without saying, the PHP source tree itself is a massive repository of sample code ripe for the picking. Because all of the bundled extensions are thoroughly documented in the PHP online manual, you won't have to guess what the purpose of a given PHP_FUNCTION() block is. If something doesn't make sense, you can be sure that someone watching the PHP mailing lists will be familiar with it and able to explain it to you. Best of all, with the exception of a few bundled libraries and some scattered reproductions, the majority of the PHP source tree is released under the extremely liberal and friendly PHP license.

Within this readily available collection of source files, you'll find detailed examples of nearly every task you'll want to implement. After all, most of the abilities to interact with PHP and extend it exist because one bundled extension or another requires it.

For help working your way through the PHP Source tree, take a look at http://lxr.php.net. This handy tool, regularly regenerated from the sources in CVS, shows PHP's source files with direct, contextual linking to related parts of the source tree. For example, say you're looking at the following code block and wondering what it does:

```
void *php_hacer_una_thingamajig(int foo, double bar) {
    return ZEND_GROK_THE_CASBAH(foo + foo * bar);
}
```

You could sort through pages of `grep` output looking for where `ZEND_GROK_THE_CASBAH()` was defined, but that can become tedious when you need to trace a definition through a dozen source files. LXR solves this by displaying every macro, function call, constant, or difficult-to-track-down symbol as a hyperlink to the source file and line it was defined on.

Linking Against Third-Party Libraries

As you already saw back in Chapter 17, "Configuring and Linking," extensions such as `zlib` serve as useful templates for designing `config.m4` and `config.w32` files that can search for, test, and link against required third-party libraries. This extension, as well as `mysql`, `bcmath`, and others, provide excellent examples for exploring optional functionality and enabling a range of variable feature sets depending on the host environment at hand.

Exporting Resources

Chapter 9, "The Resource Data Type," covered the well established API for registering, fetching, and cleaning up resource data types. Because this is the only method, prior to the availability of Zend Engine 2 objects, to store complex internal data structures, you'll find them used in some form or another in many of PHP's bundled extensions.

To begin, consider taking a look at the uncomplicated `sockets` extension for a reference to using this essential feature. Because this extension shares few API calls with other parts of the PHP Core and links against no external libraries—except for libc, of course—it provides a relatively simple look at using this otherwise mysterious data type.

Implementing Streams

The stock distribution of PHP includes wrapper implementations for the FTP and HTTP layer 4 protocols, the source code for which can be found in the `ext/standard` folder in the `ftp_fopen_wrapper.c` and `http_fopen_wrapper.c` source files. The `php_stream_wrapper` structures associated with these are then registered in `basic_functions.c`, found in the same directory.

The HTTP wrapper implementation provides a thorough yet easy-to-follow demonstration of using context options to modify the behavior of a stream during the open phase. The FTP wrapper, on the other hand, provides a more complete value as a reference thanks to its coverage of all the optional wrapper operations.

Implementing Filters

Included with the base distribution of PHP are a collection of filters found in `ext/standard/filters.c`. These include the `string.*` class and the `convert.*` class. Referring to the `string.rot13` filter should give the most easily parsable example of implementing a PHP stream filter.

Also bundled with PHP are the compression filters found in `ext/zlib/zlib_filter.c` and `ext/bz2/bz2_filter.c`. The overall structure of these two files is nearly identical, differing primarily in terms of the specific external library function called. Although the work being done is slightly more complex than the aforementioned `string.rot13` filter, they may serve as clearer examples as they're presented in isolation: one filter, one source file.

PECL as a Source of Inspiration

Since its inauguration just after the turn of the century, the PHP Extension Code Library, or PECL—pronounced "pickle"—has grown to house more than 100 extension and SAPI modules that can be optionally built into a PHP installation. These packages include rudimentary extensions, robust API collections, opcode caches, and even modifications to the language syntax itself.

The Traditionalists

The most useful extensions to use as reference during your early stages of development will be the kind that have marked the PHP language since the beginning: the basic glue extension.

In this category, extensions like `expect` and `openal` demonstrate simple one-to-one mappings of PHP userspace functions to their library implementations. Here you'll find examples of mapping data types, linking, and general resource management.

PHP5 Object Implementations

The ZE2 object model offers significant advantage over its earlier incarnation; unfortunately, few examples of using this exist in the wild. `flitetts` offers one such implementation in a fairly small, easy-to-parse package. More robust implementations exist in `pdo` and other extensions, but these are attached to more complicated application logic. When designing an internal class implementation, it's best to start with the most basic functionality and build from there.

Opcode Caches

Opcode caching has been implemented by a number of projects, and provides performance improvement to websites by saving the compiled opcode form of scripts and only performing recompilation when necessitated by a change in the source script. The opcode cache used by www.php.net, and the one you'll be able to learn from most easily, is APC, the Advanced PHP Cache.

APC hooks into the Zend Engine by replacing the built-in compiler with a caching system that redispatches requests only when the compiled version is not already available in memory. This implementation also makes heavy use of shared memory using its own cross-platform compatible allocation system. It's not a topic to jump into on your first day, but it should eventually provide you with a healthy dose of reliable and reusable ideas.

The Wilder Side

For a look at some topics not covered in this book and unlikely to be found anywhere else, turn to runkit, which exposes the function and class registries and uses the TSRM layer to embed requests within one another. Other unusual examples of manipulating the PHP interpreter include operator, which overrides the meaning of several opcodes, and VLD, the "Vulcan Logic Decoder," which turns compiled scripts into human readable representations. VLD, in particular, allows you to steal a unique look at how the engine ticks, and may serve as its own inspiration for future development down as yet unimagined roads.

The topics covered by these esoteric extensions are well beyond the scope of this book and generally inapplicable to real-world uses, although they demonstrate the extent to which PHP and the Zend Engine allow themselves to be customized to suit third-party needs.

PECL as a Design Platform

PECL is not only a source for looking at other people's code. If you're planning to release an extension as an open source project, you could find a much worse home for it than here. Apart from offering a speedy and reliable CVS repository, PECL extensions and SAPI implementations are afforded the opportunity to house their documentation in the official php.net manual. What's more, extensions hosted within PECL that have a valid config.w32 file are automatically built into usable DLLs by the pecl4win build system and made available at http://pecl4win.php.net.

Elsewhere in the PHP CVS Repository

In Chapter 4, "Setting up a Build Environment," you saw instructions for checking out the PHP Source tree from the php-src module at cvs.php.net. Other modules that can be found on this server include pear and pecl, the phpdoc manual and all of its translations, and one project—almost out of place—in the embed repository: php-irssi.

This project was designed to serve as an exemplar for using the embed SAPI introduced in Chapter 19, "Setting up a Host Environment." It demonstrates linking against libphp5.so to provide access to the PHP interpreter from within the popular IRC client `irssi`. Examples of graceful error handling, output capture and redirection, and simultaneous extending and embedding can be found in this simple and stable stub library.

Places to Look for Help

One of the disadvantages of developing against an open source project like PHP is the lack of paid support channels. There's no guarantee of response time on queries, and no assurance that the person who's answering you actually knows what he is talking about.

One of the great advantages of developing against an open source project like PHP is also the lack of paid support channels. Because PHP is in widespread use by so many individuals who are actually familiar with its internals, finding a reliable source of information on a given topic usually requires nothing more than asking.

Bear in mind that most of these resources are volunteers helping out for nothing more than the satisfaction of passing on knowledge. Ask nicely and be patient in waiting for answers; you'll catch more bees with honey than you will with vinegar.

PHP Mailing Lists

The most official of these information resources are the mailing lists hosted by the PHP project itself. Mailing lists such as `internals@lists.php.net` and `pecl-dev@lists.php.net` are routinely monitored by the PHP language developers themselves and answers to any well asked question can usually be had within a day, if not within the hour.

The `pecl-dev` list is typically the best place to go for instruction on how to accomplish a specific task in an extension or embedding project. Don't let the name of the list put you off; it's all right to ask for help in developing closed-source and proprietary code. PECL is simply the driving force behind most projects developed here.

The `internals` list, on the other hand, aims to focus on developments in the language itself. At the time of publication of this book, this list is focused on the overhauls taking place for PHP6. If you want to keep an eye on what APIs are being changed and how your extension or embed project will need to adapt to fluctuations in the language, this is the list to watch.

IRC

Several networks carry general purpose PHP scripting support channels. In some of these, such as the `##php` channel on Freenode, you'll find a few individuals with experience developing with the PHP internals. Spend some time browsing through the IRC networks out there and you'll probably find someone up at any given time of day or night to answer that 11th hour question.

Summary

You're not the first to embark down the road of PHP development, and those who have come before often leave their mark in the form of a HOWTO or tutorial on the subject. Spend some time searching the web, referring to existing source code, and seeking out your fellow developer, and you'll be able to save hours upon hours of headache.

Index

Symbols

A

resources, 356

superglobals, 172, 259-260

decoding

base64 strings, 332

resources, 116-118

URLs, 349

default stream contexts, 226

DEFINE() macro, 242

del_ref() handler, 152

delayed destruction, 122-123

deleting. *See also* **destroying**

directories, 318

hash table elements, 294

linked list elements, 298

dependencies

dependent libraries, looking for, 236

optional functionality, 238

scanning for headers, 236-237

testing actual behavior, 238-239

testing for functionality, 237-238

enforcing

configuretime module dependency, 239-240

runtime module dependency, 240-241

PECL_Gen, 248-249

destroying. *See also* **deleting**

HashTables, 106

resources, 115-119

delayed destruction, 122-123

forced destruction, 118-119

__destruct() method, 146

destructors, 356

development, configuring PHP for, 50-51

digests (message), computing, 363-364

dir_opener() function, 203

directories

closing, 319

creating, 318

opening, 319

reading, 319-320

removing, 318

directory access (streams), 189-190

displaying INI settings, 179-180

diverting streams

filters

applying, 227-228

defining, 228-232

stream contexts

default contexts, 226

options, retrieving, 222-223

options, setting, 221-222

parameters, 224-225

dl() function, 61

doubly linked lists, 92

downloading PHP source code, 49

dtor method, 119

E

each() function, 101

early departure (resources), 127

Easter eggs, declaring, 311

ecalloc() function, 39, 299

efree() function, 37, 39

EG() macro, 20, 171

email, sending, 338

emalloc() function, 39, 299

embed life cycle, 15-16

Embed SAPI, 253-254

embed startup, overriding, 268-269

$_EMBED, declaring, 259-260

embed1.c application, 254-256

embed2.c file, 261-262

embed3.c file, 265-267, 274

embed4.c file, 266-267

embed4_log_message() function, 272

embed5.c file, 273-274

embedding

calling back into PHP, 261-262

alternatives to script file inclusion, 262

calling userspace functions, 263-264, 286, 357-358

J-K-L

M

P

Q-R

returning values
  passing by reference, 73
    call-time pass-by-ref, 74
    compile-time pass-by-ref, 75-78
  reference values, 71-73
  return_value variable, 67-70
  return_value_ptr variable, 73
  return_value_used variable, 70-71
reusing resources, 125-126
RINIT (Request Initialization) method, 11
rmdir() function, 203
RSHUTDOWN (Request Shutdown) method, 11-12
RSRC_DTOR flag (php_stream_free() function), 195
runkit, 368
runtime module dependency, 240-241

S

safe_emalloc() function, 40, 299
safe mode, 309-310
safe_pemalloc() function, 299
sample_array_range() function, 71
sample_byref_calltime() function, 74
sample_byref_compiletime() function, 75
SAMPLE_G() macro, 17
sample_hello_world() function, 68
sample_long() function, 67
sample2.c file, 132-133
sample4.c file, 160-161
SAPI
  gobals access, 18-19
    threading, 19-20
    tsrm_ls pointer, finding, 21
  life cycles
    CLI, 13
    embed, 15-16
    multiprocess, 14-15
    multithreaded, 15-16

  shutdown process, 11-12
  startup process, 9-11
  thread safety, 16
    thread-safe data pools, 17
    when not to thread, 18
sapi_error, 272
sapi_module_struct structure, 268, 270
scanning for headers, 236-237
scripts
  calling back into PHP, 261-262
    alternatives to script file inclusion, 262
    calling userspace functions, 263-264, 286, 357-358
  error handling, 264-265
  including on command line, 255-256
  timeouts, setting, 288
SEEK_CUR flag, 193
SEEK_END flag, 194
SEEK_SET flag, 193
seeking streams, 193-194
sending
  cookies, 334
  email, 338
SEPARATE_ZVAL() macro, 139
separation, 42-45
  forced separation, 84
serializing variables to string values, 346
$_SESSION variable, 172
__set() method, 146
SHA1 digest operations, 348
sha1.h, 348
shared modules, loading, 60-61
shutdown process. *See also* **startup/ shutdown cycles**
  MSHUTDOWN (Module Shutdown) method, 12
  PHPAPI calls, 309
  RSHUTDOWN (Request Shutdown) method, 11-12
sizeof() function, 31-32
skeleton code, 351

W

WARNING() macro, 243

win32build.zip file, 48

Windows systems

compilers, 48-49

compiling PHP on, 52-54

config.w32 file, 241-243

extensions, building statically, 62

tools, 48-49

—with option (PECL_Gen), 248

—with-extname option (./configure), 56

wrappers (streams), 202-203, 331-332

dir_opener(), 203

implementation, 203-212

mkdir(), 203

opendir(), 213-214, 216

php_varstream_mkdir(), 218

php_varstream_rename(), 217

php_varstream_rmdir(), 219

php_varstream_unlink(), 217

rename(), 203

rmdir(), 203

stream_closer(), 202

stream_opener(), 202

stream_stat(), 203

unlink(), 203

URL parsing, 212-213

url_stat(), 203

writing

change on write, 43-44

copy on write, 42-43

streams, 192-193, 315, 361-362

WRONG_PARAM_COUNT macro, 85

X-Y-Z

xport parameter
(php_stream_xport_create() function),
188

Zend, 275. *See also* **macros;** *specific*
functions

array manipulation, 289

classes, 277-278

constants, 300-301

exceptions, 285

execution, 285-288

hash tables, 290-296

INI settings, 288

linked lists, 297-299

memory, 299-300

miscellaneous functions, 302-303

objects, 283-284

parameter retrieval, 275-276

properties, 279-283

resources/lists, 296-297

thread safety, 16

thread-safe data pools, 17

when not to thread, 18

variables, 301-302

ZendMM (Zend Memory Management),
37-40

allocator functions, 39-40

memory_limit setting (php.ini), 38

persistent allocations, 38

ZEND_ACC_ABSTRACT flag, 145

ZEND_ACC_FINAL flag, 145

ZEND_ACC_PRIVATE flag, 145

ZEND_ACC_PROTECTED flag, 145

ZEND_ACC_PUBLIC flag, 145

ZEND_ACC_STATIC flag, 145

zend_alter_ini_entry() function, 258, 288

ZEND_ARG_ARRAY_INFO()
macro, 77

ZEND_ARG_INFO() macro, 77

ZEND_ARG_OBJ_INFO() macro, 77

ZEND_ARG_PASS_INFO() macro, 77

zend_bailout() function, 303

ZEND_BEGIN_ARG_INFO() macro,
76, 86

ZEND_BEGIN_ARG_INFO_EX()
macro, 76, 86